CONTEMPORARY FRANCE: ILLUSION, CONFLICT, AND REGENERATION

CONTEMPORARY
FRANCE
ILLUSION, CONFLICT, AND REGENERATION

Edited
with an Introduction by
JOHN C. CAIRNS

Modern Scholarship on European History
Henry A. Turner, Jr.
General Editor

New Viewpoints
A DIVISION OF FRANKLIN WATTS
New York | London | 1978

944.081
C 761

New Viewpoints
A DIVISION OF FRANKLIN WATTS
730 Fifth Avenue
New York, New York 10019

Library of Congress Cataloging in Publication Data

Main entry under title:

Contemporary France.

(Modern scholarship on European history)
Bibliography: p.
Includes index.
CONTENTS: Sternhell, Z. Paul Déroulède and the
origins of modern French nationalism.—Andrew, C.
M. and Kanya-Forstner, A. S. The French "Colonial
Party."—Kemp. T. The French economy under the
franc Poincaré. [etc.]
    1. France—History—20th century—Addresses, es-
says, lectures. I. Cairns, John Campbell, 1924-
DC361.C66   944.081   77-16101
ISBN 0-531-05398-9
ISBN 0-531-05608-2 pbk.

ACKNOWLEDGMENTS

The editor wishes to express his appreciation to the following for permission to translate and/or to publish the papers included in this book: Zeev Sternhell and the editors of the *Journal of Contemporary History* for "Paul Déroulède and the Origins of Modern French Nationalism"; Christopher Andrew and Sydney Kanya-Forstner and Cambridge University Press for "The French 'Colonial Party': Its Composition, Aims and Influence, 1885–1914"; Tom Kemp and the editors of *The Economic History Review* for "The French Economy Under the Franc Poincaré"; Annie Kriegel and the editors of *Annales. Economies. Sociétés. Civilisations* for "Le PCF et la question du pouvoir (1920–1939)," which has been translated by John F. Flinn; Arthur Mitzman and the editor of the *International Review of Social History* for "The French Working Class and the Blum Government (1936–37)"; Stephen Wilson and Cambridge University Press for "The 'Action Française' in French Intellectual Life"; Philip C. F. Bankwitz and the editor of *French Historical Studies* for "Maxime Weygand and the Army-Nation Concept in the Modern French Army"; Roger Bourderon and Henri Michel and Presses Universitaires de France for "Le régime de Vichy, était-il fasciste?", which has been translated by John F. Flinn; Richard F. Kuisel and the editor of the *Journal of European Economic History* for "Technocrats and Public Economic Policy: From the Third to the Fourth Republic."

CONTENTS

INTRODUCTION

The essays in this book are about France in the twentieth century. No single theme is dominant in them. All the same, they are related: They illustrate a certain view of France during the Third and Fourth Republics and the wartime *Etat français* that linked them. Historians spend much of their time trying to isolate origins and set limits, seeking to identify the intelligible unit and to justify the problem or the period that concerns them, imposing their artifice upon the raw phenomena of the world. It is a convention, the unity and discreteness of their historical construct, the natural consequence of art without which history, like life itself, would be incomprehensible. Nonetheless, it is only a convention and it may be useful from time to time to remind oneself of this fact. Readers will require no prompting to see that this collection of papers on aspects of contemporary France has no great internal coherence, no dramatic beginning or end. These essays have been chosen simply because they suggest a variety of significant issues in France from the end of the nineteenth century to that point in the twentieth beyond which perhaps the shape of things becomes too uncertain to proceed.

In a sense, of course, it is true that what one observes across these five or six decades is the final emergence of a French nation that, though old as nations are counted, scarcely achieved cultural unity until something like our own times.[1] One sees plainly that after the nineteenth century the spirit of nationalism, transformed, probably less generous than it had been in another age, the vehicle of more fears than hopes, did at last suffuse the whole of France, with both happy and unhappy consequences. It is evident that the great French colonial empire, so often the remote symbol of individual or small-group enterprise, came to be accepted as a talisman of national status, if also no more than an intermittent, discontinuous preoccupation of the nation as a whole. Like the Great War, 1914–1918 (so much written about and about which, in so far as its overall impact on France is concerned, so little of a scholarly nature has been written), the economic and financial crises of this century left few untouched, had repercussions in every corner of the country. In the wake of older political conflicts, so often confined to a relatively small arena, out of which the Republic had emerged triumphant by 1879, came a new ideological warfare of rival twentieth-century authoritarianisms on both the left and the right, originally urban movements, but reaching ultimately deep into the provinces. In this century few escaped: The shock of war and defeat, the immense debate about responsibilities and the future of the French nation in Hitler's European empire were disseminated throughout the land by the radio and the cinema and the press. Finally, in the rather dispirited post-Liberation period, despite very clear instincts to return to the remembered securities of the past, the apparatus of technological change and state-sponsored planning came to propel the nation forward and to direct the activities of citizens whether they inhabited the remote highlands or the cramped inner cities of France.

How much change was there over the half-century or so? How different had the passage of two wars and two generations rendered this France? One could guess that a young boy or girl who had passed under René Binet's grandiose and controversial Porte de la Concorde to enter the grounds of the great Paris Exposition of 1900 and paused between the two slightly eccentric neo-baroque palaces to look back over the river toward the Invalides might, fifty or sixty years after, have found much the same spot and much the same view, without immediately remarking great changes in the perspective down across the elegant Pont Alexandre-III. Nevertheless, he or she would have known that in fact the country had been fundamentally altered by the intervening years.

The noisy shouts and cries rising from the vendors of the old nationalism during the *belle époque* had long been silenced, although some residual and even powerful echo of their activities, deep within the nation, was to prove more permanent than one might have thought. Of France's vast overseas empire, at its height in 1914, which from time to time when the European scene darkened had been remembered and celebrated as the vital compensation for declining continental power and the measure of her world authority, little remained following the general devolution of colonial hegemonies after the ruinous Second World War. The *fin de siècle* fears of tampering with the apparently orderly securities of a peasant and bourgeois economy may have left behind generic secretiveness and hostility to the tax-collector, but in the generation following the Peace of Paris, 1919, even the French became accustomed to the need to adapt in the face of depression, war, and defeat, and a subsequent national effort of reconstruction. As for opponents within the city, the kind of Socialist and anarchist harassment that troubled without seriously shaking the middle-class Republic before 1914 had given way to the largely verbal attacks of institutionalized "revolutionary" parties, their apocalyptic Marxist or Marxist-Leninist programs faded, clearly at home in the Republic, perhaps even co-opted by the regime. Something that could scarcely have been imagined at the turn of the century (at least, outside the ranks of the Socialist faithful), a government speaking in the name of the working class, had taken office between the two wars, before vanishing swiftly to leave in the long run less the virulent hatreds of the moment than a peculiar nostalgia and hope on the left that a stronger coalition might one day more truly gain and hold power.

In the half-century gone by, that antirepublican extremism on the far right that was just beginning to be heard as the Paris Exposition opened its gates would rise shrilly and divisively before subsiding in the wreck of Vichy's attempt to find a favored place in the Nazi New Order, cruelly sullied by the charge of treason, leaving behind only dwindling bands of irreconcilables to conjure ghostly visions of the counterrevolution. And all the proud sense of patriotism and *grandeur* represented by the Dôme of the Invalides, sheltering Napoleon and, later, his son, was shaken and muddied by the century's experience of war: Certainly military parades would never after 1940, if not 1919, have quite the secure, comforting implications they had held for admiring weekend crowds in the years immediately prior to the outbreak of war in 1914. Something fundamental had been altered in the relationship between the army and the people. No one in those days, unless sworn to the coterie of the counterrevolution, could have imagined the century would bring about an abrupt suspension (it threatened to be the termination) of the republican form of government; let alone, in the deepest national humiliation of modern times, far more painful than the remembered hurt of Sedan and the Treaty of Frankfurt, 1871, a total occupation of the country by German and Italian troops, in the course of which Frenchmen, ostensibly led by a marshal of France, were permitted to exercise a residual sovereignty and to remodel their public institutions along alien lines. What, however, the young lad or lass of 1900, looking out over the marvels of the 1900 Exposition, might conceivably have guessed was that these things heralded the emergence of a technologically advanced society, governed less by the elected representatives sitting in the Palais Bourbon across the Seine than by ministerial experts, professional men, businessmen, practical men not lawyers, as Henri de Saint Simon had prophesied it must and would be very long ago.

The papers in this book speak to all this. The choice is personal but representative, I hope, of what French, American, British, Canadian, and Israeli historians have been writing about certain aspects of France in the contemporary world. They belong to no school; they reflect quite different concerns, styles, approaches. But they contribute collectively to a view of France through three regimes.

Contemporary history has normally a more fragmented character than the history of the more distant past. An observer of his own times must simply guess what may one day seem to have been the principal issues of his age. And an editor must regret acutely having to omit all that must be omitted and bear the responsibility for the omissions, which here means everything from education and religion to foreign policy (still more must he regret the lack of a suitable paper on a very great theme, as is the case, in my view, where the general impact of the Great War on France is concerned). Some of these articles appeared quite recently, some a little longer ago: Experience teaches the familiar lesson that while progress in historiography is as apparent as in almost everything else, there is no inherent superiority in *le dernier cri*. These papers have been chosen because they shed light on problems extending out from the more particular aspect of the French experience with which they deal. If there is a controlling assumption about chronology, it is that, however fragile the conception of an intelligible French unit in this contemporary period, to begin with a late-nineteenth-century theme of confidence before the onset of the war of 1914, and to conclude by emphasizing the renovation of the Republic after the trial of 1939–1945, may not wholly distort the general thrust of French public affairs in recent times.

Notes

1. On all this see the remarkable work of Eugen Weber, *Peasants into Frenchmen: The Modernization of Rural France 1870–1914* (Stanford, 1976).

CONTEMPORARY FRANCE: ILLUSION, CONFLICT, AND REGENERATION

1. PAUL DÉROULÈDE AND THE ORIGINS OF MODERN FRENCH NATIONALISM

by Zeev Sternhell

Three wars put their stamp on the face of contemporary France. Doubtless every one of them—official propaganda to the contrary— was something less than a totally absorbing experience for all Frenchmen. We know of indifference, apathy, and hostility to these wars, and it must be set beside the well-known enthusiasms and massive spirit of patriotic sacrifice. But the results of them could not be escaped. Whether they ended in disaster (1870–1871, 1939– 1940) or victory (1914–1918, 1944–1945), they all had profound material and intellectual consequences for the whole nation. Obviously they did not mark the beginning or the end of things in many spheres of life, but where the public activities of the French were concerned they undeniably constituted landmarks of some importance. Thus there is some truth to the claim that the contemporary history of the French emerges from the lost battles of the Franco-Prussian War. It was easy enough to sweep away the Second Empire in the wreck of the French army; it was much more difficult to establish and define the Republic that replaced it. And though formally institutions were in place within five or six years, the argument about the Republic has in some ways lasted for more than a century.

In this article, Zeev Sternhell contends that the ideas and concerns of Paul Déroulède, so often remembered only for his political blunders and noisy revanchism ("the last witness who continued to relive the année terrible 1870," *said* Le Figaro *on his death in 1914), have continued to live on in the nationalism of the later Third and Fourth and Fifth Republics, as the French seek to come to*

*terms with their place in the world, with the problems of democracy
and the social question. Mr. Sternhell, Chairman of the Department
of Political Science, The Hebrew University of Jerusalem, is the
author of* Maurice Barrès et le nationalisme français *(Paris, 1972),*
La droite révolutionnaire 1885–1914 *(Paris, 1977), and many scholarly articles. This paper first appeared in the* Journal of Contemporary History *6, no. 4 (1971): 46–70. It is reprinted by kind permission of the author and the editors of the* JCH.

From September 1870 until the outbreak of the Great War the
shadow of the disastrous defeat at Sedan hung over the French
Republic, and the Alsace-Lorraine question constituted one of the
constants of its political life. Indeed, the years following the loss of
the two provinces form an exceptional period in which the essential
themes of a particular nationalism aroused broad and fervent support, and in which the very expression of this nationalism tended,
in the massive shock of defeat, almost to become confused with that
of the national consciousness as a whole. The crisis in French
thought was deep and enduring; the response was an immense effort
at regeneration undertaken by the Republic and more particularly
by the republican schoolhouse.[1] At the same time the shock of the
disaster, the territorial amputation, and the ensuing humiliation received their true dimension from the fact that the internal crisis
came riding on the incoming wave of a new intellectual climate.

Certain phenomena thus appeared in France, as well as in Germany,
Austria-Hungary, and Italy, in which a basic likeness came to override the purely local features. For all these countries were suffering
from the same disease. And this, despite the many and varied forms
it was to take, was everywhere recognizable by its fundamental
doubts, its questioning of the whole body of ideas and institutions
characteristic of industrial civilization, and by a systematic rejection
of the values inherited from the eighteenth century and the French
Revolution. In this way men and movements which had been developing under dissimilar political conditions arrived at identical
conclusions. These were the first stirrings of a new world.

The changes which were to occur, within the space of a single
generation, were so profound that it is no exaggeration to speak of
an intellectual revolution, which announced and prefigured, in its
themes as in its style, the mass politics of our own century. For the
vast movement of thought in the 1890s was above all a movement of
revolt—against the world of matter and reason, against materialism

and positivism, against the mediocrity of bourgeois society and the muddle of parliamentary democracy. We are here witnesses to a crisis whose consequence was a popular and authoritarian nationalism, a nationalism which was anti-bourgeois and anti-parliamentarian, a nationalism of diatribes against the rich and against economic injustice—a demagogic and quasi-socialist nationalism. It was during this period—essentially, the last ten years of the century—that the new nationalism forged its ethic, its ideology, and its style of combat, and fixed its vocabulary for the next half century to come. Above all, the new nationalism was one aspect of the revolt which, having called the spiritual foundations of the Republic into question, reflected the desire to transcend the banality of the bourgeois world, the materialism of industrial society, and the dull level of liberal democracy.

In this sense, the nationalism of the end of the nineteenth century presents features which can be defined as proto-fascist or as harbingers of fascism. It is very close to the emotional and sentimental fascist ethos; it had the same cult of youth, adventure, and heroism, the same hatred of bourgeois values, and the same faith in the power of the unconscious. It also exhibits that romanticization of action, the activist mystique and spirit of negation which were to reappear in fascism. On the social level the nationalists, who showed the same fear of industrial society, technical progress, and great cities, professed the same hostility to capitalism, and enunciated the dogmas of a national socialism. The following to which these men addressed themselves was essentially petty-bourgeois: Drumont, too, understood that it was this social category, the one most threatened by the rise of industrialism, which would be the most open to a call to arms. For him, as for Déroulède and Barrès, anti-semitism became the means *par excellence* for mobilizing this vast body of the petty bourgeoisie, ill-adapted to the modern world and responding neither to the Marxist call nor to that of liberal democracy.

There was no lack of men from the extreme Left—communards and Blanquists—within the nationalist camp; here again the resemblance to fascism is striking. However, the nationalism of those days could not avail itself of a mass of unemployed workers, of impoverished peasants, and ruined and frightened petty bourgeois; the economic and social conditions at the end of the nineteenth century had not yet produced the shock-troops for a right-wing revolutionary movement. The Boulangists and nationalists were not yet outlaws, the anti-dreyfusards were not yet *déclassés*; and for this reason the revolt, which gathered strength throughout the last ten years of the century, did not erupt into a movement capable of translating the mass of feeling borne along by nationalism into political action. It was, however, to exercise a determining influence in the formation of the future fascist climate.

Considered independently of the end-of-century climate of revolt, the fascism of a Brasillach, a Drieu La Rochelle, a Valois or even a Déat would seem to be an isolated phenomenon, divorced from the milieu which gave it birth. But the fact is that the process of 'permeation by fascism' which one notes in the history of French nationalism was no accident, and did not appear as something totally new within the French nationalist tradition.[2] At the level of ideology and state of mind there would appear to exist that continuity and concordance which constitute the essence of a political tradition.

The same holds for the connection between the political ideas of the Vichy regime and pre-1914 nationalism, a connection which points up sharply the complexity of French nationalism. In fact, the nationalist ideology prefigures the two aspects of the Vichy regime: its dynamic and romantic side, its exaltation of youth and the revolutionary masses, of the values of heroism and struggle, blood and soil; and, on the other hand, the regime's bourgeois and conservative side, its vision of a static society governed by the values of order and hierarchy, a rural and paternalistic society sustained by sound Catholic principles.[3]

It is precisely here that one sees the originality of the turn-of-the-century nationalism: its synthesis of a romantic and dynamic nationalism with one which was socially and politically conservative. A particular political situation might force one of these elements to conceal the other, but never to the point of totally obscuring it. In this respect it constitutes a landmark in French political history, for by the last years of the nineteenth century it already contained almost all the elements which, right up to the present, were to go into the making of the various forms of French nationalism. It not only foreshadows the future fascist and conservative nationalisms, but also proclaims that new form of nationalism which links a 'certain idea of France' with the Republic and the idea of democracy. For in the final analysis does not Gaullism itself pay homage to its fundamental principles and postulates? The grandeur of France, the social question transcended by national unity, direct democracy—do not these three principles of Gaullism recall the components of the nationalism of a Déroulède or a Barrès? Do not Gaullism and early twentieth-century nationalism express the same unease and anguish at seeing the dilapidation of that unique entity in the history of civilization which is the French heritage? Does not defence of this heritage—internally in the social order and externally in a recovered sense of power—determine Gaullist policy just as much as it did that of the turn-of-the-century nationalist movements?

At the level of political action, the themes given expression day after day by the nationalist leaders bear a strange resemblance to those to be developed by the Gaullist *Rassemblement du Peuple Français* and *Union pour la défense de la République*. In both cases we find the appeal to the people and the cult of the leader, disdain for the representative system and recourse to the true will of the people, the desire to re-establish the authority of the state and to give that state a head. In both cases there is the same distrust of professional politicians, parties, and their machines. Against these, and the particular interests they represent, is opposed the appeal to the people, in the name of national unity and of the higher interests of France.[4]

On the social level, the association of capital with labour, the participation in profits and management advocated by Naquet, Laisant, Barrès and Déroulède (along with several more obscure Boulangists) present a striking resemblance to the ideas developed by the Gaullist left wing. The same is true on the institutional level; for does not the Constitution of the Fifth Republic recall the various projects for constitutional reform worked out in the 1880s by the future Boulangists or nationalists? This agreement in themes and modes of thought shows both the place that the nationalism of the beginning of the century occupies in the French political tradition and the scope of an ideology which can rightly claim to have nourished—and still to be nourishing—most of the forms French nationalism has taken in the last fifty years. But what it makes most conspicuous is the stability and continuity of nationalism; the vocabulary, structure and style change, the fundamental ideas evolve, but their essence is retained. A vision of the world and a set of political and moral traditions born in the last years of the old century go on shaping consciousness, providing the basis for a system of values, and determining choices and collective loyalties.

Paul Déroulède, who was rapidly to acquire enormous popularity, was the first of the nationalist leaders to appear on the political scene. More than anyone else within this heterogeneous movement, he personifies the idea of *revanche* and the work of regeneration. He was the living embodiment of a political approach that subordinated every other imperative of the nation's life to this single end. The moment he reached the conclusion that liberal democracy was incapable of providing the country with its proper standing in the world—of ensuring the grandeur of France—Déroulède turned against the regime.

Of course, the nationalism of a Déroulède or a Barrès expresses forces which at the end of the nineteenth century were as active among the victors as among the vanquished; their origin cannot be found in the Franco-Prussian war alone. In France, however, there was the unique additional factor of the shock of defeat, which contributed powerfully towards creating an atmosphere extremely favourable to a revision of the old republican values. Déroulède was the first in the republican camp to call publicly into question the old revolutionary heritage; it was in the name of patriotic feeling that the *Ligue des Patriotes* was gradually transformed into a weapon for use against the Republic. This was why the revolt against the existing order of things—and thus against the ideology which supported it—acquired an added dimension in France: for this ideology, which was held responsible for the defeat, was at the same time seen as unable to help in overcoming that defeat.

Déroulède's work provides a remarkable illustration of this new intellectual climate. It also illuminates the nature of the process through which French nationalism, in an astonishingly short time, advanced from being official republican and Jacobin ideology to becoming mainly the common ideology of the right-wing opposition; and it shows how a movement exhibiting the most pious republican orthodoxy was transformed step by step into a right-wing mass movement aimed at bringing down parliamentary democracy.

The point of departure for the work undertaken by Déroulède was a complete recasting of the ideas left by the preceding age. 'The hour has come', he wrote on the morrow of the defeat, 'for national egoism . . . for an absorbing national passion as jealous as all passions are.' He returned to this idea each time the occasion presented itself: 'As to the brotherhood of peoples', he said at the founding of the League, 'we'll talk about that again when Cain has returned what he's taken from us.' For the present Frenchmen had to devote themselves to themselves and to their mutilated country; their sole duty was to forge the instrument of *revanche* so that Might might ultimately be made to serve Right. Like many another Frenchman raised in the old republican tradition, Déroulède attempted a complete revision of the doctrines inherited from his elders: 'Before the disasters of 1870 . . . we had Michelet for prophet and Louis Blanc for doctor. How astonished we would have been had someone disturbed our glorious quiet *vis-à-vis* the outside world and told us that alongside the human right called Freedom we would one day have to think about defending and recapturing that national right called Independence.'

The shock of the disaster had upset the entire scale of values inherited from the revolutionary and universalist tradition. This tradition Déroulède held responsible for France's territorial mutilation, and loss of status in the world.[5] The universalist ideology, he wrote, by allowing 'the military spirit to die out', had engendered 'a national peril'. Consequently the first step towards recovery consisted in protecting the country from all internationalist doctrines— these being nothing more than the 'exploitation of France by foreigners' [6]—and from all universalist chimeras, and, in general, in calling into question all the values left over from the preceding period.

The League of Patriots was founded on 18 May 1882, during a gymnastic exhibition. The historian Henri Martin, a disciple of Michelet, was its first President,[7] and Victor Hugo agreed to be its patron, contributing a patriotic poem to the 3 March 1883 number of *Le Drapeau*, the League's weekly organ; Gambetta, 'the great patriot' whom Déroulède was almost to idolize to the end of his days, was one of the first to join. After the disappearance of the architect of the *Défense Nationale*, who would always be the symbol of republican grandeur and the image of what the Republic might have been for him, Déroulède transferred his enthusiasm to 'that last political godson of Gambetta', Waldeck-Rousseau, who as Minister of the Interior in 1883 presided over the meetings of the gymnastic societies. Many years later, the government of this same Waldeck-Rousseau was to clamp down on nationalist agitation and bring Déroulède before the High Court. But for the moment, at any rate, there could be no doubt: enjoying the patronage of the highest figures in the regime and officially subsidized by the republican establishment, the League made its debut in an aura of perfect republican orthodoxy. Déroulède himself served on a commission headed by Paul Bert (Minister of Public Instruction in Gambetta's government), which had been charged with setting up a military training programme in the schools. A patriotic organization whose *raison d'être* was preparation for the glorious day of *revanche*, the League saw its first responsibility as being the banishment of any and every divisive element. It preached national unity and fought the 'spirit of particularism'.

For Déroulède, who had thoroughly assimilated the lesson of the defeat, preparation for *revanche* took the form of an immense educational effort based on that hatred for the adversary, 'that nation of vandals, mercenaries, and hangmen', which is the beginning of patriotism.

> Yes, this lesson of hate is indeed enough;
> We shall learn it by heart, we shall say it often.[8]

The system of education recommended by Déroulède rested on two basic principles. The first stipulated that 'Patriotism, which is also a religion, has its own symbols and rites just as it has its own apostles and martyrs.' For children to be given 'a deep and reasoned love for their nation and soil', it was the teacher's duty to bring them up on French *gloire* and to inculcate the heroism of every moment in the history of France. This was also the way to restore unity, to integrate the old France and that born of the battlefields of the Revolution in a single cult, and thus to bridge the gap dividing secular France from believing France, the grandsons of the emigrés from the descendants of the regicides.[9] From Gaul to Valmy all Frenchmen had to commune in the same spirit of heroism and abnegation, for French continuity ran from Joan of Arc to the soldiers of the Year II of the Revolution.[10] Above all its political forms and the institutions governing it stood the Nation.

At a time when the task was to rally 'all the national goodwill', it was vital to rise above all divisions. Déroulède managed this on the political level quite as well as on the social or religious one. 'There is no greater solvent than politics', he said in 1885 in excluding internal politics from the League's field of interest. He refused to become involved in the religious question; although anxious for 'the military virtues to be supported by the Christian ones', he nevertheless declared himself satisfied the moment love of country replaced revealed religion.[11] Equally, he rejected anti-semitism: 'A nation only gets the Jews it deserves . . . and I recognize that since 1789 France has deserved good Jews and has got them.' [12]

Déroulède was equally aware of the problem posed for French recovery by the social question: the way to national unity went via the integration of the working class into the national collectivity. But the solutions he contemplated were rather unrealistic. Prisoners of the idea of national unity, these men could barely envisage anything beyond a sketchy protectionism, even when they were genuinely preoccupied with the condition of labour. Indeed, Déroulède conceived of the social problem in terms of defending the French proletariat against foreign labour and of defending trade and industry against foreign competition. Solidarity of capital and labour constituted the cornerstone of this programme, protection of the French workers being achieved through a coalition of unions and employers. The new nationalism was one of defence at all levels, but if it showed some social concern it nevertheless revealed little understanding of the needs and aspirations of the working class. It was poorly equipped for attacking the social question, which remained a side issue, its postulates lying too far from the interests of the proletariat for the establishment of a durable common front.

The League's second principle was cultivation of the military spirit. This, and the presence of the Army and of military training in the schools had been the programme of the Paul Bert commission. Jules Ferry's assumption of the ministry put an abrupt stop to these projected reforms, with military training becoming no more than physical education. Now, for the first time, Déroulède found himself in opposition to the Republican government—*De l'Education militaire*, which he published in 1882, was an anti-Ferry lampoon. In this he was still addressing his reproaches to only one man and that man's policy; by 1884 he was already attacking principles of action. Colonial policy, with its dispersal of the national power, served as the first target of a discontent which was to grow perceptibly from year to year. Of course, Déroulède was also afraid lest this policy distract the French from the only problem really worthy of their attention.[13]

By 1885 Déroulède had taken a great step forward. We can now discern the first criticism, veiled yet firm, of the system and of its political *mores*. It was now clear that the League was undergoing a slow transformation. On 7 March, Anatole de la Forge, on resigning from the presidency, indicated in a letter to Déroulède the reason for his decision—the manifest incompatibility of their political positions. One phrase is significant: 'You are an authoritarian patriot; I am a liberal one.'[14] In October, in a speech at the Place du Trocadéro praising the spirit of discipline reigning in the rifle and gymnastic societies, Déroulède made his first clear allusion to the crises and incoherence of the parliamentary system.[15]

By 1886 the tone had hardened. For the first time Déroulède took a stand on a fundamental problem of domestic politics. The unity of the country had to be saved at all costs, and authoritarianism would not be too high a price to pay. All 'sectarian' activity, which could only lead to 'internal disintegration', had to be forbidden. Measures should be taken against the red flag and against every other expression of particularism. 'Perhaps the day will come when, less authoritarian if not more liberal, we will see fit to grant the individual greater scope and more rights, but this will only come on the morrow of the day when justice and peace, reconciled in glory, embrace on the banks of the Rhine. Until that day let us not dissipate any of our strength.' [16] Shortly after this, pressing forward on the path of opposition to the system, Déroulède, now President of the League, openly deplored 'this eternal confusion of executive and legislative power'.[17] One can measure the distance travelled in less than four years: the League, that creation of the Republic, had not only come to criticize the system; it was now even suspected of plotting against it. From 1886 Déroulède had in fact become convinced that the parliamentary Republic, because of its inherent defects, could never make a success of the work of *revanche*. He was thus ripe for Boulangism.

In the person of the new Minister of War, Déroulède believed he had found the strong man. Shortly after the formation of the Freycinet cabinet in January 1886, he proposed a *coup d'état* to Boulanger, and in the autumn undertook a vast campaign in favour of *revanche* in the minister's name.[18] Revanchist and authoritarian Boulangism, the Boulangism disposed towards a *coup d'état*, had been born; patriotism was for the first time turned against the Republic. In the name of *revanche* and of the country, parliamentary institutions were called into question. The nationalist base had shrunk strikingly: having already attacked the red flag and denounced political liberalism, Déroulède now attacked the keystone of the regime—the parliamentary system. Convinced that only a strong regime could prepare France for the day of *revanche*, he looked to the providential man for the solution.

Nationalism had now taken the path it was henceforward to follow: the individual was subordinate to the national collectivity, national imperatives were opposed to the liberal order, and individual fulfilment was to be found in service to the nation. Xenophobic patriotism and the unreserved cult of the Army linked the idea of the *patrie* to the idea of war. The patriotic education undertaken by republican circles in the first years of the Third Republic took on an even more accentuated militarism, to which were added the cults of the leader, of discipline, of sacrifice, and of death, themes which present a striking resemblance to certain fascist phenomena.[19]

A new aggressive note marked Déroulède's thought and the articles in *Le Drapeau*; the work of regeneration undertaken with dignity and fervour fifteen years earlier had degenerated into cul-

tural chauvinism, an embarrassing and often swaggering self-glori-
fication, and above all into a frankly anti-democratic trend of
thought. The new nationalism was anti-liberal and anti-democratic
because the bourgeois and parliamentary Republic, through its constant foundering in power crises, presented the country with daily
proof of its impotence. Incapable of preparing the country for war,
it acquiesced in its humiliation before Europe and, by launching itself on distant colonial ventures, made final the loss of Alsace-
Lorraine. In this sense Déroulèdian nationalism was to constitute one
of the basic factors in the two great crises which shook the Third
Republic, but it did not lie at the origin of either. Its real importance resides in the additional dimension it lent to the crisis of
liberalism and democracy; in fact, Déroulède's nationalism was
the first to set the traditional Jacobin clientele against the Republic;
it was only at the turn of the century, in the smoke of the great
battles surrounding the Dreyfus affair, that nationalism shifted de-
finitively to the right.

Boulangism, as we know, arose from the opposition of the radical
Left to the government Republicans; on the institutional level its
roots lay in the anti-parliamentary trend, nourished by opposition
to the 1875 Constitution, which existed within the Left and was
represented in the early 1880s by such men as Naquet, Rochefort,
Laisant, Laguerre, and Francis Laur. On the social level, Boulangism was a reaction against what one could call the immobilism of
the Centre government. Indeed, it was not by chance that since
May 1881 Alfred Naquet, the future philosopher of Boulangism,
had been deploring a system which imposed upon the country a
mediocre 'hybrid ministry drawn from the entire centre of the
Assembly'.[20]

On the other hand, the campaign undertaken by the militant wing
of the radicals with the support of Rochefort's *L'Intransigeant*
(which enjoyed enormous popularity in the Paris suburbs) was
greatly facilitated by the impact of the economic crisis of 1882 on
the working class, and which was heightened by a number of financial scandals.[21] The Republic had demonstrated that it could be as
corrupt as the Empire. The regime was troubled by the social
question, by political immobilism, and by a serious crisis of confidence. The October 1885 elections, by bringing three almost equal
blocs to the Chamber, speeded up the oppositional process, since
the equilibrium established between opportunists, royalists, and radicals guaranteed the regime's impotence. The triumph of the Right,

which won 200 seats as against its previous 90, had wiped out the political results of eight years of the Republic; in the minds of several of the most advanced Republicans, such as the senator Alfred Naquet and the deputy Henri Michelin (President of the Paris Municipal Council in 1884 and, as such, standard-bearer for the extreme left-wing Republicans), there gradually dawned the idea of taking action outside of strict legality in order to save the Republic.[22] In this uneasy atmosphere, Déroulède's patriotism converged with the political and social preoccupations of the radical Left. This was all the more natural since, as René Rémond has shown, a kind of vibrant, romantic, and flag-waving patriotism was at the time still the property of the revolutionary Left.[23] These were the original constituent elements of Boulangism, and it was this synthesis which explains the movement's strength and gave it its mass character.

Déroulède occupied a special place within the Boulangist movement. To it he brought his iron integrity, his disinterestedness, and his Gambettist past. With other extreme left-wing elements, such as the Blanquists and the former communards, and with other quasi-socialists of authoritarian and revolutionary temperament, he shared the appearance of being the authentic guardian of the old Jacobin tradition of chauvinistic patriotism, ferocious anti-monarchism, and direct democracy. In the name of national interest and of the outraged and diminished *patrie* he launched the appeal to the people over the heads of their leaders and against their representatives. To Boulanger, compromised by his monarchist alliances, Déroulède was of considerable use in presenting a façade to the country and in reassuring the General's republican and patriotic following.

Déroulède's political ideas received their final shape through Boulangism. The Parti National experience was decisive for him in this respect, and its weight was to be felt throughout his career, both on the ideological level and in his political behaviour. Elected deputy in 1889 for Angoulême, he played the role of chief of the Boulangist group in Parliament. In a speech to the Chamber on 24 December 1892, he contrasted the image of a true Republic founded on the direct appeal to the people with the false democracy of parliamentary representation. He recalled the anti-democratic and reactionary origins of the 1875 Constitution and the anti-republican motivations of the Versailles Assembly. The system governing this 'so little republican' Republic, he said, engendered 'an absolute lack of equilibrium among the ruling bodies, thrown together pell-mell in an organization without counterweights; a perpetual muddle in the conduct of business; and the near-impossibility of regular operation on the part of the governmental machine'. These themes were to recur throughout the years following the Parti National débâcle and the later collapse of anti-dreyfusism. From his exile in San Sebastian after the abortive coup of February 1899 until his death, Déroulède harped incessantly on these elements of the revisionist programme. His attack on liberal democracy was made in the name of the purest republican tradition, and it was under the aegis of 'the Fathers of the Republican Church' that he conducted his campaign against parliamentary institutions and in favour of an authoritarian system and personal power. In this synthesis one sees the originality of the stream of thought represented by a Déroulède, a Barrès, or a Rochefort, and it is in this respect that leftist Boulangism and republican anti-dreyfusism prefigure modern mass movements.

Against the parliamentary Republic Déroulède invoked the authority of Montesquieu, Rousseau, Mirabeau, Danton, Saint-Just, and Gambetta; the principles of '89 and '48, 'the immortal declaration of the Rights of Man', which sanctified the principle of popular sovereignty, so cynically violated by that monarchist creation, the parliamentary Republic, governed by the 'most distorted, abnormal, anarchic and tyrannical' of constitutions. He emphasized that, far from it ever having been for him a matter of attacking the Republic, what he had been aiming at was the replacement of 'the parliamentary sovereignty which has led us to where we are now by that national sovereignty which alone can pull us out again and give us a Republic divorced from the hereditary idea, from dynasties and pretenders. Thus it has been and thus will it be now if you really wish to have a true democracy.' Democracy had nothing to do with the Assembly system, and could be based only on the application of the vital principle of separation of powers: 'The keystone of all democracy is a President of the Republic who is independent in the origin and exercise of his power.' The goal of every democrat should be the destruction of a system which had confiscated the people's sovereignty in the interest of a new caste which was exercising 'an irresponsible and anonymous collective tyranny'. For this reason he was working for a 'return to the system championed by the fathers of our first Revolution—the Appeal to the People'.

This meant, of course, a regime resting on the principles of the plebiscite, of separation of powers, and of direct election of the chief of state by universal suffrage; the ministers, responsible to him and chosen from outside Parliament, would cease to be politicians and become technicians. Déroulède was advocating a strong regime and attempting to stabilize the authority of the government at the expense of Parliament. The Chamber was not to be abolished, but since what was involved was the restoration to the executive of its 'power of execution', and since 'all evils flow from the parliamentary regime', the Chamber would cease to constitute the sole embodiment of popular sovereignty. In cases of conflict between it and the executive a plebiscite would settle the question. On every issue except the budget, the President of the Republic had to have the right to dissolve the Chamber.[24]

Social immobilism, the supremacy of the money power and the misery of the working classes were other aspects of the system's bankruptcy. Here Déroulède's thinking merged with a populism drawing its inspiration from a particular militant and radical doctrine. Having contrasted the merits of direct democracy with the vices of the representative system, he advocated the possibility of a plebiscite whenever one-fifth to one-third of the electorate should call for one, and having appealed to the old revolutionary and Jacobin tradition which had demolished other systems of oppression, Déroulède presented his plan of action as a movement for the reconquest of the Republic. Its popular and republican character was constantly and vigorously reaffirmed, for from Boulangism until the Place de la Nation affair the League of Patriots had to defend itself against the charge of being merely a smoke-screen for the forces of reaction.

Déroulède dealt with this by preaching a return to the people and by making ample use of the theme of popular grandeur. The goal of this revolt against the parliamentary Republic was to recover by and for the people the sovereignty which the new aristocracy had made off with so easily, and to eliminate the corrupt, the politicians, the influence-peddlers and the moneymen. The President of the League set himself to arouse the working classes to the immense injury that had been done them: during the nineties he remained faithful to the 'social' orientation of left-wing Boulangism.

In the general débâcle the success of the twenty leftist Boulangists acquired notable significance; in labouring circles, as yet untainted by Marxism, and among the most deprived sectors of society, Boulangism for a moment played the role later to belong to socialism. Déroulède, the apparent leader of the Boulangists, was not slow to draw all the possible conclusions, and in the Chamber elected in 1889 he set out on a policy of close cooperation with the socialist deputies. On 11 July 1891 he openly demanded an amnesty for the militants sentenced the previous spring, declaring that

the workers' solidarity is growing stronger from day to day. They rely on themselves and they rely on you, and unless you show yourselves to be compassionate and magnanimous . . . one fine day you will be awakened by an explosion a hundred times worse than that of '93, worse and more justified as well, for though children of the Revolution and the Republic, you will have misunderstood both Republic and Revolution.

The Boulangists did not stop at this; they took the initiative with a series of proposals for social legislation and supported all the bills introduced by the socialist deputies. This collaboration was all the easier because the two had already travelled a long way together. The socialists had adopted rather divergent attitudes towards Boulangism, but on the whole their anti-Boulangism lacked zeal. Lafargue's gestures towards Boulangism (which Engels severely criticized) are well known. If, as has been pointed out, the Parti Ouvrier did follow a different line under Jules Guesde, it still refused to designate Boulangism as the main enemy.[25] And those socialists who had fought against Boulangism in 1888–9 found in the nineties that their only worthwhile allies lay among the men of the old Parti National. Together they formed an opposition firmly committed to harassing the majority and to doing everything possible to bring down the regime.

These attempts to rally all the opposition factions were unable to withstand the shock of the Dreyfus affair. The socialists, the overwhelming majority of whom recognized in the anti-dreyfusard camp their own enemies, were opposed at all levels of political action to the former Boulangists, who with Déroulède, Barrès, and Rochefort now preached a nationalism markedly further to the right than was Boulangism. Something far more modern than the bizarre group which gathered in the train of General Boulanger was involved here.

The nationalist populism underlying anti-dreyfusism appealed to the little man's hatred of privilege and to the sense of equality. Déroulède attacked the 'egoistic money-nobility' with its 'feudalism . . . far stronger than the feudalism of old' that was monopolizing the country's wealth and had marshalled all its forces to oppose reform of the system. It was these 'new aristocrats' who had brought about the ruin of the small tradesman and artisan while permitting colossal fortunes to be built up. This bourgeois aristocracy was squandering public funds, maintaining 900,000 bureaucrats, three-quarters of whom were working for the parliamentarians, and had covered itself with shame by raising the salaries of the latter.

These are the classic themes of anti-parliamentary demagogy, themes which from Boulangism to Poujadism have hardly varied. They were designed to entice the widest possible range of followers, to attract all the 'little men', the leftovers and disinherited of the industrial society to which Déroulède, like Barrès, Rochefort, and most of the Boulangists had never adjusted themselves. But they did not call for any structural change. Quite the contrary; the nationalists moved to the right during the turmoil of the Dreyfus affair because they wanted to preserve things as they were. Revolt was now thundering in the enemy camp, and the nationalists consequently became the guardians of order. That was why, though Déroulède did speak out against poverty, exploitation, and injustice, he blamed the parliamentary system rather than the social and economic structure. Though he pilloried the various political and economic scandals, he attributed responsibility for them to political rather than to economic liberalism; and though he supported the demands of the workers, he fiercely attacked socialism, which called for 'the confiscation of profits' and 'the right to be lazy'. Déroulède seemed to be dreaming of a golden age for the France of the 'ordinary people', a France of understanding and of harmony of interests between normally antagonistic social classes. But such links of solidarity could be forged only when the political structure reflected a similar harmony and when a similar harmonization of interests was established on the political level.

Here we see why this social question has never had and never can have a parliamentary solution. What is needed is a strong power, neither hereditary nor life-long but stable and solid, which can promise only what it is willing to give and which will be at the same time wise enough and bold enough, vigorous enough and fair enough, to impose the necessary sacrifices of the one group while limiting excessive demands on the part of the other.[26]

The same argument was repeated again and again: democratic liberalism was the root of all evil. The parliamentary system bore sole responsibility for the workers' poverty and for the difficulties facing a lower middle class threatened with proletarianization, for the corruption, the scandals, and the unsuccessful foreign policy, and in general for all events unfavourable to the interests of France as these were understood by the President of the League of Patriots. It was a case which made an easy appeal to the man in the street. Like Barrès, Rochefort, and Drumont, and of course like such street toughs as Guérin and Morès,[27] Déroulède was already thinking in terms of mass politics. There was no point in debating the respective merits of this or that political system; in order to succeed, one had to simplify reality and present easily absorbed ideas capable of channelling discontent and mobilizing the masses. The best way of doing this was to place the responsibility for all the trouble on one single factor—in Déroulède's case, on liberal democracy. The most simplistic solutions were offered for the most complex problems. All evils were due to one sole factor; once that was eliminated, the golden age would dawn. Primitive, but already clearly discernible, the mythic politics of our own century were taking shape.

Another element in Déroulèdian populism was a violent anti-intellectualism whose origins went back to the Dreyfus affair. Indeed, Déroulède and Habert blamed the intellectuals for the affair, contrasting them with the simple people, whose instincts could be trusted. It was on the 'popular soul' that they relied to save the land from anarchy: 'for the past twenty-eight years', Déroulède wrote, 'it [this soul] has been everything and done everything, acting for itself alone to the profound disarray of matters and men. How often have we seen it hovering over judicial assemblies, strengthening wavering wills and enlightening clouded minds, demanding and ensuring that France be defended and her enemies punished.'

> While the shabby and labyrinthine soul of literary and scientific egoism and of financial calculation wanders among vain subtleties and false hypotheses, the popular soul goes straight to the point and rips away the tainted veil of falsehood to disclose to the eyes of certain well-meaning dupes the obvious fact that there are now but two parties: the party of the foreigner and the party of France. And the popular soul does not waver; it is always and everywhere of the party of France.[28]

Here Déroulède was exploiting the traditional distrust of theoreticians and ideologues, and of intellectuals in general. He accused them of having lost touch with popular feeling and the general interest. Like most nationalists, he relied on that demagogic populism which, in order to exalt the virtues of the people, casts suspicion on any man capable of a too-facile command of arguments and abstract ideas. Against the 'rootless' intellectuals (Barrès' famous formula) Déroulède set the virtues of racial instinct and tradition, invoking Catholicism as a major component of the national tradition and inveighing against the plot hatched by 'the sect which is doing its utmost to demilitarize and decatholicize France'.[29] It was always the same forces—those of liberal democracy or those which encouraged parliamentary anarchy—that were attacking the spirit of France: cosmopolitan high finance, the men of the Bloc, authors of anti-religious laws, or those parliamentary Republicans who were getting along so well under the 'odious Constitution', which was nothing but an 'Anglo-German travesty contrary to all our traditions and to all our old Gallic instincts'.[30] These were the diverse elements of the coalition mounting the assault against the old France. It would be a public-health measure to stop the process, and to achieve this no means were illegitimate or illegal.

Déroulède was thus one of the first Republicans to think in the 1880s in terms of a *coup d'état*, but he was never able to bring off any of his attempts. The first lost opportunity was on 27 January 1889—the day on which Boulanger was elected deputy for Paris by an overwhelming majority. He was expected to install himself in the Elysée by nightfall. Certain members of his entourage, Déroulède in particular, urged him to attempt a coup; Boulanger refused. In his *Appel au Soldat*, in his *Cahiers*, and implicitly in his articles for the *Courrier de l'Est*, Barrès, the historian and poet of Boulangism, gave some reasons: the general was paralysed by the memory of Louis Napoleon's *coup d'état*. 'The 2nd of December weighed constantly on the Empire. I do not wish to make blood flow', he made Boulanger say. He had him take the same tone before Déroulède and Thiébaud, who were urging him to give the parliamentary Republic its *coup de grâce*. He attributed Boulanger's failure of nerve to 'prejudices of education'.[31] Barrès and Déroulède realized that what was involved was not one man's loss of nerve but rather the bankruptcy of an ideology: a prisoner of the old republican tradition, Boulanger did not know how to exploit what was already a revolutionary situation. Déroulède, on the other hand, was free of the prejudices paralysing Boulanger: on the night of 27 January he wanted to march. He had mobilized the League's cadres, the Bonapartist committees, and the Blanquist elements, but beyond that he had no idea of how to constrain the authorities to accept dissolution and revision, the two frail pillars of the meagre Boulangist programme. It all came down to obtaining new general elections for a Constituent Assembly which would give France a new constitution. Thus even Déroulède, perhaps the warmest partisan of direct and ideologically unfettered action, scarcely imagined anything beyond a kind of popular circus during which authority would collapse of its own weight.

Straddling the nineteenth and the twentieth centuries, Boulangism was confronted with problems of a new nature, to which it could make no adequate response. Déroulède had of course sketched in the elements of a response, but other and more decisive elements were lacking, particularly on the level of revolutionary strategy. He knew that direct action could only be mass action, but he still thought in terms of the *journées* of the Great Revolution, thus proving that he was himself only imperfectly weaned from the old revolutionary mythology. He was no more able than Boulanger to conceive a plan of attack against democracy. In fact, he was facing a situation unknown till then: for the first time what had to be a popular insurrection would be directed against a regime born of universal suffrage which, though much decried and already in many ways discredited, still occupied a central place in the popular consciousness. Anger and unease were, to be sure, widespread, but these had to be assembled into a coherent ideological system, and directed and channelled by a powerful machine. This was not done, and Boulangism, which operated within the framework of the system and accepted its postulates, was reduced to impotence.

Ten years later, on 23 February 1899, at the height of the antidreyfusard agitation, Déroulède, re-elected deputy for Angoulême the year before, attempted to revive Boulangism without Boulanger. The nationalists felt the ground slipping from beneath their feet; their strongest supporter, the President of the Republic, had just died. According to the testimony of Barrès, Déroulède had made preparations for a coup which was to be carried out by the Army, but Félix Faure's sudden death forced his hand.[32] For the day of the funeral the President of the League of Patriots worked out his extraordinarily infantile plan of attempting to lead General Roget's troops to the Elysée when they were about to return to barracks. To attempt a coup after having announced it a few days earlier, and without making any serious preparations, was something perfectly in line with the Déroulèdian idea of a *coup de force*, reflecting that same sense of exaltation and trust in the strength of popular spontaneity, that same atmosphere of popular festival which ten years earlier was to have brought down the regime. For the old Boulangists the doctrine of a coup based on a popular insurrection was always unquestionable. Like Boulanger in 1889, Déroulède in 1899 refused to spill blood, seeking instead to justify his coup by appeals to the 1791 and 1793 Declarations of the Rights of Man, to Mirabeau and La Fayette, Gambetta and the men of 4 September, and finally by recalling the illegality of the Constitution. He was still dreaming of a 'popular insurrection supported by the Army'. The attempt collapsed in ridicule, Déroulède having a difficult time even getting himself arrested. Brought before the Seine jury, he was acquitted, only to be later sentenced by the High Court on 5 January 1900 to ten years' banishment.

Déroulède's trial was the last important event of his career. Pardoned in 1905 after five years of exile, he was defeated in the 1906 elections. He made a reappearance during the electoral campaign of 1910, harping on the old Boulangist themes and casting anathemas upon liberal democracy. But on the eve of his death in 1914, against the background of the nationalist revival which characterized the years leading up to the war, the chief of the League of Patriots seemed the representative of a bygone age. Indeed, with the victory of the *Bloc Républicain,* the first period in the history of post-1870 nationalism had ended, a period embracing tentatives for renewal and reform or for open struggle against the regime, but starting from the fundamental postulate of acceptance of the Revolution. May 1902 showed that such a road led nowhere, that the regime could not be overcome from within. A break with the old revolutionary tradition now seemed a vital necessity for the preservation of nationalism, and so Action Française, which was quickly to unite the majority of the leading nationalists apart from Barrès and Déroulède, was born.[33] But Déroulède, who like Barrès had always refused to make a choice within French history, remained faithful to the original nationalism—republican, authoritarian, and plebeian, a nationalism which was at once the product of the crisis of liberal democracy and of the reaction to the humiliation of defeat. This was the deeper meaning of Déroulèdian Boulangism, and its importance lies in the fact that it was the first great manifestation in the series of assaults which French democracy was to endure from the turn of the century, and whose roots lay in the Jacobin Republic. 'Opportunist' liberalism, which under the threat of succumbing to the combined assault of Left and Right could do no more than perpetuate political and social immobilism, was now forced to face the revolt of a part of its traditional following. Jacobin anti-parliamentarism had thus managed to mobilize authoritarian temperaments on the left around an ideological platform which was primarily a negative criticism of the system's weakness, incoherence, and impersonalism. To stabilize authority, strengthen the Executive, and give the state a head and a brain were Déroulède's objectives, the preconditions for a French renaissance. The League of Patriots, initially an implement of *revanche,* was progressively transformed until it became an organization designed to manipulate the masses outside of political parties and of Parliament, or even against them.[34]

In regard to the organization and technique of the *coup d'état,* Déroulède and the League remained a nineteenth-century phenomenon, completely unadapted to the conditions of an industrialized society. It is also true that they lacked a mass of unemployed or impoverished peasants and frightened petty bourgeois. But on the ideological level the Déroulèdian synthesis already foreshadowed the twentieth century. Authoritarianism, anti-parliamentarism, and anti-capitalism were combined with a violent anti-Marxism: it formed the basis of Boulangism and later of anti-dreyfusard nationalism. Against the institution which was the very embodiment of liberal democracy, Déroulède made a direct appeal to the people; against the parliamentary circus he called for direct action, and against Assembly impotence he looked to the strong man. He made great use of revolutionary imagery, but this evocation of the Revolution retained nothing of its partisan and Jacobin meaning; all that remained was a certain vocabulary, with its content jettisoned. Emptied of the humanism, universalism, and appeal to liberty which the Revolution had conferred upon it, this vocabulary of revolt now served to mobilize the masses against the Republic. This was a new phenomenon: for the first time Rousseau, Michelet, and the Revolution of '48 were brought in to justify a popular *journée* whose beneficiary was to be a saviour, that strong man so despised by the old republican tradition. For the first time it was possible to appeal to large sections of the populace and obtain their enthusiastic adherence, in the name of political authoritarianism; the new nationalism placed itself resolutely, at one and the same time, under the banners of authoritarianism and of universal suffrage, of the man elected by the popular will, and of social reform.

In the name of safeguarding national values, the new nationalism begot authoritarianism, cultural chauvinism, xenophobia, the absolute subordination of the individual to the collectivity, and, finally, racism. It ended in a violent anti-intellectualism, accusing the intellectuals of spawning individualism, stifling vitality, and dulling the energies. Like Barrès, Jules Soury, Daudet, Marchand, or the majority of the leading nationalists, Déroulède worshipped at the shrine of heroism, energy, and the will to action. The nationalism he advocated was that of Barrès, which laid the foundations for a nationalism of defiance and adventure, for a romantic and mystical nationalism which explained why life was worth living, which sought to give life a new meaning and a new dynamism, and which strangely prefigures fascism. It is this form of nationalism which merged with the Right, once the latter had made it an essential part of its doctrine.[35]

Of course, the Right has never had a monopoly of nationalism, nor has it ever formed a homogeneous whole. Far from it. And the same holds for nationalism; if it does teeter to the right, it nevertheless retains two clearly distinct tendencies. There is a nationalism which is nationalist before it is rightist, and a bourgeois nationalism which is rightist before it is nationalist. Déroulède's nationalism belongs to the first category. Though it came to lean to the right, it did not merge outright with the traditional Right; and at the outset it rejected the latter's social choices. Nevertheless, as its social consciousness points essentially to the integration of the proletariat within the national community, to the elimination of every form of particularism, and to the defusing of the social question, nationalism must clash with Marxism and in this way become the ally of the Right as a whole. Henceforward it was the petty bourgeoisie that was to furnish the big battalions it needed to play any political role at all; it was this bourgeoisie which provided the following of the League of Patriots—a connection which was to endure until the Leagues of the nineteen-thirties.

Notes

1. Cf. Raoul Girardet, *Le nationalisme français (1871–1914)*, Paris, 1966, 15, 70–84; Claude Digeon, *La crise allemande de la pensée française (1870–1914)*, Paris 1950, indispensable for the study of the intellectual reaction in France after 1870. For the notable contribution of Ernest Lavisse, the official ideologue of Republican education, to the exaltation of national feeling, see Pierre Nora, 'Ernest Lavisse: son rôle dans la formation du sentiment national', *Revue Historique*, July–September 1962.

2. Raoul Girardet, on the other hand, considers this new colouring which French nationalism took on in the five or six years before the war of 1914 as something totally new and original in its history: 'Note sur l'esprit d'un fascisme français', *Revue Française de Science Politique*, July 1955.

3. On the two sides of the Vichy regime see Stanley Hoffmann, 'Aspects du Régime de Vichy', ibid., January 1956.

4. It is hard to imagine a work more inspired by pre-1914 nationalism —more 'Barrèsian'—than André Malraux's latest book, *Les Chênes qu'on abat*, Paris 1971. The resemblance is striking between the themes of this dialogue and those which dominate the works of the nationalist writers of 1890–1914.

5. Paul Déroulède, *La Défense Nationale, conférence faite à Rouen le 22 juin 1883*, Paris 1883, 6; *Le Livre de la Ligue des Patriotes, extraits des articles et discours* (hereafter *Le Livre de la Ligue*), Paris 1887, 2, 5, 65; 'Vive la France', in *Chants du Soldat*, Paris 1909, 7. The collection

Chants du Soldat includes *Chants du Soldat* (1872), *Nouveaux Chants du Soldat* (1875), *Marches et Sonneries* (1881), *Refrains Militaires* (1888), and *Chants du Paysan* (1894). Déroulède's popularity can be gauged from the fact that in the 1878 catalogue of the Bibliothèque Nationale mentions 49 editions of *Chants du Soldat* and the 1883 catalogue records 91 for *Nouveaux Chants du Soldat*. In the single year 1894 *Chants du Paysan* ran through 19 printings. The entire collection was translated into Italian in 1882, with a preface by Edmond de Amicis. The history of the League of Patriots has yet to be written, having been treated so far only in a paper presented by Raoul Girardet to the Société d'Histoire Moderne et Contemporaine on 20 April 1958 (summarized in the *Revue d'Histoire Moderne et Contemporaine*, supplement 3, 1958). Girardet points out the League's obedience to the Gambettist line, its connections with the opportunist establishment, and its officially non-political character.

6. Paul Déroulède, *De l'Education Militaire*, Paris 1882, 22; *Le Livre de la Ligue*, 171–2.

7. On its own estimates, the League and the associations grouped about it had a membership in 1887 of some 200,000, drawn mainly from the 'lower classes and the younger generation' (see the foreword to the *Livre de la Ligue*). It is impossible to verify this figure; in fact, Girardet has shown that the League drew the bulk of its membership from among the lower middle class and retired military men. Déroulède became the League's president on 13 May 1885, after the resignation of Anatole de la Forge, who had succeeded Henri Martin. Until then Déroulède had held the post of Délégué Général.

8. Déroulède, *De l'Education Militaire*, 3–4; *Chants du Soldat*, 19; *Le Livre de la Ligue*, 4–5, 231.

9. Déroulède, 'La Madone de la Patrie', *Le Drapeau*, 21 July 1883, 333; *De l'Education Militaire*, 12, 14–16, 25.

10. Déroulède often returned to the subject of Gaul; see for example *Le Livre de la Ligue*, 80, 84, 87. He exalted Joan of Arc in *Chants du Soldat* (36), and managed the same enthusiasm for the myth of the French Revolution (93).

11. Déroulède, *Le Livre de la Ligue*, 4; *Le Drapeau*, 14 November 1885, 544; *De l'Education Militaire*, 7–8. Article 30 of the League's charter stated that the League 'does not engage in either religious or internal politics'.

12. Déroulède, *Le Défense Nationale*, 11. Déroulède, in fact, did not become an anti-semite until the time of anti-dreyfusard nationalism, when he invoked Catholicism as one of the pillars of patriotism and of the military spirit; but by then he had reached the end of his evolution.

13. Déroulède, *Le Livre de la Ligue*, 124, 135; *Chants du Soldat*, 65. At the same time he was making it plain that the Republic itself was not in question: 'The fault, I know, is not in its laws. It has made the effort and is pointing the way.'

14. *Le Drapeau*, 7 March 1885, 112.

15. Ibid., 14 November 1885, 544.

16. Ibid., 23 January 1886, 65.

17. *Le Livre de la Ligue*, 270.

18. Adrien Dansette, *Le Boulangisme*, Paris 1946, 63–4; cf. Déroulède, *Qui vive? France! 'Quand même'—Notes et Discours, 1883–1910*, Paris 1910, 88; and the work by the former Boulangist deputy Francis Laur, *L'Epoque Boulangiste—Essai d'histoire 1886–1890*, Paris, 2 vols., 1912–14, I, 177.

19. Déroulède, *La Défense Nationale*, 2: 'The leader must be coarse, and he must be totally obeyed.' See 'Les funérailles d'Henri Rivière', *Le Drapeau*, 7 February 1885, 65: 'Belonging to the Army means belonging to duty, danger and death, means no longer belonging to oneself and almost no longer being oneself.'

20. Alfred Naquet, *Questions Constitutionelles*, Paris 1883, 129.

21. On this see Jacques Néré, 'La crise économique de 1882 et le mouvement boulangiste', unpublished doctoral thesis, University of Paris, 1959.

22. See Maurice Barrès, *L'Appel au Soldat*, Paris, 1900, 48; Jacques Néré, *Le Boulangisme et la presse*, Paris 1964, 87; cf. Henri Michelin's speech in the Chamber published in *L'Action*, 8 December 1886.

23. René Rémond, *La Droite en France—de la première Restauration à la Vème République*, Paris 1963, 160.

24. For Déroulède's ideas on the parliamentary Republic, the powers of the President, plebiscites, etc., see *Cours d'assises de la Seine, 29 juin 1899. Affaire de la Place de la Nation. Procès Paul Déroulède—Marcel Habert. Discours de Paul Déroulède . . .*, Paris 1889 (hereafter *Affaire de la Place de la Nation*), 16; Déroulède, *L'Alsace-Lorraine et la Fête Nationale*, Paris 1910, 30–1; idem, *Les Parlementaires*, Paris 1909, 9, 11–12; idem, *Qui vive? France! 'Quand même'*; idem, *Discours prononcé le 23 mai 1901 à Paris au Manège Saint Paul*, Paris 1902; idem, *La Patrie, la Nation, l'Etat*, Paris 1909, 17; Déroulède's speech in the Chamber of Deputies, *Journal Officiel*, 23 December 1892.

25. Claude Willard, *Le Mouvement Socialiste en France (1893–1905) —Les Guesdistes*, Paris 1965, 37. On the leftist aspect of the nationalist movement see Z. Sternhell, 'Barrès et la gauche: du Boulangisme à la Cocarde', *Le Mouvement Social*, April–June 1971.

26. 'Fraternal amelioration of their lot is not the only thing which Socialism holds out for the workers; there is also the defeat and disappearance of the bosses. It's no longer a more equitable distribution between wages and profits, it's the confiscation of profits. It's no longer each man attaining a happier state in his turn, it's the immediate attainment of the same state by all, as if general ruin could give birth to individual prosperity.' *Affaire de la Place de la Nation*, 12.

27. On Guérin and Morès, see Jules Guérin, *Les trafiquants de l'antisémitisme:* La Maison Drumont et Cie, 208–209; Georges Bernanos, *La grande peur des bienpensants: Edouard Drumont*, Paris 1939, 348–9; R. F. Byrnes, 'Morès, the First National Socialist', *Review of Politics*,

July 1950. Morès' group, known as 'The Friends of Morès', was an organization of gangsters recruited from the Paris underworld, not unlike the fascist and Nazi stormtroopers of a later day.

28. *Qui vive? France! 'Quand même'*, 25–6. The article was written on 4 December 1898.

29. *La Patrie, la Nation, l'Etat*, 7.

30. *Affaire de la Place de la Nation*, 16. See also *La Patrie, la Nation, l'Etat*, 24; *De l'Education Militaire*, 7–8; *Hommage à Jeanne d'Arc*, a speech given at Orleans on 8 May 1909 at a banquet of the League, Paris 1909, 2–5.

31. Maurice Barrès, *L'Appel au Soldat*, 200, 208, 210, 443; *Le Courrier de l'Est*, 31 August 1890; *Mes Cahiers*, I, 203.

32. Maurice Barrès, *Scènes et Doctrines du Nationalisme*, Paris 1925, II, 242–62.

33. Cf. *Enquête sur la Monarchie*, Paris n.d. [1925], 476; Léon de Montesquiou, *Les Origines et la Doctrine de l'Action Française*, Paris 1918, 12–14.

34. See the chapter on France by Eugen Weber in Hans Rogger and Eugen Weber (eds.), *The European Right: A Historical Profile*, University of California Press 1966.

35. Cf. on this subject, J. L. Talmon, *The Unique and the Universal*, London 1965, 176–80.

2. THE FRENCH "COLONIAL PARTY": ITS COMPOSITION, AIMS AND INFLUENCE, 1885–1914

by C. M. Andrew and A. S. Kanya-Forstner

Fierce debate and political conflict, leading to rebellion and the threat of civil war, suggested in the later twentieth century an intensity of commitment to colonial empire that the French did not earlier feel for their overseas possessions. The great additions to France's imperial holdings that were made through the nineteenth century, especially after 1871, certainly occasioned no serious public protest; but no more were they made in response to a ground swell of popular enthusiasm. The French may not have collected their empire in a fit of absence of mind, but they appeared in general to be little attracted by overseas empire, to have no strong imperial vision. Anticolonial opinion may have fallen away pretty steadily from the mid-1880s; it is less sure that it was replaced by an activist colonial sentiment. Hence the continued interest in the problem of how it was that this nation, evidently so considerably indifferent to the second greatest colonial empire in the world, came to assemble and hold it before 1914. It has long been recognized that part of the explanation lies with the special interest groups linked to the geographical societies, and with the explorers, the administrators, the soldiers and sailors who worked their will either at home or on the far colonial frontiers. Above all, it has been known that there was a "colonial party." Just what the party was has been less sure, though its principal spokesmen were in full view in parliament, in the press, and in public meetings.

The authors of this article undertake to explain the paradox of a relatively small pressure group that had so powerful an influence on the public life of the nation. Christopher Andrew, Director of

Studies in History, Corpus Christi College and University Lecturer, Cambridge University, is editor of Historical Journal *and author of* Théophile Delcassé and the Making of the Entente Cordiale *(New York, 1968) and* The First World War: Causes and Consequences *(London, 1970). Sydney Kanya-Forstner, Professor of History, York University, Downsview, Ontario, is the author of* The Conquest of the Western Sudan: A Study in French Military Imperialism *(Cambridge, 1969) and, together with Dr. Andrew, of various articles on aspects of French imperialism and international relations. This paper first appeared in* Historical Journal *14 (1971): 99–128. It is reprinted, with slight revisions in the light of new evidence, by kind permission of the authors and the publisher.*

I

In all three great imperial powers of Western Europe, imperialism acquired a popular following only in the 1890s. This change in public attitudes was particularly striking in France. For most of the 1880s the French public had seemed at best indifferent, at worst violently hostile, to colonial expansion.[1] The Tunisian expedition had helped to bring down Jules Ferry's first ministry in 1881; the proposed Egyptian expedition brought down Freycinet in 1882. Three years later Ferry was hounded not merely from office but virtually from public life after an insignificant military setback in Tonkin. At the elections of 1885 the Opposition reserved its most virulent invective for the attack on colonial expansion, and even the Moderate Republicans felt obliged to condemn the *politique d'aventures* which they had previously supported.[2] Ferry himself had to plead in self-defence: 'L'expédition du Tonkin . . . est terminée . . . Notre politique coloniale doit désormais se limiter à l'organisation et à l'exploitation des colonies nouvellement acquises . . .'[3] The election results—the anti-colonialist Right gained over 100 seats—confirmed the unpopularity of overseas expansion. Even France's existing Empire now seemed in danger. Two months after the elections, the Chamber approved the Tonkin and Madagascar Estimates by only three votes, and as late as 1888 the Government's majority on Tonkin fell to nine.[4]

By 1890 the mood of public opinion had been transformed. In May Parliament enthusiastically applauded the Colonial Under-Secretary's sweeping territorial claims in West Africa. During the summer public support for the creation of a vast African empire was extravagant enough to alarm the Government and disturb even the colonialists. By 1893 Far Eastern expansion too had become popular. During the Siamese crisis of that year it was the French Government, not the French public, which lost faith in a forward policy.[5]

This sudden change of opinion was less profound than it appeared. The anti-colonialism of the 1880s drew its strength almost as much from domestic as from colonial controversies. Moderate governments, treading their wary path between radicalism and reaction, made enemies on both flanks. But the major issues—the separation of Church and State, the laicization of education, constitutional reform—all reflected the polarization of Left and Right. Only on colonial questions could the two extremes unite to attack the Centre. For the same reason, however, Moderate deputies were driven to support the Government's colonial policies in order to defend the *République opportuniste* against its enemies. The Republicans who deserted Ferry in March 1885 never deserted his successors and, as the passions of 1885 subsided, some Radicals and Conservatives also came to accept the permanence of the new French Empire. By 1889 opposition to colonial expansion was already losing its electoral appeal. Only 84 successful candidates condemned overseas expeditions in their *professions de foi*, and half of them were Conservatives extracting what little advantage they still could from the Tonkin defeat of 1885. In 1893 only 28 still condemned colonial expansion, while 40 deputies now called for 'la prompte organisation d'une armée coloniale'.[6]

But by far the most important reason for the Empire's new-found popularity was the growing involvement of colonial expansion with *European* rivalries. The new attitude to Africa in 1890 was less the reflection of a genuine imperialism than of indignation at the Anglo-French agreement of that year and its apparently deliberate neglect of French interests. The Siamese crisis of 1893 was regarded not simply as a struggle with the Siamese but principally as a struggle with the English for influence in Siam. Théophile Delcassé, the Colonial Under-Secretary and the only member of the Government anxious to make Siam French, privately admitted that his strength in Cabinet lay in his reputation not as a partisan of French expansion but as 'the man who insists on not giving way to John Bull'.[7] Anglo-French rivalry converted many nationalists into imperialists; Franco-German rivalry after 1904 seemed to convert the rest. When Germany decided to challenge French influence in Morocco, *Revanchards* whose patriotism had previously been limited to Europe suddenly espoused the French cause in North Africa. All nationalists were now united in defence of an imperial interest, just as all imperialists were united in opposition to Germany. 'L'Allemagne', said one such imperialist, René Millet, 'nous a rendu le plus grand service en faisant du Maroc une question nationale au premier chef.' [8]

But the appearance of massive popular support for colonial expansion was deceptive. At the turn of the century colonialists tried to persuade themselves that the 'progrès de l'idée coloniale' since 1890 reflected not merely French nationalism but a love of the Empire for its own sake.[9] After 1905 their optimism rapidly evaporated. As soon as Morocco ceased to be the focus of a Franco-German crisis, it also ceased, along with the rest of the Empire, to hold the interest of the French public. The *Ligue Coloniale Française*, founded in 1907, was an attempt to remedy this situation by creating a mass colonialist movement which was to undertake the 'colonial education' of the French people. It failed. In 1913 the total membership of the *Ligue* stood at a paltry 2,600, and the following year its official bulletin gloomily admitted that 'l'éducation coloniale des Français demeure entièrement à faire'.[10] Except in Paris and a few provincial cities with overseas connexions, Frenchmen remained stubbornly indifferent to colonial affairs; for all their nationalism, they became colonialists only in a moment of national crisis. On the eve of the First World War the French colonialist movement, the *parti colonial*, represented, and knew itself to represent, only a tiny minority of the French people.

II

Of whom did this minority consist? Generally speaking, the 'colonial party' comprised the members of various societies, each with an interest in a particular area or a particular aspect of French expansion.[11] For the most part these members were professional men—journalists, writers, businessmen and politicians—either in or on the fringes of public life. A few had achieved distinction in their chosen fields: Eugène Melchior de Vogüé had a major literary reputation and a seat in the *Académie Française;* Paul Leroy-Beaulieu was one of France's leading economic theorists, and Eugène Etienne was one of the most powerful deputies in Parliament. But the majority were undistinguished. Even some of the most influential, journalists like Harry Alis, Paul Bourde and Robert de Caix, were obscure figures in their own time and are now completely forgotten.

By far the richest of the colonial societies was the *Union Coloniale*

Française, founded in 1893 as 'un syndicat des principales maisons françaises ayant des intérêts aux colonies'.[12] Its high subscription rates enabled it to spend more than 1,000,000 frs on its activities during its first ten years.[13] It published its own periodical, the *Quinzaine Coloniale*, and subsidized the *Politique Coloniale*, for many years the most widely read colonialist newspaper. Its relations with the Government were good, and it regularly tried to influence official policy either by lobbying or by mounting propaganda campaigns. Some of its opponents at least feared that it might eventually become 'le véritable ministère des colonies'.[14]

But the importance of the *Union Coloniale* should not be overestimated. It began life as 'un humble satellite de la Chambre de Commerce de Paris', and its first president, Emile Mercet, was chosen only after several other candidates had refused the position.[15] Although it had connexions with important financial concerns like the *Comptoir national d'escompte* and the *Banque de l'Indochine*, most of its members were small or medium-size firms with exclusively colonial interests.[16] Most of its funds were spent on the *Quinzaine Coloniale* and on the collection of information about commercial prospects in the colonies.[17] For all its wealth, the *Union Coloniale* remained essentially a *service de renseignements* without any significant influence on expansionist policy. Nor was the *parti colonial* as a whole primarily an economic pressure group. Its only major economic campaign during the 1890s was for the creation of chartered companies on the British model, and even that was by no means completely successful. Although the campaign began in 1891, the Congo was not given over to concessionary exploitation until 1899, and by 1905 the experiment was generally recognized to have failed.[18] Most colonial societies, like the *Union Coloniale*, devoted their energy to the organization of lectures, conferences and, above all, banquets. *Gourmandisme*, indeed, was the best known characteristic of the *parti colonial* and gave it its nickname: 'le parti où l'on dîne'.[19]

The only colonial society for which 'la question coloniale n'est pas un prétexte à banquets et à discours tapageux' was the *Comité de l'Afrique Française*.[20] Its founder, the journalist Harry Alis (Henri-Hippolyte Percher), had become interested in West Africa through his friend, the explorer Paul Crampel, and in January 1890 he helped to organize Crampel's unofficial mission to Lake Chad. Alis was convinced that the clauses of the Anglo-German agreement relating to the territories south of Chad posed a serious threat to French plans for the creation of a north-west African empire. On

19 July, a week after the terms of the agreement became known, he approached the Colonial Department with a plan for sending Lieutenant Louis Mizon on a secret mission along the Benue to establish French influence over Bornu and Bagirmi.[21] On the 27th he wrote to Prince Auguste d'Arenberg, a prominent Conservative deputy and a contributor to the Crampel mission, stressing the danger of British expansion and suggesting the creation of 'une sorte de petite association' to give 'une forme organisée à l'initiative qui a été prise lors de la préparation de l'expédition Crampel'. Arenberg agreed, and in October 1890 the *Comité de l'Afrique Française* was formally constituted. Its specific objective, mirroring its origins, was 'l'union, à travers le Soudan, du Congo français, du Sénégal et de l'Algérie-Tunisie'.[22] The driving forces behind this plan for unification were the *European* rivalries created by the scramble for Africa. 'Cette question d'Afrique', wrote Arenberg to Alis in April 1891, 'prend chaque jour une nouvelle importance, et les événements récents prouvent une fois de plus combien notre action doit être active et rapide si nous ne voulons pas laisser l'étranger nous devancer dans cette conquête'.[23]

The *Comité* was a small organization. It had only 30 members at its foundation, 48 in 1900, and never more than 1,500 subscribers (*adhérents*). Although it contained a number of former *Gambettistes*, its political centre of gravity remained slightly but consistently to the right of centre. Alis was secretary-general of the *Union Libérale*, a moderately conservative political group to which six other members of the *Comité*—Aynard, Greffulhe, Loreau, Leroy-Beaulieu and Melchior de Vogüe—also belonged. Auguste Terrier, Alis's brother-in-law and the *Comité*'s secretary-general after 1899, was at one time a member of the *Ligue de la Patrie Française*.[24]

The *Comité* was not simply an association of disinterested patriots, and its high-minded claim to be 'absolument étranger à toute préoccupation d'affaires' was false. Individual members did at times use the organization as a cover for their private schemes,[25] and the *Comité*'s official activities sometimes had economic motivations. When Alis chose Mizon for the secret mission to Bornu, the explorer was already acting as an agent of the *Syndicat français du Haut-Bénito*, a group of businessmen seeking a concession in northern Gabon, and the *Syndicat* continued to act as Mizon's ostensible employer.[26] When Mizon ran into difficulties with the Royal Niger Company, the *Comité* energetically supported the *Syndicat*'s claims for an indemnity, raising the matter in the Chamber and applying pressure directly on the Quai d'Orsay.[27] The second Mizon expedition, launched in 1892, exhibited an even closer identity of commercial and political interests.[28] Georges Berger, its principal organizer, saw the expedition not merely as a move in the *Comité*'s general strategy but also as 'un acte commercial . . . un jalon positif, encourageant, bien orienté pour un avenir d'affaires'. For Berger at least, there was no distinction between commercial and political objectives: 'l'un protège et aide l'autre pour l'honneur du pays et notre fortune commerciale.' [29]

But the significance of these commercial involvements should not be exaggerated. The *Comité* was a nationalist rather than an economic organization. Between 1891 and 1914 it received subscriptions totalling some 1,000,000 frs, of which less than 5 per cent came from financial, industrial or transport concerns. Of the banks, the largest subscriber was *Rothschild frères* who had no West African interests but whose directors had personal ties with the *Comité*.[30] The most important contributors were wealthy individual sympathizers, the largest of them members of the *Comité* and their families. As far as can be judged, the motives for their generosity had little to do with economic interests.[31] The overriding preoccupation of the *Comité* remained the defence of *national* interests against foreign competition. 'Il fallait avant tout', said Arenberg on his retirement as president in 1912, 'arriver les premiers partout où des territoires africains étaient encore sans maître.' [32]

Most of the *Comité*'s revenue was spent on subsidies to treaty-making expeditions in Africa rather than on propaganda; between 1891 and 1898 these subsidies accounted for more than two-thirds of its total income.[33] During this period, correspondingly little was spent on publicity. Estimated expenditure for 1892 was 60,000 frs, of which only 11,000 frs was set aside for the *Bulletin*, the *Comité*'s principal organ of propaganda. The *Bulletin* was never intended to achieve a mass circulation, and even in the twentieth century only 4,000 copies of each issue were printed. The size of the printing in 1894 was 3,300, of which 1,500 were intended for *adhérents* whose subscriptions automatically entitled them to receive the *Bulletin* free of charge.[34] These priorities were not in the least surprising. The *Comité* always regarded itself as a 'comité d'action' and set out deliberately to avoid the noisy propaganda campaigns organized by other colonialists. Its stated policy was to 'réunir des fonds et, de concert avec le gouvernement, à organiser sans bruit des explorations dont on apprend le départ en même temps que le succès'.[35]

Much of the *Comité*'s influence derived from its determination to act 'de concert avec le gouvernement', and the personal connexions which enabled it to do so. Both Alis and Patinot were former colleagues of Ribot (Foreign Minister 1890–3) on the *Journal des Débats*, and Alis in particular was 'très bien vu et très légitiment apprécié' at the Quai d'Orsay.[36] Ties with the Colonial Department were particularly close. Etienne (Under-Secretary 1887–8, 1889–92) was a friend of Alis, gave the *Comité* every assistance while in office, and became a member soon after his resignation in 1892. Of Etienne's two chief advisers on African affairs one, Jacques Haussmann, was a founder-member of the *Comité*, and the other, Jean-Louis Deloncle, although never formally a member, was an active and influential supporter.[37] After Haussmann and Deloncle left the Colonial Ministry in 1895, the *Comité* retained its influence through the ministry's new Director of Defence, General Louis Archinard. And by the time Archinard left the ministry in 1897, Gustave Binger, one of the *Comité's* founder-members, had been appointed head of the *Bureau d'Afrique*. Both the Foreign Ministry and the Colonial Department gave their financial support as well. Indeed, the Colonial Department's contribution of 45,000 frs in 1891–2 was the largest amount ever received from any single organization.[38]

Government support was vital for the success of the *Comité's* activities in West Africa. Etienne, recognizing Alis and his friends as valuable allies in his own policies of African expansion, had already co-operated with them on the organization of the Crampel mission. After the signature of the Anglo-French agreement in August 1890, he secured Cabinet approval for a series of expeditions, including that of Mizon, designed to consolidate French influence in the Niger Bend and lay the diplomatic foundations of the Chad empire.[39] The Colonial Department contributed to the Mizon expedition, to the Dybowski mission which the *Comité* sent to reinforce Crampel, and to the Maistre mission, sent to reinforce Dybowski.[40] Haussmann and Deloncle ensured official support for the second Mizon expedition, and a similarly close relationship was maintained during Delcassé's period of office, first as Under-Secretary (1893) and later as Minister of Colonies (1894–5). Delcassé organized all his West African expeditions with the help of the *Comité*, using its money when the official funds available proved inadequate.[41] The *Comité's* influence in the ministry survived the departure of Delcassé, Haussmann and Deloncle in 1895. Although the ministry at first refused to approve plans which the *Comité* drafted in 1896 for exploring the territories north of the Say-Barruwa line, it reversed its decision as soon as Binger became head of the *Bureau d'Afrique*. Overriding the objections of the minister's own private office, Binger arranged to pay the expedition's salaries out of departmental funds and even secured a subvention of 15,000 frs from the Quai d'Orsay. On 14 February 1897 Terrier could finally inform Captain Cazemajou, the leader of the expedition: 'La mission a été décidée dans une entrevue qui a eu lieu hier . . . entre le prince d'Arenberg, Binger, de La Martinière [secretary-general of the *Comité*] et moi. Et voilà!' [42]

The parliamentary section of the *parti colonial* was the *groupe colonial de la Chambre*, formed in the summer of 1892 when Anglo-French colonial rivalry was at its height. Its membership epitomized the change in the Chamber's attitude to expansion since 1885. Of the 32 founder-members of the *groupe colonial* who had been deputies in March 1885, only 13 had approved Ferry's forward policy in Indochina. But on crucial colonial votes during the next Parliament (1885–9), they invariably supported the Government. [43] As early as 1886 the colonial and Algerian deputies seem to have formed an organized group. [44] Proposals for a broader parliamentary association not limited to colonial representatives were made immediately after the 1889 elections but then temporarily shelved: probably because Etienne, already the recognized leader of the colonialist deputies, remained a member of the Government. Etienne left office in February 1892; four months later the *groupe colonial de la Chambre* was formed. [45]

The new organization grew steadily in size and influence. By the time it was reformed after the 1893 elections, its original membership of some 110 had risen to about 130, 50 of whom had joined since 1892. By 1902 the membership was probably about 150. [46] In 1898, 28 senators formed the *groupe colonial du Sénat*, and after 1902 the two bodies frequently held joint meetings. [47] All colonial and Algerian deputies, with one exception, belonged to the *groupe colonial de la Chambre*, and all cities with colonial interests, except Bordeaux, were represented in it. [48] The political complexion of the group justified its claim to include 'un grand nombre de députés siégeant sur les bancs les plus divers, mais tous réunis par le désir d'assurer la force et la grandeur de la France coloniale et extérieure'. Although the *groupe colonial* embraced all shades of opinion from *Légitimiste* to *Extrême-Gauche*, however, a large majority of its members were always moderate Republicans. [49] Despite its divisions on domestic policies, the *groupe colonial* did formulate coherent policies on major issues of foreign and colonial affairs, and it pressed for their adoption both in debate and through direct approaches to the Government. It quickly became 'the Parliamentary nursery of Colonial Ministers', producing five of the seven ministers between 1894 and 1899. Its members formed an important bloc in all parliamentary Budget Commissions between 1890 and 1896, and a majority of the *Commission des Affaires Extérieures et Coloniales* which was set up in 1895. In a Chamber without disciplined parties the colonialists were at least 'men who know definitely what they are about and what they want'. As such, they were a pressure group to be reckoned with.[50]

The *groupe colonial* had close links with the other sections of the colonial party. Thirteen of its founder-members, including Etienne and the first vice-president, Arenberg, were members of the *Comité de l'Afrique Française;* one of them, Jean Charles-Roux, was in addition president of the *Comité de Madagascar.* The *groupe colonial* championed the same causes. Its first action was to organize a banquet for Mizon; its second was to seek an increase on the colonial missions estimate of 200,000 frs, half of which was immediately allocated to the second Mizon expedition.[51] It was equally active on Far Eastern affairs. In February 1893 it called for a firm stand against Siamese violations of the Indochinese frontier and sent its demands to the Quai d'Orsay with the signatures of more than 200 deputies. Knowledge of massive parliamentary as well as public support enabled Delcassé, himself a founder-member of the *groupe colonial,* to force the Government's hand during the crisis which followed.[52] The *groupe* also demanded energetic action to make a reality of the French protectorate over Madagascar. One of its members, the former Resident-General Le Myre de Vilers, was sent by the Government to the island, and he delivered the French ultimatum on 22 October 1894. Four days later, the *groupe colonial* called publicly for military action and the provision of the necessary funds. On 26 November the Chamber, by a large majority, approved plans for a military expedition and voted credits of 65,000,000 frs.[53]

III

During the first few years of their existence, both the *Comité de l'Afrique Française* and the *groupe colonial de la Chambre* held regular and well attended meetings. The *Comité* met fifteen times in 1891, fourteen in 1892 and eight in 1893. The *groupe colonial* held sixteen meetings in the eighteen months before the 1893 elections and ten during the first year of the next Parliament. At one such meeting, over 100 members were present. After 1894, however, the number of formal meetings rapidly declined. The *Comité* met only sixteen times in all between the summer of 1894 and January 1900; the *groupe colonial* also abandoned regular meetings during the summer of 1894, thereafter assembling only on an *ad hoc* basis to discuss specific issues. The continued growth in its membership gave a misleading impression of the real level of colonial enthusiasm in the Chamber. In 1902, when its numbers reached their peak, only some twenty deputies expressed any support at all for colonial expansion in their election manifestos.[54] Most members, having declared their membership at the opening of each Parliament, took little further part in the *groupe*'s affairs.

This decline in the organized activity of the *parti colonial* was due in part to the changing context of colonial expansion. The *Comité de l'Afrique Française* had been formed to deal with the threat of European rivalry to French plans for a unified African empire. By 1894 the immediate danger of European competition was passing. The Anglo-German and Franco-German agreements completed the diplomatic partition of the Chad area, and Anglo-French disputes in the Niger Bend also became a matter for negotiations. By March 1895 Delcassé, the principal organizer of the expeditions into the Niger Bend, was convinced that 'en Afrique, dont le partage définitif . . . sera bientôt accompli, il n'y a plus qu'à fournir . . . les moyens de consolider et de compléter les résultats acquis . . .'[55] In the Chamber too the passions aroused by Anglo-French rivalry were beginning to cool, and with them the enthusiasm for colonial expansion. In November 1894, for example, Parliament and the press had acclaimed the invasion of Madagascar, hailing it not so much as a glorious colonial venture as a blow to British pretensions.[56] As rivalry with Britain became less intense, the enthusiasm for Madagascar evaporated. 'De tous les côtés', complained the *Politique Coloniale*, 'dans presque tous les milieux, dans la plupart des journaux, s'élèvent des plaintes, s'exhalent des récriminations . . .' For several months, until the final success of the expedition silenced criticism of it, the *Politique Coloniale* actually feared a return to the violent anti-colonialism of 1885.[57]

The transformation of the *parti colonial* during 1894–5 also reflected a change in its tactics. Its leaders had always been suspicious of relying too heavily on propaganda and on public demonstrations of enthusiasm. Both Etienne and Alis were convinced that public statements of colonialist ambitions would, by arousing foreign and domestic opposition, simply make their ambitions more difficult to achieve. On the other hand, their preferred tactic of exerting pressure directly and privately on the Government had already proved its effectiveness. By 1895 the importance of the *parti colonial* was recognized more in official circles than by the public; indeed the influence attributed to it at times reached absurd proportions. François Deloncle, a prominent member of the *groupe colonial*, visited Egypt in the spring of 1895, claiming quite falsely to have secret instructions from the Quai d'Orsay, and threatening to mobilize colonialist opposition against the French minister, Cogordan. Hanotaux immediately disavowed him, but Deloncle was nevertheless able to persuade many of Cogordan's subordinates, including his second-in-command, that he really did have secret instructions and that his friends could force the minister's recall.[58] Some leaders of the *parti colonial*, however, did favour the greater use of publicity. In 1902 Joseph Chailley-Bert, one of Etienne's closest lieutenants, called on him to state openly France's claims to Morocco and Siam. But Etienne stood firm. 'Je crains que ce programme . . . trop net', he replied, 'n'éveille pas au dehors quelques alarmes . . . Là où les conventions internationales laissent des questions ouvertes, n'est-il pas prématuré de crier trop haut comment nous entendons les régler?'[59] And Etienne had his way. In June 1905 the *groupe colonial* unanimously resolved to ask for the restriction of parliamentary debates on foreign affairs to those occasions when public discussion would not interfere with diplomatic negotiations.[60]

The preference for private, rather than public, pressure inevitably necessitated the concentration of initiative in relatively few hands. The *groupe colonial* as a whole was too amorphous a body to be kept in a permanent state of mobilization or to maintain the necessary secrecy. It continued to have its uses, but only as a loosely organized reserve whose weight could be added to private pressure whenever a suitable occasion arose, as it did during the Siamese crisis of 1902. Like the *groupe colonial*, the *Comité de l'Afrique Française*, particularly after it had ceased to meet regularly, was controlled by its leaders and permanent officials. Although broad lines of policy continued to be discussed at general meetings, the real decisions were taken by only a few individuals, often without reference to the *Comité* as a whole.[61] From the mid-1890s onwards, a small inner circle: the officers of the *groupe colonial*, the leaders of the *Comité de l'Afrique Française* and its twentieth-century offshoot, the *Comité du Maroc*, dominated the *parti colonial* and determined its policies.

Fashoda was the first dramatic demonstration of this inner circle's power. The attempt to reopen the Egyptian question by establishing a French presence on the Upper Nile was the boldest and most dangerous gambit in the African partition, but it did not originate

in the French Government. The scheme was first advanced seriously
in 1892 by Harry Alis, the secretary-general of the *Comité de
l'Afrique Française*.[62] Alis, it is true, was by then a paid agent of
King Leopold II who was anxious to promote a French expedition
to the Upper Nile because it would necessitate a prior agreement on
the Franco-Congolese frontier. But almost every French newspaper
of note, and many individual journalists, accepted bribes from foreign governments.[63] In urging the French Government to negotiate
with Leopold, Alis was not acting against French interests.[64] The
leaders of the *parti colonial*, Etienne and Arenberg, did not need the
Belgians to arouse their interest in the Upper Nile. To end the British
occupation of Egypt was the aim of almost every colonialist in France.

Until the autumn of 1892 it had been possible to believe that
Gladstone would honour his promise to withdraw British troops
when he returned to power. By the end of the year this belief was
clearly an illusion. A foothold on the Upper Nile now seemed the
only way to force Britain's hand. With the appointment of Delcassé
as Under-Secretary for Colonies in January 1893, the *parti colonial*
gained the means to make the Fashoda expedition government policy. In planning the mission, Delcassé bypassed all the official channels. The Foreign Ministry first learned of it from press reports, and
even Delcassé's permanent officials were deliberately kept in the dark.
Instead, the Under-Secretary relied solely on the support of a sympathetic President of the Republic, Sadi Carnot, and of the *Comité*.
The man first chosen to lead the expedition, Parfait-Louis Monteil,
was one of its members, and the *Comité* was also called on to organize the Maistre mission, intended to reinforce Monteil from the
east. Even when seeking the agreement with Leopold which he too
recognized as necessary, Delcassé continued to ignore the Quai
d'Orsay and conducted private negotiations, using Alis as his go-
between.[65]

Diplomatic complications with both Leopold and the British eventually prevented Monteil's departure and ended the attempt to by-
pass the Cabinet. But on 17 November 1894 Delcassé, now Minister
of Colonies, was able to override the opposition of Hanotaux, the
Foreign Minister, and gain Cabinet approval for sending Liotard,
the *Commissaire du Haut-Congo*, on a second attempt to reach the
Upper Nile.[66] The backing of Sadi Carnot's successor, Casimir
Périer, was crucial, and it is significant that four of the Cabinet,
Delcassé, Félix Faure, Poincaré and Guérin—were members of the
groupe colonial, which had just called publicly for a British evacuation.[67] The *Comité*, too, continued to be deeply involved. The
evacuation of Egypt was now its first priority. Alis had thought of

little else since the beginning of 1894 and twice visited Egypt to stir up opposition to the British.[68] In January 1895 he informed the Colonial Ministry that the *Comité* would contribute 10,000 frs to the Liotard expedition and would also pay for a second mission, under a certain Georges Grimaux, to be placed at Liotard's disposition. When Grimaux reached Libreville and announced his plans, Lieutenant-Governor Dolisie was amazed: 'Mais M. Percher [Alis] n'en peut rien savoir; il n'y a que trois personnes qui soient au courant de cette question.' [69]

Liotard also failed to reach his destination, though for logistic rather than diplomatic reasons. In 1896 a third expedition left France, this time with the full approval of Hanotaux, now converted to the Fashoda strategy. Its leader, Captain Marchand, was not an agent of the *Comité*, but he was a protégé of General Archinard, the Director of Defence at the Ministry of Colonies and one of the *Comité*'s most influential members. It was Archinard who persuaded his minister to approve the expedition against the advice of the civilian officials.[70] Even before Marchand left, he was profuse in his thanks for 'tout ce que vous [the *Comité*] faites pour moi et pour la mission'. Once in Africa, he regarded the *Comité* as his only reliable supporters.[71]

The Marchand expedition was discussed by the Cabinet in February and June 1896. It was not discussed again until its arrival at Fashoda in July 1898.[72] Only the *Comité de l'Afrique Française* gave the expedition its serious and sustained attention. It also fostered the illusion that Marchand's arrival would give the signal for an international conference at which Russia and Germany would unite with France to force the British out of Egypt. The unfortunate Marchand certainly believed this. Much more seriously, so too did Hanotaux.[73] The Fashoda crisis destroyed these illusions but revealed for the first time the full extent of the *parti colonial*'s influence on foreign policy. President Félix Faure summed up that influence most pungently: 'Nous avons été comme des fous en Afrique, entraînés par des gens irresponsables qu'on appelle les coloniaux.' [74] There could scarcely be a more shattering indictment of the conduct of French foreign policy.

IV

The failure of the Fashoda expedition was to prove the crucial turning point in the African ambitions of the *parti colonial*. As a consequence of this failure colonialists began to consider an alternative solution to the Egyptian question: that of territorial compensation. If Britain could not be compelled to leave Egypt, she might at least be persuaded to offer France something in exchange. There were different views on where the compensation should be sought. The *Politique Coloniale,* now edited by Louis Henrique, the deputy for *Inde Française,* suggested that France might evacuate Fashoda in return for an enlargement of Henrique's constituency. The *Dépêche Coloniale* revived French claims to the Gambia, also in return for a withdrawal from Fashoda. Neither newspaper, however, dared to add what was probably in its mind: that compensation should be part of a bargain by which France not only left Fashoda but also recognized Egypt, implicitly or explicitly, as a British protectorate. Only the *Bulletin du Comité de l'Afrique Française* openly suggested the abandonment of Egypt for compensation elsewhere. Its proposed bargain—the barter of Egypt for Morocco—was adopted as the policy of a Moroccan pressure group within the *Comité de l'Afrique Française* led by Etienne. During the Fashoda crisis Etienne tried for the first time, but without success, to press this proposal on Delcassé (Foreign Minister from June 1898 to June 1905). Six years later, it was to form the basis of the Entente Cordiale.[75]

Etienne's Moroccan enthusiasts provide the supreme example of the striking disparity between the size and influence of colonialist pressure groups. All three of Etienne's closest supporters—Bourde, Chailley-Bert and de Caix—were later at pains to emphasize how small their group had been. Chailley-Bert wrote of its origins: 'Nous étions cinq ou six pressés autour de lui [Etienne], clairvoyants à force d'enthousiasme, et inquiets à force de désir, qui faisions de ce problème [Morocco] l'objet principal de nos préoccupations.' The originator of the group, 'le premier en date et le premier aussi par sa perspicacité', was Paul Bourde.[76] Next in importance was the group's convenor, Chailley-Bert himself. Appropriately for the 'parti où l'on dîne', the group originally met over lunch, becoming known as the *Déjeuner du Maroc.* In November 1902, at the height of the colonialist campaign against the Franco-Siamese treaty, the *Dèjeuner du Maroc* merged with another group, the *Déjeuner du Siam,* to form the *Dèjeuner Etienne.* But Morocco remained 'la grande, la constante prèoccupation' of the new group, which soon reverted to its old title. By 1903 the *Déjeuner du Maroc* had about twenty members, with a few others posted in the colonies attending when in Paris. They were, as Chailley-Bert once reminded them after a particularly heated discussion, almost the sum total of Moroccan enthusiasts in the whole of France.[77]

Chailley-Bert wrote later of the group's methods: 'Nous nous réunissions . . . pour causer entre nous de notre cher Maroc. Nous nous efforcions de lui gagner des partisans. Nous lancions parfois dans la presse un ballon d'essai. Nous jetions un coup de sonde dans l'opinion. Mais nous savions que nous ne pouvions rien sans les pouvoirs publics.' There was general agreement that, for the time being, 'le Maroc ne devait pas, ne pouvait pas, nous engager dans une occupation militaire'. The essential first step towards a French protectorate was the diplomatic recognition of French supremacy: 'C'est une question de politique extérieure et dans laquelle la politique jouera un rôle plus considérable que les armes.' [78] The main aim of the group, therefore, was to press on Delcassé the diplomatic solution agreed by its leading members: the exchange of Egypt for Morocco.[79]

Etienne's influence on Delcassé reached its peak during the life of the Combes ministry (May 1902 to January 1905). That influence was made possible in part by Combes's virtual abdication of Cabinet responsibility for foreign policy. On the rare occasions when such an issue arose in Cabinet, Combes was apt to remark: 'Laissons cela, Messieurs, c'est l'affaire du ministre des affaires étrangères et du président de la République.' Etienne's influence, however, was also due to his position of quite exceptional parliamentary power. He was president of the foreign affairs commission in the Chamber, of the *groupe colonial*, to which a third of the deputies now belonged, and of the *Union Democratique*, on which the Combes Government depended for its majority. 'Il est de fait', wrote Delcassé's private secretary in the spring of 1903, 'qu'Etienne a dans ses mains le sort du cabinet. Son groupe constitue l'appoint qui est indispensable à celui-ci pour vivre.' The strength of Etienne's parliamentary position gave him a decisive voice in the formulation of foreign policy. His campaign against the Siamese treaty which Delcassé negotiated in October 1902 was so successful that it threatened to drive Delcassé out of office. In February 1903, having weathered the storm for four months, the Foreign Minister was forced to give way to it and renegotiate the treaty. At almost the same moment he finally decided to seek an agreement with England based on the barter of Egypt and Morocco. It is reasonable to suppose that this decision also reflected, at least in part, the influence of Etienne.[80]

In December 1903, four months before the signing of the Entente, the *Déjeuner du Maroc* became the nucleus of a new *Comité du Maroc* with Etienne as its first president.[81] Part of Etienne's purpose in transforming an informal pressure group into a formal organization was doubtless to raise funds. In this he was eminently successful. During its first year the new committee collected 180,000 frs, of which over 50 per cent came in large subscriptions of 1,000 frs or more from financial institutions. There is little doubt that the benevolence of the banks was prompted by expectations of financial reward, the expectation, in particular, of the *Comité du Maroc*'s assistance in arranging a series of lucrative loans to the Sultan. The largest single donation after its first year—12,000 frs in 1910 from a syndicate of Paris banks which had just negotiated a new Moroccan loan—seems to have been given in recognition of such assistance.[82]

The *Comité du Maroc*'s opponents inevitably sought to brand it as 'an organization of financiers . . . the value of whose securities stood to rise with a French occupation'.[83] But anxious though it was to encourage French investment in Morocco, the *Comité* was equally anxious to prevent an uncontrolled scramble for concessions. 'Les appetits se dechaînent beaucoup trop vite du côté du Maroc', declared its secretary, Robert de Caix, in May 1904: 'Ce n'est pas pour préparer ou favoriser une sorte de curée que s'est constitué notre comité marocain.[84] And though eager to establish French control of Moroccan finances, it was privately critical of the extortionate terms imposed on the Sultan by the banks.[85] The *Comité du Maroc*, like Etienne's original Moroccan pressure group, was dominated not by businessmen but by writers and academics: Bourde, de Caix, Chailley-Bert, Bernard, de Castries, Houdas, de Vogüé, Terrier. Bourde, the originator of the group, was also the most completely devoid of any possible financial interest in a French Morocco.[86] Etienne and Charles-Roux did possess substantial business interests, but there is no convincing evidence that these interests inspired their devotion to the Moroccan cause. Etienne insisted: 'Il ne s'agit pas pour nous au Maroc, comme nous l'avons fait dans d'autres régions, d'établir notre domination pour y développer nos intérêts économiques. Au Maroc c'est vraiment l'avenir de la France qui se joue d'une façon irremédiable . . .'[87]

The *Comité du Maroc* quickly spent its first year's revenue. Through the French legation in Morocco, with which it had close links, it founded a pro-French Arabic newspaper and established two new French schools. It also commissioned a geological survey of Morocco and subsidized expeditions to various parts of the country.[88] These expeditions were presented to the public simply as geographic explorations. In reality they were meant to map out the land for an eventual military occupation by General Lyautey's forces on the Algerian border. One of the explorers, Segonzac, was described by Lyautey's deputy, Saint-Aulaire, as an 'éclaireur de notre armée'.[89] In addition the *Comité du Maroc* secretly gave Lyautey funds to assist, by bribery, the 'discreet penetration' of Morocco which he pursued in defiance of his orders from Paris. Jonnart, the Governor-General of Algeria, urged the *Comité* to continue the good work: '. . . Le meilleur moyen, le seul moyen . . . de nous assurer le concours des chefs politiques et religieux qui ont une influence de l'autre côté de la frontière, c'est d'y distribuer un peu d'argent.'[90]

By the beginning of 1905, therefore, the *Comité de l'Afrique Française* and its Moroccan offshoot could—and did—feel that they had achieved their objectives in Africa. They had taken the initiative in securing the unity of France's African empire and, although they had failed to turn back the clock in Egypt, they had been the first to see the sacrifice of Egypt as the way to a French Morocco.

V

In Asia, its second main area of interest, the *parti colonial* was far less successful. The great majority of French colonialists in the 1890s considered the conquest of Indochina not as an end in itself but only as the first stage in the construction of a much larger Asian empire. They looked on Siam, 'a dying nation', as the first candidate for absorption, and in 1893 they enthusiastically supported Delcassé's attempts to establish French hegemony. 'Nous allions fonder', said Etienne later, '. . . une grande Indochine avec Siam. C'était merveilleux. L'Angleterre intervient et déclare qu'elle ne reconnaîtra pas le protectorat français.' Colonialist pressure could not persuade the French Government to go through with Delcassé's plans for a protectorate and risk a war with England. But it did succeed in forcing on Siam a treaty intended to pave the way for future French expansion, giving France a narrow zone of influence on the right bank of the Mekong and the right to occupy the port of Chantabun.[91]

During the summer of 1895, following a frontier incident on the borders of Burma and Indochina, Britain and France made their first attempt to reach a *modus vivendi* in South-East Asia. In January 1896 the two governments agreed to guarantee the integrity of the Menam valley in central Siam but implicitly recognized the areas to the east and west as, respectively, French and British spheres of influence. Although opposed in principle to any limitation of French influence in the Menam valley, the *groupe colonial* reluctantly concluded, after sending a delegation to the Foreign Ministry, that for the moment no more satisfactory terms could be obtained. François Deloncle, a member of the delegation, sponsored the motion approving the treaty, which the Chamber passed unanimously.[92]

Having accepted the treaty, the *groupe colonial* proceeded to put its own interpretation on it. Supported by most Paris newspapers, but to the indignation of the British press, it insisted that France had been given *carte blanche* to occupy eastern Siam whenever she chose. 'Le Siam', said the *Politique Coloniale*, 'n'est plus que la vallée du Ménam.' [93] Even the ban on expansion into central Siam was regarded by some leading colonialists as no more than a provisional arrangement which could later be circumvented. Etienne and his lieutenants considered the beginning of the Boer War in October 1899 as the suitable moment to modify the arrangement. Just as they hoped that Britain's difficulties in South Africa might persuade her, 'désireuse de fermer sûrement . . . la porte égyptienne, à consentir à nous laisser ouvrir la porte marocaine',[94] so they counted on the same difficulties to make the British more accommodating in Siam. Chailley-Bert declared roundly in the *Quinzaine Coloniale*: 'Le Siam doit être à nous!' Etienne suggested more discreetly in the *Figaro* that France could profit from England's present weakness to open negotiations on both Siam and Morocco.[95]

Despite colonialist pressure, however, successive French governments failed either to occupy eastern Siam or to seek a revision of the 1896 agreement. One of the most frequent complaints of the *Comité de l'Asie Française*, founded by Etienne in 1900, was that, far from being strengthened, French influence in Siam was steadily declining. Robert de Caix, editor of the new *Comité*'s monthly bulletin, calculated that of the 190 foreigners in the service of the Siamese Government in 1901, ninety-five were British and only two were French.[96]

The conclusion of the Anglo-Japanese alliance in January 1902 added a new dimension to colonialist anxieties. The French minister in Bangkok complained that, with British help, Japan was now emerging as a dangerous rival in Siam.[97] Hitherto, Japanese influence had scarcely been mentioned in the *Bulletin du Comité de l'Asie Française*. By the summer of 1902, however, the *Comité* regarded the Japanese foothold in Siam as an even greater potential threat to Indochina than the British presence in Burma. Although Britain was blamed for helping to create the Japanese menace, the consequence of that menace was, paradoxically, to persuade the

Comité of the need for an agreement with Britain. De Caix insisted that the British must be blind not to see that Japanese influence was as great a potential threat to their own Asian empire as to that of France: 'Notre politique doit être de ne cesser de travailler à ouvrir les yeux des Anglais à la solidarité profonde des deux pays au Siam.' In Asia as in Africa, the leaders of the *parti colonial* were reconciled by the summer of 1902 to a policy of cooperation with England. The aim of colonialist policy, which for the past decade had been based on rivalry with Britain in Siam, was now on the contrary to secure 'une sorte de loyal condominium anglo-français' and so preserve both empires from the emergence of a new and menacing Asian rival.[98]

The French Government, however, seemed bent on surrendering what remained of its influence in Siam. Colonialist resentment at its ineffectiveness came to a head in October 1902 with the signature of a new treaty abandoning most of the gains of 1893 in return for frontier adjustments which Etienne condemned as derisory.[99] The success of his campaign against the treaty—in Parliament through the *groupe colonial* and the Foreign Affairs Commission, in public through the press and the *Comité de l'Asie Française*—provided the most convincing public demonstration of the *parti colonial*'s ability to dictate the foreign policy of the French Government. The fact that most French newspapers had at first approved the treaty made this victory all the more striking.[100]

But the success of the campaign could not conceal how far the *parti colonial* had been forced to lower its sights since 1893. By the summer of 1902, nine years after the abortive plan for a Siamese protectorate, even the *Comité de l'Asie Française* aimed only at gaining equal influence with the British at Bangkok and at making 'une réalité de notre sphère d'influence dans le bassin du Mékong'.[101] Both these more limited aims were substantially achieved. A new and far more favourable treaty with Siam, negotiated as a result of Etienne's campaign, was signed in February 1904. In April the Entente Cordiale gave formal recognition to the spheres of influence implicit in the agreement of 1896, though restating the determination of both powers to preserve the integrity of the Menam valley. 'Siam', noted *The Times*, 'was quick to see the great change that had taken place in international relations': that Britain, in other words, had ceased to be an ally against French encroachments in the east. In 1907 Siam formally ceded to France both the areas most coveted by her in the Mekong valley, the provinces of Angkor and Battambang.[102]

Siam was originally regarded only as the first step in the expansion of Indochina. The ultimate prize for many French colonialists during the 1890s was Yunnan and South China. It was wrongly but widely assumed that the nineteenth-century scramble for Africa would be followed by a twentieth-century scramble for China.[103] China's humiliation by Japan in 1895 and the scramble for concessions which followed seemed the prelude to this partition. The outbreak of the Boxer rebellion in the summer of 1900 and the dispatch of an international force to Peking appeared to give the signal for the partition to begin. Just as the *Comité de l'Afrique Française* had been founded in response to the scramble for Africa, so Etienne, in anticipation, now founded the *Comité de l'Asie Française*.[104] But the aftermath of the Boxer rebellion was anticlimactic. The partition which almost all colonialists had assumed to be inevitable never happened. By 1903 even the *Bulletin du Comité de l'Asie Française* openly acknowledged that China was likely to remain intact for at least a generation, and that France could do no more for the moment than strengthen her commercial influence.[105]

The *parti colonial* was now forced to look on Indochina not as the foundation for a much larger empire but as the *limit* of French expansion in Asia. This sudden contraction of Indochina's horizons encouraged doubts about its economic and military viability. The French Consul in Yunnan insisted that the Eldorado in South China to which the French colony was supposed to be the commercial gateway simply did not exist. General Borgnis-Desbordes, one of the heroes of African expansion, declared bluntly in 1900: 'L'Indochine serait en cas de guerre à qui voulait la prendre.' Paul Bourde privately regarded it as 'matière à échange'.[106] A few were prepared to say as much openly. Onésime Reclus in 1904 published a book with a title which became famous: *Lâchons l'Asie. Prenons l'Afrique.* Only a minority of the French colonialists were in fact prepared to abandon the Asian Empire. But, significantly, both the colonialist press and the Colonial Ministry felt sufficiently alarmed by the undercurrent of opinion favourable to Reclus to denounce his slogan publicly.[107]

Even the majority who still had faith in the future of the Asian Empire felt a declining sense of its importance: partly because their hopes for its expansion had been frustrated, partly because they recognized the far greater importance of the African Empire. One of the commonest images in colonialist writing during the early twentieth century was the vision of a Greater France reviving the Empire of the Romans on both shores of the Mediterranean, with an

African hinterland running south to the Congo.[108] The myth that 'La Méditerranée traverse la France comme la Seine traverse Paris' was already capturing the colonialist imagination. Even Etienne, the founder of the *Comité de l'Asie Française*, insisted that only in North Africa could the French spread 'l'air de notre civilisation': 'Partout ailleurs . . . même si demain nous étions appelés à prendre notre part dans ce bloc d'immenses richesses latentes qu'est la Chine, nous ne pouvons plus espérer que des développements economiques.' [109]

VI

Until 1905 the *parti colonial* prided itself on its ability to unite men of almost all political persuasions in a common devotion to the Empire. Even the sharp differences which emerged among colonialists at the turn of the century over the treatment of France's subject peoples had little immediate effect on this unity. Etienne's two chief lieutenants in his Moroccan pressure group, Bourde and Chailley-Bert, were two of the champions of the *indigénophile* movement in Algeria, while Etienne himself led the settler lobby. The members of the *groupe colonial* were similarly divided on the question of the *indigénat* (the system of summary native jurisdiction in Algeria and the colonies).[110] Yet the *groupe colonial*, the *Déjeuner du Maroc* and the *Comité de l'Afrique Française* were all proud that their members, whatever their political views, could always meet 'sans que la moindre discussion politique soit venue altérer leurs bons rapports'.[111]

When the *parti colonial* did divide in 1905, it was over a domestic rather than a colonial issue: the separation of Church and State. The split began when the *groupe colonial* was forced to decide whether Separation, and the anti-clerical legislation preceding it, should also apply to the Empire. Perhaps significantly, the split occurred while Etienne was a minister and the *groupe* was temporarily deprived of his leadership. On 27 March Clémentel, the Minister of Colonies, appealed for continued unity, but at a meeting of the *groupe colonial* three days later, a majority called for the application of the Separation Laws to the colonies.[112] The depth of the division in their ranks was illustrated by the vote on the Raiberti amendment (July 1905), the first vote clearly to distinguish the supporters and opponents of Separation.[113] In January 1906, a month after the separation law was passed, the split within the *parti colonial* led its anti-clerical wing to establish the *Comité*

d'action républicaine aux colonies. Besides its general aim of foster-
ing French expansion, the new group was also committed to the
rooting out of clerical influence. The split over Separation also
brought differences over the *indigénat* into the open. *The Comité
d'action républicaine,* boycotted by the conservative deputies who
had previously belonged to the *groupe colonial,* adopted a programme which was clearly *indigénophile* as well as anti-clerical.[114]

The disintegration of the *parti colonial* was confirmed by the
failure of the *groupe colonial* to reform after the spring elections
of 1906.[115] Etienne remained predictably aloof from the *Comité
d'action républicaine.* His *Ligue Coloniale,* founded in 1907 to undertake the 'éducation coloniale des Français', also aimed to reunite
all colonialists and show that 'les questions coloniales ne sont pas
des questions de parti'.[116] Unfortunately, the fact that the *Ligue
Coloniale* was at the same time intended to act as a counter-balance
to the *indigénophile* propaganda of the *Comité d'action republi-
caine* prevented if from achieving this objective either. Despite this
failure, however, Etienne still retained his own position as the undis-
puted leader of colonialist opinion, both in the Chamber and in the
country as a whole. And he remained a force to be reckoned with.
The French legation in Morocco, according to Saint-Aulaire, felt that
its most effective means of influencing the Government's Moroccan
policy was to work through Etienne rather than apply pressure
directly on the Quai d'Orsay. And it felt confident, too, that in a
crisis, 'le parti colonial, plus puissant que nombreux, Eugène Etienne
en tête, tonifierait, s'il le fallait, le cabinet'.[117]

The other reason for the malaise which descended on the *parti
colonial* after 1905 was that, with one exception, the aims of its first
decade had either been realized or abandoned. After the Algeciras
Conference had concluded the first Moroccan crisis, almost no one
in France except the socialists—and they half-heartedly—challenged
the principle of French supremacy in Morocco. But only a small
minority of deputies were prepared to envisage what the *Comité de
l'Afrique Française* and the *Comité du Maroc* saw as the necessary
consequence of that supremacy: the establishment of a protectorate.[118] The *Bulletin du Comité de l'Afrique Française* more than once
complained that the hostility of the 1880s had been less difficult to
overcome than the all-pervasive apathy which followed the first Moroccan crisis: 'Sans doute la politique d'expansion eut à soutenir d'âpres
luttes de 1885 à 1890. Mais peut-être l'hostilité dogmatique d'alors
valait-elle encore mieux que la trop fréquente indifférence où il faut
bien convenir que nous sommes arrivés aujord'hui.' [119]

In the decade before the First World War the *parti colonial*, partly as a result of its own previous successes, aroused a good deal of active distrust. In November 1907 the *Comité du Maroc* denounced 'cette légende absurde que la question [marocaine] est uniquement posé par l'ardeur excessive des coloniaux "impénitents", auxquels on reprocherait même de troubler avec "leur Maroc" la tranquillité du pays'.[120] There was also a vague feeling, both in Parliament and in the country, that colonial affairs were inherently disreputable. The scandals surrounding colonial elections led even some colonialists to call for the abolition of colonial, though not Algerian, seats in Parliament. In 1909, after a particularly scandalous senatorial election in *Inde Française*, the *Comité d'action républicaine* felt it necessary to launch its own campaign in favour of retaining colonial representation.[121] The colonial seats were retained, but the distrust also remained strong. On the eve of the First World War the *Dépêche Coloniale* acknowledged:

> Un Français—et combien, en cette occasion, nos députés sont Français irrémédiablement!—ne peut admettre qu'une affaire faite aux colonies soit une affaire parfaitement honnête, ni qu'un conseil donné à l'égard des colonies soit un conseil parfaitement désintéressé. Celui qui, à la Chambre, s'occupe des questions coloniales, si lointaines, si peu assimilables, est frappé immédiatement de suspicion.[122]

VII

The *parti colonial* was rescued from the doldrums by the growth of unrest in Morocco during 1910 and the prospect, in consequence, of moving at last towards a French protectorate. Probably because of the situation in Morocco, Etienne was able to inject new life into the *groupe colonial* after the 1910 elections. Although smaller than its predecessors, the new *groupe* managed to overcome the differences which had almost destroyed it five years before. Its members, most of whom were hard-core activists, included both clericals and anticlericals, and Algerian deputies as well as *indigénophiles*.[123] The reunification of the *parti colonial* was further marked by Etienne's first appearance, in 1911, at the annual banquet of the *Comité d'action républicaine*.[124]

Early in 1911 Etienne also organised a further series of *Déjeuners*, attended by some of the Algerian generals, at which projects for intervention in Morocco were discussed.[125] The details of the collusion between Etienne and the generals were, unsurprisingly, not committed to paper. But that there was collusion seems clear. Stéphen Pichon (foreign minister from October 1906 to March 1911) was well aware that a plot was being hatched. 'Je trouve notre situation au Maroc aussi bonne que possible', he wrote to his ambassador in Berlin, Jules Cambon, in January 1911; 'ne donnons pas aux militaires et au parti colonial trop de prétextes à tronquer le mouvement et à nous lancer dans des aventures.' [126] Cambon himself was equally concerned by what he called 'la politique des déjeuners' of Etienne and the generals.[127]

Happily, from a colonialist point of view, the height of the Moroccan rebellion in the spring of 1911 coincided with the establishment in France of the weakest Government for more than twenty years, and one particularly vulnerable to colonialist pressure. The three key figures were: Monis, the Prime Minister, a nonentity 'dédaignant systématiquement les questions de politique extérieure'; Cruppi, the Foreign Minister, 'aussi novice en affaires coloniales qu'en questions diplomatiques'; and Berteaux, the Minister of War, a man consumed by the ambition to become the next President of the Republic.[128] The weakness of Monis, the inexperience of Cruppi and the ambition of Berteaux were all essential elements in the success of Etienne's pressure for the creation of a French Morocco.

It was clear that, however serious the rebellion in Morocco became, the *groupe colonial* had no immediate prospect of persuading the Chamber to approve the establishment of a French protectorate. But Etienne calculated that, by acting on the Cabinet instead, he could present Parliament with a fait accompli. A protectorate did not have to be imposed at a stroke. It was necessary only to persuade the Monis Government to send a military expedition to Fez, ostensibly as temporary protection for French nationals. Its continued presence could then be shown as necessary, and its successive reinforcement would gradually amount to a military occupation. Etienne's scheme was not new; it had been almost exactly prefigured in his successful plan for the occupation of In Salah and the Tuat oases eleven years before.[129] On both occasions Parliament accepted after the event a military operation launched without its knowledge.[130]

The Fez expedition was ordered during the Easter recess, when only three ministers—Monis, Cruppi and Berteaux—remained in Paris. Messimy and Caillaux, the only ministers to have left accounts of the incident, both agree that the decision was taken by Cruppi and Berteaux, and then approved without discussion by Monis.[131] Cruppi agreed to the expedition because of his inexperience. He seriously believed that 'l'expédition à Fez n'etait pas autre chose qu'une colonne de secours, qu'aussitôt nos compatriotes délivrés et la garnison chérifienne secourue, les troupes françaises se hâteraient de rejoindre leur base de départ et de regagner la côte'. His naiveté caused a good deal of amusement in the Ministry of Colonies, which had no doubt about the eventual outcome.[132] Berteaux, however, had no illusions about the expedition which he proposed to Cruppi. According to Victor Bérard, a usually reliable observer of Moroccan affairs, Etienne was present at the meeting between Berteaux and Cruppi when the decision was taken. Berteaux, said Bérard, 'a cédé aux instances d'Etienne parce qu'il était candidat à la présidence de la République et qu'il avait besoin des 40 voix du parti colonial'.[133] There is no reason to doubt Bérard's account; both Etienne's manoeuvre and Berteaux's reaction were entirely in character. In 1897 Etienne and his fellow Algerian deputy Thomson had used the promise of their votes to purchase the removal of the Governor-General, Jules Cambon, whom they had found insufficiently disposed to follow their instructions.[134] Berteaux, the object of Etienne's advances in 1911, had on previous occasions used bribery to further his political career.[135]

The expedition's orders were signed on 17 April. 'Les ministres convoqués en conseil de cabinet le 23 avril seulement', wrote Messimy later, 'ne purent que sanctionner le fait accompli.'[136] L'Humanité was not the only French newspaper to detect evidence of colonialist pressure. Even before the expedition was ordered, the usually conservative Revue des Deux Mondes reported that 'les partisans d'une politique d'intervention militaire au Maroc . . . ne perdent aucune occasion de pousser le gouvernement dans le sens de leurs vues et . . . à tort ou à raison comptent sur leur impressionnabilité'. Etienne's tactics were most accurately analysed, however, by the English Nation:

> The art of conducting this game lies in creating at each stage a situation which leads inevitably to the next . . . It avoids the presentation of a clear issue to the electorate and Parliament, with whose consent to the ulterior plans the manipulators of the manoeuvre contrive to dispense. There can be little doubt that if the French people or the French Chamber were asked to answer with a 'Yes' or 'No' whether they desire to embark upon the conquest of Morocco, their decision would be an emphatic and nearly unanimous negative.[137]

By the time French troops reached Fez most European diplomats already saw that a French protectorate was inevitable. This realiza-

tion prompted the German Government to send a gunboat to Agadir
in an attempt, as Kiderlen-Wächter put it, 'to thump the table' and
force the French to offer compensation. The Agadir crisis ended in
November 1911 when Germany recognized the French protectorate
and received a large slice of the French Congo in return. The *parti
colonial* was agreed both in deploring the sacrifice and in accepting
it as a necessary consequence of the Government's earlier hesitation
in Morocco. A few colonialists, as a sign of their displeasure, voted
against the treaty in the Chamber, safe in the knowledge that it
would go through nonetheless. But the whole of the *parti colonial*
accepted Barrès distinction of the issues at stake: 'Le Maroc: question nationale. Le Congo: question coloniale.' [138]

Colonialist influence was as obvious in the organization of the
Moroccan protectorate as in its origins. General Lyautey, a prominent member of the *Comité de l'Afrique Française,* was chosen as
the first Resident-General. Both the President of the Republic and the
Prime Minister had their own candidates for the post but were
overruled by their colleagues, who were perhaps influenced by the
Comité du Maroc's press campaign in favour of Lyautey.[139] Instead
of establishing an office in Paris on the lines of the *Office Algérienne*
or the *Office Tunisienne,* Lyautey at first used the *Comité du Maroc*
as his official representative.[140] When business grew too large for the
Comité du Maroc to handle and an *Office Marocaine* had to be set up,
its first secretary was Auguste Terrier, the secretary-general of both
the *Comité du Maroc* and the *Comité de l'Afrique Française.*[141]

The establishment of the protectorate, however, removed the last
issue capable of reconciling the differences within the *parti colonial.*
During 1912 the old dispute over the *indigénat* re-emerged in an
acute form. In December the *indigénophiles* in the Chamber formed
a new *groupe parlementaire d'étude des questions indigènes,* swiftly
denounced by its opponents as 'cet instrument de guerre contre les
colons'.[142] At almost the same moment the *groupe colonial* disintegrated once again. In its place there emerged at the beginning of
1913 a new *groupe interparlementaire des représentants des colonies,* which by 1914 called itself simply the *groupe colonial.* Thus
the wheel had turned almost full circle since the 1880s. Before the
foundation of the *groupe colonial* in 1892, the colonial deputies had
already formed a cohesive bloc, dominated by Etienne and the Algerians. When the *groupe interparlementaire des représentants des
colonies* re-emerged in 1913, it was attended by representatives of all
parts of the Empire *except* Algeria.[143] The reason why Etienne
and the other Algerians boycotted the new group is simple. Unlike

them, the colonial representatives all had substantial native electorates and all supported the gradual removal of inequalities between *colon* and *indigène*.[144] This final split was a reminder that the *parti colonial* in Parliament, and to a lesser extent in the country as a whole, had never been a settler lobby. By the First World War, indeed, all three colonialist groups in Parliament—the *groupe interparlementaire des représentants des colonies*, the *groupe interparlementaire d'étude des questions indigènes* and the *Comité d'action républicaine aux colonies*—were committed opponents of the *colon* interest.[145]

VIII

Two characteristics of the *parti colonial* stand out above all others: its diminutive size and its enormous influence. The colonialists before 1914 were never more than a tiny minority of the French people; on the eve of the First World War there were probably no more than 10,000 of them. The colonialists who mattered were a much tinier minority still. Yet they decisively influenced French overseas policy for more than twenty years. Africa was the scene of their most impressive achievements. They unified the scattered territories in the west. They led France to Fashoda and the most serious Anglo-French crisis since the fall of Napoleon. They then produced the African formula which six years later became the cornerstone of the Anglo-French entente. Finally, they added Morocco to the Empire and realized their dream of a Greater France.

The secret of their influence lay not just in their own enthusiasm but in the attitudes of French society and in the structure of French government. Except in moments of international crisis, the French people and their parliaments were almost totally apathetic to foreign and colonial affairs. The most hotly debated colonial issue on the eve of the First World War was the reform of the *indigénat* in Algeria. The parliamentary debates on it continued for more than eight weeks, yet never more than thirty deputies took part. When a special morning session was called to hear a statement by the Governor-General, only seven turned up.[146] In the prevailing climate of apathy, a determined and skillful pressure group could wield an influence unthinkable in any other circumstances.

Although the colonialists were few, their opponents were fewer still—and much less determined. Even the socialists, despite their theoretical anti-imperialism, were not completely opposed to colonial expansion. In 1903 Jaurès declared: 'Si nous avons toujours combattu la politique d'expansion coloniale guerrière, la politique d'expéditions armées et de protectorats violents, nous avons toujours secondé et nous sommes toujours prêts à seconder l'expansion pacifique des intérêts française.' [147] Although colonial rivalries failed to create a lasting enthusiasm for the Empire, the nationalist feelings they aroused had at least destroyed the violent hostility to colonial expansion so evident in 1885.

To bring its influence to bear on policy, the colonialist minority depended on the weakness of French government. The ministries of the Third Republic, often precarious, usually preoccupied by domestic affairs, rarely attempted to impose Cabinet control over foreign and colonial policy. Major decisions could be taken by a single minister and approved by the Cabinet without serious discussion, or even implemented without Cabinet approval at all. Ministerial instability sometimes left the permanent officials in control of policy, so opening another door to the colonialist pressure group. Significantly, the *parti colonial* exercised its greatest influence on those occasions when Cabinet control was weakest: during the succession of ministries which presided so ineffectually over the origins of the Fashoda expedition; during the Combes ministry, preoccupied by the battle between Church and State; during the Monis ministry, which was scarcely a ministry at all.

The *parti colonial* also had its weaknesses. It possessed only a tenuous organization. Although it shared a belief in the *mission civilisatrice*, it was deeply divided on what that mission meant. That it retained any unity at all was due largely to one man: Eugène Etienne, *Notre Dame des Coloniaux*, its uncrowned but also unchallenged leader. He provided the one common focus of loyalty for the colonialist movement as a whole. For its inner circle he was 'le guide, le chef, le maître, l'ami'.[148] His leadership made the *parti colonial* one of the most powerful pressure groups in the history of the Third Republic. At a number of crucial moments—in the making of the Entente Cordiale, in the establishment of the Moroccan protectorate—the influence of the *parti colonial* was, in effect, the influence of Eugène Etienne.

But if Etienne could influence the French Government, his movement could not educate the French people. The *parti colonial*, throughout its life, remained a pressure group. Like all pressure groups, it was far more capable of changing the policy of government than the climate of opinion. The colonialists were able to win public support only when they succeeded in presenting colonial issues as questions of national prestige. Colonialism divorced from nationalism had little popular appeal. Camille Fidel, one of the colonial party's most active propagandists, wrote in 1918:

Malgré les efforts incessants de nos différents groupements et organes coloniaux (lesquels, sans le concours de la grande presse, ne peuvent malheureusement atteindre qu'un public restreinet) l'éducation coloniale de la grande masse de la population n'est pas encore faite, et il n'existe pas en France une opinion coloniale, un sentiment 'impérial' . . . A Paris, on a l'impression de n'être que dans la capitale de la France; à Londres, on a l'impression d'être dans la capitale de l'Empire britannique: c'est là une différence essentielle qui permet d'expliquer bie des choses.[149]

The *parti colonial* was never a mass movement.[150]

Notes

This essay is a preliminary statement of research on which we are currently engaged. We acknowledge our debt to Professor Henri Brunschwig's *Mythes et réalités de l'impérialisme colonial français* (Paris, 1961), the pioneer study of the *parti colonial*, on whose foundations we have tried to build.

Abbreviations used in the notes: A.E.: Archives du Ministère des Affaires Etrangères; A.N.: Archives Nationales; A.N.S.O.M.: Archives Nationales (Section Outre-Mer); *B.C.Af.F.: Bulletin du Comité de l'Afrique Française; B.C.As.F.: Bulletin du Comité de l'Asie Française;* B.N.: Bibliothèque Nationale; *D.C.: Dépêche Coloniale; D.D.F.: Documents Diplomatiques Français; J.O. D.P.C.: Journal Officiel, Débats Parlementaires, Chambre; P.C.: Politique Coloniale; Q.C.: Quinzaine Coloniale.*

1. On a few occasions, it is true, particular colonial projects did arouse some enthusiasm, but such enthusiasm was always short-lived. For examples, see A. S. Kanya-Forstner, *The Conquest of the Western Sudan: A Study in French Military Imperialism* (Cambridge, 1969), pp. 60–3; C. W. Newbury and A. S. Kanya-Forstner, 'French Policy and the Origins of the Scramble for West Africa', *Journal of African History*, x (1969), 270–1.

2. See *Recueil des textes authentiques des programmes et engagements électoraux des députés proclamés élus . . .* , *J.O.D.P.C.*, no. 683, 17 Apr. 1886.

3. Jules Ferry, 'Déclaration aux électeurs [des Vosges]', 23 Aug. 1885, ibid.

4. Even these figures give a misleadingly favourable picture. In De-

cember 1885 the seats of twenty-two invalidated Conservative deputies remained unfilled, as did six Radical seats. Even then, the Prime Minister, Brisson, could only obtain his majority by ordering the Cabinet to vote, contrary to usual Parliamentary procedure. In February 1888 the Chamber approved only the reduced estimates; the vote on the Government's original demands had been tied.

5. For a fuller discussion of these African incidents, see A. S. Kanya-Forstner, 'French African Policy and the Anglo-French Agreement of 5 August 1890', *Historical Journal*, XII, 4 (1969), pp. 628–50. On Siam, see C. M. Andrew, *Théophile Delcassé and the Making of the Entente Cordiale* (London, 1968), pp. 32–4.

6. *Recueil des . . . programmes . . . électoraux*, *J.O.D.P.C.*, no. 493, 25 Mar. 1890; no. 532, 15 Mar. 1894. These figures are based on our own calculations. The summarized lists given in the introduction of each *recueil* are inaccurate.

7. Delcassé to his wife, 27 July 1893, A.E. Delcassé MSS.

8. Speech by Millet at the annual banquet of the *Comité du Maroc*, 30 Nov. 1909, *B.C.Af.F.*, Dec. 1909.

9. 'Le progrès de l'idée coloniale', *B.C.Af.F.*, July 1899.

10. 'La Ligue Coloniale Française, son but et ses statuts', *P.C.*, 24 Apr. 1907; 'Bulletin de la Ligue Coloniale Française', *D.C.*, 1 July 1913, 2 Feb. 1914.

11. Saint-Germain [Secretary of the *Ligue Coloniale*], 'L'Expansion coloniale de la France', *P.C.*, 13 June 1907: 'Tous nos coloniaux métropolitains font partie de ces sociétés: éminents ou modestes, ils apportent tous à la propagande coloniale un dévouement et un labeur incessants.' The most prominent of the societies listed by Saint-Germain were: the *Société de Géographie*, the *Société de Géographie Commerciale*, the *Société des Etudes Maritimes et Coloniales*, the *Comité de l'Afrique Française*, the *Union Coloniale Française*, the *Comité de Madagascar*, the *Réunion des Etudes Algériennes*, the *Comité de l'Asie Française*, the *Comité de la Guyane*, the *Mission Laïque Française*, the *Action Coloniale et Maritime*, the *Comité du Commerce et de l'Industrie de l'Indochine*, and the *Comité du Maroc*.

12. *B.C.Af.F.*, Aug. 1893.

13. *Q.C.*, 25 Nov. 1903.

14. Colonel Louis Archinard, Note personnelle et confidentielle, 13 July 1894, A.N. 81 AP 6 II, Rambaud MSS.

15. *Q.C.*, 25 Mar. 1897, 25 July 1908 (Mercet's obituary).

16. *P.C.*, 11 July 1893, gives a list of the *membres sociétaires*. Mercet was a director and later president of the *Comptoir national d'escompte*. The treasurer of the *Union Coloniale*, Stanislas Simon, was the director-general of the *Banque de l'Indochine*.

17. *Q.C.*, 25 Dec. 1905.

18. *B.C.Af.F.*, Mar., May, July, Oct. 1905.

19. e.g. *P.C.*, 11 July 1906.

20. Marchand to Terrier, 25 Nov. 1897, *Institut de France*, Terrier MSS 5904.

21. *B.C.Af.F.*, Mar. 1895 (Alis's obituary); Alis to Etienne, 19 July 1890, A.N.S.O.M. Missions 6, Mizon.

22. Alis to [Arenberg], 27 July 1890 [draft], Terrier MSS 5892; Arenberg to Alis, 31 July 1890, 18 Sept. 1890, Terrier MSS 5891. *B.C.Af.F.*, Jan. 1891.

23. Arenberg to Alis, 13 Apr. 1891, Terrier MSS 5891.

24. Letter-heading on *Compte Crampel*, n.d., Terrier MSS 5891; Baud to Terrier, 2 Jan. 1898, Terrier MSS 5894.

25. e.g. General Derrécagaix to Reinach [both members of the *Comité*], 4 Jan. 1892, B.N. n.a.fr. 13535, Reinach MSS: 'Je viens d'être appelé à donner mon avis sur le tracé du chemin de fer d'Aïn Sefra *vers* Djénien Bou Rerg, et j'ai lieu d'espérer qu'il sera écouté. Une campagne de presse en faveur des idées que je vous ai exprimées devient donc moins nécessaire. Peut-être jugerez-vous qu'il suffirait d'en dire un mot à M. de Freycinet [Prime Minister and Minister of War] pour le décider au besoin. En tout cas, vous pourriez attribuer mon opinion au Comité de l'Afrique Française afin qu'on ne puisse se douter de la part que j'aurai prise au petit projet dont il s'agit.'

26. Note, 1 May 1890, A.N.S.O.M. Missions 6, Mizon; Mizon to Alis, 26 June 1890, Terrier MSS 5892.

27. *J.O. D.P.C.*, 22 Jan. 1891 (speech by Arenberg); Arenberg to Ribot, 14 May 1891, A.E. Nouvelle Série Afrique 2. The first statement of the *Syndicat du Haut-Bénito*'s claims was in fact drafted by Alis. See Deloncle to Alis, 24 Oct. 1890. Terrier MSS 5891.

28. Mizon's ostensible employer this time was the *Compagnie Française de l'Afrique Centrale*, formed by members of the *Comité de l'Afrique Française*, the *Société d'Economie Industrielle et Commerciale* (the parent body of the *Syndicat du Haut-Bénito*), the *Compagnie des Chargeurs Réunis*, and the *Banque de l'Industrie et du Commerce*. See *B.C.Af.F.*, Sept. 1892, May 1894.

29. Berger to Alis, 5 Nov. 1893, Terrier MSS 5891. Berger, a director of the *Chargeurs-Réunis*, joined the *Comité* soon after the second Mizon expedition set out.

30. These figures are calculated from the subscription lists published monthly in the *B.C.Af.F.* Edmond de Rothschild was a friend of Georges Patinot, put up most of the money for the Crampel expedition, and also contributed 20,000 frs to the second Mizon expedition. Patinot was the Editor of the *Journal des Débats* and, with Alis, one of the *Comité*'s originators. See *Compte Crampel*, n.d., Terrier MSS 5891; Alis to Patinot, 6 Aug. 1890, Terrier MSS 5892; *B.C.Af.F.*, Sept. 1892.

31. The five largest contributors were: the comtesse Greffulhe (wife of a member): 39,900 frs; the duc de Chartres: 18,200 frs; Armand Templier (treasurer of the *Comité*) and his widow: 15,150 frs; the duc d'Aumale: 13,000 frs; and Alphonse de Rothschild: 10,000 frs. These figures represent total subscriptions over the period 1891–1914.

32. Arenberg's speech to the *Comité*, 11 Dec. 1912, *B.C.Af.F.*, Jan. 1913.

33. Between 1891 and 1898 the *Comité*'s income was 562,000 frs (in-

cluding 60,000 frs from the *Legs Giffard*). During the same period it spent 384,000 frs on expeditions. *B.C.Af.F.*, Jan. 1906. The *Comité*'s income is calculated from the subscription lists, taking into account certain errors of addition. The calculations on which Professor Brunschwig based his conclusion that the *Comité* was principally a propaganda organization are incorrect.

34. Alis, Rapport, 15 Nov. 1891, Terrier MSS 5891; Service du Bulletin [1894], Terrier MSS 5893.

35. Alis to [Arenberg], 27 July 1890 [draft], Terrier MSS 5892.

36. Deloncle to Alis, 26 Oct. 1890, Terrier MSS 5891. For the use they made of these connexions, see, for example, Ribot to Alis, 14 Nov. [1890], Terrier MSS 5892; Patinot to Ribot, 18 July 1892, A.E. N.S. Afrique 2.

37. Deloncle's letters in the Terrier MSS 5891 make clear his close relations with Alis and the *Comité*. See especially Deloncle to Alis, 26 Oct. 1890.

38. Alis, Rapport, 15 Nov. 1891, Terrier MSS 5891. The contribution, given in three instalments, is shown in the *Comité*'s subscription lists under the initial C. The Quai d'Orsay's subscription of 5,000 frs is shown under the initals A.-E.

39. Crampel to Etienne, 12 Mar. 1890, A.N.S.O.M. Missions 5, Crampel; Etienne to Foreign Ministry, 9 Aug. 1890; Foreign Ministry to Etienne, 19 Aug. 1890; Etienne to Foreign Ministry, 7 Sept. 1890; A.E. N.S. Afrique 1. We are grateful for these references to Mr T. R. Roberts of the University of Aberdeen.

40. Rapport au soussecrétaire, 25 Aug. 1890, A.N.S.O.M. Missions 6, Mizon; Arenberg to Alis, 23 Sept. 1891, Terrier MSS 5891.

41. Delcassé to Toutée, 17 Nov. 1894 (Copy), Terrier MSS 5934; Toutée to Terrier, 25 Sept. 1895, Terrier MSS 5908.

42. Arenberg to André Lebon, 18 Apr. 1896; Lebon to Arenberg, 20 Apr. 1896, A.N.S.O.M. Missions 11, Cazemajou; Terrier to Cazemajou, 19 Dec. 1896, 14 Feb. 1897, Terrier MSS 5896.

43. On the combined Tonkin and Madagascar estimates in December 1885, 30 future members of the *groupe* voted in favour, thirteen against, and one abstained. On the Tonkin credit in November 1888, 35 voted in favour, seven against, seven abstained and four were absent. The larger number voting in 1888 was the result of by-elections since 1885.

44. *Avenir de la Marine et des Colonies*, 11 Feb. 1886.

45. *Le Siècle*, 18 Oct. 1889; *P.C.*, 18 June 1892.

46. See C. M. Andrew and A. S. Kanya-Forstner, 'The *Groupe Colonial* in the French Chamber of Deputies, 1892–1932', *The Historical Journal*, xvii, 4 (1974), 838–40.

47. *Q.C.*, 25 Feb. 1898.

48. See H. Sieberg, *Eugène Etienne und die französische Kolonialpolitik* (Cologne, 1968), p. 98.

49. *B.C.Af.F.*, July 1892. Brunschwig, *Mythes et réalités*, p. 144, has attempted to classify the members of the *groupe colonial* by political

affiliation, and his general conclusions are accurate. But the detailed breakdowns are not so reliable. The number of Boulangists and Revisionists, for example, is exaggerated. Arenberg, who had run as a Revisionist in 1889, was by 1892 a leader of the moderate Right. Martineau, who had stood as a Boulangist, broke with the movement in January 1890. Before 1910, the political affiliations of deputies are impossible to determine with complete accuracy. In 1910, when membership lists of political groups in the Chamber first become available, all the office-holders of the *groupe colonial* belonged to the government majority. Etienne and Rozet were members of the *Gauche démocratique;* Hubert, Clémentel and Carpot of the *Gauche radicale;* Métin and Le Hérissé of the Radical-Socialists.

50. *The Times,* 27 Jan. 1896. Of the Colonial Ministers, Delcassé, Chautemps, André Lebon and Guillain were members of the *groupe colonial,* and Ernest Boulanger, the first holder of the post, later became a member of the *groupe colonial du Sénat.* The *groupe colonial*'s membership on the Budget Commission (33 members in all) varied between 10 and 15. Twenty of the 33 members of the Colonial Affairs Commission in 1895 were also members of the *groupe colonial.*

51. *P.C.,* 25 June 1892; *B.C.Af.F.,* Sept. 1892.

52. *P.C.,* 28 Feb., 2 Mar. 1893.

53. *P.C.,* 7 Dec., 14 Dec. 1893; *B.C.Af.F.,* Nov. 1894 (reporting the meeting of the *groupe colonial* on 26 Oct.) ; *J.O. D.P.C.,* 24 Nov., 26 Nov. 1894.

54. *Recueil des . . . programmes . . . électoraux, J.O. Doc. Parl. Chambre,* no. 1162, 3 July 1902.

55. *J.O. D.P.C.,* 2 Mar. 1895.

56. Cf. de Lanessan in *Le Rappel:* '. . . si les millions furent votés sans compter . . . n'est-ce pas encore parce qu'on était dominé par le désir de "donner une leçon à l'Angleterre"?', reprinted in *P.C.,* 12 Sept. 1895.

57. *P.C.,* 8 Aug. 1895: 'On se croirait revenu au temps où Jules Ferry fut renversé du pouvoir.' See also *P.C.,* 12 Sept. 1895.

58. Cogordan to Hanotaux, 6 Apr., 20 Apr., 11 May 1895. A. E. Hanotaux MSS vol. xviii; Cogordan to Reinach, 18 May 1895, B.N. n.a.fr. 13534, Reinach MSS. As a result of the incident, Cogordan conceived an abiding distrust of 'les enragés du parti colonial . . . le parti agité français'. Cogordan to Hanotaux, 14 Apr. 1897, cited in Marc Michel, 'La Mission Marchand', unpublished *thèse de 3ᵉ cycle* (Paris, 1967), p. 146.

59. *D.C.,* 11 Sept., 14–15 Sept. 1902. Though secretary-general of the *Union Coloniale Française,* Chailley-Bert's real importance was as a member of Etienne's Moroccan pressure group; see Andrew, *Théophile Delcassé,* p. 109.

60. *P.C.,* 18 June 1905.

61. See, for example, Toutée to Terrier, 20 Sept. 1895, Terrier MSS 5908. In November 1894, four months before his death, Alis had used *Comité* funds to finance Toutée's expedition, without informing most of the *Comité*'s members.

62. The origins of the Fashoda strategy are most fully discussed in J. Stengers, 'Aux origines de Fachoda: l'expédition Monteil', *Revue belge de philologie et d'histoire*, xxxvi (1958), 436–50, xxxviii (1960), 366–404, 1040–65.

63. See, for example, A. Raffalovitch, *L'abominable vénalité de la presse française* (Paris, 1921).

64. The Belgians knew this as well as anyone. Cf. Janssen to Alis, 27 May 1894, Terrier MSS 5892: 'Nous ne nous attendons pas à ce que vous défendiez notre agrément avec l'Angleterre [the Anglo-Congolese agreement of May 1894] . . . nous nous attendons à vous trouver toujours très bien français et habile à rendre service à votre pays.'

65. Stengers, 'Aux origines de Fachoda', loc. cit. pp. 444–50; Andrew, *Théophile Delcassé*, pp. 24–5, 41–4; Alis, 'Note écrite de la main de M. Delcassé . . . pour que je tâche d'amener M. Janssen à intervenir en faveur de cette solution', Terrier MSS 5891.

66. *D.D.F.*, 1st ser., xi, no. 285.

67. G. Hanotaux, 'Carnets', 10 Mar. 1895, published in *Revue des Deux Mondes*, 1 Apr. 1949, p. 402; *B.C.Af.F.*, Nov. 1894, reporting meeting of *groupe colonial*, 26 Oct. 1894.

68. *B.C.Af.F.*, Mar. 1895 (Alis's obituary).

69. Note [13 Jan. 1895], Terrier MSS 6010; Chautemps to Alis, 16 Feb. 1895, Terrier MSS 5891; Grimaux to Terrier, 31 Aug. 1895, Terrier MSS 5900.

70. For a full discussion of the role of Hanotaux and Archinard in the preparation of the Marchand expedition, see Michel, 'La Mission Marchand', pp. 36–63.

71. Marchand to Terrier, 16 Mar. 1896, 25 Nov. 1897, Terrier MSS 5904.

72. Michel, 'La Mission Marchand', p. 51; idem, 'Deux Lettres de Marchand à Liotard', *Revue française d'histoire d'outre-mer*, lii (1965), 51; Félix Faure, 'Fachoda (1898)', *Revue d'histoire diplomatique*, lxix (1955), 30.

73. Andrew, *Théophile Delcassé*, pp. 94–6.

74. Faure, 'Fachoda (1898)', loc. cit. p. 34.

75. Andrew, *Théophile Delcassé*, pp. 45–52, 103–10.

76. J. Chailley-Bert, 'Le traité anglo-français', *Q.C.*, 25 Apr. 1904. On the small size of the Moroccan pressure group, cf. R. de Caix, 'Le traité de Fez', *B.C.Af.F.*, Apr. 1912, and Bourde's obituary in *B.C.Af.F.*, Aug.–Dec. 1914.

77. V. Jean, *Les origines du protectorat de la France au Maroc, 1830–1912* (Rabat, 1940), p. 27; *Le Figaro*, 28 Nov. 1902, 12 Feb. 1905. We owe these sources to Sieberg, *Eugène Etienne*.

78. *Q.C.*, 25 Sept. 1903, 25 Apr. 1904.

79. Even René Millet, who 'ne cessait jamais de représenter l'opposition' at the *Déjeuner du Maroc* (*Le Figaro*, 12 Feb. 1905), accepted the principle of an Egypt-Morocco barter; with characteristic perversity, he later suggested that England would have agreed to such an arrangement as early as 1900. See. R. Millet, *Notre politique extérieure de 1898 à 1905* (Paris, 1905), p. 23.

80. Andrew, *Théophile Delcassé*, pp. 64, 196–200.

81. Etienne described the new *Comité* as 'une branche du Comité de l'Afrique Française', *B.C.Af.F.*, Jan. 1904.

82. The subscription lists of the *Comité du Maroc* were published in the *B.C.Af.F.*, which also acted as the *Bulletin du Comité du Maroc*.

83. E. D. Morel, *Morocco in Diplomacy* (London, 1912), p. 111.

84. *B.C.Af.F.*, May 1904.

85. See the confidential report prepared for the *Comité* in January 1905 by de Labry, 'A.s. de la situation de l'influence française au Maroc', Terrier MSS 5951.

86. The *Comité*'s founder members are listed in *B.C.Af.F.*, June 1904; on Bourde, see Andrew, *Théophile Delcassé*, pp. 108–9.

87. Speech by Etienne to the annual banquet of the *Comité du Maroc*, 30 Nov. 1909, *B.C.Af.F.*, Dec. 1909.

88. De Labry, 'A.s. de la situation . . .', Terrier MSS 5951; Saint-René Taillandier to Etienne, 29 July 1904, B.N. n.a.fr. 24327, Etienne MSS.

89. Comte de Saint-Aulaire, *Confession d'un vieux diplomate* (Paris, 1953), p. 267; Saint-Aulaire said that he used this expression 'dans toute la force du terme'. De Labry had insisted in his report, cited above, on the need for 'une reconnaissance rapide, pratique, terre à terre, du pays— chemins, fleuves, ressources, état des esprits, influence' to prepare for an eventual military occupation.

90. Lyautey to Terrier, 14 Dec. 1904, Terrier MSS 5903; Henrys to Terrier, 19 Jan. 1905, Terrier MSS 5900; Jonnart to Terrier, 26 Feb. 1906, Terrier MSS 5901.

91. *Q.C.*, 10 Nov. 1898; Andrew, *Théophile Delcassé*, pp. 32–4.

92. *P.C.*, 21 Jan. 1896; *J.O. D.P.C.*, 27 Feb. 1896.

93. *P.C.*, 21 Jan. 1896.

94. *B.C.Af.F.*, Dec. 1899.

95. *Q.C.*, 25 Nov. 1899; *Le Figaro*, 7 Nov. 1899.

96. *B.C.As.F.*, Jan. 1902.

97. *D.D.F.*, 2nd ser., II, no. 280.

98. *B.C.As.F.*, July, Aug. 1902.

99. Etienne, 'Encore le traité franco-siamois', *D.C.*, 28 Oct. 1902.

100. De Caix at first complained of 'l'enthousiasme plus ou moins spontané' of most of the French press for the treaty, *B.C.As.F.*, Oct. 1902.

101. *B.C.As.F.*, June 1902.

102. *The Times*, 25 Mar. 1907.

103. Paul Cambon, the most respected French ambassador of the time, wrote to Delcassé in 1899: 'Cette question chinoise . . . va dominer les vingt-cinq premières années du nouveau siècle'. Delcassé agreed: 'J'y pense depuis longtemps.' *D.D.F.*, 1st ser. XV, no. 171.

104. Etienne, 'L'oeuvre du Comité', *B.C.As.F.*, Jan. 1901.

105. De Caix, 'Les intérêts français en Chine', *B.C.As.F.*, May 1903.

106. M. Bruguière, 'Le chemin de fer du Yunnan. Paul Doumer et la politique d'intervention française en Chine (1899–1902)', *Revue d'histoire diplomatique*, LXXVII (1963), 263; *D.D.F.*, 1st ser. XVI, no. 113; Andrew, *Théophile Delcassé*, p. 255.

107. *P.C.*, 11 Oct. 1906; speech by Clémentel to colonial banquet, 1 Mar. 1905, *B.C.Af.F.*, Mar. 1905.

108. Millet, *Notre politique extérieure*, p. 177; O. Reclus, *Lâchons l'Asie. Prenons l'Afrique* (Paris, 1904), pp. 95ff; speech by Lyautey to the *Académie Française*, cited in *B.C.Af.F.*, Oct. 1912; M. Barrès, *Mes Cahiers*, IX (Paris, 1935), 215; R. F. Betts, 'The French Colonial Frontier', in C. K. Warner, *From Ancien Régime to Popular Front* (London, 1969), p. 135.

109. *B.C.Af.F.*, Jan. 1904.

110. Albin Rozet, secretary of the *groupe colonial* from 1893 to 1898 and vice-president thereafter, was the most outspoken *indigénophile* in the Chamber.

111. *Le Figaro*, 12 Feb. 1905. Even the violent animosities aroused by the Dreyfus affair had failed to disrupt the unity of the *Comité de l'Afrique Française*. See Terrier to Marchand, 10 Mar. 1900 [draft], Terrier MSS 5904.

112. *P.C.*, 29 Mar., 2 Apr. 1905.

113. Of the officers of the *groupe colonial*, four (Etienne, Gerville-Réache, Chaumet, Vigouroux) voted for Separation, three (Guillain, Lebrun, Rozet) against, two (Flandin, Carnot) abstained, and Siegfried was absent. *J.O. D.P.C.*, 4 July 1905.

114. *P.C.*, 11 Jan. 1906.

115. The *groupe colonial* was reformed by Etienne in December 1907, but we have no record that it met at all before the 1910 elections. *Le Mois colonial et maritime*, Dec. 1907. We are grateful to Dr. Peter Grupp for this reference.

116. *P.C.*, 25 Apr. 1907.

117. Saint-Aulaire, *Confession*, p. 180.

118. 'C'est à dire que l'immense majorité des députés se rend compte que nous ne pouvons déserter notre tâche au Maroc, mais se refuse encore à voir les conditions dans lesquelles cette tâche peut s'accomplir avec un minimum de sacrifices et de difficultés.' *B.C.Af.F.*, Feb. 1908.

119. *B.C.Af.F.*, Nov. 1907.

120. Ibid.

121. Comité d'action républicaine aux colonies, *Pour la représentation coloniale au Parlement* (Paris, 1909).

122. *D.C.*, 25 May 1914.

123. Andrew and Kanya-Forstner, 'The *Groupe Colonial* in the French Chamber of Deputies', *loc. cit.*, 841 and Appendix VI.

124. *D.C.*, 20 June 1911.

125. De Caix to Terrier, 23 Jan. 1911, Terrier MSS 5896; Jules Cambon to Paul Cambon, 22 Apr. 1911, *D.D.F.*, 2e série XIII, no. 248.

126. We are grateful for this quotation to Mr David Miller, who is at present preparing a thesis on Pichon at Cambridge University.

127. Jules Cambon to Paul Cambon, 22 Apr. 1911, *D.D.F.*, 2e série, XIII, no. 248.

128. A. Messimy, *Mes souvenirs* (Paris, 1937), pp. 34, 48, 56; J. Caillaux, *Mes mémoires* (Paris, 1942–7), II, pp. 43, 65–6.

129. For the manner in which the oases were occupied, see Andrew, *Théophile Delcassé*, pp. 153–4. Credit for the occupation was publicly ascribed by Chailley-Bert to Etienne: 'C'est à lui qu'elle est due, personne ne me démentira.' *Q.C.*, 25 Mar. 1900.

130. Even when faced with the fait accompli of the Fez expedition, most deputies at first failed to appreciate its significance. 'Je ne comprends pas cette Chambre', wrote Barrès. 'Que croyait-elle qu'on faisait? Est-ce que vraiment tout le monde ne comprenait pas qu'on allait à Fez, qu'on s'acheminait vers la tunisification du Maroc.' Barrès, *Mes Cahiers*, IX, 213.

131. Messimy, *Mes souvenirs*, p. 56; Caillaux, *Mes mémoires*, II, 65–6.

132. Messimy, *Mes souvenirs*, p. 56. Bertie, the British Ambassador, agreed: 'I believe that Cruppi really thinks that he will be able to fulfil his pledge as regards withdrawing from Fez and keeping within the terms of the Algeciras Act. The Colonial Party will not be pleased if he succeeds.' Bertie to Grey, 14 June 1911, Public Record Office, F.O. 800/52 Grey MSS.

133. *Les carnets de Georges Louis*, II (Paris, 1926), 110. Victor Bérard was professor of Mediterranean geography at the *Ecole Supérieure de la Marine*. From 1904 to 1911 he was secretary-general of Lavisse's influential *Revue de Paris*, specializing in foreign affairs. One of his best-known works was *L'Affaire Marocaine* (Paris, 1906), based on his close contacts with the Quai d'Orsay.

134. President Faure wrote of this incident in his journal: 'Ainsi, afin d'avoir les voix de Thomson, Etienne et consorts, s'est-il [Méline] engagé à leur donner satisfaction en déplaçant Cambon.' Note personnelle XXVII, 13 Apr. 1897, Faure MSS (in the possession of Monsieur François Berge). In April 1911 Jules Cambon was among those who believed that the plan for the Fez expedition had been devised by Etienne and the Algerian generals.

135. We are indebted for this information to the researches of Mr. Peter Morris, Emmanuel College, Cambridge, in the Paris police archives.

136. Messimy, *Mes souvenirs*, p. 55.

137. *Revue des Deux Mondes*, 1911 (3), p. 239; 'Modern Methods of Conquest', *Nation*, 6 May 1911.

138. Barrès, *Mes Cahiers*, IX, 215.

139. President Fallières wanted a civilian; Poincaré, the Prime Minister, proposed a fellow Lorrainer, General d'Amade. Alexandre Millerand, 'Souvenirs' (unpublished typescript in the possession of Monsieur Jacques Millerand), p. 70.

140. Typewritten note by Terrier, 'Entrevue du 2 décembre 1912 avec le général Lyautey', Terrier MSS 5903.

141. *D.C.*, 13 Jan. 1914.

142. *D.C.*, 6 Dec., 12 Dec. 1912; C.-R. Ageron, *Les algériens musulmans et la France, 1871–1919* (Paris, 1968), p. 1103.

143. *D.C.*, 23 Feb. 1913, 9 Mar. 1913, 25 June 1914, 23 Dec. 1914.

144. On 22 February 1913, the *groupe interparlementaire* gave its

unanimous approval to a report on the *indigénat* prepared by Lucien Hubert, a prominent supporter of reform. *D.C.*, 23 Feb. 1913.

145. The *Comité d'action républicaine*, although open to Republicans outside as well as inside Parliament, was dominated by its parliamentary members. All three organizations, of course, had an overlapping membership.

146. Ageron, *Les algériens musulmans*, p. 1110; *L'Illustration*, 14 Feb. 1914.

147. *J.O. D.P.C.*, 23 Nov. 1903.

148. Chailley-Bert, open letter to Etienne, *D.C.*, 11 Sept. 1902: '. . . vous me guiderez, vous m'ordonnerez, vous me commanderez. Et je vous obéirai.'

149. C. Fidel, *La paix coloniale française* (Paris, 1918), pp. 5–6.

150. In 1921 the *Ligue Coloniale* did merge with the *Ligue Maritime* to form the *Ligue Maritime et Coloniale*, which was to have 600,000 members by 1925. But many of these were schoolchildren, and it was in any case the naval rather than colonial element which dominated the new group. The *Ligue Maritime* had eighty of the hundred seats on the *Conseil Général* and nine of the thirteen places on the *Comité de Direction*. *Mer et Colonies*, 25 Mar. 1921.

Authors' Note: Some of the arguments advanced in this article have since been developed further in: C. M. Andrew and A. S. Kanya-Forstner, 'The *Groupe Colonial* in the French Chamber of Deputies, 1892–1932', *The Historical Journal*, xvii, 4 (1974), 837–866; C. M. Andrew and A. S. Kanya-Forstner, 'Gabriel Hanotaux, the Colonial Party and the Fashoda Strategy', in E. F. Penrose (ed.), *European Imperialism and the Partition of Africa* (London, 1975), pp. 55–104; and C. M. Andrew, P. Grupp, and A. S. Kanya-Forstner, 'Le parti colonial français de 1890 à 1914: organisation et effectifs', *Revue française d'histoire d'outre-mer*, lxii, 4 (1975).

3. THE FRENCH ECONOMY UNDER THE FRANC POINCARÉ

by Tom Kemp

Notoriously, France before 1914 was a stable society, affluent, satiated, with an apparently well-balanced economy, substantial savings, and a relatively low level of social discord. Equally notoriously, France two decades later had begun to look like a sick man of Europe. When other states in the 1930s began to recover from the Great Depression, France lagged behind and was only moving up slowly when the war of 1939 swept over her and the enemy in succeeding years ruined her economy. Another decade passed before a strong revival set in, based upon demographic change, planning, and rationalization. Through much of the first half of the century, however, it appeared as if the pre-1914 brilliance of the belle époque *had been a last guttering of the candle, as if the conditions that had produced the effect, genuine or spurious as it may have been, had gone forever. The war of 1914 and its tumultuous aftermath had evidently wrecked the foundations of the French economy, despite the recovery of the 1920s. Only with the upsurge of industrial and agricultural prosperity during the later Fourth Republic did the nature of the pre-1914 affluence and the post-1918 stagnation seem clearer, as optimism replaced the profound pessimism suffusing so many analyses of the French condition in the 1940s and 1950s.*

Tom Kemp places the still contentious question of France's economic performance between the wars in a broad social and psychological context, refusing to accept merely technical monetarist explanations for the slow recovery and the two decades of severe difficulties that plagued the country. Reader in Economic History, University of Hull, he is the author of Theories of Imperialism

(London, 1967), Industrialization in Nineteenth-Century Europe *(London, 1969)*, Economic Forces in French History *(London, 1971)*, The French Economy 1913–39 *(London, 1972), and of various scholarly articles. This paper first appeared in* The Economic History Review, *2d ser. 24 (1971): 82–99. It is reprinted by kind permission of the author and the editors of the* EHR.

The period between the adoption of the *franc Poincaré* in June 1928 and the abandonment of the gold standard by the Blum government in September 1936 is a distinctive one in French economic history. It covers an entire trade cycle from the peak of prosperity through a deep and protracted depression to the early signs of recovery. It offers a striking contrast with the response to the world economic depression of other countries, most of which began their recovery from 1933 or 1934. It witnessed perhaps the last sustained attempt to impose deflation as the remedy for depression. It broke a secular trend of steady and sustained growth in the French economy which extended back to the late nineteenth century and had been resumed after the interruption brought about by the 1914–18 war. It initiated a phase of stagnation from which the economy did not really revive until the 1950's.[1]

The main question which is raised by the peculiarities of the French response to the trends of the 1930's is whether they are to be explained mainly as a consequence of mistaken policies or reflect structural weaknesses which have their roots in the previous century or even earlier. The economist is perhaps tempted to adopt the former position, which would amount to saying that if only the right exchange value for the franc had been found French recovery would have been at least as rapid as that of similar countries. The historian is more likely to stress the structural resistances to change which were expressed in the marked inflexibility which most sectors displayed in the face of the new situation created by the world economic depression. Opposition to devaluation and tenacious adherence to the *franc Poincaré* also had deep roots in the social and economic structure and virtually ruled out devaluation as a deliberate act of policy. The approach of this article may be summed up by saying that while the problem assumed a monetary form, and was thus seen most often by contemporary observers, it was essentially a reflexion of a deep-seated crisis of confidence in bourgeois France which, in different forms, exists to this day.

I

To understand the almost pathological addiction to monetary stability and orthodoxy which prevailed in France in the 'thirties to the virtual exclusion of all other considerations it is necessary to begin with a brief reference to previous monetary experience. Throughout the nineteenth century and until the outbreak of the First World War, the so-called *franc germinal* had maintained a fixed gold value. This stability of the franc was taken for granted, especially by the numerous middle-class rentier public; the monetary unit seemed as unchanging as the metre or the gramme. The inflationary waves of war and reconstruction rudely shook this confidence at a time when many of the comforting landmarks of the pre-war world were being swept away. Anxiety about the currency was understandable on the part of those whose patrimony consisted to a large extent of fixed-interest securities. Bourgeois families, already stricken by the war and the other fears and dangers of post-war Europe, badly needed assurance in the mid-'twenties that the franc would not go the way of the currencies of central and eastern Europe.

French inflation had its source in the war. War finance had been a model of ineptitude; the method and scale of payment to war contractors and the looseness of the control over government expenditure had led to excessive prices, notorious cases of profiteering, and some unsavoury scandals.[2] Hard-pressed, it is true, by the seriousness of the war situation, the government had not exercised sufficient control over the costing of supplies and depended upon borrowing rather than upon higher taxation to raise the money it needed to pay for them. Inflationary pressures, kept under some restraint while wartime controls were in operation, burst forth once they were relaxed.

In financing the urgent reconstruction required in the war-devastated areas of northern and eastern France the government continued to borrow heavily between 1919 and 1925, unwisely assuming that the cost would eventually be borne by reparations from Germany.[3] The generous compensation payments made to industrial firms permitted the re-equipment and modernization of a substantial part of French industry and contributed in no small way to its prosperity and competitiveness in the 1920's. However, the inevitable counterpart was continuous inflationary pressure at home, the depreciation of the franc on the foreign exchanges, and loss of confidence in the monetary unit. While the falling value of the franc assisted exporters and helped the tourist trade to flourish, it had a devastating effect on the confidence of the rentiers. A "flight of capital", in which large holders of funds obviously joined, hastened the process of depreciation and struck further blows at the owners of fixed-interest securities. An effort to halt the inflation by some means became imperative to reassure the holders of capital, check the drain of gold, and enable both the state and the business sector to continue raising the capital which they required from the public. The limit to further inflation was thus met in the shape of the unwillingness of the public to hold depreciating paper and, more particularly, its political pressure to restore a stable currency.[4]

The battle to restore confidence in the franc was complex and long drawn out, involving as it did problems of mass psychology, public finance, and the political instability which dogged post-war France. Between March 1924 and July 1926 eleven ministries came and went, and in the ten months before Poincaré took office eight Ministers of Finance had grappled unsuccessfully with the problem of the franc. There were serious divisions of opinions between politicians and between them and the Governor of the Bank of France about the rate at which the franc should be stabilized and about the requisite fiscal measures. The advent of Poincaré took place in an atmosphere of acute national crisis, accompanied by street demonstrations and an extraordinary wave of xenophobia.[5] At its lowest point the franc had reached 235 to the pound, in July 1926. The Poincaré government was able to restore confidence rapidly with a programme which included the conversion of part of the dangerously large short-term debt on to a long-term basis, reductions in government expenditure, and increases in taxation. The announcement in August by the Bank of France that it would buy pounds at 122.25 marked the re-establishment of financial confidence. The temporary stabilization thus achieved *de facto* by the end of the year was followed in a quite different atmosphere by the law of 25 June 1928, whereby the franc was formally placed on the gold standard at the existing rate of exchange, that is at an exchange rate equivalent to 66.6 milligrammes of fine gold, one-fifth of the value of the *franc germinal*. For the first time France was on a full gold standard, but convertibility was confined to ingots worth approximately 215,000 francs. At the same time, exchange controls on gold and capital movements were brought to an end. Under Poincaré a remarkable restoration of confidence in the franc took place.[6] Gold flowed back to the Bank of France which thus entered the next period in an exceptionally strong reserve position.

The parity decided upon by Poincaré represented the final abandonment of the hope, cherished by wide circles of opinion, of a return to the pre-1914 parity.[7] The choice was a conservative one which resisted such pressures. According to Jacques Rueff, Poincaré was influenced by Léon Jouhaux, Secretary of the Confédération Générale de Travail, who pointed out to him that too high a parity would result in unemployment.[8] As it was, Poincaré's domestic measures did have the effect of temporarily dampening down demand, but the undervaluation of the franc at the rate adopted in 1926 but the undervaluation of the franc at the rate adopted in 1926 permitted France to participate fully in the boom of the late 'twenties.

II

The experience of the French economy during this period raises the question of the relationship between the policies adopted to maintain monetary stability and the underlying factors affecting the long-term rate of growth. There has been a tendency to see the French economy in stereotypes of stagnation and retardation.[9] The literature composed in the period from the 'thirties to the 'fifties was no doubt influenced in its emphasis by the predominance of these traits at the time. However, the economy had grown at a rate before 1914 which compared favourably with that of other countries.[10] The basis was then laid for large-scale and technologically advanced industries, a modern banking and financial structure was built up, and there were evidences of concentration and combination in these sectors.[11] Industrialization in the unoccupied areas proceeded rapidly during the war though there was inevitably a sharp fall in aggregate production at the beginning.[12] France was potentially a more highly industrialized country in the early 'twenties than before the war. The factory proletariat had increased in absolute and relative social weight—a factor which further aggravated the crisis of confidence with which the bourgeoisie was already beginning to become afflicted.

With the peace France recovered not only the industrial areas which had been occupied by the enemy and stripped of their equipment or rendered economically useless by their proximity to the war zone, but also Alsace-Lorraine—that is to say centres of advanced textile industry, resources in iron ore and potash, and modern steel plants. An intensive programme of reconstruction was put into effect in the devastated areas which enabled the very important and varied industries which they possessed before the war to be rebuilt and equipped on the most modern lines.[13]

Reconstruction was an important element in the prosperity of the 1920's, but there were a number of other specifically French factors which have to be taken into account in this period. For example, in contrast with Britain, there was not a serious problem of unemployment or depressed export industries at this time. As a result of France's later start in industrialization the major export industries were turned not towards the markets of the less developed countries but rather to the high-income markets of the advanced countries of western Europe and North America. Thus, for example, while French textiles had little to lose from Japanese or Indian competition they gained from the growth in incomes in the countries which were booming during the 'twenties. Of the other typically depressed industries of the period, coal-mining benefited from reconstruction and the French industry was unable to meet home demands, while shipbuilding was not of sufficient importance for its depressed state to have widespread effects. It was characteristic that unemployment was negligible during the 'twenties.

However, it would be a mistake to separate French growth in that decade from world market trends. Every step towards a more highly industrialized economy strengthened French dependence on international trade. For example, the expansion in iron and steel exports in the late 'twenties was a reflexion of the relative inelasticity of supply of the industries of other countries during the last stages of the investment boom. French luxury or semi-luxury exports prospered on the strength of the purchasing power of the international rich. Also, this period saw a striking advance of the tourist trade, the opening up of the Côte d'Azur mainly for rich visitors, and investment in and prosperity for hotels, restaurants, casinos, and similar facilities. This tourist boom was, of course, assisted by the undervaluation of the franc after 1926. It was also accompanied by prosperity in those industries which had always been patronized by foreign visitors and constituted concealed exports, industries which were often organized on small workshop and artisan lines.

One of the main constraints on expansion in the 'twenties was labour supply, a situation, again, which contrasts very strikingly with British experience. The explanation of the relative labour shortage is to be found in the demographic trend established during the nineteenth century among the bourgeoisie and the peasantry and which, by the end of the century, had reached the working class as well. The war, which struck into the ranks of the young able-bodied men, thus aggravated an already existing situation which was different from that in the other belligerent countries. The consequence was that in the 'twenties France became a country of large-scale immigration by foreign workers.[14] Immigration made an indispensable contribution to reconstruction and expansion, by providing large numbers of workers who were, moreover, more mobile and more ready to take on arduous manual work than new recruits to the industrial labour force from the peasantry, and posed fewer problems as far as housing and other services were concerned.

The picture in the 'twenties is thus a very favourable one: rapid recovery from the war speeded by large government outlays and growth in production and in industrial investment; continued industrialization and modernization; expansion in exports and in invisible earnings. The ending of the inflation and wild speculation of the early 'twenties and the restoration of confidence which resulted in the repatriation of funds which had taken refuge abroad were the first fruits of Poincaré's stabilization of the franc in 1926. By early 1928 the situation had once more assumed a stable shape. The international conjuncture was now very favourable; when the franc was restored to a convertible gold basis by Poincaré's law of June 1928, many must have believed that a new and indefinite era of currency stability was beginning. The parity chosen undervalued the franc and thus gave French exporters and the tourist trade an advantage. Foreign purchasing power was at its height. The gold reserves of the Bank of France had been built up to an impressive level; to all appearances the franc was now a solid money once again.

III

The economic successes of the 'twenties have to be seen in the context of certain structural inflexibilities whose ability to restrict adaptation and growth was to be demonstrated in the next decade. A number of these deserve special mention, although this is not the place to accord them detailed treatment.

(1) *The demographic problem.* There are many well-known studies of this problem by Landry, Froment, Sauvy, Spengler, Kirk, and others. The French population was virtually stagnant. Within the post-war frontiers (including Alsace-Lorraine), despite the immigration of some two million people, it grew by only about 1 per cent from 1911 to 1936 from 41.5 to 41.9 million. As a result of this, and reflecting the heavy losses of the younger male population dur-

ing the war, the proportion of under-twenties fell from 34 per cent
to 31 per cent over this period while the proportion of over-sixties
rose from 12 to 14 per cent.[15] The adverse consequences of a stagnant and ageing population made themselves felt precisely in the
period of the depression.

(2) *The excessive weight of agriculture.* Considered over the same
period, 1911 to 1936, one of the outstanding trends in the French
economy is the decline in the weight of agriculture. However, in
the longer historical perspective, what remains impressive is that
agriculture, dominated by small-scale units in the hands of the
peasantry, should have continued to play such an important role in
the economy. For instance, in 1931 approximately one-third of occupied males were engaged in agriculture.[16] Although many French
writers, even economists, extolled the virtues of rural life, and
thought this contributed to the "balance" of the economy and compared the situation favourably with "over-industrialized" Germany
or Britain, the continued heavy weight of agriculture hardly appears
to be a matter for self-congratulation. At least, it scarcely needs to
be argued now that this heavy commitment of resources to the
agrarian sector was a constraint on growth and kept down *per capita*
income.

(3) *The prevalence of artisan and small-scale industry.* The
weight of the artisan sector and its capacity to survive were closely
connected with the preservation of peasant agriculture and had
tended to diminish with it.[17] Undoubtedly artisan production and
small-scale industry were constantly being undermined by the competition of large capital. The point again is that this sector conserved
considerable weight and embodied the resistance of artisan producers and small-scale entrepreneurs to change. Statistical estimation
of the size of this sector is imperfect but the figures leave no doubt
that it was of considerable importance. One estimate suggests that
there were 1.2 million artisans in the towns and 800,000 in rural
areas.[18] Much production in the textile industries, particularly silk,
was carried on in small workshops or by outworkers.[19] The important luxury and semi-luxury industries were still organized to a
large extent on a small scale and gave employment to artisans and
workers in their own homes. Even advanced industries, such as
motor-cars, found it advantageous to employ outworkers and small-
scale sub-contractors for the supply of such parts as carburettors.
During the depression, moreover, small producers could hang on,
with their low overheads, by cutting prices or simply by making do
with fewer orders. Some skilled men and women formerly employed

Table 1. *Percentage Distribution of Population
by Size of Commune*

Number of inhabitants	1911	1936
Less than 500	12.9	13.4
501–1,000	16.5	13.7
1,001–5,000	32.5	26.0
5,001–10,000	6.5	7.5
10,001–20,000	6.8	7.2
20,001–30,000	3.4	4.5
30,001–50,000	3.9	4.8
50,001–100,000	4.3	6.9
100,001–1,000,000	7.3	9.2
Over 1,000,000	7.3	6.8
Proportion in communes of		
over 30,000	22.8	27.7
over 50,000	18.9	22.9

Source: *Rev. d'écon. pol.* LIII, (1939), 18.

by bigger firms might even set up on their own as an alternative to unemployment. In fact, during the depression the process of industrial concentration was not only brought to an end but also reversed in this sense.[20]

(4) *The role of the small town and the petty bourgeoisie.* Rural France gave sustenance to numerous small towns as centres for the sale and processing of agricultural produce and as the source for the goods and services purchased by the still numerous peasantry. As Table 1 shows, the proportion of the population living in the larger towns remained relatively small. In the small towns there nestled, as there had for generations, a large army of small shopkeepers, traders, and artisans, as well as professional men such as doctors, lawyers, surveyors, auctioneers, teachers, and journalists. Coming largely from traditionally property-owning families long established in the vicinity, these people composed a numerous middle class, or petty bourgeoisie, a generally conservative force of cautious spenders, savers, and investors. This large small-town middle section, hit by the loss of investments in Russia or elsewhere, whose fixed-interest securities and savings bank deposits fell in real value as a result of the post-war inflation, made up a large part of the rentier element and, of course, of the electorate. In matters of financial policy it was this large, traditionally influential but still

largely amorphous force to which politicians claimed to defer. These were the sort of people who wrote abusive and threatening letters to Reynaud, when, in the 'thirties, he espoused the cause of devaluation.[21]

IV

The chronology of the cycle in France in the 'thirties lagged two or three years behind other countries. Thus, if the onset of the world economic depression be dated from the Wall Street crash, the signs of its impact in France were scarcely visible for about two years.[22] The undervaluation of the franc helps to explain this relative immunity, and for France the devaluation of the pound sterling and the competitive exchange depreciation which followed in its wake was the crucial turning-point. From that moment the franc became an overvalued currency; French exports were priced out of foreign markets and a severe blow was administered to the tourist trade.[23]

However, before concluding that the main responsibility lay with monetary policy it is necessary to mention some other features in the situation. It was hardly likely that France would remain insulated for long from the depression in the rest of the world for the obvious reason that the resulting fall in incomes in the advanced countries was bound to cut spending on French exports and lead to a reduction in the flow of foreign visitors to France. The overvaluation of the franc could only have intensified a tendency which would have operated in any case. As it was, direct trade to the other advanced countries fell sharply while trade with the colonies also fell as a result of the collapse in the world prices of primary products, which reduced their capacity to buy French goods. In the 'thirties, therefore, there was a catastrophic fall in the output of the main export industries and especially in silk and other textiles, leather, and the luxury trades.[24] In 1931 a significant fall in total industrial production was recorded. The trend continued during the following year with a slight recovery in 1933 and further falls in the next two years.[25] The fall in exports was as spectacular as their growth in the late 'twenties, and there were signs that the fall was even greater than could be attributed to the overvaluation of the franc. Thus in 1934 *The Economist* remarked, "French exports are now beaten everywhere, not only by the countries off the gold standard, but actually by other gold countries." [26] The collapse of exports and their failure to show signs of recovery suggest cost rigidities and a falling off in competitiveness in crucial sectors of industry, old and "new" alike.

If the depression reached France somewhat belatedly and in a muted form it then struck with considerable force. The devaluation of the pound in 1931 and then of the dollar in 1933 were severe blows. While other countries showed more or less vigorous signs of recovery from about 1933 or 1934, the trough of the depression in France did not come until 1935. Only from about the middle of that year were there signs that the worst was over and a slow recovery continued in the early part of 1936.

It was after 1931 and during the depression that the maintenance of the *franc Poincaré* became a barrier to recovery, as *The Economist* pointed out in its comments on the French financial situation at this time.[27] In France the argument against the *franc Poincaré* did not begin to find much public expression until about 1934. Only a few economists, such as Bernard Nogaro, added their voices to left-wing criticism. But it was clear from the reception received by Paul Reynaud, the only prominent politician to espouse devaluation publicly, that there was no prospect of a devaluation *à froid* as a deliberate policy to stimulate the economy. The experience of the inflation and depreciation of the 'twenties had a traumatic effect on the French rentier who saw devaluation as a step little better than expropriation. Not a single important organ of the press supported Reynaud and a solid bloc from the Regents of the Bank of France to the Central Committee of the Communist Party demanded that the 1928 parity should be maintained.[28]

The result was that the successive coalitions which governed France during this period had in common a determination to save the franc—which meant a deflationary budgetary policy, and thus a further aggravation of the depressive trends in the economy. Those governments thus tried to cut expenditure and produce budget surpluses. At the same time they made no attempt to limit the right of capital holders to exchange francs for gold and to export gold or currency. If this dedication to the franc did not have worse deflationary effects it was only because consistent deflation proved impossible to carry through and governments were not able to attain the hoped-for budget surpluses.

The sanctity of the *franc Poincaré* had a powerful hold on expert economic thinking as well as upon the rentiers and the politicians. While *The Economist* was already "modern" and Keynesian even before *The General Theory*, French opinion stood by orthodox monetary theories; the division between the French and the Anglo-

Saxons on monetary policy did not begin with the Fifth Republic.[29]

The obvious point about the deflation—devaluation dilemma, then, is that the latter was simply not practical politics in France at that time. But whether devaluation to the extent of about 15 per cent, in 1932, or probably 25 per cent by 1935, which would have been necessary to bring the franc into line with other countries' currencies, would have solved the problems of the French economy remains a doubtful and clearly unsettled point into which enters the possible retaliatory action of Britain and the U.S.A. If the view is taken that devaluation could have produced recovery, then in logic it must be assumed that British recovery was principally dependent upon the devaluation of the pound, American recovery upon the devaluation of the dollar, and so on. This seems to go against current fashions which have stressed other reasons for these recoveries such as the rise of new industries, the boom in housing, and government pump-priming. However, it is possible that in these cases effects have been taken for causes, or that recovery was much more a quasi-automatic response to a period of stagnation in investment and falling costs and prices.

V

In the 'thirties the French economy displayed all the symptoms of deceleration. There was a heavy decline in exports which in some branches reached catastrophic proportions as, for example, in the Lyons silk industry and the fashion and dress trade. The fall in industrial production was also severe and in some industries output fell not only below the level of 1929 but also below that of 1913. More significant than this falling off in exports and production, which was common to all the industrial countries, was the belated and weak character of the recovery. There was, for example, no sign of a big push forward of the newer industries. The production figures in the motor-car industry may be taken as representative of the newer sectors.[30] Nor was there any sign of a house-building boom; on the contrary, after some speculative over-building in the 'twenties new building fell off and remained at an exceptionally low level throughout the 'thirties.[31] In Paris and the large towns new construction virtually ground to a standstill.[32] Since building was pre-eminently a "sheltered" industry, its performance has to be explained principally from the character of home market demand.

While in the 'twenties some new industries such as chemicals and motor-cars had gone through a phase of expansion, they showed no sign of taking the lead in recovery after the depression. Where could an expansion in demand come from for such industries? The aggregate purchasing power of the large agrarian sector had declined in real terms.[33] Likewise, incomes in the artisan sector also probably fell. Although real wages tended to rise, the total paid out in wages also fell because the labour force was reduced by as much as two million.[34] Into this pattern there obviously appear, as causative factors, the demographic stagnation and ageing and the dependence on home supplies of foodstuffs which prevented advantage being taken of falling world prices for primary products. Government policy, which of course was deflationary, also enters in as a further factor dampening down demand.

What happened to the incomes of the middle classes is more difficult to say. Property owners dependent upon rents were adversely affected by rent controls, which also discouraged new building. Those on fixed incomes gained from falling prices. On the other hand, industrial share prices and dividends paid out on many shares tended to fall. It was characteristic that the middle class hoarded on a vast scale. Large quantities of gold went into hoards and a high proportion of the additional note circulation of the Bank of France was also held by the public as a precaution against the unknown.[35] Those with discretionary purchasing power tended to spend cautiously and in a traditional way. Thus middle-class car-owners kept their vehicles on the road longer. Modern forms of merchandising and credit selling were, in addition, poorly developed, or even frowned upon, so that the potential market for the new consumer durables among lower-income people remained largely untapped.

Nevertheless, however sharp the effects of the depression on industry, tourism, and exports, there were signs of small but steady improvements in living standards. It was typical, however, that the gains in real wages seem mainly to have gone not on manufactured goods but on more or better food.[36] The existence of a large peasantry and an artisan sector offered a kind of cushion against impoverishment. Most important, for reasons which must now be examined, France did not experience an unemployment problem on the same scale as the other industrial countries. The highest annual average recorded as in receipt of benefit was 433,700 in 1936.[37]

It must be said, however, that the volume of unemployment was much higher than was general even in bad times before the 'thirties. Still, its level seems modest by British or American standards of the time. Since it was less of a problem, too, it was no doubt measured less accurately. Relief was on a local basis and the figures quoted are those of unemployed people receiving assistance, so that it must be a minimum figure and may not represent the numbers actually available for work.

If the problem is looked at from the standpoint of the number of jobs available it becomes more serious. There was a serious shrinkage in demand for labour during the 'thirties which cut down the number of jobs by approximately two million.[38] It has been calculated that about 600,000 foreign workers left France. The ageing of the population, together with accelerated retirement, reduced the labour force by roughly the same number. By 1935 there were 425,000 wholly unemployed on average. In addition, some industries, notably textiles and clothing, practised systematic short-time working. The balance was made up of juveniles who stayed at school longer and the smaller number of new recruits to the labour force.[39]

No doubt, too, the peasant and artisan sectors concealed a large volume of underemployment, including temporary urban workers who went back to the villages and artisans who simply had less work. The wholly unemployed were concentrated heavily in the Seine department and a few industrial areas. But it was also characteristic that some industries which in other countries were chronically afflicted by unemployment, notably mining, were not much affected in France. In the case of coal this arises obviously from the fact that this resource was a scarce factor and home supplies were insufficient to meet normal needs.

These peculiarities of the labour market, which account for the relatively modest level of unemployment, were later to turn out to be a brake on recovery. In fact there was never a great surplus of manpower waiting upon reflation for its re-employment. A large proportion of the unemployed were older people (32 per cent were over 50 in 1936), women, and the unskilled.[40] Since there was not a great reserve of labour, the recovery in the late 'thirties saw the chronic labour scarcity of the 'twenties appear once more.

Finally, a significant aspect of French unemployment was that, although relatively modest, it continued to increase between 1932 and 1936 while it fell in most other countries. This was symptomatic of the stagnation of the economy under the *franc Poincaré*.

VI

It is evident that the policy of deflation could only handicap the recovery of exports and tourism and make necessary, through tariffs and quotas, further efforts to insulate France from the world market. At the same time, exchange controls were resisted on the grounds that they interfered with an essential freedom and would have been a step towards a state-controlled economy. The main argument for devaluation was that by ending the overvaluation of the franc it would contribute to an export-led recovery. But it really implied, also, a reversal of the trend towards self-sufficiency which logically meant the lowering of tariffs and closer integration with the international economy. The continuation of monetary chaos for which it was held that the French, with their strict adherence to the gold standard, were not to blame weakened the case for such a shift in the emphasis of economic policy. Opinion at the time made it most unlikely that devaluation would be carried out *à froid* as a deliberate act of policy. Adherence to the *franc Poincaré* thus deprived the government of the possibility of meeting the depression at home by pump-priming; all policy was subordinated, as the Laval decrees of June 1935 made plain, to the need to "avoid devaluation of the money".

But it may be asked whether the failure to devalue, or even the deflationary budget policy which this entailed, can be held fully responsible for the extent and prolongation of depression and stagnation. The foregoing analysis suggests that other factors have to be taken into consideration in explaining the failure of the home market to reverse the trend. There was a built-in inflexibility to change and adaptation which represented inherited structural weaknesses that had remained unobtrusive during the secular expansion of the previous half-century. These weaknesses, which were reflected in the timidity and caution of investors and businessmen, were reinforced psychologically by the general crisis of confidence which afflicted people of their class during the inter-war years.

Advocates both of deflation and of devaluation expected more or less instantaneous and predictable results to follow from these measures. The sustained effort to deflate showed how slowly costs, incomes, and habits in general changed. The resistance to it was so great that it remained very largely a budgetary matter and, while that meant that the franc did not experience the hoped-for revival in strength, it also prevented its depressive effects from being as great as they might have been. On the other hand, the response of industry to the depression only aggravated its symptoms; a halt was called to new investment, equipment aged, and, in view of the modernization taking place elsewhere, the international competitiveness of French industry deteriorated.[41]

Turning to the home market, it has been seen that there was a general decline in aggregate purchasing power despite a rise in individual real incomes. Some specifically French responses to the depression help to account for this but it was also a consequence of the preservation of a large peasant and artisan sector and the slowness of the shift in general consumption habits to the products of the "new" industries. This was coupled with a demographic situation unfavourable to growth and enterprise to which some economists have ascribed considerable if not major responsibility for the poor performance of the economy between the early 'thirties and the 'fifties. It would be dangerous, however, to isolate one factor as being the unique or principal cause. The demographic trend was itself closely intertwined with a particular social and economic structure, and until some shift could be made in the habits and responses bound up with that it was doubtful whether remedies applied specifically to the population problem could have much effect on the economy as a whole.

VII

It may be repeated that there was also no question of government expenditure being consciously used to counteract the depression. The battle to preserve the *franc Poincaré* ruled out such a policy and imposed instead one of budgetary economies, including cuts in capital outlays on such projects as electrification and railway modernization. The situation would no doubt have been worse if the deflationary policies of the Flandin and Laval governments had been more successful. In fact they did not succeed in pushing down the structure of costs and incomes in any consistent way or to an effective degree. They remained mainly budgetary deflations and even in that sense were not successful. It is probable that the recovery which began to take place in the latter half of 1935 and continued in early 1936 was a reflexion of this: despite its deflationary professions the government was confronted with shortfalls in tax receipts coupled with rising expenditures. It financed this unintended deficit by short-term borrowing from the Bank of France which increased note circulation and thus global purchasing power.[42]

Different sectors of the economy responded in divergent ways to the depression. Those which had captive markets, such as public utilities, or which enjoyed high tariff protection, were able to maintain profitability better than those which had depended upon exports or were operating under highly competitive conditions.[43] The growth of monopoly and combination and a closer interconnexion between banks and industry had become discernible from the end of the nineteenth century when the great expansion of heavy industry began. The big monopoly groups pursued a policy of live and let live as far as the smaller independents were concerned, except where they stood in their way. Their response to the depression was to maintain prices and profits by cutting back production. Although they were thus able to show a higher profit rate than the unsheltered sectors, a large proportion of these profits, it has been alleged, was retained in liquid form rather than reinvested in new plant and machinery.[44] These liquid funds might be held in government bonds or bank deposits, used for speculation, or sent abroad for safety. In fact, in the year before the coming to power of the Popular Front, the fear of an eventual devaluation and growing political uncertainty led to a steady flight of capital.

Even at this distance historians can say little with certainty about the policy decisions and influence on the government of the powerful business interests which dominated the most advanced sectors of the economy.[45] We can make some inferences but to back them up with documentary evidence remains impossible, as much for these years as for the period of the "Blum experiment". That new investment in industry was neglected can, however, be deduced from what followed. At the end of the 'twenties French industry had gone through a process of modernization and investment which had expanded capacity and brought important sectors up to world competitive standards. During the 'thirties, however, the average age of machines and machine tools seems to have progressively lengthened.[46] The technical weaknesses of crucial sectors of industry became visible during the recovery and rearmament of the late 'thirties. For instance, the bottlenecks which appeared in industry in late 1936 and early 1937 are frequently blamed on the untimely reduction in hours of work imposed by the Matignon Agreement of June 1936. However, while it has been admitted that the labour reserve was in fact much smaller than the global number of unemployed suggested, the policy of the big firms in fields such as engineering had been to cut their labour force to a minimum, to reduce the intake of apprentices, and to invest little in new labour-saving machinery.

VIII

It is possible but not proven that recovery would have been more rapid during and after 1934 had there been a different sort of government with a different policy. However, it is clear that no party or coalition of parties would have been elected which included devaluation and exchange control in its programme. The Communist Party, for instance, vigorously opposed the inclusion of devaluation in the programme of the Popular Front, since it believed that this would lose the votes of the rentier and small property holders if not for itself, at least for its coalition partners, which included the Radical Party. Further, it is very obvious that the policy of budgetary deflation which had been pursued with increasing rigour from 1934 onwards had contributed to the intensification of social and class conflict. In fact, it has been said with some justice that the final instalment of deflation, initiated by the Laval decrees of 1935, amounted to electoral suicide since it hit at civil servants and large sections of the salaried middle class and swung them towards the Popular Front or the extreme right.[47] If devaluation was unpopular with the rentier middle class the alternative, deflation, was equally so with wage and salary earners. Since no section willingly accepted the cuts in money incomes which deflation required, the government had either to abandon consistency when it met opposition or give up the attempt. In practice, then, the deflation was not consistent but discriminated against the least vocal or well-organized sectors, while government policy actually aimed at maintaining or raising incomes in others for political or social reasons, notably in the agrarian sector.

What was needed for a revival of business confidence was the expectation that profitability would be restored. In fact the anxiety about the franc discouraged investment and operated against the recovery of profits. At the same time it is difficult to know to what extent the commitment of banking and financial interests, together with the rentiers, to the *franc Poincaré* was shared by the industrialists. The measures taken to defend the franc, such as cuts in the wages and salaries of government employees, while they may have reassured the financiers and rentiers, aggravated social tensions and prepared the way for the victory of the Popular Front in the elections of May 1936. The principal contradiction of the "Blum experiment" which followed lay in its failure either to restore the profitability of business or to satisfy fully the claims of the working class, while antagonizing the large middle layers who held the political balance.

Making a balance sheet of gains and losses for the different classes of the population during the period of the *franc Poincaré* poses some difficult problems. Spokesmen for peasants, rentiers, small-

and medium-sized businesses, and wage-earners all claimed that they had lost during these years. In fact, since prices were falling, real incomes of wage and salary earners who did not suffer from unemployment tended to rise. However, the deflationary measures had severe psychological effects while the modest gains in real earnings passed unnoticed. The peasantry lost in money income as a result of the sharp price decreases of the early 'thirties. Subsequently government measures to safeguard the peasantry, which cut across the deflationary policy, brought some relief. However, it was at this period that for the first time for many years the peasants began to organize on a large scale in defence of their corporate interests and to become a politically more coherent force.[48] Generally speaking, any interest group which was strong enough could put pressure on the government to obtain some kind of protection or privilege. This made for an incoherent body of legislation the general sense of which was restrictionist, and helped to render nugatory the deflation to which the government was committed.

Whether or not the rentiers and property owners suffered as much as they believed, they remained uneasy and lacked confidence in the future. They viewed with alarm the claims of the working class, granted the 1928 parity of the franc an almost mystical virtue, and, as Reynaud pointed out, feared the worst while their several efforts to safeguard their individual or sectional interests made it all the more probable that the worst would happen. Those who could sent their liquid capital for refuge abroad whenever the franc was under pressure; and the flight of capital was already going strong a year before the Popular Front took office. By timidity in spending and in investing they made it all the more difficult for the depression to be overcome. By their unwillingness to procreate while proclaiming the virtues of the family their class had created a demographic pattern unfavourable to economic growth. The *franc Poincaré*, which was their life-line in a world which they increasingly failed to understand, was in practice a treacherous friend. Whether or not devaluation would have solved all the problems of the French economy it would certainly have alleviated some of the most pressing. In the meantime it is clear that depression and deflation between them reduced aggregate demand in the home market, which for structural reasons was narrower than it might have been, and thus excluded, or at least delayed, the possibility of renewed growth based upon "new" industries such as consumer durables. The general lack of confidence and the preference for liquidity in the same way prevented recovery in industrial investment. In the sequel it took the stimulus of rearmament to produce the incomplete recovery of the late 'thirties.

IX

The policy of deflation which the attempt to maintain the *franc Poincaré* imposed upon successive governments from 1928 to 1936 was not the unique cause of the troubles of the French economy, but it certainly intensified them. What has to be explained is the specific failing which produced the twenty years' regression after 1931. Adherence to monetary orthodoxy through the early years of the depression was one symptom of a deeper underlying malaise which gripped large sections of French society. It displayed itself even more disastrously in the restrictionist policies of government and business: concerted action to adjust production to falling demand. The term "economic malthusianism" has been customarily used to describe this response which, while it resembles in an aggravated form policies adopted elsewhere, can be related also to the historically rooted characteristics of French entrepreneurship and the paralysis of will in the bourgeoisie as a whole which prevented its leaders from grasping radical solutions.[49] Even the programme of the Popular Front professed its adherence to the principle of "reflation without devaluation". Not easy to prove or to document, it is this prevailing crisis of confidence which, more than anything else, paralysed the decision-making powers of businessmen and politicians and made them as incapable of facing up to the depression as the army and the administration were of undertaking the tasks of modern warfare in 1940.

The deep fear of inflation and the desire to preserve monetary stability may have been an irrational sentiment in the circumstances of the 'thirties, but it was a material reality which every politician had to contend with and a point of view which most of them shared. Yet, while large numbers of Frenchmen feared for their money, and, by their timidity, made recovery from the depression more difficult, others contributed to the weakness of the franc by hoarding gold and exporting capital funds. It was this lack of confidence, in the money, in the government, in the future of the country, which resulted, eventually, in the inevitable devaluation carried through by the Blum government in September 1936. The short-lived era of the *franc Poincaré* which had begun with one national crisis had been ended by another.

Imprisoned in orthodox monetary doctrines, French policy-makers were unable to stimulate recovery by government spending and deficit financing. The balanced budget was as much a fetish as the stable franc. The special features of the home market also restricted and delayed the possibility of a spontaneous recovery, or more accurately delayed and weakened it. The contraction in the labour force and the unfavourable demographic trends must be accorded some importance, though it is difficult to say how much. Aggregate demand in both the agrarian sector and the working class fell off badly during the depression. The continued rise in real earnings per head of wage and salary earners did not have an appreciable effect in shifting demand to the products of the new industries and thus encouraging a higher rate of investment in them. The reluctance of savers to lend and of business firms to invest in the face of a threatened fall of the franc acted as a constant brake on recovery and perhaps did more harm than deflation *per se*. France's self-sufficiency in the major foodstuffs proved to be something of a handi-cap to industrial recovery since the working and middle classes did not benefit, as in Britain, from the fall in world food prices.

Comparing the 'thirties with the 'twenties the contrast seems to be very great. The brilliant performance of the latter decade gave place to a period of stagnation and decline. Yet for special reasons, some of which have been mentioned, France did not suffer the misery of mass long-term unemployment or the extremes of poverty and distress which afflicted other countries during the depression. The weight of the peasant and artisan sectors impeded industrial recovery but the traditionalists may have been right in seeing them as a stabilizing social force. Certainly there was a strong opinion in some circles which was opposed to further industrialization, extolled the "balance" of the French economy, and praised the virtues of rural life.[50] While it may be true that the very incompleteness of French industrialization dampened the impact of the depression and was a guarantee of social stability, this "advantage" was only of short-run significance. It may be said against such a view that the French economy suffered a continuous relative as well as absolute decline which further undermined confidence and prepared the way for the Armistice of 1940. The affinity of the anti-industrial view with the policies of the Vichy period hardly needs to be underlined. The net negative result of pre-war stagnation, the military defeat and occupation to which it contributed, and wartime destruction was very considerable in economic terms alone, and it was not until the 1950's that the French economy once again began to show clear signs of dynamic growth.

Notes

1. This article is part of a longer study of the French economy in the inter-war years which has been assisted by a grant from the Houblon-Norman Fund.

2. "The financial policy of France during the Great War of 1914–1918 will remain a model of what *should not be done*. A worse financial administration would be difficult to conceive".—G. Jèze, *The War Expenditure of France* (New Haven, 1927), p. 112.

3. For the reconstruction period and the effects of inflation see William F. Ogburn and William Jaffé, *The Economic Development of Post-War France* (New York, 1929). A total of nearly 85 billion francs had been paid out for the repair of war-damaged property by 1926.

4. For the monetary history of the period down to the stabilization see in particular Eleanor Lansing Dulles, *The French Franc, 1914–1918* (New York, 1929).

5. Marguerite Perrot, *La Monnaie et l'opinion publique en France et en Angleterre de 1924 à 1936* (Paris, 1955), pp. 110, 162–3.

6. For an account of the struggle to save the franc and the reasons for Poincaré's success, see Alfred Sauvy, *Histoire économique de la France entre les deux guerres* (Paris, 1965), I, chs. II–IV and the bibliography on p. 59.

7. Perrot, op. cit., provides many illuminating insights into French opinion on monetary questions at this time. In the event Poincaré's stabilization proved popular as even Blum and the Socialist opposition had to recognize. See Hormis Ziebura, *Léon Blum et le parti socialiste, 1872–1934* (Paris, 1968), ch. 7, *passim*.

8. Jacques Rueff, 'Sur un point d'histoire: Le niveau de la stabilisation Poincaré', *Revue d'économie politique*, LXIX (1959).

9. For example, Shepherd B. Clough, 'Retardative Factors in French Economic Development in the Nineteenth and Twentieth Centuries', *Journal of Economic History*, VI (1946), supplement; Rondo E. Cameron, 'Economic Growth and Stagnation in France', *Journal of Modern History*, III (1958); David S. Landes, 'The French Entrepreneur and Industrial Growth in the Nineteenth Century', *Jnl. Econ. Hist.* IX (1949).

10. M. Lévy-Leboyer, 'La croissance économique en France au XIXe siècle', *Annales*, no. 4 (1968), p. 799, gives a growth-rate of 2.66 per cent per annum for industrial production between 1885 and 1905 and 4.42 per cent between 1905 and 1913.

11. See the present author's *Economic Forces in French History* (1971), ch. IX.

12. Arthur Fontaine, *French Industry during the War* (New Haven, 1927).

13. See the works by Ogburn and Jaffé and Fontaine already cited. The reports to the Department of Overseas Trade in Britain on *Economic*

Conditions in France by Sir Robert Cahill are an invaluable source of information. See for example the report dated June 1934, Department of Overseas Trade, pp. 54–581 (H.M.S.O. 1934).

14. See Cahill, report for 1934, pp. 636–8, which suggests an immigration of 1¾ million for the period 1922–31 plus several hundred thousand illicit entrants.

15. The article by H. Ulmer, from which these figures are taken, provides a useful summary of French population history from 1911 to 1936. Entitled 'Structure Humaine', it forms part of the special number of *Revue d'économie politique*, LIII (1939), entitled *De la France d'avant guerre à la France d'aujourd'hui*.

16. See the article by M. Augé-Laribé in *Rev. d'écon. pol.* LIII (1939). Approximately three-quarters of holdings were worked by their owners, one-fifth were worked by tenants, and one in 20 by *métayers*.

17. Artisan industry is taken to be a form of production in which the owner of the enterprise executes the same tasks as his employees. This is the definition suggested by T. J. Markovitch in 'L'industrie française de 1789 à 1964—sources et méthodes', *Cahiers de L'I.S.E.A.*, no. 163 (July 1965), who points out that it still remains more widespread in France than is often assumed.

18. J. Denuc, 'Structure des Entreprises', *Rev. d'écon. pol.* LIII (1939), p. 222, gives the following figures based on the Census of 1931: 1,050,000 male small masters; 158,000 male domestic workers (*à façon à domicile*); 657,000 female small employers (*petites patronnes*); and 260,000 female domestic workers.

19. The breakdown of workers in manufacturing industry in 1931 was as follows:

> 2,651,134 in units employing from 1 to 10
> 438,714 in units employing from 11 to 20
> 670,172 in units employing from 21 to 50
> 576,897 in units employing from 51 to 100
> 2,356,826 in units employing over 100

For more detailed tables see Denuc, op. cit. p. 223.

20. Denuc, loc. cit.

21. As recorded in his autobiography: *Mémoires I: Venue de ma montagne*, I (Paris, 1960).

22. The contrast between comparatively prosperous France and the other countries of Europe comes out very clearly in the journalist Hubert H. Tiltman's *Slump! A Study of Stricken Europe Today* (1933).

23. Receipts from tourism are estimated to have fallen from 8.5 hundred million francs in 1930 to 2.5 hundred million in 1932.—*Rev. d'écon. pol.* LIII (1939), p. 539.

24. The following figures (in millions of francs) of some French manufactured exports in the early years of the depression give an idea of the disaster which was especially serious for the textile industries, whose exports fell by 80 per cent.

	Cotton	Silk and rayon	Woollens	Clothing	Iron and steel	Motor vehicles
1928	2,963	3,819	2,339	2,096	2,871	1,541
1929	2,713	3,439	2,095	1,844	2,632	1,608
1930	2,145	2,866	1,571	1,662	2,405	1,123
1931	1,414	1,989	1,099	691	1,929	837
1932	971	1,083	419	192	1,108	549

Source: Cahill, op. cit. App. II, pp. 701–2.

25.   French Industrial Production, 1928–38
(Annual Average): 1928 = 100

1928	1930	1931	1932	1933	1934	1935	1936	1937	1938
100	108	96	83	90	89	82	86	90	95

Source: Sauvy, op. cit. II, Table VII, 3, p. 533.

26. The Economist, 21 August 1934, p. 871.

27. The Economist followed economic developments in France closely both with regular and detailed information and with feature articles of a high analytical standard; see the articles of 27 April, 30 Nov., and 21 Dec. 1935.

28. The Economist noted, 11 Aug. 1934, that Reynaud's speech in the Chamber of Deputies in favour of devaluation had received a cool reception and that not one paper had taken up his views.

29. While some economists considered devaluation as desirable they did not make the case for it very strongly. In Prof. Rist's editorials in Revue d'économie politique he avoids making a clear statement. Thus, in introducing the number on 'La France économique en 1934', he assumes the necessity to preserve "a strong money"; he continues, "Le problème qui se pose à l'économie française est donc entièrement nouveau. Il ne s'agit pas d'une déflation modeste, il s'agit d'une déflation profonde, plus étendue qu'aucune de celles que nous avons connues dans le passé . . . Il s'agit enfin, et c'est ce qu'il y a de plus grave, d'une déflation, dont il est impossible d'apercevoir la limite puisque, à chaque instant, la monnaie anglaise, et peut-être aussi, la monnaie américaine, en baissant brusquement, peuvent bouleverser chaque nouvel équilibre, si péniblement atteint qu'il soit."—Rev. d'écon. pol. XLIX (1935). In the absence of a drastic deflation Prof. Rist considered that the problem could not be solved without a general monetary stabilization.

30.   France: Production of Motor Vehicles (000's)

1926	1927	1928	1929	1930	1931
192	191	223	253	230	201

1932	1933	1934	1935	1936	1937
163	189	181	165	204	201

Source: Ingvar Svennilson, Growth and Stagnation in the European Economy (Geneva, 1954), Table 40, p. 149.

31.
France: New Dwellings (000's)

1926	1927	1928	1929	1930	1931
110	80	111	122	199	145

1932	1933	1934	1935	1936	1937	1938
138	117	119	116	86	73	67

Source: Ibid. Table 47, p. 242.

32. It was estimated that in 1945 30 per cent of the stock of houses were over 100 years old; in 61 towns with over 30,000 inhabitants the average age of houses was 57 years and 19 per cent were over 100 years old.— Marc Aucy, 'Habitations et logement', *Rev. d'écon. pol.* LVII (1947), 1686.

33. M. Augé-Laribé, in the article cited, attempted to measure the total purchasing power of the agricultural sector. According to him this fell after the war to 80 per cent of the 1913 level which was not attained again until 1925. By 1931–2 it had fallen to 86 per cent but deteriorated again in 1934 to 77 per cent and went down to 63 per cent in 1935, despite price supports, tariffs, and quotas.

34. The estimate of the total wage and salary bill (in billions of francs) made by L. Dugé de Bernonville, 'Revenus privés et consommations', *Rev. d'écon. pol.* LII (1939), gives the following results:

1930	1931	1932	1933	1934	1935	1936	1938
123.7	118.4	107.4	102.5	93.8	87.4	119.7	133.0

The cost of living was, of course, falling to 1936. The index of 213 articles constructed by J. Singer-Kérel, *Le coût de la vie à Paris de 1840 à 1954* (Paris, 1961), fell 20.7 per cent in 1935 by comparison with 1930, and her statistics show all the indexes of real wages increasing until 1936; see p. 149.

35. *The Economist* quoted an article by P. Strohl, General Secretary of the Bank of France, which drew attention to the large-scale hoarding of newly issued notes of 500 and 1,000 francs denomination. It suggested that "between 1928 and 1931 26,000 million of notes were issued against gold, which had been repatriated as a result of stabilisation and have since been hoarded through fear of various complications inherent in the economic and political crisis".—21 December 1935, p. 1257.

36. For instance, total meat consumption rose from 1,381,000 tons in 1928 to 1,535,000 tons in 1936, milk from 107.3 million hectolitres in 1928 to 128.9 million hectolitres in 1936, and groundnut oil from 186,000 tons in 1928 to 237,000 tons in 1936. On *per capita* consumption the calculations of L. Dugé de Bernonville yielded the following results: between 1928–30 and 1933–5 the increase for meat was 5.1 per cent, for potatoes 7.7 per cent, for coffee 7.5 per cent, for oranges and bananas 57 per cent, and for cooking oil 4.7 per cent. However, *per capita* consumption of beer, salt, and tobacco fell. See 'Les Salaires et les consommations', *Rev. d'écon. pol.* L (1936).

37.   *Unemployment in France (000's in receipt of benefit)*

1929	1930	1931	1932	1933	1934	1935	1936	1937	1938
0.9	2.4	54.6	273.8	276.3	341.6	425.8	433.7	351.3	374.1

Source: Sauvy, op. cit. p. 554.

38.   *Index No. of Employment in France*

1929	1932	1933	1936	1937
100.0	80.9	79.4	74.1	78.6

Source: *Ministry of Labour Gazette, London*, XLVI (1938), 134. The basis for the estimate is not given.

39. Free use has been made of the important article by Jean-Charles Asselin, 'La semaine de 40 heures, le chômage et l'emploi', *Le Mouvement Social*, no. 54 (1966).

40. Ibid.

41. There is no shortage of observations to this effect. Thus, in 1934, an economist reported, with reference to machinery and machine tools, "les achats de la clientèle nationale sont tombés à un niveau faible; si dans quelques cas plutôt exceptionnels, des usines ont jugé opportun de moderniser leur equipement en vue de comprimer leur prix de revient la plupart des entreprises hésitent, au contraire, à rénover ou à aggrandir leur parc de machines." Nevertheless, he went on to add that despite tariffs, foreign machine imports were competing successfully with French products.—Henri Laufenburger, 'Les industries métallurgiques et méchaniques', *Rev. d'écon. pol.* XLIX (1935), special number on 'La France économique en 1934', p. 861. See the articles on other industries in the same number, and also 'La production industrielle' by P. Jéremac.

42. As *The Economist* put it, "The fact is that the Government and the Bank of France, despite their orthodox canon, have been driven by the exigencies of the situation in the direction of credit expansion" (30 December 1935). The persistence of depression kept down budget receipts so that, despite economies in expenditure, borrowing on short term from the Bank of France became inevitable. See also for a discussion of this, Sauvy, op. cit. II, 165 f.

43. For a comparative study of the profitability of the "sheltered" and "unsheltered" sectors see Jean Dessirier, 'L'économie française devant la dévaluation monétaire: secteurs "abrité" et "non-abrité" ', *Rev. d'écon. pol.* L (1936).

44. Charles Bettelheim, *Bilan de l'économie française, 1919–1946* (Paris, 1947), pp. 156–8.

45. As Jean Bouvier puts it in *Histoire économique et histoire sociale* (Geneva, 1968), p. 34: "Que savons-nous du pouvoir *économique* de la bourgeoisie d'entreprise et d'affaires? du grand négoce? de la grande banque? Qu'en savons-nous surtout entre les années 1880 et 1930? Un demi-siècle de croissance capitaliste et de pouvoir effectif de la grande bourgeoisie échappe, dans une mesure considérable, à nos investigations.

Il semble que dans l'historiographie française sociale contemporaine, nous avancions bien plus vite dans la connaissance des classes dirigées que dans la connaissance de la classe dirigeante. C'est une constatation qui me paraît même s'aiguiser à mesure que le temps s'écoule."

46. Thus the average age of machine tools at the end of the Second World War was stated to be twenty-five years against six or seven in the U.S.A. and Russia and seven to nine in Britain.—Jean Fourastié and Henri Montet, *L'économie française dans le monde* (Paris, 1946).

47. Sauvy, op. cit. II, 162; on this point, and for the depression period, see his article 'The Economic Crisis of the 1930s in France', *Journal of Contemporary History*, IV (1969).

48. See Gordon Wright, *Rural Revolution in France* (Stanford, 1964), chs. II and III.

49. Sauvy, op. cit. ch. XXII, 'Le malthusianisme économique'; and Bettelheim, op. cit. pt. II, 'Causes de la régression de l'économie française'. Sauvy places main emphasis upon the demographic factor, especially the ageing of the population; Bettelheim attaches more importance to the growth of monopoly. Clearly, a considerable field for research is open here.

50. This is to be seen in the pages of conservative journals such as *La Revue des Deux Mondes* during the 'thirties. Thus, in 1936 one reads statements of the kind 'La France, il ne faut pas l'oublier, en effet, ne conservera jamais sa richesse que si elle demeure un pays essentielle-ment agricole'.—Paul D'Espe, 'Les répercussions des nouvelles lois sociales', *Revue des Deux Mondes*, XXXIV (1936), 756.

4. THE FRENCH COMMUNIST PARTY AND THE PROBLEM OF POWER (1920–1939)

by Annie Kriegel

Translated by John F. Flinn

One of the characteristics of the Republic in the twentieth century has been the presence of political groups that opted out of "the system" and thus considerably narrowed the ground from which the parliamentary governing majority might be chosen. This was true even before 1914 with both die-hard survivors of intransigent monarchist or imperial loyalties and the rising Socialist party. The Great War that brought about an active Socialist participation in government initially limited but ultimately strengthened this leftist refusal to be compromised in a bourgeois system. What particularly cramped the situation of the Socialist party between the wars, however, was the emergence of the French Communist party, elements of which did not hesitate on occasion to preach dissidence and treason. Should they assume ministerial responsibility in bourgeois governments, the Socialists could be outbid on the left by their Communist rivals. Not until the crises of the mid-1930s, and with the approval of Moscow, did their mutual hostility end in a truce. Even then, the Communist party did not participate in the government of the Front populaire, *1936–1937, in which the Socialists shared power with their Radical Socialist allies, though it supported the government for many months. On the other hand, with the Nazi-Soviet Pact and the outbreak of war in 1939, the Communist party was condemned and virtually driven underground by the ruling conservative majority in parliament, whereupon it pursued subversive and defeatist activities. Nor were some of its adherents strangers to collaboration with the German occupant following the armistice of 1940. This wartime episode, lasting from the autumn of 1939 to the summer of 1941 (when the Soviet Union was invaded by Germany), has continued to seem difficult to reconcile with other aspects of the Communist party's behavior before and since.*

The author of this article proposes an explanation that, in the continued absence of firm documentation, is as plausible as it is ingenious. Annie Kriegel, Professor of Political Sociology and Chairman of the Department of Social Sciences, University of Paris-X, Nanterre, is author of Aux origines du communisme français, 2 vols. *(Paris, 1964),* La croissance de la C.G.T. (1918–1921) *(Paris, 1966), and of numerous other books and scholarly articles. This paper first appeared in* Annales E. S. C. 21 (1966): 1245–1258. *It is reprinted by kind permission of the author and the editors of that periodical.*

In the first volume of his *Histoire du Parti communiste français* Jacques Fauvet came to the following conclusion:

> From the occupation of the Ruhr to the operation in the Rif, from the war in China to the war in Spain, and from Munich to the German-Soviet Russian agreement, the Communist party succeeded neither in swaying French policy nor even in having any real influence on public opinion. Undoubtedly it bore witness, and its witness went to the point of martyrdom. But it failed.[1]

Considered solely from the author's viewpoint, this conclusion probably calls for some slight modification. Would it for example be of no use to make a distinction between two periods of unequal length, one extending from 1920 to 1934, the other from 1934 to 1939? During the first period the importance of French communism as a current of public opinion, as a party, and as a parliamentary group, steadily declined so that in reality it was no longer in a position to intervene in the creation of any combination or in the conduct of any policy, whether of the right or the left. From 1934 to 1939, on the contrary, as a current in public opinion, a party, and a parliamentary group the Parti Communiste Français was the contributing factor that was indispensable in the formation of a majority of the left.

But Jacques Fauvet's conclusion, interesting as it is from the point of view of internal French politics in the period between the two wars, above all risks leading to a misunderstanding of the real nature of the Communist phenomenon, particularly in its relationship to the problem of power. It is in fact sound to judge any human experience in terms of success or failure only in relationship to the values which that experience has agreed to be measured against: To be rich or not to be rich is a success or a failure only if becoming rich was the initial objective.

Now, in the case that concerns us, must we think that the original vocation of the PCF was "to sway French policy"? Not exactly.

THE NATURE OF THE COMMUNIST PHENOMENON

French communism is in fact the specific and original product of a grafting: the grafting of Russian bolshevism on the body of that form of French socialism dominated by the thought of Jean Jaurès. In this operation, as in any grafting, the elements involved were not equally divided at all levels. If at the outset the particularities of French socialism were predominant in determining the features of the *terrain*, that is to say the people, their number, their territorial and professional implantation, on the other hand the contribution of Russian bolshevism was decisive in defining the announced aim of French communism, for the simple reason that it existed outside of and in opposition to traditional socialism.

To discover the ultimate meaning of the French Communist phenomenon, consequently, we are driven to the necessity of discovering the ultimate meaning of Russian bolshevism. Naturally the historians, sociologists, political scientists, and philosophers give multiple and often contradictory versions of this "ultimate meaning." For my part, perhaps because I am a historian and consequently *time*—that is to say the observation of the juncture—is an essential dimension in my intellectual way of proceeding, I believe that I can grasp it by going back a little in time.

Is it indeed not suggestive to note that in the 1900s the two great spiritual currents that ran through the nineteenth century, venerable Catholicism and young socialism, underwent together a major doctrinal crisis, which would be called "modernism" in the first case and "revisionism" in the second? Is it rash to think that perhaps both these crises, in the specific form that each assumed from the specific nature of the current involved, had the same origins: the development of the industrial society and the triumph of the parliamentary Republic?

In any case, under the heading "revisionism," the fundamental problem with which the Socialist movement had been confronted, since the turn of the century and proportionately to its own growth, had been the following: How was it to conceive of the relations of the working class with the Establishment so as to prevent it from being gradually integrated into the Establishment society and to maintain its final purpose, the founding of a radically new society, the Socialist society? In political terms this problem can be formulated as follows: How were the relations between working-class organizations and the established power to be conceived so as to prevent them from being gradually associated with that power and to maintain their final purpose—the acquisition of power (for the champions of the Marxist-Socialist school), or its destruction (for the champions of the Anarchistic-Socialist school)?

Now, in the period 1895–1917, doctrine and history decidedly seemed to tend to recognize the supremacy of the factors favoring integration over the forces of rupture and isolation. This was true in France in an early stage when the "Millerand Case" and the so-called ministerial affair raised the question of the Socialist attitude toward the state. It was truer still at a later period when the *Union Sacrée*, in August 1914, settled the question of the attitude of the Socialists toward the nation in the manner that we all know. Moreover, must we not recognize in the fact that the tendency toward strengthening social cohesion won out, the final explanation of the breaking-up of revolutionary syndicalism, which in the years preceding the First Great War was in France the most logical, ambitious, and lucid enterprise for creating a truly and exclusively proletarian society, civilization, and world, in opposition to the bourgeois ones?

Seen in this light, bolshevism, in the form it assumed when the ordeal of the war led it to break off angrily from the Second International, of which it was originally an offshoot, in the form it assumed in the Russian Revolution and in which it spread through the channel of the Communist International, and about whose subtle connection with revolutionary trade unionism we do not know enough, can then be interpreted as a global attempt to break up completely the tendency toward integrating the working class and its organizations into the established society and power, a tendency that up till then had appeared to be unbeaten and unbeatable.

If that is indeed the "profound meaning" of bolshevism, then it is from that point of view that the success or failure of the PCF must be judged. It is through this starting point particularly that we manage to formulate the following hypothesis: If we look beyond the changes in policy due to circumstances, the sudden switches that have so often been denounced, the alternations that are too quickly called sectarianism and opportunism, the superficial balancing between falling back defensively upon one's self and conquering the others offensively, then the attitude of the French Communists toward the problem of power in the period between the two wars was remarkable and impressive in its continuity.

BOLSHEVISM AND THE PROBLEM OF POWER

Bolshevism was not content with being a plan of resistance to the process of integration of the workers: It defined and put into place the mechanisms capable of constituting the obstacles, hitherto unknown, upon which their creators intended that the tendency toward strengthening social cohesion, in existence for several decades, would be broken, and it is that which assured bolshevism of a prominent place in the gallery of great political doctrines.

Among those mechanisms I should like to mention three that to my mind are essential:

1. The size of the revolutionary enterprise, which was to be created immediately, on a worldwide scale;

2. The nature of postrevolutionary power: the demand for dictatorship of the proletariat had prerevolutionary implications;

3. The construction of a party that fulfilled, among other functions, not just that of a simple party, but of a proletarian society within and opposed to the dominant bourgeois society.

1. *The Size of the Revolutionary Enterprise*

Defining bolshevism as a strategy of revolution is a necessary initial approach, because it does not inevitably follow from the fact that bolshevism claims kinship with Marxism. Indeed, there seems to be no doubt that during his lifetime Marx envisaged alternatively two processes, or rather two tempos according to which the Socialist society could emerge from within capitalist society.

But that is an insufficient approach: Certainly bolshevism can be defined as a strategy of revolution, but as a *worldwide* strategy. For Lenin the October Revolution was only a prelude, and not even a decisive one: "The complete victory of the socialist revolution," he declared before the Congress of the Soviets in 1919, "is impossible in a single country; it requires at the very least the active assistance of several progressive countries, among which Russia does not figure."

As a revolution, the Russian Revolution could appear as an event, cease being an episode of secondary importance due to circumstances, and acquire a meaning, a destiny, and perhaps even a future, only when the Third International, the institutional expression of the plan for world revolution, was founded in its wake and at its call.

This was a change of scale inseparable from the Bolshevist enterprise; it was this that gave its Marxist rationality to the attempt to establish socialism in Russia, an economically backward country. It was this above all that prohibits thoughtlessly trying to settle the debates that split international socialism and every national party during those years. When for example Léon Blum pointed out at Tours that the conditions for an early proletarian revolution were not assembled in our country, he was unquestionably right; when the Austrian Marxists demonstrated in Vienna that they could do nothing else than what they did in the Austria of 1918–1919, they were unquestionably right; when the German Social Democrats demonstrated in Berlin that they could not do better than set up the liberal and progressive Republic of Weimar, they were unquestionably right. But they were right on one condition, which bolshevism rejects: that only the relative forces within national frameworks are to be taken into consideration.

From then on proletarian internationalism was no longer what it had been when it assumed concrete form in the First International: a form of collective sensitiveness linked with the sentiment of belonging to a community without frontiers of oppressed and exploited peoples. It was no longer what it had been when it thrilled the congresses of the Socialist élites of the Second International. It was still in large measure a form of behavior, an ecumenical attitude, ethical and humanistic in character. Henceforth it was above all a strategy, a certain concrete idea of the technical manner in which the planetary Establishment could be overthrown.

Long expositions are not necessary to understand why as a result of this the Communist parties, sectorial elements of an enterprise that was nothing less than worldwide, found in this type of strategy an obstacle of exceptional quality that the tendency toward integration ran up against. Certainly those parties were evolving within the established national societies on the one hand (which allowed them to take root in them and to draw from them an indispensable nourishment), but on the other hand, and perhaps that was the essential element, they belonged congenitally to a supranational world that had no "bourgeois" homologue. Does not the prestige of French communism, for example, derive from the delicate combination that results from its double role, that which it plays in French political life because it belongs to the worldwide Communist movement, and that which it plays in the worldwide Communist movement because it represents France?

2. *The Nature of Postrevolutionary Power*

It is not possible at this point to go into the mysteries of Bolshevist theory concerning the dictatorship of the proletariat. They can be found in concentrated form in "Les Thèses du camarade Lénine sur la démocratie bourgeoise et la dictature prolétarienne," which were presented to the First Congress of the Communist International and published in May 1919 in the first issue of the periodical *L'Internationale Communiste*. The key theme is that "there is no middle course between the dictatorship of the bourgeoisie and that of the proletariat." Consequently, the proletariat can only aim at overthrowing the dictatorship of the bourgeoisie, seizing the power of the bourgeoisie as it is incarnated in the bourgeois state, and putting in its place a power of the proletariat in the form of a proletarian, centralized state with an hierarchical organization and equipped with the attributes of every state: police, army, and so forth.

From this key theme there undoubtedly follow other important themes such as the *temporary* nature of the dictatorship of the proletariat (since the only aim of this dictatorship is to continue the class struggle until classes have been *destroyed*), or the form of the proletarian state (Lenin saw it as being nonparliamentarian, non-trade-unionist, but based upon the system of soviets).

But it is the key theme that remains firmly implanted in the heart of Communist thought and behavior, for by itself it banishes everything that might raise the illusion of reformism.

3. *The Nature of the Party*

It is not possible at this point for me to go into the very complex Bolshevist theory concerning the party as a means to seizing power and exercising power in the postrevolutionary period as it is set forth in the 19-point resolution adopted by the second congress of the Communist International on "the role of the Communist party in the proletarian revolution," a *new* party, a *proletarian* party, a *worldwide* party, but also a *single* party with the task of beating back all external opposition, a *unified* party with the task of proscribing all internal opposition, a *centralized* party whose structure is strictly formed on the hierarchical system.

Here too we must pick out the key theme: the party as a world-wide countersociety in miniature that prefigures the Socialist society to come. Again it is incumbent to interpret the theme correctly. In itself a party that represents a form of society is not necessarily an agent of revolutionary decomposition of established society. It may simply be an agent for creating a pluralistic structure in that society. That was exactly what happened with the Scandinavian, Belgian, and German Socialist parties of the Second International, which, long before the Communist parties of the Bolshevist sort, were able to transform themselves into autonomous social powers. Does not the great strength of Belgian socialism still reside in the immense network, which will soon be a hundred years old, of trade unions, cooperatives, "maisons du peuple," welfare activities, as a result of which a Belgian Socialist can live his life, feed and dress himself, take care of himself, defend his interests, relax, without ever ceasing to have a Socialist outlook? Conversely, is not the great weakness of the SFIO the fact that in France it disposes of this infrastructure only in certain regions, where, besides, its influence remains dominant as a result?

Like the Socialist parties, the Communist parties also aspired to plunging into the masses: Like them, they were consequently in part parties and business managers together. At the same time they did not shut their eyes to the fact that such a setup is a dangerous one: The tens of thousands of administrators that it requires are more concerned with the financial stability of the businesses—in the normal and commercial sense of the term—for which they are responsible than with killing capitalism, and I know some whom the prospect of an economic depression throws into perplexity—it is perhaps good for revolution, but it certainly is bad for business, even Communist business.

But, and here we are diametrically opposed to the spirit of Social Democracy, the Communist parties intend at the same time and contradictorily to remain "separate." The setting-up of a *ghetto*, which, with the passage of time, one no longer knows whether it developed freely or under compulsion, presents three advantages: It allows a minority group to preserve its originality and, through its homogeneity and the intensity of its inner life, to defend itself against assimilation, day after day and for a long time; again, it allows that group to exercise on the less tightly knit society outside of it, an influence that is out of proportion to its real size; and finally, it puts forward a parallel hierarchy and consequently forms of social mobility that are reserved strictly for its inhabitants, an indispensable condition for the birth of a specific elite.

FROM 1920 TO 1934: A PERIOD OF DOCTRINAL ASSIMILATION

Through the simple fact of having wanted to be a section of the Communist International, the PCF had officially *adopted* the Bolshevist doctrine. It still had to *adapt* it to the facts as they existed in France, to assimilate it enough to have it become little by little part of daily practice. That was what would be done with great effort in the period from 1920 to 1934.

The balance sheet of that effort is complex: It can be summarized in three points.

1. After many different crises and adventures difficult to follow, the PCF did actually succeed in situating itself concerning the problem of power on the positions contained in Bolshevist doctrine. This showed up in a stiffening within its ranks, a kind of coagulation: The global microsociety to which I referred and which was coiled up inside official society, was constituted. After eliminating little by little, from 1920 to 1925, those adherents from the prewar period who had been trained on other models, the Communists acquired a mentality and a form of behavior that assimilated them to "voluntary exiles of the interior." As such the PCF became in effect an advance detachment of the worldwide revolutionary enterprise, whose headquarters, the Executive Committee of the International, was in Moscow; a corps of snipers whose task was to harass the capitalist front from behind the lines.

2. This hard core of resistance to social integration exercise in addition such an attraction on its periphery that the SFIO itself was profoundly affected by it. In the discussion opened in 1926 on the theme: "Must the SFIO participate in the formation of a coalition government, or not?" the majority of the Socialist leaders answered in the negative, preoccupied as they were with the advantages that the Communists might obtain from a possible participation by the Socialists in a government, whatever it might be, or whatever might result from it.

3. On the other side, however, the Communist party, while able to resist the lures of the ruling society, was at the same time unable to attract those persons of any social origin, including of course those

members of the working class who had not taken up a position of rejecting that society overall, of breaking completely with it. Therefore, during the twenties, a period of capitalist stabilization, when the tendency was toward greater social uniformity and cohesion, the party deliberately went against the current and transformed itself little by little into a sect, not in the political but in the sociological sense of the term. When one gets to the bottom of it, that is the explanation of the astounding drop in numbers of Communists between 1920 and 1934. A sect, that is to say a complete society that functions in a closed circuit and reconstitutes in miniature an ideal society made up of working-class traditions, Socialist utopias, and Russian and Soviet realities that have been more or less conventionalized and transposed.

FROM 1934 TO 1939: IMPROVEMENTS CARRIED OUT ON A STABLE DOCTRINAL FOUNDATION

This first period of simple assimilation of doctrine was followed by a second period, the analysis of which requires greater development because during it a significant variant began to take form on a stable doctrinal foundation. Indeed, the PCF inaugurated a new policy that did not trespass upon its *position of remaining outside bourgeois power* but nevertheless brought it *inside* the government majority.

A. *The New Communist Policy: The PCF Outside Bourgeois Power but Inside the Majority.*

1. The shift in the Communist policy was spectacular. A short time before, the French Communists had been absolutely hostile to any form of collaboration with the group in power, whatever the color of that power, which could only be power held by the bourgeoisie; yet there were the French Communists in the period 1934–1936 entering for the first time into a coalition movement, then into an electoral alliance with the other two parties on the left of the political chessboard [Radical Socialists and Socialists], and finally reaping benefits from the creation of a government majority, even though they remained outside the government which depended upon that majority.

2. Who took the initiative for this shift in policy? On this point Communist historiography hesitates between two temptations.

The first is, in order to assert the Communists' merit, to attribute to the Communist party all the political initiatives that had made possible the alliances of the *Front populaire*. We can go back very far, but as early as 1931, in the struggle against the "Barbé-Célor group," Maurice Thorez is supposed to have outlined the themes that would receive definitive form in 1932 in the campaign around the international congress in Amsterdam.

This argumentation is in large measure specious: The same terms of *Front unique* and *Unité d'action* were probably used at the beginning of the thirties and in 1935–1936, but in both cases they referred to two diametrically opposed policies. Even the events of February 1934 contributed only to a certain degree to bringing together the Communist and Socialist organizations, and this particularly in the provinces, where the differences between schools of thought were less bitter. They did not suffice to bring about a summit aggreement: Afterward as before, the leadership of the PCF and its authorized newspapers multiplied the most virulent attacks against the Socialist leaders, who were guilty of defending the Republic of the bourgeoisie. In the February 19, 1934, issue of *Humanité*, Vaillant-Couturier was still writing: "Defend the Republic!, says Blum? As if fascism were not already the Republic, as if the Republic were not already fascism." It was not until June 26, 1934, at the national conference that the PCF held at Ivry, that, following instructions from the Communist International, the decisive step was taken, when the fruitful watchword "Unity at any cost" was substituted for the sterile demand of "Unity at the base."

The second temptation was to cast upon the SFIO the sole responsibility for the earlier division of the working class, to make the shift in policy in 1934 the corollary of the change in attitude on the part of the Socialist party alone: Under the pressure of the working-class masses the Socialist leaders were supposed to have been forced to accept the unity of action that up till then they had stubbornly refused. At this point Blum's well-known remark about the united front being "inevitable" would be quoted. But it would be useful to specify that if unity was "inevitable," it was because the Communists rallied to the democratic and national policy of the Socialist party, to the policy—and these are key words—of "defense of republican liberties" and "national defense": The new Communist policy in the period 1934–1939 was characterized by a review of the problems of democracy and the nation.

This is not the place to inquire into the grounds for the new Communist orientation. Let us confine ourselves to recalling that this

orientation seemed essentially to spring from a decision of a strategic nature—the recognition of Hitlerism as the principal enemy.
This was a decision that carried two corollaries. The first was that
there was a convergence, albeit a temporary one, of the concerns
of French diplomacy and those of the Communist movement, within
which the French section (which, since the catastrophe that had
swept away the German Communist party, had become the most important of the non-Russian sections in Europe) carried particular
weight. The second corollary was that everything had to be done to
prevent Hitlerism and foreign Fascist movements, particularly the
French one, from coming together. On the one hand this implied
avoiding the German model by not repeating in France the errors of
the Communists across the Rhine, and on the other it implied avoiding the Spanish model by not carrying a class war to its conclusion,
with the risk of tipping the French bourgeoisie into the camp of the
rightist extremists and bringing on a Nazi counterrevolutionary
intervention.

B. *Did This New Policy Involve a Change*
in the Bolshevist Doctrine Concerning Power?

What interests us in this question is not so much the motives for
the new policy and its consequences as the following question: Was
it the same process of integration, under a new disguise, which was
resumed after a brief pause? This interests us all the more as it is
disturbing to observe that the process of integration had already
started at the turn of the century on the same two fundamental
problems of democracy and the nation.

Now, the reply was a straightforward: No. When circumstances
had again changed, in the summer of 1939, the PCF was to give
evidence that it had kept its fundamental singularity. After that it
was possible to assert that the braking action that had been thought
up to resist the process of integration had proved effective. But it
must be added that in order to pass this test successfully the PCF,
under the direction of the Communist International, took three major precautions.

*1. The refusal by the Communists to participate in the Léon Blum
government.* The Communists justified the decision not to participate
in the government that came out of the victorious elections in
April–May [1936] with an argument that on the surface was linked
with their new policy: They did not want, they said, to run the

risk through their presence in the government of alarming the middle classes and the centrist groups. But this argument was trotted out *a posteriori* during the months of May and June. After all, the Communists knew perfectly well that if their refusal to share in the responsibilities of governing could help to reassure the lower middle class, it could not fail on the other hand to worry the Socialists: Didn't Léon Blum have to fear playing Kerensky's role?

In actual fact the Communists' refusal to take part in the government was linked with the technique called "parallel power," which had enabled the Bolshevists to create the conditions for the Russian October in six months.

Unlike the other political parties, the Communists had not had to consult together on May 6, 1936, about their attitude with regard to the Léon Blum government: Exactly eight months before they had discussed it at the highest level, and since that time their most authorized leaders had written hundreds of articles and delivered hundreds of speeches on the subject. Indeed, the Seventh Congress of the Communist International, which had met in Moscow in August 1935, had laid down in the most detailed fashion the three conditions on which Communists would be authorized to appoint representatives in a non-Soviet government.

   a. "When the bourgeoisie's machinery of the State is seriously paralyzed, to the point that the bourgeoisie is not in a position to prevent the creation of such a government;
   b. When the great masses of the workers rise up violently against fascism and reaction but are not yet ready to revolt in favor of Soviet power;
   c. When a considerable part of the social-democratic organization and of the other parties that are taking part in the common front are already demanding ruthless measures against the Fascists and other reactionaries and are ready to engage in a common struggle with the Communists for the application of those measures."

For the Communists, then, a *Front populaire* government was called for before the take-over of power, but at a point where the revolutionary torrent was sufficiently swollen to be capable of sweeping away later obstacles; in short, within the framework of an acute political crisis. Dimitrov summed this up in a vigorous formula: "*On the eve* of the victory of the Socialist revolution and *before* that victory."

If the Communists did not participate in the Blum government in May 1936, it was not because they were taken by surprise by the

event. Nor was it because their principles prevented them from joining any government in a capitalist regime. It was quite simply because the Blum government, by its very nature, did not correspond
to the idea that they had formed in their minds of a "real" *Front
populaire* government. Maurice Thorez had, moreover, warned of
this on several occasions during the preceding months: He had made
a very clear distinction between what he called, on the one hand,
a "government of the left," a government composed of a parliamentary coalition "such as those in which the Socialist parties are
participating in Belgium, Czechoslovakia, and Spain," and, on the
other hand, "a *Front populaire* government" or "real government
of the people." In short,

> So long as conditions do not allow the formation of a *Front populaire*
> government *as we conceive of it*, we are resolved to support with our
> votes the government that is in accordance with the interests and the
> will of the people of France. (January 22, 1936)

2. Critical harassment of the Léon Blum government. Not only
did the Communists not take part in Léon Blum's government, but in
addition the "total support" that they had promised the leader of
the SFIO very quickly became so critical that one could not tell
very well whether or not they were "on the side of the government."
As early as June 13, 1936, Jacques Duclos, from the speaker's
platform of the Chambre des Députés, took his distance with a single
sentence:

> We are going to give you our votes, *but* outside the walls of this room
> there is a whole nation that wants its legally expressed will to be
> respected.

After which, all the articles in the *Correspondence Internationale,*
the official periodical of the Comintern, which dealt with France
under the signature of its editor in chief, Joanny Berlioz, followed
the same line: An opening paragraph summarized in a few lines
the grounds for satisfaction that the victory of the *Front populaire*
had legitimately procured; then followed three pages of rather
harsh remarks in which the journalist listed everything that had not
been done, everything that still had to be done.
Finally, when the summer and fall had gone by in this way, the
last stage was passed: on December 12 one could read under the
title "Blum and the action for peace":

> We did not associate ourselves with a governmental formation because
> of the men who constitute it nor because of the intentions they may

have, but only as a means of carrying out resolutely the electoral promises that were made in common.

And further on:

The fate of the Cabinet is one thing, the powerful *Front populaire* movement is another.

Thus the conditions in which the technique of parallel power was applied in France little by little approached those that had existed in Russia in 1917. At the beginning the difference was considerable, since in France the Communists were *outside* the *Front populaire* government but *inside* the political majority that supported the government, while in Russia the Bolshevists, at least from the time when Lenin was again at their head, were outside *both* the provisional government *and* the majority—in the narrow sense of the word—that supported the provisional government. But some months later, by the end of 1936, the French Communists were also outside *both* the Blum government *and* practically outside the majority—in the parliamentary sense—that supported that government. From then on, as formerly in Russia—and that is the third precaution that I mentioned earlier—the French Communists used fundamentally the technique of parallel power to gain the majority *within* the majority—that is to say the left, the majority in public opinion.

3. *The winning-over of the masses*. This was in reality what, in a formula that was as alluring as it was incautiously revealing (it created a scandal), Vaillant-Couturier called: exercising "the ministry of the masses."

For this winning-over of the majority within the majority the French Communists tried, moreover, different courses. In 1935 they had attempted the traditional course of *Front populaire* committees, committees whose function was to be similar to that of the Russian soviets. But in refusing to be a party to the creation of such committees Léon Blum and the SFIO had nipped the undertaking in the bud.

Therefore in 1936 a hitherto unknown course appeared: It opened up to the Communists the prospect of assuming the direction in its fundamental structure of the working-class movement without have recourse to the expedient of the *Front populaire* committees. It was a historically new course, since never up till then and nowhere, even in Russia and even after October, either on the level of the party proper or of the electorate, had the Communists disposed directly, in a favorable conjuncture, of the majority within the Socialist movement. Now, in May 1936 the membership of the PCF exceeded that of the Socialist SFIO, 131,000 against 127,000. Six months later, in November, the PCF could claim 284,659 adherents as against 200,000 for the SFIO. From that time on the Communists put the emphasis on the need to achieve very quickly the organic unity of the two parties that called themselves Socialist. From the moment the Communists largely outnumbered the Socialists, unification would mean that the whole of the movement inspired by socialism would come *under the leadership* of its Communist wing. This was a condition that, as we know, the Communists considered fundamental for taking over power, and that up till then they had brought about only through the roundabout way of taking control of the soviets or the trade unions.

To be sure, this did not happen; organic unification failed in 1937 as it would again fail in 1945–1946. But henceforth the political gains from demands for unity would go to the Communists.

In short, from 1934 to 1939 the Communists worked out on a solid doctrinal foundation an original theoretical development. Undoubtedly their major preoccupation remained what we said it was at the beginning: not to set in motion again the earlier and fatal process of integrating the working class with the Establishment. But the obstacles devised to resist this process—in particular the world-wide dimension of the revolutionary enterprise and above all the construction of a party on the model of a global microsociety—appeared sufficiently sound for an original experiment to be attempted; the principle of remaining absolutely outside power was toned down, and the idea of participating in *one aspect* of power was adopted: joining the governmental majority. The precautions taken to prevent this experiment from going off the track were, besides, considerable: no participation in government and even a critical position with regard to the governmental aspect of power, while efforts were pursued to win another majority, no longer the governmental majority but a majority within the organized working class. This was, in a word, a resurgence of the technique called parallel power that had been perfected by Lenin in 1917, with the considerable but not crucial difference that the Bolshevists had proclaimed their hostility to the Social-Democratic government, whereas the French Communists in theory gave it their support.

The gains from this comprehensive arrangement were considerable. On the one hand, proof was given that the PCF was indeed a force standing completely outside established society: It "held on" when the Socialist parties in the Second International had not resisted. On the other hand, the PCF became in actual fact the foremost of the two parties in France that claimed to be Socialist: We are well enough aware of the extent to which the problem of the relative strength of the Communists and Socialists has dominated French political life over the last twenty years and of how it continues today.

CONCLUSION

Before the war the French Communists would not go further into the problem of power. Although they had already foreseen the final stage, they would not enter upon it; it was not until 1945 that they would consider that they were capable of taking their place not only *within* the majority that the Left disposed of in public opinion, not only *within* the governmental majority, but *within* the government itself, without giving up because of that their position of remaining completely outside the established regime. In the Eastern European countries it would even be this formula of parallel power, right up to and including the governmental level, that was to direct the complete acquisition of power in its different aspects.

From 1936 on, it is true, the question of participation in the government had been a stormy one. In the second edition of *Fils du peuple* Maurice Thorez felt that he had to make clear, as he had not done in the first edition, that he had personally put forward the idea of participation by the Communists in the government, but that he had had to give in to the opposition of the party's *Bureau politique*. One may dispute the reality of the fact that this detail is intended to establish (the detail is, besides, expressed in rather vague terms: in particular the date of the discussion by the *Bureau politique* is not given). On this point Auguste Lecoeur, who was not an eye-witness but who probably had the oportunity on many occasions to discuss these problems at the highest level, maintained that Duclos and Frachon, much more than Thorez, were favorable to participation.

On the other hand there is no doubt about the fact that the International had to reopen discussion on this problem in the following months: In September 1936 the Spanish Communists were authorized, for the first time in the world, to participate in a *Front populaire* government that was not an outrightly revolutionary government. Finally, after the fall of the first Blum government and when the possibility of another government headed by the Socialists again loomed up at the beginning of 1938, the French Communists announced that they were ready to belong to the combination. We know that finally this did not happen until 1943, but we can deduce from it that between May and September 1936 the Communist International realized fully that Communist participation in *Front populaire* governments was no longer a problem of principle but a tactical one governed by circumstances.

Thus from 1920 to 1939, under the Third Republic, and afterward in the period 1945–1947, the Communists maintained intact their capacity for appearing as the heralds of the only society of the future: This did not prevent them from thinking up nevertheless, on this constant doctrinal foundation and in keeping with circumstances and the successes they obtained, bold variations in their relations with the Establishment.

Should not the historian at this point hand the torch over to the political scientist? Does the question that is on everyone's lips today: "Have the Communists changed?" not amount to wondering whether since 1956 it is not the doctrinal foundation that in a confused sort of way is in question, whether the long and victorious struggle against the formidable process of social integration and cohesion will finally have been simply a delaying action, whether once more the revolution is behind us, whether the separateness of the Communists is no longer anything but a holdover? Just as it took sixty years for a certain type of Christian modernism to triumph, so a certain type of Socialist revisionism—shades of Bernstein!—may well win out inevitably one day, if it has not already done so.

In that case one would still wonder whence contemporary society draws its exceptional force of assimilation, its unconquerable tendency toward homogeneity, its final indifference to utopia.

Notes

1. Jacques Fauvet, *Histoire du parti communiste français*, 2 vols. (Paris, Fayard, 1964–1965), I: 269.

5. THE FRENCH WORKING CLASS AND THE BLUM GOVERNMENT (1936–37)

by Arthur Mitzman

The Front populaire *may well be the best-known political event of the Third Republic. Long after so much of what once seemed important in the seventy years from the fall of the Second Empire to the establishment of the* Etat français *has been forgotten, the memory of the first government claiming to represent the working-class population of France remains clear. Clear but at the same time much in dispute, the inevitable fate of a movement that was at once the bearer of so many high expectations and the herald of so many social fears, and that ended its brief career amid vast disappointment and vicious class schism. The* Front populaire *exists still as myth and is likely to continue therefore very nearly independent of the evidence and the historical inquiry about it. No doubt the fierce hatreds that grew up around it and that it polarized have gone, or are mostly going to rest with that generation, but so too has much of the most bitter disenchantment that was experienced on the left. The* Front populaire *is likely to remain as a creative myth.*

Arthur Mitzman reconstructs the events of that year 1936–1937 to show why, in his view, an enterprise so hopefully begun came to so unhappy an end and, as he sees it, with such baleful effects for the strength and unity of the nation. Professor of History, University of Amsterdam, he is the author of The Iron Cage: An Historical Interpretation of Max Weber *(New York, 1970) and* Sociology and Estrangement: Three Sociologists of Imperial Germany *(New York, 1973), as well as various articles in learned journals. This paper was first published in the* International Review of Social History *9 (1964): 363–390. It is reprinted by kind permission of the author and the editor of that periodical.*

To the French Left in May 1936, the electoral triumph of the *Front Populaire*—a coalition of the Communist, Socialist, and Radical Parties—signified nothing if not the victory of legal republicanism over the criminal machinations of domestic fascism. Consequently, embarrassment—not to mention confusion—was widespread, when the proletariat chose to greet this victory with a wave of sit-down strikes that was at once massive, spontaneous, joyful, and utterly illegal. It is true that the roots of the strikers' grievances went much further back than the political campaign of recent months. Five years of lowered wages, poorer working conditions, and the indifference of many employers to the lot of their men [1] were behind the workers' monumental audacity. Nevertheless, the coincidence of the strikes with Leon Blum's accession to office was far from accidental.

In part, the Left's sweeping victory at the polls meant to the workers that striking was no longer to involve the chance of police repression and mass dismissals.[2] This feeling of assurance was certainly an important reason for the walkouts. But possibly more important was that, for the proletariat, this new government, soon to take office, had become a beacon of hope. Since the First World War, the French working class had seen one continental democracy after another destroyed by fascism and reaction. In Italy, Germany, and Austria, it had witnessed the defeat and dissolution of free labor parties and trade union organizations that had been the pride of pre-war social democracy. After February 6, 1934, there was reason to fear that France herself was next. Only a few days before Austrian Socialism was crushed in armed struggle with Dollfuss' police, right-wing rioters at the Place de la Concorde were threatening to lynch the members of the National Assembly.

Indeed, during the years preceding the victory of the Popular Front, right-wing leagues, notably the *Croix de feu*, had made countless demonstrations and threats against the republican order. No one at the time was sure how much of their display was smoke and how much, fire. But the excellent showing of the left parties in the 1936 elections gave hope that at last a stand, or, better, a counteroffensive might be made against the encroachments of fascism. If some workers were wary of doing anything to antagonize external fascism, because of the war danger, there was no such inhibition regarding the domestic brand. A great feeling of elation filled the partisans of the *Front Populaire*, and this elation, accompanied as it was by a steep decline in the morale and popularity of the supporters of the Right, encouraged the workers to take a step which without the general exuberance would have been very unlikely.[3]

To be sure, the strikes do not show the workers to have had any child-like faith in the omnipotence of the new regime. They certainly did not see it, as some of their more rabid antagonists did, as a government of Red Revolution. The very fact of locking themselves in and their employers out of the struck plants, while it signified a belief that Blum would not use the *Gardes mobiles* against them, also showed little confidence in the government's ability to keep their employers from running the plants with strikebreakers. And such a lack of confidence would have been most inappropriate under a truly Bolshevik regime. Indeed, several chronicles of the period present the strikers as feeling the need to "push" Blum into doing something for the workers.[4] But at least Blum was seen as capable of being "pushed" in the right direction, as distinct from the usual chief of state, who when pushed would merely push back with all the armed force at his disposal. Thus, there can be little doubt that despite these reservations, and apart from all other factors producing the strike wave, the strikes indicated the workers' enthusiastic support of the new Popular Front government. In return for their support, the workers expected a strong stand against fascism and a major improvement in their conditions of labor.

Little more than a year later, this government, under heavy pressure from the banks and the Senate, was forced out of office. By then the attitude of the workers to the Blum regime had changed drastically. I have seen no better indication of this change than the following statement by a conservative opponent of the Popular Front:

> It had been commonly admitted that the fall of the cabinet would have as an immediate consequence a general strike of the Parisian working class, indeed, large-scale riots. Some spoke of revolution. Now it is a fact that never has a ministerial fall left the street, the public square, so indifferent. Not a movement, not even a cry. No armed force employed. None of our fellow citizens, even among the most confident, could have hoped for such an easy, regular defeat of the cabinet.[5]

The purpose of this study will be to show how and why this monumental indifference developed out of the workers' initial enthusiasm.

I

It is traditional to assign to the Communists a role that is not merely Machiavellian but all-powerful in turning the working class against the Popular Front. Noting the strange mixture of ultra-patriotic and left-extremist demagogy in the Communist propaganda output for 1936–37, some of the most acute observers have considered that the Party aimed both at forming right-wing alliances and at turning the working class against Blum, the former, to serve Stalin's policy of the moment, the latter, to prepare a base for an ultimate conquest of power.[6] The conclusion is then reached that while they failed in the attempt to gain right-wing allies, they were most successful in turning the workers against the Blum regime.[7] Nevertheless, though there is no question of the duplicity of the Communists, I do not believe that the workers' growing disillusionment with the Popular Front was so much a result as a cause of the confusing maneuvers of the French Communists in 1936–37.

The basic aim of Stalin's European policy in the period following the Laval-Stalin pact and continuing at least until the fall of 1937 was to prevent the rapprochement, in a massive European combination directed against Russia, of France and Italy on the one hand and Germany and England on the other.[8] There is little doubt that fear of this combination, coupled with fear of the already existing Berlin-Tokyo axis, was communicated to the French party in no uncertain terms, and that its whole energy was directed to winning the sympathy of the French people and government for Russia and against Germany.[9] Up to the autumn of 1936, this tactic is most unequivocal. The Communists showed themselves as super-patriots to the electorate in the election campaign of April 1936.[10] They in no way sought the strike wave of May-June 1936, and, though they capitalized on it very well, for reasons I shall explain shortly, they did everything they could to convince the strikers to go back to work at the earliest possible moment.[11] When the Spanish Civil War broke out towards the end of July, they consistently played down the revolutionary character of that war, and stressed the need for a "French Front" of all Frenchmen, to save the republican cause and keep France from fascist encirclement.[12] Their entire appeal was directed not to the working class—though at massive outdoor rallies in August 1936 they gathered great numbers of people, of whom a large proportion were probably workers—but to the parties and adherents of the Right and Center.[13]

For reasons which are inexplicable in terms of the demands of Russian foreign policy, however, this line of action seemed to stop rather abruptly in September 1936. The "French Front" slogan was dropped and two large-scale protest strikes against Blum's non-intervention policy signified the beginning of an attack on the Blum regime *from the Left*.[14] The most plausible interpretation of this shift is that the working class had maintained considerable autonomy vis-à-vis its environment, including that part of its environment which embodied the propaganda and charisma of the Communist Party. A few brief reflections on the role of the Communist Party in the June strikes and its later relations to the proletariat makes this clear.

In May and June 1936, the Communists came to control the greater part of the rejuvenated labor movement not by attracting the workers to its slogans, but by falling in line with the slogans of the workers. In a sense, the Party was made a prisoner of its working-class base. For years, it had had as the substance of its organization factory cells, which were practically identical with the quasi-legal Communist union locals (CGTU). Because of the strictly centralized hierarchical and conspiratorial nature of these cells, they managed to persist in many areas where CGT locals, with their looser structure and more open operations, were quickly disrupted and dissolved by the dismissals of their members.[15] Thus the CGTU militants, through the very fact of their continued existence and agitation, and though their numbers were very small, were often held in high, almost mystical esteem by their co-workers.[16]

But this regard was based on the identification of the workers' hopes, however vague and inarticulate they were, with the actions of the local Communist militants.[17] The distant and obscure international aims of the Party had practically no influence on the mass of semi- and unskilled workers in the factories colonized by the Communists. It was the local and class issues, of significance primarily to the factory in which they worked or, at best, to the class with which they identified themselves—pay rates, hours, conditions of work, etc.—that appealed to the workers and could be used by the Communists in appealing to them. So that when a conflict arose between the macrocosmic demands of Party policy, and the microcosm of a factory or class situation, the local militants, despite instructions from above to prevail in the name of the Party, had either to go along with the class demands of the microcosm or see themselves bypassed.

In May and June, the local militants agreed to take over the leadership of the stay-in strikes despite the discrepancy between the illegal nature of the strikes and the law-and-order pose of the Communist leadership at the time, because if they did not, their own personal influence and that of the Party (it must have been extremely difficult to separate the two) would be dissipated.[18] After the Matignon Agreement, the Party leaders lost no time in exhorting the proletariat to return to work, and in resuming their pose as defenders of the Republic.[19]

Their tactic was again interrupted, however, and this time permanently, by the renewal of labor unrest in the fall of 1936. Through the month of August, the workers had shown little more than contempt for the French Front, and the Socialists took no little pleasure in flaying the Communists for their total abandonment of even the theory of class struggle.[20] These annoyances could be endured, but only as long as there was no reason to fear the wholesale defection of the Party's new working-class supporters. And such a defection could come about through a new strike wave, in which the Communists, trapped in their new principles of class collaboration, would be completely bypassed. When in late August and early September, this new series of strikes began in the north of France, where, as Thorez well knew, the Socialists were more powerful than the Communists, the Communist leadership was forced to choose between the implementation of its long-range policies and its working-class hegemony.[21] Since the organizational basis of the party was more than ever in the factory cells, the decision was virtually forced on the top leadership of the Party to call off the French Front slogan, and lend its support to the strikers.[22]

But this tactical maneuver to hold together their working-class organization by no means meant that the Communists had abandoned completely the goal of a new *Union Sacrée*. If, in the ensuing months, Communists were to belabor the government for its Spanish policy with increasing vigor, it was because this was the only issue open to them which both remained congruent with their basic policy of keeping France at odds with Germany and Italy, and could be used to distract the working class from economic conflicts, thus holding alive the possibility of a future *Union Sacrée*. In December 1936, the Communists disclosed the intensity of their opposition to non-intervention by making it the only issue in Blum's year of office on which they abstained from supporting him in the *Chambre*.[23]

But there can be no doubt that if the Communists had their reasons for pushing Blum on the Spanish issue, so had the workers theirs, and the latter were by no means identical with the former. The Communists' continual denial of the revolutionary character of the war in Spain did not hide this character from the average French worker, who felt keen bonds of sympathy for the Spanish workers' militias, and was often enough aware that Russian aid to the Loyalists had been slow in coming and meager when compared to the oratory of the French Communist Party.

An interesting example of this awareness—and one which sheds additional light on the conditional nature of the Communists' control over the workers—emerges from the record of the February 1937 Congress of the "Union of Unions of the Paris Region", the most important regional labor organization under Communist control in France.[24] In the course of an attempt by a small group of revolutionary syndicalists to have deleted from the organization's official report an endorsement of the Moscow trials and the Stalin Constitution of 1936,[25] Communist hecklers from the audience told the speaker to "go to Mexico", which had just granted asylum to Leon Trotzky. In reply, the speaker pointed out that Mexico had aided Spain before the USSR. Efforts of the Communist leadership to keep control of this meeting extended to cutting off the power supply for a microphone being used by an oppositionist delegate. We may gauge the power which the Communists wielded in this organization, which was thought even by a high CGT official to be totally under Communist control, by the fact that the leadership, fearing to put its line on the trials to a vote, voluntarily withdrew the praise of Stalin's terror and his bogus constitution from their report.[26]

The workers' growing indifference to the Blum regime can thus be understood in its own terms, apart from the maneuvers of the Communists. It developed from three major disappointments, all of which were, with more or less justification, laid at the door of the government: non-intervention in Spain, which they felt to be a betrayal of the government's anti-fascist pledges; the refusal of their employers to recognize their newly won rights and privileges; and, finally, the material dissipation of the wage gains of Matignon by steep price increases.

II

It is certain that the desire to lend material support to the Spanish Republic, far from being a mere Communist maneuver, was an instinctive reaction of almost the entire French Left. Everyone regarded the *Frente Popular* a sister-grouping to the *Front Populaire*, and the two coalitions were elected to office within ten weeks of each other. When Spanish generals attempted a coup d'etat in July 1936, they carried most of the army with them, and the sole defenders of the republic and the *Frente Popular* were poorly trained bands of Anarchist, Socialist, and trade-union militiamen.[27] It was only through the resistance of these units that the coup was turned into a civil war and the republic was given the time in which to build up a new regular army. In the week after the insurgent attack, the Socialist *Le Populaire* reported many resolutions of support for the Spanish workers from union locals, Socialist sections and Popular Front committees. On July 28, the miners' union, controlled by non-Communists,[28] sent a message of solidarity to the Spanish miners. On July 30, the interunion committee of the Paris printers, among whom non-Communists also predominated,[29] voted a resolution containing the following statement:

> Considering, furthermore, that only popular pressure will put an end to the blackmail of the French fascists and permit to be given to the Spanish proletariat the moral aid and material supplies which it needs for its victory; the interunion committee of the Parisian printers resolves that our reunified CGT should take the initiative as soon as possible for a vast demonstration in favor of Republican Spain.[30]

The day before the printers' resolution was issued, the highest leadership of the non-Communist workers, in the International Federation of Trade Unions and the Socialist International, mirrored and furthered the sentiments of the rank-and-file with an appeal to "The International Proletariat" that said in part:

> Comrades! You have all felt that if the Republic and democracy were conquered in Spain, a fearful blow would be carried to the cause of liberty in the entire world. No sacrifice will be too heavy to defend such a cause. To those who, down there, are giving their blood and their lives, let us give all the material and moral support that we can bring to bear. Everywhere and in all circumstances demonstrate your real solidarity with the Spanish workers. Demand of the democratic states that, in conformity with the constant rules of international law, the regular and legal government of Spain be able to obtain the necessary means for its defense.[31]

Indeed, according to one labor historian, it was felt in France at the time that the dispatching of two French divisions at the outset of the war would have quickly brought victory to the Loyalists.[32]

Blum's declaration on non-intervention of August 1, 1936, prompted as it was by Britain's refusal to back France in case aid to Spain produced a war with Germany, did not turn off the flow of appeals by Socialists and trade-unionists.[33] In *Le Populaire* for August 19, 1936, Jean Longuet's column was headed "Justice for Spain" and concluded: ". . . either immediate and complete neutrality or . . . the British and French governments ought to grant to the Spanish government the material it needs." And on August 22nd, the Administrative Commission of the CGT, fully controlled by non-Communists, demanded "for the constitutional government of Spain the guarantees of international law, which allow it to supply itself freely for its defense against the rebel generals in the service of fascism".[34] Perhaps the height of feeling against the government came with the fall of Irun on September 4th, 1936. A small town in the Pyrenees near the French border, Irun could only be supplied by the Spanish government through French territory. The necessary supplies and ammunition were allowed into France, but not out again. As a result, the defenders of Irun, after an heroic struggle that was in the headlines of the French workers' press for days, were forced to give up the town.[35]

Blum, who did his best not to lose touch with the workers' sentiments,[36] had had ample opportunity before Irun to feel the pressure mounting against his policy. As early as the end of July, a speech of his in memory of Jaurès had been interrupted by cries of "Airplanes for Spain".[37] Shortly after the fall of Irun, therefore, at Luna-Park near Paris, Blum made an impassioned plea for the workers to give their support to his policy:

> Do you think I do not share your feelings? . . . When I read in the papers about the fall of Irun and the agony of the last militia-men, do you think that my heart was not with them too? . . . And do you think me suddenly incapable of reflection and foresight? Do you think I do not understand what it all means? Believe me, If I have acted as I have done, it is because I knew that it was necessary.[38]

The necessity, Blum went on, derived from the fact that if France renounced non-intervention, so would Germany and Italy, whose heavy industries could more easily supply arms for the rebels than could those of France for the Loyalists. He added that there was not a single piece of evidence supporting the claim that Hitler and Mussolini were violating the non-intervention Pact; that France, having been the originator of this pact, could hardly tear it up when the ink was still wet on it,[39] and that, finally, intervention might well lead to war with Germany.

The audience which Blum addressed appeared to be mollified if not won over by his arguments. But whatever the victory won by Blum at Luna-Park, his definitive statement that the government would not, because it could not, aid the republicans of Spain, seriously harmed his future relations with the proletariat. For even among those who were convinced by him, the hope for a determined stand against fascism, which had been placed in the *Front*

Populaire government, must have been severely shaken. Here was a regime which was swept into office on the basis of an essentially negative program—defense against fascism—and whose triumph was interpreted as a turning point in the world struggle between fascism and democracy. To be sure, it had dissolved the *Croix de feu* and other paramilitary bands. But since the fall of the conservative Doumergue government in late 1934 did not produce the fascist putsch which had been threatened for that occasion, most people came to realize that the threat of French fascism had been over-rated.[40] While the threat of domestic fascism was waning, however, that of the international variety grew. The French Left had suffered the passivity of its government during the Italian conquest of Ethiopia and Hitler's reoccupation of the Rhineland without becoming demoralized because, after all, it was a *bourgeois* government that had behaved so spinelessly. But when the workers saw their own political leadership behaving in the same manner, and offering good (if not sufficient) reasons besides, the good will that marked Blum's first weeks in office received its first douche of cold water.

Thus, the workers entered the fourth month of *Front Populaire* government with a bitterness that was soon to be increased by renewed conflict between labor and capital. Though they had probably not yet turned their backs on the Popular Front, they were soberly impressed by its limitations, and impatient of them.

III

The greatest strike wave France had ever experienced reached its crest in the second week of June 1936, when over a million men downed their tools.[41] Thereafter, the major demands of the strikers having been satisfied, strikes slowly subsided. By the third week of July, all but 33,000 people had returned to work,[42] and on August 17th and 18th, for the first time since May, *Le Temps* failed to print a line of strike news. This calm was quickly broken by a new surge of unrest that had little of the peaceful character of the earlier sit-down strikes and seemed to be caused as much by employer intransigence as by a rapidly rising cost of living.[43]

On August 19th, one of the first strikes reported after the mid-August hiatus was a strike of government workers.[44] This was a particularly bad omen for the Blum regime. The Civil Servants' Federation had always been noted for its *lack* of the endemic *in-*

civisme which made so many Frenchmen view their government as an independent predator rather than an embodiment of the public interest. And of all the trade union groups, the civil servants were considered closest to the Socialists.[45] Indeed, according to André Delmas, the *fonctionnaires* were "the elements on which [Blum] counted on being able to support himself with most security".[46] If this was all Blum could expect from his friends, what must his enemies be preparing!

The plans of Blum's enemies in the reorganized employers' federation soon became clear. Through a resolute campaign of resistance to organized labor, the new *Confederation Générale du Patronat Français*, was determined to prevent any new gains by labor and to take back as many of the concessions granted at Matignon as possible.[47] One of the most anti-union of the employers' sub-groups, because of the nineteenth-century paternalism of most of its members, was the textile employers' federation.[48] This group was even more eager to recoup the losses of June than the CGPF, which it had left in disgust after Matignon and refused to rejoin. Thus, the strikes of late summer and early fall, 1936, had four principal characteristics. A great many of them took place in textile mills, which were concentrated in the north of France. They were frequently touched off by dismissals of union workers, and the fear of lockouts. They were aggravated, where not actually caused, by sharp rises in the cost of living.[49] They were usually prolonged by the refusal of the employers—especially the textile employers—to negotiate until their workers left company property.[50]

On August 19th and 20th, this new pattern began to appear with strikes in the Nord and other departments over dismissals and lay-offs of workers. On August 22nd another strike in the Nord, at Lille, developed over the employment of non-union labor: on the 24th, a sympathy strike was declared in nearby Roubaix and Tourcoing. All three of these cities were major textile centers. The festive mood of the June strikes was absent: at least one case occurred where strikers went to the home of a non-striking worker and destroyed property.[51]

On August 25th, the Talbot factory locked out 1,000 workers in the Paris area, claiming it could not meet the new wage rates. The workers countered that orders were plentiful and that the only reason for the lockout was to exert pressure on the government to obtain credits. More lockouts were feared. On August 29th, 1,100 men occupied a plant in Belfort. On August 30th, more strikes, especially in the Nord, over dismissals of union members, were reported. On

August 31st, 5,000 coal miners of the northern region left their pits.

The pace of the new strike wave accelerated almost daily. On September 3rd, 1,800 weavers sat down in their plants at Amiens, while strikes for higher wages involved 1,400 men in Soissons. The 4th saw 6,000 metallurgy workers leave their jobs in Grenoble. The next day, presumably under the pressure of their employers' refusal to negotiate, the weavers of Amiens agreed to leave their plants for the duration of the strike. In the following four days, a rash of strikes by dockers and shipyard workers broke out in La Seyne, Cherbourg, and La Rochelle. On the 10th of September, 10,000 metallurgy workers in the Nord struck for wage increases to keep up with the cost of living. On the 11th, 30,000 textile workers locked themselves into their factories in Lille.

Two days later, the Lille strikers, under government pressure, agreed to evacuate their plants, only to reoccupy them on the 14th after their employers broke off negotiations. On the 17th, 24,000 textile workers in the Vosges struck, while the Lille strike continued. After an attempt at government arbitration failed because of the employers' refusal to cooperate with the government, the strike in Lille was settled by a compromise on the 19th. On the same day, the Hotchkiss workers in Clichy walked out because of feared dismissals, and returned only when assured they would not take place.

The next day, September 20th, *Le Temps* reported major strikes in progress at Douai and Marseilles in metallurgy, and at Amiens, in the Vosges, and at Lyons, in textiles. On the 21st, textile workers in Roubaix and Tourcoing prepared to strike, while a small textile plant in Lille, employing 70 men, closed down because it could not afford to pay new wage rates. The Roubaix-Tourcoing strike was avoided, but on the 24th, the epidemic of metal workers' walkouts reached Paris, and sent men out by the tens of thousands. The strikes of textile workers in Vosges and Lyons remained unsettled, and, on the 26th of September, a special meeting of the CGT's national committee was called to review the situation.

In his speech before this body, Jouhaux condemned both the provocations of the employers and the inexperience of the workers and ended with an important new list of demands for government intervention to control the situation. He condemned the press reaction to the strikes, asserting that ". . . every move of the workers is savagely exploited to create an atmosphere of panic from which our adversaries hope to gain profit".[52] He admitted the unreasoning impulsiveness of the great mass of newly unionized workers, who wanted "immediately, full satisfaction for all their demands", and denounced "troublemaking elements inside each factory", who used this impulsiveness. His conclusion was that it was necessary to "develop in the masses a sense of discipline", which could only be done "by guaranteeing all the acquired rights". To obtain such a guarantee, Jouhaux made three demands: 1) That factories be closed by the government during strikes so that neither workers nor management could get into them; 2) That a mobile scale be established for workers' wages, to keep pace with the cost of living; 3) That a system of compulsory arbitration be established by the government for handling labor disputes. All three of these points were in marked contradiction to the CGT's traditional stand against government regulation.[53] But with a friendly government, and an unfriendly management, which as the Lille strike showed was obviously not amenable to any voluntary procedures, the CGT realized it had more to gain than to lose by its proposals.

Neutralization of struck factories would have virtually ended all need for sit-down strikes by removing their most important cause: the workers' fear that struck factories would be run by strikebreakers. Neutralization, however, was bitterly opposed by all employers, and this position, probably coupled with the French public's traditional mistrust of government authority, prevented the measure from even being proposed under the Blum regime.[54] The mobile wage scale was proposed by Blum a few days after the CGT conference, as part of the devaluation law, but it was quickly rejected.[55] This left only conciliation and arbitration as possible means of holding down labor conflicts. Though the *Chambre* was willing to grant Blum rather broad powers to safeguard purchasing power, including an arbitration system, the Senate rejected these on the grounds that no special powers should be given until future events showed their necessity. Blum was finally able to obtain only the authority to establish compulsory arbitration for wage claims arising out of price increases.[56]

This was obviously insufficient, since many strikes had dismissals of union members as their cause. Summing up a good part of the basis for the strike record of September 1936, *La Voix du peuple*, monthly CGT organ, complained of "numerous cases of violation of social legislation and of failure to respect the free exercise of union rights. An offensive has been unleashed by certain employers' circles to take back all or part of the advantages granted the workers".[57] The CGT then went on to repeat its proposals for a conciliation and arbitration system for all industrial disputes. However, there was little hope that the employers could be brought into a voluntary agreement with labor on such a system: "These propositions have not encountered . . . a very sympathetic response in employers' circles . . . The CGPF has recently placed at its head new men whose presence at this post, if one can judge by what one knows of them, does not appear likely to facilitate things."

This proved to be an accurate forecast of what was to happen to Blum's efforts to obtain agreement from the employers on a voluntary system. Negotiations between CGT, CGPF and government representatives started in mid-September and dragged on for ten weeks until, in late November, the employers' delegation walked out for good and Blum was forced to apply to the Assembly for a comprehensive compulsory arbitration bill.[58]

During these months, strike activity, though generally less than a tenth what it had been in June, continued at a very high level. In the last third of 1936, more strikes (2,428) occurred than in any previous year of French history, while the number of strikers (295,000) exceeded that of any year since 1930.[59] Prices rose unceasingly, and with them, the cost of living. The actual increase in weekly wages resulting from the June strikes had been about 17 per cent.[60] But the September retail price indices revealed a six per cent increase in the cost of living over May, the November ones, a 13.5 per cent increase.[61] Speaking of the strikes in this period, Joel Colton states, "Had there been no other contributory causes, the rise in prices alone would have been sufficient cause for labor unrest".[62] It may well have occurred to the workers that what the Popular Front regime had given them in human dignity and a higher standard of living, union-busting employers and rising prices were taking away. In the case of Spain, they had seen that, though Blum's heart may have been in the right place, his foreign policy was anchored in the Thames, and that consequently he could do no more for their unfortunate Spanish brothers than English Toryism would allow him—which was nothing at all. The failure of their government to defend the gains of June was even more galling, since these were, after all, *their* rights and *their* wages that were being slowly eroded. The pressure was clearly on Blum to rectify the situation. Not only was he losing vital political support, but his whole social and economic policy, built as it was around the idea of inducing economic recovery through increased purchasing power, was in jeopardy. But all Blum could do for the workers was to push compulsory arbitration through the Senate and, as we shall see, this was far from enough.

IV

The creaky mechanism of the arbitration law that was passed on the last day of 1936 can best be understood in its actual functioning. As an example of this functioning, arbitration in the Paris metal industry reveals the experience of a large and significant group of workers.

The Paris metallurgical union had grown from a membership of about 10,000 before the strike to 200,000 afterward.[63] The old CGT militants were overwhelmed by swarms of impatient new recruits who, for the reasons outlined above, were almost all Communist sympathizers.[64] For years prior to the strike of May-June 1936, the metal workers' union had attempted to enter negotiations with the industry's employers' association. All those attempts had failed because of the employers' refusal to even discuss with the union. Relations between workers and management showed no improvement in the post-strike period. Throughout the latter months of 1936, their employers made numerous, though largely unsuccessful, attempts to secure a delay in the date for enacting the forty-hour week, attempts which were probably known and resented by the workers.[65] At the same time, the price rise in the Paris area was nullifying their gains of the summer. As a result of the price rise, the long tradition of anti-unionism on the employers' part and the recent September metal strikes, relations between management and workers were a mixture of resentment and mistrust.[66] In November 1936, the metal workers reacted vigorously to the destruction of their newly acquired purchasing power by demanding a 15 per cent wage increase.[67] When it was refused, the union threatened a strike, but, realizing that compulsory arbitration would soon be passed, refrained from any more than token stoppages.

In early January the metal union submitted its demands to arbitration. The man appointed by the government to reach a decision was Professor William Oualid, a scholar known for his labor sympathies. On February 7th, 1937, Professor Oualid handed down his decision. While granting the union's claim that there had been a 15 per cent increase in the cost of living between May and December 1936, he allowed a wage increase of only 8.5 per cent, less than three-fifths of the price rise. In doing so, he pointed out that granting full compensation for the higher prices would only encourage further price inflation, and so produce more harm for the national economy than good for the workers.

The union protested vehemently against this decision, particularly since there had been a further rise in the cost of living of five per cent between its original demand and the arbitration decision. As a result of its agitation, another arbitration award was granted the metal workers in March 1937, which brought the total increase over May in weekly wages to between 12.5 per cent for the highest and 15.2 per cent for the lowest paid category of workers. But by March the cost of living had risen 20.2 per cent over May, leaving the Paris unionists, after ten months of *Front Populaire* government, with barely two-thirds of the increased purchasing power they had won for themselves in June.

A sense of mistrust in their employers' good faith had already been instilled in the workers by the persistent attempts of the Union of Metal Industries to obtain a legal delay in the application of the forty-hour week. Now the government proved a disappointment— small wonder that the workers were no longer willing to support it with militant action. Far from being an especially bad case, the experience of the Paris metal union was probably better than average. Indeed, Joel Colton maintains that "it exploited the arbitration system to the maximum and extracted all possible benefits from it . . ."[68] Summarizing the operation of the 1936 Arbitration Act, Colton says,[69]

> . . . the arbitrators had tried to hold the line against a runaway wage-price spiral, granting only a partial wage adjustment to cost of living rises, rarely granting complete retroactivity and refusing unanimously to grant automatic sliding wage scales for the future. *Their decisions represented a denial, past, present, and future, of total wage compensation for the increased living costs . . . There is no doubt that the excessive caution of the arbitrators and a consuming concern for preventing inflation resulted in many instances of injustice to labor . . .*
> (My emphasis, A.M.)

Colton adds that, from the point of view of the national economy, it could be argued that none of the wage increases were justified, since they encouraged inflation; but this statement in no way vitiates the significance of his assertion that "many instances of injustice to labor" resulted. From the standpoint of the French worker, and from my own standpoint in trying to understand the change in the workers' attitude towards the Blum regime, the crucial fact is that arbitration under a Socialist premier did not grant anything like the full compensation for price increases that the workers expected.[70]

In the *Economist* for February 13th, 1937, a report from France described the public's reaction to rising prices in the following terms:

> "What is the increase in wages worth if it is absorbed at once by the rise in prices" is the slogan invariably heard in the streets, when a further increase in the price of bread, or wine, or butter occurs. The Popular Front is anxious, and the organs of the Left demand that the rise in prices should be checked at once. The leaders of the Trade Unions are urging their followers to be patient, to "digest" the labour reforms and to safeguard the victory of the Popular Front. But their patience will not last for long.

The events of the next four weeks were to stretch this patience to the limit and finally to snap it. On the one hand, the government's supporters were urging new reforms which would cost billions of francs: a national unemployment fund; old age pensions for workers; relief for the farmers (whose prices had been fixed before the general price rises); wage increases for civil servants. On the other hand, M. Caillaux had warned that the Senate finance committee would not certify any new expenditures unless accompanied by economies in other areas; the investing public was boycotting government bonds; and Blum seemed ready to try halting the price rises by lowering import duties, which would occasion an inevitable drain on the Exchange Equalization Fund, and so cause the government more financial embarrassment.[71]

In mid-February 1937, Blum appealed to the men of the Left for a breathing space.[72] But in their eyes, practically everything the government had done since the summer was a breathing space. Thus, union leaders partial to the CGT Plan, who had been quiet since the 1936 elections in order to give Blum's social and economic policies a chance to work, now became increasingly vocal,[73] in doing so, they probably reflected and certainly stimulated the growing disaffection of their troops from the government.

The more radical voice of labor in the weeks from mid-February to early March undid Blum's efforts to gain the confidence of banking and business interests. The consequent precariousness of his financial situation was driving Blum to a complete repudiation of his social and economic policy. But this policy, after Blum had renounced any possibility of aiding republican Spain, and internal fascism had proven to be a paper dragon, was the sole remaining bond between the government and the proletariat. When, on March 5th, Blum finally gave in completely to conservative demands for an orthodox economic policy (by dropping his government's public works program and giving control of the Exchange Stabilization Fund to financial conservatives), he created an irreparable breach between himself and the workers who, for all their suspicions, had hoped for so much from the Socialist premier. The *Economist* astutely noted this breach when it commented that the great result of the policy change was the shock created in the ranks of the Popular Front, and added that "if the Blum cabinet falls, a successor may come without riots in the street. In that sense", it concluded, "the danger of a revolution is past".[74]

Ten days later, in the Parisian workers' suburb of Clichy, street riots did occur. But far from being in defense of the Blum regime, they constituted a bloody proletarian outbreak against it.

V

On March 16th, 1937, in Clichy, a movie party held by the *Parti Social Français*, legal descendant of the *Croix de feu*, provoked an angry counter-demonstration by thousands of workers. According to the account given by Blum to the *Chambre*,[75] local Communist and Socialist leaders made strenuous efforts to have the permit for the meeting revoked by the government, but the government refused. When it became obvious that the mood of the people might bring an attack on the government police guarding the theater, the Socialist mayor, the Communist deputy, the secretary of the Socialist Federation of the Seine, and a Communist general councillor of Clichy all agreed, at a last minute meeting with representatives of the Ministry of the Interior, to lead the counter-demonstration they had jointly organized away from the theater. Some 4,000 workers followed them out of the trouble area, but thousands more remained in an extremely agitated state near the theater,[76] and some, it was alleged, availed themselves of the opportunity to take pot shots at Blums' police.

Whether provoked by gunfire or not, the police fired on the crowd, and when the smoke cleared, there were five wounded workers on the ground. As soon as the workers in the procession heard the shots, they raced back to the scene of the fighting and the serious bloodshed began. As police reinforcements rolled up by the truckload, the shooting became more frequent. Certainly many of the workers, anticipating a gun battle with the police, had come armed,[77] and those who had not found no scarcity of stones and pieces of scrap metal to hurl at the *Gardes mobiles*. When Blumel,

the Premier's *chef du cabinet*, arrived, he was promptly caught in a
volley of the *Gardes mobiles* and shot twice. Marx Dormoy, Blum's
Minister of the Interior, was a little more adept at keeping out of
the line of fire, but when he tried to address the rioting workers,
he was drowned out with cries of "Dormoy, démission!" and the
fighting went on.[78] Meanwhile, the police had evacuated the frightened moviegoers through a rear exit, but when the crowd learned
that the object of its initial demonstration was no longer in existence,
it only turned with more fury on the *Gardes mobiles*. Workers from
neighboring suburbs were only kept from joining the men from
Clichy by strategically placed police barricades.[79] By the time it was
all over, there were four dead and probably several hundred
wounded workers, and about one hundred and fifty police who had
to be treated at the hospitals.[80] Of some fifty critical cases in the
hospitals, most were workers, including one who soon died of his
wounds.[81]

The Clichy riots are the clearest indication we have of the more
militant workers' attitude after March 5th. In ever greater number they were turning away from the Blum regime, deserting the
Front Populaire leadership in the unions and the Left parties, and
following left-extremists.[82] The Clichy outburst was the first and
major occasion on which left-extremists successfully contested the
authority of the Popular Front over a large group of workers.

Certainly, no other explanation fits the facts of Clichy. Many people at the time believed the Communists were behind the rioting.[83]
But it would have been madness for the Communist leadership to
have deliberately provoked the gun battle, for their main goal in
French politics was still to seek right-wing allies for a possible
Union Sacrée against Hitler. If the Clichy affair had produced a
chain reaction through the rest of the Paris area (as it threatened
to do when workers from neighboring suburbs attempted to join
their comrades in Clichy), the Communists would have been forced
to make an irrevocable choice: either follow the left-extremists into
a revolutionary adventure which, besides being almost certain to
fail, would be in flagrant contradiction to Stalin's foreign policy; or
oppose the left-extremists in the name of untiy with the French
nation and thereby insure the disintegration of their entire working-
class apparatus. Blum, completely exonerating the "responsible"
Communist leadership, hinted in his speech to the *Chambre* that
right-wing *agents provocateurs* fired first.[84] While this may have
been so, it in no way tells us why, in the first place, thousands of
workers refused to follow their elected leaders, or why, when the

shooting began, the rioters persisted in fighting the police at the peril of their lives.

Obviously, beyond the stated purpose of the demonstration, and responsible for the actual explosion, was the pent-up fury of the more militant workers over the results of Blum's policy: non-intervention, price rises, the wage-sieve of arbitration, subservience to the banks, the *pause* of February, and the retreat of March 5th. The "fascist provocations", of which the Clichy movie party was a rather paltry specimen, totally out of proportion with the reaction it produced, were no more than "justifiable" opportunities for the workers to vent their spleen against the Blum regime. The premier, for all his betrayals, was a Socialist and a republican: to riot *en masse* against him would have placed them on the side of their most detested opponents, the rioters of February 6th, 1934, and the monied interests. But to show their hostility by demonstrating first against the fascist provocation at Clichy, then against Blum's police, who protected the fascists, and finally against the Blum regime itself, was within the rules of the workers' political psychology.

On the day following the riot, March 17th, the Paris area was rife with labor unrest. Agitators haranguing the construction workers at the Paris exposition held up work until 11 a.m.[85] The Metro and Autobus unions, apparently without consulting the Paris "Union of Unions", called a twenty-four-hour strike for the 18th.[86] Faced with the *fait accompli* of the transportation strike—which would in any case prevent most of the workers from getting to work in the morning—and with widespread agitation in the workers' suburbs, the "Union of Unions" and the giant metal workers' union, both under Communist control, issued an order for a general strike.[87] In the very limited scope of the strike, which was to be of only a half day's duration, in the stated aim of the strike, which was to protest only against the resurgence of fascism and not against the government, in the refusal to allow any demonstrations, and in the openly expressed hope that the strike would serve as a safety-value for the workers' discontent, the strike leaders revealed not only the extreme nervousness and distaste with which they regarded the agitation of the rank-and-file, but also the widening gap that now separated the latter from themselves.[88]

Certainly the strike appeal of the Paris "Union of Unions", printed in *Le Temps*, was far from an inflammatory document.[89] It called on the workers "to act with calm and composure, to avoid all provocations, and all street demonstrations, to take up work everywhere in the afternoon in order to demonstrate the power and discipline of our movement". When, on the afternoon of March 18th, CGT members in several places tried to expel non-strikers from their factories, many CGT delegates opposed the expulsions, sometimes without success.[90] On the morning of March 19th, a communiqué issued jointly by the Paris Union Group and the CGT reminded the workers that the strike had been "limited in objective to the problems raised by the tragic shootings at Clichy", admitted that "at certain meetings orders of the day were voted in favor of different demands", but insisted that "Yesterday's movement should not have as a consequence the continuation of the work stoppage for these demands".[91] It ended with a virtual order for work to be resumed "everywhere".

The picture I have drawn above—of angry workers ignoring their leaders, of the Communist union leadership forced by pressure from its middle rank leaders and its rank-and-file to act in ways it would prefer not to act, of strikes getting out of the hands even of local union delegates—is mirrored in many statements by centrist and even right-wing spokesmen of the period. Léon Meyer, a deputy of the Radical Socialist Party, said after Clichy: "Even if we should admit the Communist chiefs do not desire to disturb order for the moment, we would be forced to recognize that they no longer have authority over their troops." [92] In the *Revue des deux mondes*, René Pinon says that the CGT chiefs have been pushed aside and forced to obey the dictates of anarchist and Trotzkyist elements.[93] Pinon shrewdly links the explosion at Clichy to the "riffraff's" anger over the *pause*. *La République*, a right-wing Radical daily, refers to the "unknown quality of the four million newcomers . . . ignorant of union traditions and not yet disciplined".[94] It adds, "the Communists seem no more confident than the CGT'ers before the reaction of this popular mass".

VI

With the militant workers in such a mood of rebellion against their official leaders, it is no wonder that they could view the demise of the Blum Ministry with equanimity. But when Blum resigned, it was not only a cabinet that fell in France. It was the last hope of binding together a terribly divided nation.

Perhaps that hope was lost in June 1936, when a bold program of nationalizations and exchange control might well have tied the workers firmly to the regime without alienating the bulk of the middle class. But Blum had been caught unawares by the strikes of June and did not know how to use them.

Since the Blum regime failed to make the necessary basic economic reforms, it was impossible to prevent a continual, though losing, struggle on the part of the workers to preserve their gains of the summer. This struggle pushed the workers to the left, while Blum drifted to the right. The workers became progressively more hostile to the government and less receptive to patriotic appeals. While the government shift to the right continued under Chautemps and Daladier, left extremism increasingly gave way to apathy. As the workers, deprived of virtually all their gains by price rises and the revocation of the forty-hour week, saw the Popular Front disintegrating, the government turning against them, and the union movement splitting into hostile factions over the war issue, many of them tore up their union cards in disgust.[95]

The failure of the general strike of November 1938, undertaken at a time when union militants were no longer being followed by the rank-and-file, led to severe reprisals by employers and a mass exodus from the CGT.[96] By the end of 1938, 3,000 of the CGT's 18,000 local unions had disintegrated.[97] Nine months later, at the beginning of the war, CGT membership had fallen back from its peak of five million in 1936–37, to what it had been in January 1936—one million.[98] The great workers' movement that had been spawned by the Popular Front victory in 1936 was broken.

Notes

1. Speaking of employer attitudes in the years preceding the Blum regime, Henry Ehrmann, Organized Business in France (Princeton, 1957), p. 12 says: "Absorbed by a constant fight for a share in an always limited and now still-narrowing market, beset by credit difficulties, cynical about domestic policies, many employers knew nothing about the living conditions and the mentality of their own workers." In the same work, on p. 6, Ehrmann refers to the "shocked" and "ashamed" reaction of the employers' representatives at the Matignon Conference in June '36, when CGT leaders presented statistics showing the low wage rates in many industries. See also Henri Prouteau, Les Occupations des usines en Italie et en France (Paris, 1937), p. 104.

2. Cf. Simone Weil, La Condition Ouvrière (Paris, 1951), p. 168. The traditional treatment meted to strikers once calm was restored has been described in fictional form in the first part of La Grande Lutte (Paris, 1937), by Tristan Remy.

3. Cf. Salomon Schwarz, "Les Occupations d'usines en France de Mai et Juin, 1936", in: International Review for Social History, Vol. II (1937), p. 51.

4. Alexander Werth, Destiny of France (London, 1937), p. 304. A fictionalized account of the 1936 strike, Les Belles Journées by Maurice Lime (Paris, 1949), p. 128, also makes this point.

5. Bernard Lavergne, "L'Expérience Blum", in: L'Année politique française et étrangère, June 1937, p. 191.

6. Franz Borkenau, European Communism (New York, 1953), pp. 158, 198; André Delmas, A gauche de la barricade (Paris, 1950), pp. 116–130, passim.

7. Borkenau, p. 198; Delmas, idem.

8. Max Beloff, The Foreign Policy of Soviet Russia (London, 1946), Vol. I, 1929–1936, pp. 90–91. Also cf. Maurice Ceyrat, La trahison permanente parti communiste et politique russe (Paris, 1947), pp. 40–44, and Borkenau, op. cit., p. 167.

9. Both Borkenau and Ceyrat hold that the achievement of this friction was the major reason for the Communists' attempt to push France into the Spanish Civil War.

10. Cf. Alexander Werth, The Twilight of France (New York, 1942), pp. 77–78.

11. On June 10, 1936, Maurice Thorez somewhat threateningly declared in L'Humanité that it was necessary to know how to end a strike once the essential demands were satisfied. In the July 25, 1936, number of Cahiers du Communisme Jacques Duclos told the proletariat that the workers could make their demands triumph not only without recourse to sit-down strikes, but even without striking, since before stopping work, the workers could use other means of pressure on the employers.

12. The "French Front" line was gradually brought out in L'Humanité between July 24th and August 3rd, 1936.

13. In two huge meetings alone, reported in L'Humanité for August 10 and 31, 1936, 700,000 people were gathered. Social issues were deemphasized, national ones stressed, at these gatherings. Joan of Arc and the composer of the Marseillaise replaced Marx and Lenin as Communist saints; the supporters of Franco were compared to the aristocratic intriguers against the French Revolution; and Charles V was adduced to show the menace to France of a Spanish-German coalition.

14. On Sept. 3, 1936, Thorez, in a speech before 15,000 Renault workers, commended a proposed protest strike against the blockade (L'Humanité, Sept. 4, 1936). On Sept. 7, the metal workers of Paris struck for one hour to protest, among other things, Blum's Spanish policy. These were the first protest strikes on Spain to be sanctioned by the Communist leadership.

15. Michel Collinet, "Masses et militants: la bureaucratie et la crise actuelle du syndicalisme ouvrier français", in: Revue d'histoire économique et sociale, Vol. 29, 1951, pp. 65–73. Delmas, op. cit., p. 104, offers further reason for Communist control over the union in the ability

of the Communists to send their men into the new unions and, because of the workers' lack of sophistication, to get these militants appointed to key positions.

16. Collinet, op. cit., loc. cit.

17. This point is made very clearly in M. Lime, Les belles journées (Paris, 1949), pp. 128 ff. which is described by the labor historian Eduard Dolléans as "une image romancée, mais exacte de la réalité" (Histoire du mouvement ouvrier, Paris, 1953, Vol. III, p. 153). Lime shows how, when the local Communist leader fails to back a strike that has begun spontaneously, he is simply ignored until, contravening the orders of his superiors, he agrees to join the strike committee.

18. Delmas, op. cit., p. 93, says that during the June strikes, "in the conversation of one militant to another", the Communists admitted "that the workers' demands mocked all their slogans, and declared that the wisest thing was to let themselves be carried by the popular current in order to give the impression that they were leading it".

19. See note 4.

20. In Le Populaire for August 9, 1936, see Emile Farinet's column, "The Spanish War is a Class War". On August 14, Marceau Pivert condemned the French Front in the Socialist paper, and also stressed the class struggle in the Spanish War. In the August 31st Populaire, Louis L'Hévéder sarcastically rebuffed Thorez' repeated pleas for a government "from Reynaud to Marcel Cachin". As for the proletariat, Delmas says that "in the workers' meeting the speeches in favor of the French Front only encountered skeptical smiles and jeers". Op. cit., p. 124.

21. In an article apparently written in mid-September, Thorez said, "Let us emphasize the fact that strikes are beginning in a district like the Nord, where the Socialists have remained stronger than we". This very interesting article, which strongly suggests the mental anguish of the Communist bureaucracy at being torn away from its "moderate" pose by the resurgence of class conflict, appeared as "The People's Front and Tasks Facing the Communist Party of France", in Communist International, 1936, pp. 145–71.

22. On September 12, 1936, in the name of working-class unity, the Communists renounced the French Front slogan in L'Humanité.

23. Journal Officiel, December 5, 1936, pp. 3377–3378.

24. The congress was given extensive coverage in Le Peuple for February 7, 1937, and La Révolution Prolétarienne, February 10, 1937. In my narrative, I have combined these accounts.

25. According to the Bulletin of the International Federation of Trade Unions for February 17, 1937, the phrases in question were, "the vanguard of Fascism has been revealed and destroyed in Moscow", and "the workers and peasants of Russia, who form one bloc with their government, have recently given themselves the most democratic constitution in the world, which allows of the Trade Unions fulfilling their most useful task".

26. Le Peuple, February 7, 1937, and La Révolution Prolétarienne,

February 10, 1937, article by Simone Weil. The CGT official was André Delmas in his A gauche de la barricade, p. 127. The ostensible reason given by the CP, according to Le Peuple and Weil, was the preservation of unanimity. But surely the Communist leadership must have been aware of the presence of non- and anti-Communist syndicalists among the 800 delegates, who were not going to vote for the report as presented. At any rate, the fact that the Communists only withdrew the passages after a fairly influential bloc of old syndicalists came out against them, shows rather clearly that more than a fear for mere unanimity impelled the leadership.

27. Cf. Franz Borkenau, The Spanish Cockpit (London, 1937), pp. 64 ff.

28. Delmas, op. cit., p. 105.

29. Idem.

30. Le Populaire, July 30, 1936.

31. Le Populaire, July 29, 1936.

32. Eduard Dolléans, op. cit., p. 162.

33. There is much opinion that asserts, to the contrary, that non-intervention was proposed entirely on the initiative of France. However, the account of Pertinax in the Gravediggers of France, p. 433, quoted approvingly in Claude Bowers' My Mission to Spain (New York, 1954), p. 281, is very explicit and, unless fabricated out of whole cloth, leaves no room for doubt that, though the announcement came from France, England was primarily responsible. Werth, Destiny of France, p. 379 also supports this account.

34. Le Populaire, August 22, 1936.

35. The French refusal to allow Spanish munitions to cross back into Spain is recounted in Claude Bowers, op.cit., pp. 280–283.

36. According to Sturmthal, Blum's contact with the working class was "far more intimate than Ramsay MacDonald or any German Social Democratic minister had ever thought necessary". And Delmas supports this in relating how, at the Matignon Conference, Blum urged Communist union officials: "Don't call me Mr. President; I have done nothing to merit this. Call me Blum, as always". Adolf Sturmthal, Tragedy of European Labour (London, 1944), p. 234; André Delmas, op. cit., p. 94.

37. Sturmthal, idem.

38. Quoted in ibid., p. 234. With the exception noted below, all the other details of the Luna-Park speech are from this source.

39. Delmas, op. cit., p. 117.

40. Cf. Alexander Werth, Destiny of France, pp. 72–92, 250; and Franz Borkenau, European Communism, p. 116.

41. Henry W. Ehrmann, French Labor from Popular Front to Liberation (New York, 1948), p. 41.

42. Le Populaire, July 21, 1936.

43. Cf. Joel Colton, Compulsory Arbitration in France, 1936–1939, p. 28; Michel Collinet, L'Esprit du Syndicalisme, p. 127; and John C. De

Wilde, "The New Deal in France", in: Foreign Policy Reports, Sept. 1, 1937, esp. p. 140.

44. Le Temps, August 19, 1937.

45. Eduard Dolléans, Histoire du Mouvement Ouvrier, Vol. III, p. 144.

46. Delmas, op. cit., p. 47.

47. At the time C. J. Gignoux, the new head of the employer group, though he stated his belief that the 40-hour week was a "serious error", denied that he desired the revocation of the social reforms granted in June 1936. Cf. his Patrons, soyez patrons (Paris, 1937), pp. 7, 33. But in a work written under the German occupation, Gignoux showed a bitter hostility to certain of the reforms, especially to the 40-hour week, which he now less temperately described as an "insanity". Cf. C. J. Gignoux, L'Economie française entre les deux guerres, 1919–1939 (Paris, 1942), pp. 307 ff. Ehrmann says that "the CGPF flatly turned down requests by the government to facilitate the working of the new legislation through a new and more elaborate understanding with labor". H. W. Ehrmann, Organized Business in France (Princeton, 1957), p. 37.

48. Henry W. Ehrmann, in Organized Business in France, discusses the relation of the textile employers to the new CGPF on p. 15. An article in the left Radical La Lumière for Sept. 19, 1936, titled "Le Conflit du textile du Nord: Premier vague d'une grande offensive des féodaux de l'industrie", referred to "the desire for combat of the great conservative families: Michelin and Clermont-Ferrand; the cotton manufacturers of the Vosges; the textile masters of Lille . . . They want to break the union power and dissolve the Popular Front."

49.   TIME SERIES ON WAGES AND PRICES

Average male hourly wage for 43 "professions" (all cities outside Paris): October, 1935—3.80 frs.; October, 1936—4.42 frs. (percentage increase: 16.3%).

Average female hourly wage for 7 "professions" (all cities outside Paris): October, 1935—2.26 frs.; October, 1936—2.62 frs. (percentage increase: 15.9%).

Retail Price Index for 34 Articles,
April-Nov. 1936 (July 1914 = 100):

	Towns of more than 10,000 inhabitants	Paris
April		451
May	429	459
June		461
July		461
August	453	477
Sept		494
Oct.		515
Nov.	508	534

Cost of living Indexes for Paris and France
(Indexes reflect the expenses for supplying a worker's family of four):

France (1930 = 100)		Paris – 1936 (1914 = 100)	
Nov. 1935	77.8	1st Quarter	486
May 1936	80.3	2nd Quarter	497
Nov. 1936	91.1	3rd Quarter	504
		4th Quarter	540

(Figures reflect quarterly averages)

Source: Statistique général de la France (quarterly bulletin).

50. On Sept. 23, 1936, Le Temps reported that 100 textile employers meeting in Tourcoing refused to negotiate with the unions under the menace of force: presumably meaning sit-down strikes. On the same day, the Cotton Syndicate of the East reportedly refused to discuss with the union as long as union pickets forbade entry into the textile plants, which had already been evacuated. On the 28th of October, 1936, Le Temps reported that coal dealers in Roubaix-Tourcoing would not talk with strikers until they evacuated the yards and withdrew their pickets.

51. Le Temps, August 24, 1936. All dates given in this and the next four paragraphs are the date on which the strike report appeared in Le Temps.

52. Le Temps, Sept. 26, 1936. For an extended argument on the same theme, see "Une manœuvre contre la CGT" by Robert Bothereau, in the October 30, 1936, Vendredi.

53. The reasons for the CGT's reversal of policy are detailed in Colton, op. cit., pp. 36–38.

54. Neutralization was later proposed to the Chambre by Chautemps in January 1938, but it was not passed. Colton, op. cit., p. 61.

55. See pp. 381–382.

56. Idem.

57. La Voix du Peuple, October 1936.

58. See pp. 381–383.

59. See tables in Colton, op. cit., pp. 13–14.

60. M. Kalecki, "The Lesson of the Blum Experiment", in: Economic Journal, March 1938, p. 26. Kalecki believes the official figures of 13% for Paris and 16% for the rest of France were too low, since they failed "to account sufficiently for the big augmentation of wages in many enterprises where trade union rates were not observed during the depression".

61. See table in Colton, op. cit., p. 31.

62. Ibid., p. 33. Also cf. Michel Collinet, op. cit., p. 126.

63. Collinet, op. cit., p. 123. Colton, op. cit., p. 81 gives the membership as 350,000 in 1937.

64. Collinet says that 90% of the 200,000 voted the Communist theses. Ibid., p. 123.

65. These attempts were discussed in the Rapport annuel de L'union

des industries metallurgiques et minières, presented at the General Assembly on February 18, 1937. A 3,000-word excerpt was printed in La Voix du Peuple, March 1937, pp. 176–179.

66. On June 10, 1936, Simone Weil had described the working conditions in a metallurgy factory, where she was then taking part in a strike, under the headings of hunger, poverty, fatigue, fear, and coercion. "La Vie et la grève des ouvrières métalles", reprinted in La Condition Ouvrière (Paris, 1951), pp. 162–174. Originally appeared in La Révolution Prolétarienne, June 10, 1936, under the name S. Gaulois.

67. I am indebted to Joel Colton, op. cit., pp. 81–86, for all my information on arbitration in the metal industry.

68. Ibid., p. 81. For other wage adjustments under arbitration in 1937, see ibid., p. 84. The effects of inflation on the income of less aggressive workers is seen in Collinet's statement that between 1936 (one presumes the beginning of the year) and 1938, the real wages of civil servants decline by 18%. Collinet, op. cit., p. 126.

69. Ibid., p. 86.

70. The Economist of February 20, 1937, commenting on Blum's appeal to the civil servants "for a breathing space, for a respite in expenditure", argues that "a breathing space for wages would be an absurdity if not accompanied by a pause in the rise of prices".

71. A summary of the CGT's criticism of arbitration as it functioned from its inception to its replacement by a more precise law in May 1938, is given in the Compte rendu sténographique des débats of the CGT Congrès confédéral de Nantes—1938, pp. 62–63. Immediately following is an analysis of the first two hundred arbitration decisions, as reported in the Journal officiel for September 3, 1937, and February 3, 1938.

72. The Economist, February 20, 1937.

73. At the same time that Blum was soliciting support for the "pause", Jouhaux was urging nationalization of banks and industry. Cf. The Economist, February 27, 1937.

74. The Economist, March 13, 1937.

75. Le Temps, March 25, 1937. Except where indicated, other information in this and the following paragraph is from the same source.

76. The figures are from the account in the Socialist Prolétaire de Clichy, reprinted in La Révolution Prolétarienne, April 10, 1937.

77. The London Times, on March 19, 1937, summed the reason up for this by pointing out that: "In France, every policeman openly carries a loaded automatic pistol, and the gardes Mobiles are equipped with steel helmets, pistols and carbines. When the police, with no weapons but firearms, are hard pressed by the crowd, it is likely that the firearms will go off sooner or later, and when demonstrators know that the police will be armed, they are apt to arm themselves also."

78. Le Temps, March 18, 1937.

79. Idem.

80. The hospitals only received about 80 workers, but in the press, it was generally thought that untold numbers of workers had not reported to the hospitals for fear of punishment. At any rate, the number of wounded police is a good indication that the number of wounded workers was several times eighty.

81. London Times, March 18, 1937.

82. For Alexander Werth's description of left-extremism and an excerpt from the speech of a revolutionary syndicalist at the 1938 Congress of the CGT, see Appendix.

83. André Delmas, op. cit., p. 127; Pierre Lazareff, in a chapter on Clichy in Deadline, and Franz Borkenau, European Communism, p. 208.

84. Le Temps, March 25, 1937.

85. London Times, March 18, 1937.

86. La Révolution Prolétarienne, April 10, 1937.

87. Idem. André Delmas, relating the very confused situation on March 18, implies that the Communists wanted to use the strike as a means of stirring trouble for the Blum regime. But the actual facts he gives correspond to the account in La Révolution Prolétarienne, whose conclusion that the Communist-led Union of Unions and Metal Workers Union were forced by rank-and-file agitation and by pressure from the Metro Union to call the strike makes more sense than Delmas' notion of a plot.

88. Michel Collinet astutely argues that the arbitration system was responsible for this gap, first by removing the union leadership from its role as organizer of a real class struggle and transforming it into a simple intermediary between the workers' demands and the government arbitrator; secondly, by putting the leadership in the position of accomplice to the erosion of real wages under arbitration. Esprit du syndicalisme, pp. 126–127.

89. Le Temps, March 19, 1937.

90. Ibid., March 21, 1937, and London Times, March 23, 1937. The incidents continued for several days after the strike.

91. Le Temps, March 20, 1937.

92. Ibid., March 18, 1937.

93. Revue des deux mondes, April 1, 1937, p. 714.

94. Le Temps, March 20, 1937.

95. Probably the best account of this process is in Ehrmann, op. cit., pp. 77–125. Also, see Collinet, Esprit du syndicalisme, pp. 126–127.

96. Ehrmann, op. cit., pp. 115–120.

97. Collinet, op. cit., p. 127.

98. Collinet, op. cit., p. 125. Ehrmann, using an estimate supplied by union officials in the summer of 1939, says there were probably still two million CGT members at the outbreak of war. But Collinet was an active trade unionist at the time, and the discrepancy between his and the semi-official figures can probably be attributed to the desire of the officials only to reveal losses which absolutely could not be hidden or denied.

6. THE "ACTION FRANÇAISE" IN FRENCH INTELLECTUAL LIFE

by Stephen Wilson

*In retrospect it is difficult to understand why a movement so ec-
centrically placed in the political sphere, so narrowly focused, so
ungenerous in its instincts, and in so many ways in conflict with the
Republic should have survived so long and shone with such a terrible
brilliance. But there can be no doubt that the* Action française *that
emerged from the political and social disarray of the Dreyfus affair
was among the most enduring and powerful legacies of the nineteenth to the twentieth century. Politically it represented the for-
lorn cause of the counterrevolution long after no more than a comparative handful of the monarchy's* amants inconsolables *existed to
exhale their grief and their hostility to the republican regime. As
late as the 1930s, still led by Charles Maurras, still under ban by
Rome for its flagrant atheism in practice (despite its celebration of
throne and altar in theory), the* Action française *had the power to
agitate, provoke uproar, sow distrust of the established order. And
momentarily, after the defeat of 1940, it appeared to believe its
hour had come round at last. The* Action française *expired in the
disintegration of the Vichy regime, but its influence lived on in
several generations of Frenchmen powerfully under its literary and
nationalist spell, however differently it had worked itself out in them
and however divergent the paths they, as individuals, took through
the century.*

*The author of this article is concerned with the rich literary as-
pect of Maurras's movement. Stephen Wilson, Lecturer in European
History, University of East Anglia, has published numerous scholarly articles on aspects of the Action Française, on anti-Semitism,*

and on religion. This paper was first published in the Historical
Journal *12 (1969): 328–350. It is reprinted here by kind permission of the author and the publisher.*

The *Action Française* was neither a widespread nor a powerful nor
a successful political movement, and its political objectives were
anachronistic to the point of absurdity. Its intention to carry out a
coup d'état could not be taken seriously when its leaders were so
eager to find reasons for avoiding or postponing action.[1] Critics of
the movement rightly claimed, for this reason, that it did not deserve its name.[2] Of course, the Action Française always claimed to
have considerable political influence, but its very poor showing in
the elections of 1919 and 1924,[3] when what influence it had was
probably at its height, only emphasized the movement's real complexion. In spite of its slogan of 'Politique d'abord', the movement's leaders were from the start fully aware that its strength
did not lie in the purely political sphere. Charles Maurras wrote in
October 1910: 'Nous avons cessé d'être un "parti" subsistant de ses
forces anciennes et ralliant des cadres une fois comptés: nous
sommes devenus une idee conquerante.'[4] And it is as 'une idée conquérante' that the Action Française's main significance in modern
French history lies; its became a centre of intellectual attraction, a
school to which writers belonged or through which they passed, and
as such it exerted an influence for a period of over fifty years that
can be compared only with that of the Catholic Church, the Communist Party and perhaps *La Nouvelle Revue Française*. The purpose
of this article is to give some indication of the nature and extent of
this influence.

I

The ostensible aim of the Action Française was to prepare for the
restoration of the monarchy in France 'par tous les moyens', but in
practice the means were predominantly propaganda aimed mainly
at an intellectual élite. Maurras explained: 'La réforme de la nation
française commencera par la réforme du gouvernement de la France;
mais pour que cette réforme soit, il convient qu'une élite, aussi
petite que fera l'hasard, mais dont l'influence peut être sans borne,
s'exerce à penser et à sentir en commun afin de réagir de même.'[5]
This small body would carry out a 'coup d'état intellectuel et moral';

it would maintain 'l'opération de police intellectuelle'; and it would constitute a 'Contre-Encyclopédie' to defeat and replace the reigning ideas of democracy.[6] These, Louis Dimier wrote 'avaient semé la ruine, en littérature, en histoire, en pédagogie, comme en politiqué', and therefore 'sur tous ces points, quoique étrangers en apparence au retour du prince exilé, il y avait donc des idées d'Action Française'.[7] As another leader of the movement, Henri Vaugeois, put it: 'Nous sommes en pédantocratie. Il faut parler en maîtres d'Ecole.'[8] But the claim that this emphasis on propaganda and education was merely a means to an end, or something forced on the royalist movement by the circumstances of its struggle against democracy was never very convincing; as the coup d'état became indefinitely postponed, it became difficult to see the propaganda as anything but an end in itself. As a liberal Catholic critic said: '. . . la restauration monarchique paraît même intéresser infiniment moins ses chefs que l'établissement d'une dictature intellectuelle dont ils seraient les bénéficiaires';[9] and several members of the movement became convinced that Maurras was concerned 'non . . . de créer un fait, mais . . . de faire une démonstration logique'.[10]

But the relationship of propaganda and action, for the Action Française, was not one of simple antithesis. Maurras's reply to his critics, that propaganda was action,[11] was not pure sophistry. His logical or, more properly, his historiographical demonstration of the necessity of monarchism, the whole 'Contre-Encyclopédie' constructed and developed by the Action Française, was not merely or necessarily an alternative to political action, but performed rather a function similar to Georges Sorel's myth of the General Strike.[12] The intransigent monarchism and Catholicism of the Action Française must be seen in this light; they were attractive because they were extreme, because they were absolutes, and hence they flourished on the disavowal of the Pretender and the condemnation of the Pope. The Action Française took a delight in being extremist and paradoxical; Maurras referred to 'la volupté de faire quelque chose de difficile, mais de grand . . .'.[13] But at the same time Action Française thinking and behaviour operated on a more rational level. Maurras had been very cautious in introducing monarchism into the movement,[14] for example, and during the Great War he put his royalism into cold storage and rallied temporarily to the republican régime. Similarly, although Maurras based his defence of Catholicism on political and cultural grounds, and refused to submit to the Pope, he and several other Action Française leaders eventually became converted in the purely religious sense.[15] This dichotomy is also evident in the writing and propaganda of the movement. There was an aim at intellectual dominance, a repetition 'tous les jours, sans se lasser . . . (of) les mêmes mots à effet, les mêmes images obsédantes, les mêmes romans hallucinants . . .',[16] but at the same time, and this has often been ignored, Maurras did attempt to counter the irrationalist tendency of much right-wing thinking, and placed his doctrines under the aegis of Reason.[17]

The possible appeal of the Action Française was therefore complex, and operated on different levels, and this found reflexion in the organization and orientation of the movement. The Action Française was founded, at the time of the Dreyfus affair, largely because the Ligue de la Patrie Française had been felt to be too diverse in membership and too vague in intention,[18] and it always remained a close-knit dogmatic group with a strict membership: 'Entrer en Action Française, c'était prononcer des vœux, accepter une discipline . . .' wrote Albert Thibaudet in 1931.[19] Yet Maurras claimed quite sincerely that the movement was 'une image de la France, des raisons et des passions de la France, de ses points d'unité et de ses innumérables diversités';[20] and he referred to '. . . le statut de l'Action Française . . . suivant lequel vivent et s'accordent des légitimistes de race, des petits-neveux de conventionnels régicides, des incroyants, des catholiques'.[21] More significantly he dedicated his *Enquête sur la Monarchie* 'à tous les Français mécontents. . .', and always denied that the movement was right wing or reactionary in the accepted sense.[22] There was a time, too, when, under the influence of Georges Valois, the Action Française had directed its appeal towards the working classes, though, as Xavier Vallat commented later, the very intellectual quality of the movement prevented its influence from penetrating 'les couches populaires'.[23]

In assessing the intellectual influence of the Action Française this wider appeal is evidently most important, for it went beyond or even against certain tenets of the movement, and it was even expressed in organizational terms. Maurras claimed that France was ruled by the anti-national 'quatres états confédérés', the Jews, the Protestants, the Freemasons and the 'métèques' or foreigners, and these four groups were the special objects of Action Française attack and abuse. Nevertheless Maurras and others pointed out with some pride that a Protestant, Frédéric Delebecque, was on the *comité directeur* of the movement, and that many 'Juifs bien nés' supported it.[24] The deputy Xavier Magallon even claimed to be a 'républicain d'Action Française',[25] an apparent contradiction in terms. Those who could not accept the whole doctrine of the Action Française were accommodated in the specially organized Alliance d'Action Française. Xavier Vallat, a great admirer of the Action Française, was able to tell Maurras after the Second World War that

> l'efficacité de son œuvre ne consiste pas uniquement, loin de là, à avoir fondé la Ligue d'Action Française et ses filiales, mais à avoir ensemencé des centaines de milliers d'esprits qui, pour n'avoir pas côtisé ou avoir cessé de côtiser à ces organismes, n'en pas ont moins gardé une reconnaissance et une admiration infinies au chef d'école qui leur a révélé la vérité politique . . .[26]

As Vallat suggests, the influence of the Action Française was increased by the fact that it was, in Raoul Girardet's words, 'un lieu de passage'; [27] Beau de Loménie, at one time a member of the movement, wrote that 'l'histoire de l'Action Française . . . a été l'histoire d'une série de dissidences successives. . .'.[28] Those who repudiated or broke with the movement retained its mark, and as Thierry Maulnier, also at one time an admirer of Maurras, has pointed out: 'l'étendue d'une influence . . . ne se mesure pas seulement aux adhésions, mais (aussi) aux oppositions suscitées'.[29]

Two further questions arise in connexion with the wide zone of influence of the Action Française. How far was this diffusion part of the evolution of the movement? And what was left of Action Française doctrine when it had been shorn of its royalism, its Catholicism and its antisemitism, for these were probably the most exclusive aspects of its doctrine? While Maurras's ideas were inflexible, the complexion of the Action Française did change over the years. Maurras retained his bohemian habits and the newspaper continued to be run in the old inefficient way, but the anti-bourgeois, anti-conservative student intransigence of the early days did tend to give way, as the movement became established, to a kind of 'Orléanisme', symbolized by the entry of many of the leading figures of the movement into the Academy. This move towards respectability was certainly aided by the circumstances of the Great War, when the Action Française's brand of extreme nationalism became widely acceptable, and after the War the movement felt in a position to implement its policy of 'par tous les moyens' by presenting candidates in the parliamentary elections. It is hard to say precisely how this change affected the influence of the movement. It is obvious that the prestige and the sales of its writers were increased, for example, when they could put 'de l'Académie Française' on the covers of their books but, on the other hand, those who wanted action and no compromise with the established régime tended in the thirties to gravitate away from

the Action Française towards the new Fascist-type organizations, as
did Drieu La Rochelle. And of course the desire to shock never left
the Action Française.

What did the Action Française mean for those on the edges of the
movement? Besides royalists of traditional or modern type, political
Catholics and nationalists, it attracted those who wanted to have firm
convictions or to belong to a group, those who feared 'Bolshevism',
those whom the government and administration of the Third Republic repelled or neglected and, most significantly for our purpose,
those for whom Maurras was the defender of civilization against bar-
barism, and order against anarchy. This last factor should be taken
seriously, for if it is ignored, the attraction of the Action Française,
however temporary, for such men as Gide and Malraux, Bernanos
and Maritain, Léautaud and Proust, Joseph Lotte and Georges Sorel,
T. S. Eliot and Daniel Halévy, becomes difficult to explain. The
movement's willingness to advocate violence, its antisemitism, its
xenophobia undoubtedly won it converts, but so did its appeal to
simple nostalgia, to the desire for an ideal and to a concern for
traditional values. Gérard de Catalogne must have expressed a fairly
widespread opinion, when he wrote in 1941:

> Les idées que nous défendions, ce patrimoine occidental . . . non seule-
> ment sans l'Action Française, nous serions bien loin d'en soupçonner
> la valeur mais sans elle, nous n'aurions pas sans doute le sentiment
> qu'il y ait là aucun problème essentiel et sur lequel il importe avant
> tout autre soin de prendre nettement position.[30]

and he was writing not in Occupied or Vichy France, but in Canada.

One further observation on the nature of the Action Française's
intellectual influence is necessary. While the movement attracted
literary critics and novelists, and even those who practised the non-
literary arts, most of the intellectuals to whom it appealed were in
some way historians. This was not surprising, for as Jean Longnon
wrote in 1924:

> Un disciple de Barrès et de Maurras attache forcément une importance
> capitale à l'histoire: la doctrine de la Terre et des Morts, comme celle
> de l'Empirisme organisateur, trouvent en elle leur fondement; elles
> prétendent enrichir le présent de tout le passé, rechercher dans celui-ci
> une doctrine éparse, un milieu favorable.[31]

Much, perhaps most, Action Française writing was devoted to an attempt to show from a study of history that 'la Monarchie est le
gouvernement qui convient à la France'.[32] But the movement's emphasis on history was not merely an aspect of its royalism; it was

something larger, more serious and more compelling. Maurras had arrived at his political beliefs from an acute sense of the fragility of civilization and of human effort, and hence of the need for constant vigilance to preserve the fruits of both:

> Il faut une cité debout, des murs intacts, des frontières sûres, un ordre intérieur à peu prés résistant pour maintenir la vie commune de l'esprit ailleurs que dans la grotte des ermites . . . Pas de vie intellectuelle, pas de cercle pensant si l'on ne maintient une société générale qui seule garde ses trésors, ordonne et polit ses acquets . . . il ne suffit pas d'élever un Parthénon sur une Acropole, il faut encore le garder et le fortifier contre des forces naturelles et historiques essentiellement ennemies . . .[33]

The writers whom Maurras inspired and influenced were both attracted and marked by this passionate and sophisticated traditionalism, and this conception of history as the creation and preservation of civilization or, more accurately, of the Greco-Roman tradition, was an important element in the *rayonnement* of the Action Française.

II

For the dissemination of its ideas, in however dilute a form, the Action Française had access to a wide variety of media. For our purposes the official organs and organizations of the movement are less important, although their appeal was by no means confined to strict members. Action Française doctrine was taught at the Institut d'Action Française, founded in 1906, by means of regular lectures, some of which were published in the *Revue des Cours et Conférences d'Action Française;* but the main instrument of Action Française propaganda was the daily newspaper, founded in 1908, whose mixture of invective, scurrility, seriousness and good writing won it readers far beyond the royalist movement; its circulation reached a maximum of perhaps 90,000 in 1926.[34] The Action Française also published a monthly and an annual almanac, but none of these official publications was one to which sympathetic but uncommitted writers would contribute, and their audience was necessarily limited.

For these reasons Maurras wanted to have the platform of a review with a wider appeal and a less narrow doctrinal complexion. He thought that he had found this in the *Revue Critique des Idées et des Livres,* founded in 1908 'pour recueillir des études politiques et sociales que fournissent des écrivains nationalistes et des théoriciens de l'Action Française'.[35] But as it became more influential the

Revue became also more purely literary and in February 1914 it dropped the *devise* from its back cover declaring its adherence to the principles of *empirisme organisateur* (Maurras's political ideology), and declared that it was absolutely autonomous. The break, over the *Revue*'s tolerant attitude towards Bergsonism, was not absolute, however; the editors continued to pay their respects to Maurras and his ideas, and the marquis de Roux, one of the leading figures of the Action Française, continued to contribute his 'Notes politiques' to the *Revue* until it closed down in 1924. The *Revue Critique* is a good example of a periodical that wanted to give some support to the ideas of the Action Française, without being under the control of the dictatorial Maurras; it was run by three young disciples of Maurras, Eugène Marsan, Jean Longnon and Jean Rivain; the last played a large part in the foundation of the Nouvelle Librairie Nationale, which remained the main publisher of Action Française books until 1925. Contributors included Paul Bourget, who was a close friend of Maurras and who shared his political views; René Groos, one of the rare Jewish supporters of the Action Française; Roger Lambelin, at one time director of the political bureau of the Pretender and a notable antisemite; René Johannet, a member of the *Cahiers de la Quinzaine* circle and closely connected with the Action Française during and just after the Great War; and Gonzague Truc, a Thomist sympathetic to the Action Française.[36] Almost at the same time that the *Revue Critique* closed down, René Groos started the *Revue du Siècle*, in March 1925. Several writers from the *Revue Critique*, like Marsan and Johannet, found a refuge there, and Maurras himself wrote for the *Revue du Siècle* in its first year. Jean Héritier, one of the most scholarly of the Action Française historians, was its history critic, and later one of its directors.[37] The *Revue du Siècle* ran a publishing house which published Bainville, Héritier, Dutrait-Crozon and other Action Française writers. Although the review proclaimed its independence,[38] it was openly sympathetic to the ideas of Maurras and his school and gave them a platform. Until the mid-twenties and, in a more general way, until 1939, the *Revue Hebdomadaire* was also favourable to the Action Française and published articles by Pierre Lasserre, André Bellessort, Frantz Funck-Brentano and Bainville, all of whom were more or less definitely Action Française writers.

But none of these reviews provided the wide and lasting audience for such writers that the *Revue Universelle* did from its foundation in 1920 until 1940. Although its programme was wide: 'Refaire l'esprit public en France par les voies de l'intelligence; tenter une fédération intellectuelle du monde par la pensée française',[39] its direction by Henri Massis and Bainville ensured its fidelity to the Action Française, and Maurras was able to refer to it as 'notre *Revue Universelle*'.[40] At the start, Johannet was in charge of the Foreign Affairs section, Lasserre of Literature, Jacques Maritain of Philosophy and René de Marans of History, all men who were Maurrassians at the time. Maurras himself was a regular contributor, as was Léon Daudet, and Pierre Gaxotte, another prominent Action Française figure, was the *Revue*'s history critic in the early twenties. A list of contributors would include all those who can in any way be seen as Action Française writers; for example Beau de Loménie, André Bellessort, Charles Benoist, Bernanos, Louis Bertrand, Brasillach, Augustin Cochin, Gustave Fagniez, Bernard Fay, Daniel Halévy, Robert Havard de La Montagne, Héritier, Lambelin, Pierre de Luz, Firmin Roz, the comte de Saint-Aulaire and Georges Valois.[41] But the *Revue Universelle,* which became an important and established review, was by no means an exclusive Action Française domain, but rather an outstanding example of how the Action Française acted as a point of reference and as a guide to a far wider complex of ideas and attitudes.

The movement had a similar relationship with other more specialized reviews. The Cercle Fustel de Coulanges, aimed at preserving the traditional forms and content of French education, was directly inspired by Maurrassianism; Action Française leaders attended its banquets, and some of them contributed to its *Cahiers*. The *Revue des Etudes Historiques* gave the works of Action Française historians full and favourable reviews, and Funck-Brentano belonged to its editorial committee. The *Revue des Questions Historiques* was more closely connected with the movement; founded in 1866 by the marquis de Beaucourt, it maintained its aristocratic patronage but not its legitimist complexion. In 1913 its directors were Jean Guiraud [42] and Paul Allard, but Allard was soon replaced by Roger Lambelin; after his death in 1929 the editorial board was reorganized, and Gaxotte became a member of it. The *Revue* published articles by Fagniez, Funck-Brentano, Bellessort, Henri Massis, the marquis de Roux, Gérin-Ricard and other exponents of Action Française historiography. Another review over which the Action Française had some control was the monastic *Revue Mabillon,* directed until 1920 by Dom J.-M. Besse, a firm disciple of Maurras.[43]

But Action Française influence was never limited to reviews over which it had some control. Many of its writers contributed to provincial periodicals,[44] and the more famous ones to the big Paris reviews. The *Revue de Paris*, co-directed for a time by Lavisse who was one of the targets of Action Française historical criticism, published articles by Bellessort, Funck-Brentano, Daniel Halévy, Gaxotte, Lasserre, Johannet and Maurras himself. The *Revue de France* opened its columns to Lasserre, Jean Longnon, Funck-Brentano and the duc de Lévis-Mirepoix.[45] Even the *Nouvelle Revue Française* was not closed to Action Française influence; Julien Benda gave the movement great publicity by his continual attacks, but Albert Thibaudet maintained an attitude of sympathy; Daniel Halévy wrote for the review and the *N.R.F.* published books by Bellessort and Léon Daudet.[46] But the most important review that was open to Action Française writers was the *Revue des Deux Mondes*. Lasserre, Massis, Halévy, Funck-Brentano, Benoist, Saint-Aulaire and Roz contributed occasional articles; Louis Bertrand and André Bellessort were early associated with the review and became two of its main contributors, Bellessort also becoming its editorial secretary in the twenties.

Those connected with the Action Française were prolific writers, and published many books as well as journalism. As already mentioned, the movement's main publisher until 1925 was the Nouvelle Librairie Nationale; after that date the main doctrinal works of the Action Française were published by the Bibliothèque des Oeuvres Politiques, and the movement also controlled Les Editions du Capitole. Les Editions du Siècle have been mentioned. Maurras was not faithful to any one publisher, and his works appeared under the imprint of Calmann-Lévy, the official publishers of the Pretender, Boccard, Crès and Flammarion. André Bellessort was a director of Perrin, and Henri Massis of Plon. Action Française writers also published with La Renaissance du Livre, Les Editions de France, Tallandier, Champion, La Mercure de France and Grasset, whose collection, *Les Cahiers Verts* was edited by Halévy. Grasset also published the collection: '*Les Leçons du Passé*', 'consacrée aux hommes ou groupes d'hommes qui ont défendu . . . la cause de l'ordre et de la résistance sociale en présence des forces révolutionnaires. . .', a very Action Française programme.[47] Arthème Fayard was a personal friend of the leaders of the movement; his collection, *Les Grandes Etudes Historiques*, was almost an Action Française preserve, and his weeklies, *Je suis partout* and *Candide*, were very much Action Française concerns until they became 'fascist' in the late thirties. Hachette's *L'Histoire de France racontée à tous*, was edited by Funck-Brentano.[48] The Action Française, then, had its own monarchist publishers and press; it had the sympathetic support of general right-wing publishers and reviews; but it also penetrated into neutral and supposedly hostile zones. We must now look at some of the individual writers involved in these various networks of influence.

III

Given the complex nature of Action Française influence and its history of *dissidences*, it is sometimes hard to be precise about a writer's degree of affiliation to the movement, but a rough division can be made between those who were full-time members or leaders, and those who remained on its edges, expressing perhaps a brief enthusiasm or a distant sympathy, or displaying in their work some debt to Integral Nationalism. The number of those in either category is considerable, and we must concentrate on the major figures, beginning with the fully committed writers.

Maurras himself dominated the Action Française, and earned admiration and respect as a writer in circles far beyond the French Right. His career and his writings have received considerable attention from historians and critics, and familiarity with both can probably be assumed. Three points, however, should be made. First, despite his emphasis on history and politics, Maurras saw poetry as his real vocation; his lifelong dedication to political journalism he saw as a sacrifice of literature made for literature's sake:

> Les Lettres nous ont conduit à la Politique . . . notre nationalisme commença par être esthétique . . . ; J'ai bataillé . . . pour les traditions de goût française; mais je n'ai conçu l'espérance de les voir relevées que le jour ou j'ai conçu la possibilité de rétablir l'ensemble de nos traditions nationales.[49]

Secondly, Maurras was a propagandist and a polemicist of great talent and application; his vast output was almost entirely journalism, though journalism of the highest quality; all but three of his books were compilations of articles. This gave his work a persuasive immediacy, and an apparent lack of system. But, thirdly, Maurras was an inflexible thinker. His career as a journalist and his study of history had given him no sense of fruitful change, no ability to adapt his ideas to fit present needs.[50] He saw the past and the present in almost Manichean terms. While this aspect of Maurras alienated some followers, for others it exercized a hypnotic attraction; in his discussion of the daily affairs of French politics,

Maurras kept them in touch paradoxically with man's changeless struggle with the elements and with his nature.

After Maurras, Jacques Bainville was probably the most important Action Française writer, both in terms of interest and influence. The details of his career can be briefly described. He was one of the leaders of the movement, a regular contributor to the daily where he wrote the foreign affairs column, and a close personal friend of Maurras and other members of the group. Like many members of the Action Française, he came from a republican family. Again, not untypically, he returned from a visit to Germany in 1893 a convinced nationalist and a monarchist, claiming that the Prussian monarchy was a lesson for France.[51] He met Maurras in 1899. He had begun his journalistic career as a literary critic, and he continued to write fiction, but his first book was a biography of Ludwig II of Bavaria, and he made his reputation and his living as a popular historian. Besides contributing to the *Action Française*, he wrote for *La Liberté*, *L'Excelsior*, *L'Eclair*, *Candide*, and *Le Petit Parisien* and, as already mentioned, he was co-editor with Henri Massis of *La Revue Universelle*. With these wide interests went wide and important contacts in parliamentary circles; he was on friendly terms with Poincaré, knew Delcassé very well,[52] and was sent on a mission to Russia in 1916 by Briand.[53] Just before his death in 1936 he entered the Academy. Bainville had none of Maurras's dogmatism nor of Léon Daudet's outrageousness. Louis Dimier and Georges Valois suggested that he was rather shocked by the violence of the Action Française, and he certainly did not endorse its antisemitism.[54] Bainville's most important publications were his *Histoire de France* (1924), *Napoléon* (1931) and La *Troisième République* (1935). In the first he sought to show that France as a nation had been the creation of her kings; in the second, that Napoleon was doomed to failure since he was unable to found a dynasty or find peace, though Bainville was in fact unable to resist the Napoleonic legend and defeated his own object by Hugoesque evocations of the Promethean Bonaparte; in the third, he argued that the Third Republic had survived only in so far as its constitution was monarchic. The intention behind these, as behind his other historical essays—for they were not straightforward accounts—was the demonstration and the propagation of Action Française ideas, but the didacticism was couched in an agreeable style, and the past was rendered clear and intelligible. If one also takes account of the great vogue for popular history books between the wars in France, it is not surprising that Bainville's books became best-sellers.[55] It is not likely that anyone was converted to royalism by reading Bainville, but the elements of his appeal are clear; his Voltairean style, his desire for clarity are signs of an attitude that can loosely be labelled 'Orléanisme', and whose weightier components can be seen in his articles on investing money, in his wish that France remain a primarily agricultural country, and in his celebration of capitalism as the heroic sacrifice upon which civilization was based.[56] Bainville's work was in part the expression of a bourgeois resistance to industrialism, large-scale capitalism, and fiscal measures of a 'socialist' or 'statist' tendency, as it was the defence of classical education, individual and family effort, and thrift. But Bainville was also a foreign affairs correspondent with wide interests and great perception, and it is hard to believe that the Action Française would have drifted so far into appeasement had he been alive in the late thirties. Bainville, in fact, in spite of his closeness to Maurras, was more in touch with the realities of France and of Europe than the Action Française has often been supposed to have been, and as a writer he expressed and appealed to opinion of a traditionally 'bourgeois' rather than a royalist nature.

Léon Daudet fulfilled a similar role, although as a person he was impulsive, noisy and excitable, and a complete contrast to the cool Bainville. As the son of Alphonse Daudet, he inherited a position in the republican intellectual aristocracy; he was on familiar terms with his father's friends Goncourt, Zola, Renoir, Mistral; and his marriage to Jeanne Hugo in 1891 was 'l'une des plus brillantes et retentissantes cérémonies nuptiales de l'epoque'.[57] However, early on he had reacted against this background. He trained to become a doctor, but abandoned medicine after failing his examinations and through disgust at the spectacle of death and suffering in the hospitals and in his own home; his first literary success was a satire on the medical profession, Les Morticoles (1894). Even before this break, he had been tempted by journalism, though the final direction of his career was set by the Dreyfus affair and by his contemporaneous second marriage.[58] He broke with his republican beliefs and friends; his admiration for Zola turned to execration, his love for Wagner to hatred, his admiration for German philosophy to scorn; the bearded frequenter of the cafés of Montparnasse became a royalist, a Catholic, an antisemite,[59] and a man who rejoiced in his extreme reactionary opinions. He met Maurras in December 1904 and joined the Action Française soon after; it was with the help of money left to Daudet's wife by Mme de Loynes that the daily was launched. Daudet became its director, and he brought to the paper not only a wide journalistic experience [60] but a flair for amusing invective that greatly increased its popularity. During the Great War he achieved a certain fame through his press campaigns against defeatism and, particularly, through his accusing the Minister of the Interior, Malvy, of treason.[61] On the crest of this fame he was elected to the Chamber in 1919, where he interrupted and laughed his way to further notoriety. The death of his son Philippe in 1923 took away much of his verve, though he continued to take an active, though less picaresque part, in Action Française affairs until his death in 1942.

Much of Léon Daudet's extremism was mere naïveté and pose; he was fundamentally a generous man,[62] sociable and garrulous, and these were factors in his influence. He was well-travelled and had a vast range of acquaintances. On the political side, he showed his openmindedness by championing Clemenceau for the Presidency of the Republic; on the literary side, he used his membership of the Académie Goncourt to promote and support the reputations of Gide, Proust, Céline and Bernanos. It is hard to describe or assess his own voluminous and repetitive literary output. His many novels were popular, although through their Rabelaisian gusto they offended many Catholics and ran into trouble with the hierarchy. Probably his most interesting and most read books were his rambling and anecdotal *Souvenirs*. His contribution to right-wing ideology was as the heir to Eduoard Drumont, with whom he had had personal connexions. Daudet had worked on *La Libre Parole*, and he saw his own *L'Avant-Guerre* (1913) as a continuation of *La France Juive*. The subtitle of *L'Avant-Guerre*, 'Etudes et documents sur l'espionnage juif-allemand en France depuis l'affaire Dreyfus' sufficiently indicates its contents. However, Daudet's importance does not really lie in his rather credulous and unsystematic antisemitism, but in the fact that he made the Action Française lively and interesting to outsiders. Without him, Maurras said, the *Action Française* would have been a paper of *professeurs*.[63] As André Germain suggests, beside Maurras, that melancholy Don Quixote, Daudet played the necessary role of Sancho Panza.[64]

Pierre Gaxotte was the most important Action Française historian after Bainville. He too came from a republican family; he joined the Action Française in the twenties, and was for a time Maurras's secretary.[65] He was later director of *Candide and Je suis partout*. Like many Action Française leaders he was a talented public lecturer. His most important works which sold on the same scale as those of Bainville were *La Révolution Française* (1928), *Le Siècle de Louis XV* (1933) and *Frédéric II* (1938). These were more straightforward books than those of Bainville, although the first two were clearly inspired by the author's royalist sympathies, seeking to show that the Revolution was an unnecessary and disastrous destruction of a prosperous, ordered and slowly evolving régime. But Gaxotte's books were moderate in tone, pleasingly written and based on considerable scholarship, so that their political overtones must have played a very secondary rôle in their appeal. As a critic wrote of them in 1939: 'Chez soi, entre intimes, on est conservateur ou réactionnaire à tous crins; la plume à la main on devient opportuniste, préoccupé des opinions de cette inconnue, le lecteur anonyme.' [66] Nevertheless, the lasting popularity of Gaxotte's books indicates a wide audience for whom his political views were not distasteful, and his attack on the Revolution welcome, and they may even have helped to create such an audience. Gaxotte eventually earned recognition from the literary establishment by being elected to the Academy in 1953.

Louis Dimier, the historian and art historian, was for a time one of the leaders of the Action Française, and his *Vingt ans d'Action Française* is almost the only important source for the internal history of the movement. It seems that he was drawn to the movement through the Dreyfus affair, through his Catholicism, and perhaps his local patriotism,[67] since decentralization was one of the platforms of the Action Française. During the Great War Dimier was in charge of the Ligue de l'Action Française, and he tried to reorganize the movement's chaotic finances. Maurras's refusal to co-operate, and Dimier's conviction that the Action Française was not really working for the Restoration led him to break with it soon after the end of the War. During the time of his association with the Action Française, Dimier published two books which remained the handbooks of the movement on their respective subjects; these were *Les Préjugés ennemis de l'histoire de France* (1908), and *Les Maîtres de la Contre-Révolution* (1917). The first was a full-scale revision of republican historiography; the second an acquisitive inquiry into the intellectual origins of the Action Française. After his break with the movement, Dimier devoted himself to scholarship; he wrote a book in 1935,[68] deploring nationalism in the arts. This may have represented a break with his previous attitudes, but it seems more likely that it was not; so well-travelled and cultured a person as Dimier was unable, unlike Bainville and Daudet, to combine intellectual curiosity and a literary nationalism, especially when the latter was a substitute for political action that he had once thought possible.

Pierre Lasserre's was a similar case. He was drawn to the Action

Française by the effects of a stay in Germany, like Bainville, by the Dreyfus affair, and by his concern for literary standards. He was, for a time, the editor of the *Revue d'Action Française*, and two of his books, like those of Dimier, became part of the Action Française canon. *La Doctrine officielle de l'Université* (1912) formed the basis of Action Française's attack on the Sorbonne and its allegedly stultifying and anti-national monopoly of French education. *Le Romantisme français* (1908) was an important contribution to the attack on Romanticism, in which Maurras also played a large part, but which was by no means confined to the French Right. But Lasserre was a man of developing and widening opinions and he left the movement after the War, when Maurras tried to edit his articles. He saw the attitudes of the Action Française as necessary only during the emergency created by the Dreyfus affair, and could not for long be bound by its narrow doctrine. Before his death in 1930 he became one of France's leading literary critics; André Thérive wrote of him: 'Le titre de confesseur de son temps n'est pas indigne. . .'.[69] His main work, beside the early 'livres de guerre',[70] which he abandoned to the Action Française, was an unfinished biography of Renan,[71] whom he in many ways resembled. *Mise au point*, a collection of articles published posthumously in 1931, at his express request, was an eloquent confession of faith in liberalism.

Two other writers who remained within the strict membership of the Action Française should be mentioned briefly. The marquis de Roux, the movement's legal expert, wrote various historical works, notably *La Restauration* (1930) and *Origines et fondation de la Troisième Règublique* (1933), which displayed the usual Action Française mixture of political propaganda and readability, though in Roux's case the propaganda was muted and the scholarship more scrupulous than usual. Franz Funck-Brentano, a Luxembourgeois, was easily the best-qualified of the Action Française historians; he was an archiviste-paléographe, was employed at the Bibliothèque de l'Arsenal, was for a time a professeur-suppléant at the Collège de France, and in 1928 was elected to the Académie des sciences morales et politiques. He was a regular lecturer at the Institut d'Action Française, and seems to have remained faithful to the movement until his death during the Second World War. He was one of the most prolific popular historical writers of his time, and though most of his works tended to idealize pre-revolutionary France and particularly the Middle Ages, their political intentions were not obvious. His books include *Les Lettres de cachet* (1926), *L'Ancien Régime* (1926), *L'affaire du collier* (1901) and *La Renaissance* (1935), and although they catered for those interested in the scandals and mysteries of history, they were usually scholarly and probably presented a truer picture of the past than their republican equivalents.

IV

The writers mentioned above all had some definite commitment to the political programme of the Action Française; those sympathizers who did not go so far are perhaps a better indication of the influence of the movement, though one that is naturally much harder to measure.

André Bellessort was among the most distinguished of these. He lectured at the Institut d'Action Française and, as Beau de Loménie writes, he was 'à plus d'un point de vue lié de très près à l'Action Française . . .'.[72] Brasillach, who was once his pupil, remembered his openly avowed opinions in favour of Maurras,[73] and Bellessort himself said that he was led to react against his republican background and become a royalist in great part through the influence of Maurras.[74] Unusually for a right-winger, Bellessort was a *universitaire*, though he interspersed his Lycée teaching career with extensive travels. As in the cases of Bainville and Maurras, his experience of other nations gave him a feeling of France's weakness and vulnerability; he wrote in 1936: 'Je retirais . . . de mes voyages l'idée qu'il fallait biffer tout ce que les romantiques et tout ce que nos politiciens nous racontent de l'amour des étrangers pour la France. Les rapports entre les peuples se fondent sur les intérêts, non sur des sympathies.'[75] Bellessort had a strikingly successful literary career, in the conventional sense; he wrote a regular column for the *Journal des Débats*; he became secretary of the *Revue des Deux Mondes*; and in 1935 was elected to the Academy, of which he later became secretary. His publications include: *Sainte-Beuve et le dix-neuvième siècle* (1927), *La Société française sous Napoléon III* (1932), and *Le dix-huitième siècle et la romantisme* (1941). As these titles indicate, his main concern was with cultural history, and he wrote with sensibility and learning, avoiding, for example, both the Action Française's unthinking dismissal of the achievements of the Bonapartes and its equally crude rejection of Romanticism. But if he was a traditionalist rather than a doctrinaire, he followed Maurras in believing that there could be no civilization without faith and constant vigilance and no State 'sans monarchie gardienne de l'intérêt public . . . ,'[76] though he did not subscribe entirely to Maurras's corollary that such a belief implied the need for a rigid doctrine and political violence.

Like Bellessort, Louis Bertrand was a successful writer and an Academician, but he was in many ways very different from other writers who moved in Action Française circles. He was a friend and admirer of Maurras, but not a disciple. He developed a nationalist doctrine of his own which, although it has many resemblances to that of Maurras, ultimately separated the two men and brought Bertrand into the camp of 'fascism'.[77] Bertrand was born at Spincourt in 1866, and remained in thought and feeling a Lorrainer, a man with, as he put it, 'le sens de l'ennemi'.[78] The memory of 1870 preoccupied him as it did Barrès and Maurras. 'Le cauchemar de l'invasion me hante', he wrote; 'Le devoir, c'est de nous défendre. Nous sommes des conservateurs au sens le plus large et el plus profond de ce mot . . . Nous nous conservons, nous nous maintenons le plus possible en face de l'envahisseur qui complôte sans cesse de nous défaire.'[79] But Bertrand was not from the start a nationalist. He went to the Ecole Normale and began a conventional university career, completing his doctorate, teaching at lycées, and becoming an early Dreyfusard.[80] But in 1891 he went to teach at the lycée of Alger, and this proved to be the decisive event of his life. There, he wrote later, he lost his republican and democratic illusions, there he saw France creating something great as she had not done since the time of Napoleon or of Louis XIV. Beneath the exotic Arab façade he encountered Latin Africa, to which the French came not as conquerors but as heirs.[81] He abandoned the university and devoted himself to the task of preaching his new-found faith. He travelled extensively in North Africa, Europe and the Middle East, and his belief in Latinity and his nationalism were confirmed. Like so many right-wing writers, he came to see any idea of the fraternity of peoples as a dangerous illusion. About this time Bertrand met Maurras, who was angry with him for treating the Félibrige as a joke. Bertrand wrote later:

> La violence de Maurras avait bouleversé mes idées . . . Le félibrige ce n'était pas du tout ce que je pensais . . . une prétexte à banquets et à farandoles. C'était quelque chose de profondément sérieux: l'instinct de conservation d'un peuple qui se lève contre l'invasion étrangère, qui veut . . . sauver ses traditions, ses coutumes, sa langue . . . Ne pas se laisser contaminer, expulser l'intrus, et, contre l'anglomanie et la germanomanie stupides qui régnaient alors dresser le vieil idéal latin, exalter la Méditerranée, mère des civilisations occidentales. Voilà le programme à la fois intellectuel et politique que . . . Maurras me mettait sous les yeux d'une façon saisissante.[82]

Bertrand and Maurras had then much in common; both saw civilization as 'un petit îlot perdu dans un océan de barbarie'; [83] both
wanted to save France from foreign influences, Oriental and semitic,
German and English. Like Maurras, Bertrand saw the Catholic Church
and the monarchy as the preservers of order, Latinity and civilization, all of which France represented. Bertrand's panegyric biography of Louis XIV (1930), which sets him up as a Latin and a
hero in a way that the Action Française saw as its own,[84] marks
the highpoint of his agreement with Maurras.

But there were also profound divergences between the two men
which became more marked in the thirties. Bertrand, symbolically,
lacked Maurras's love of Greece. Like Maurras, he had visited the
Acropolis in awe, but he came to share Gobineau's opinion that
Ancient Greece had been semitic. His admiration for Gobineau was
in direct contrast to Maurras's execration.[85] If Bertrand had celebrated the Latinity of North Africa, he had also exulted over the
contact with 'le barbare'; already during the Great War he had
proposed that France find a more virile ideal 'un retour et un re-
bondissement de l'instinct d'aventure, d'audace, d'initiative et d'entreprise . . .', and had suggested 'Nous rebarbariser' as the formula
for national salvation.[86] This attitude led him to go much further
in his admiration for Mussolini than Maurras,[87] and in 1936 he
publicly expressed his admiration for Hitler as the regenerator of
his nation and Europe's defence against Bolshevism.[88] This last
stand caused Maurras to break with him. Louis Bertrand is significant
not only and perhaps not primarily as an example of a writer who
moved from traditional right-wing attitudes to Fascism, skirting
the Action Française en route, but because through his novels,
his historical works, and his books on Africa,[89] he gave French
nationalism a new direction and a new dimension. The purely Action Française writers had moved away rather cautiously from the
old right-wing view that France's colonial Empire was a diversion
from the Vosges to a celebration of a heroic creation won despite
the Republic; but Louis Bertrand was the first to put the emphasis of
his nationalism on the Empire. Africa he asserted was the real
theatre of 'l'action française'; [90] he never forgot Lorraine, but in
fact North Africa became his Lorraine, and he pointed the way to
'l'Algérie Française' and all that went with it.

It is not surprising that Daniel Halévy was interested in the Action Française for, as René Johannet noted, he had 'un flair inouï
pour pressentir les nouveautés qui compteront . . .'.[91] Yet at first
sight the possible obstacles to his sympathy are striking. He came of
a Jewish family eminent in the cultural life of nineteenth-century

France. As a young man he was both a Socialist and a Dreyfusard and, although these were both temporary enthusiasms, he never entirely repudiated either.[92] He early demonstrated his intellectual independence and earned the respect of his great contemporaries. It was Halévy who rescued Sorel's *Refléxions sur la Violence* from the obscurity of *Le Mouvement Socialiste*, and Sorel addressed the preface of the book to him. Like Sorel, Halévy was an important member of the *Cahiers de la Quinzaine* circle. His *Apologie pour notre passé* (1910), a partial recantation of his Dreyfusardism, provoked Péguy to write *Notre Jeunesse* and *Victor-Marie comte Hugo* in reply, and in spite of this difference Péguy tried to persuade Halévy to take over the direction of the *Cahiers*.[93] Halévy was also one of the first people in France to appreciate Nietzsche,[94] and he did much to create the later reputation of Proudhon.[95]

The Action Française liked to claim Proudhon as one of its masters; many of the Action Française leaders had at one time expressed great admiration for Nietzsche; and Sorel went through a period of temporary flirtation with the royalist movement which advocated violence. All three factors probably played their part in Halévy's own evolution, but probably more important were his own intellectual curiosity and his dissatisfaction with the world in which he lived.[96] His political opinions certainly moved from the Left to the Right, but not in any simple way. He abandoned his Socialism, but continued to proclaim, quoting Proudhon: 'La démopédie, non la démocratie, est mon parti.'[97] He despaired of the Republic not because he preferred the monarchy, or any other positive solution, but because the Republic failed to live up to his ideals. The Action Française was merely one place that caught his interest among others. He said that he dreamed of finding a man or a group of men who would revive a real interest in things of the intellect,[98] and at least for a time he saw the Action Française in this light. He signed the Manifeste du Parti de l'Intelligence, drawn up by Henri Massis in 1919, with Action Française support;[99] he attended the banquets of the Cercle Fustel de Coulanges; he accompanied his son, according to Maurras, to meetings of the Etudiants d'Action Française.[100] This, apart from his friendship and respect for Maurras, is as far as his association with the Action Française went, and it is hard to date it precisely. Already in the mid-twenties he was talking of the movement very much as a critical, if benevolent, outsider,[101] though his political opinions continued to veer to the Right. His nephew Daniel Guérin has recently described his behaviour on the night of 6 February 1934:

Sans attendre même que se soit levée l'aube, un homme surexcité capitalise déjà les morts. Je l'apercevrai . . . parcourant seul . . . les grands boulevards . . . gesticulant comme s'il criait vengeance: mon oncle Daniel Halévy, qui, hors de ses gonds, perdant toute retenue, rejetant tout masque, s'avoue publiquement d'extrême droite.[102]

In *La République des Comités*, dated significantly 7 February–20 April 1934, Halévy delivered a biting attack on the Radical party and the Republic of its creation, and hinted at the need for a dictatorship; and in 1940 he welcomed Pétain in ecstatic terms and gave his support to the National Revolution.[103]

Halévy's place in French intellectual history is beyond question. What did he owe to, or what did he have in common with the Action Française? First, he and Maurras admired each other and each other's works; the two men shared a common idealism, a dislike for and a feeling of alienation from the modern world. Halévy wrote that he and Maurras had often differed in their opinions but '. . . je n'oubliais jamais que, là ou se trouvait Maurras, planait au-dessus du combat la vision des murailles d'Antibes, une haute flamme et un dévorant amour'.[104] Again, in his pioneering works on the history of the Third Republic, Halévy used a modified version of Maurras's conception of 'les quatre états confedérés'.[105] But Halévy's most profound link with Maurras and the Action Française was his preoccupation with conservation and with the constants of history. The Action Française historians sought to discover the 'ossature de l'histoire . . . le principe unifiant qui se perpétue sous les vicissitudes des faits accidentels'.[106] Halévy's quest was the same: 'Il y avait . . . une France de Mgr Dupanloup, ignorante des modes, ignorée par les modes, mais qui très largement était la France, et dont l'historien doit montrer la force, la valeur, la durée.' [107] If the Action Française historians as a rule were content to find this 'ossature' in the monarchy, Halévy was not; he went beyond the Action Française, but it is of great significance that, in some sense, he also went through it.

V

To complete the list of writers who in any way came within the influence of the Action Française would be otiose; it is sufficient to have indicated some of the most important. It remains to inquire how far they consciously formed a school or a group and, if so, what were its characteristics. Although many of them were pronounced individualists, they shared their admiration for Maurras and his ideas; most of them were close colleagues or friends, and they moved in the same social and literary circles, and certainly had the sense of belonging to a group. It is perhaps surprising to discover that most of them were well-travelled, for the Action Française has often been regarded as 'un vasc clos'; however their experience of other countries only served to awaken or to confirm their nationalism. Relatively few of them were Catholics, and some of these, like Daudet and Bertrand, were really converts. The papal condemnation alienated some, but Louis Dimier's estrangement from the movement had nothing to do with his religion, and the diplomat-historian Charles Benoist came to the movement after 1926.[108] On the whole, however, the Action Française seems to have attracted people to the Church rather than alienating them from it; Jacques Maritain and Lucien Dubech, to mention only two examples, were drawn to Catholicism via the Action Française,[109] and hardened sceptics like Lucien Moreau, Henri Vaugeois and Maurras himself were received into the Church before they died.[110] The Action Française writers were rarely traditional royalists.[111] Most came from bourgeois republican backgrounds; many came to the movement from the Left. Maurras, Dubech and Valois, for example, confessed to an original anarchism; [112] Pujo and Vaugeois came from L'Union pour l'Action morale; Moreau from 'un milieu farouchement républicain et rationaliste'.[113] Although the Action Française had been created to combat Dreyfusardism, several of its later admirers had been Dreyfusards. However, most of these writers accommodated themselves to the 'Orléanisme' of the movement's maturity, and characteristically welcomed Vichy as the virtual moderate monarchy that they had hoped for.

Most of the Action Française writers were at least part-time journalists, and they all aimed at popularity and often attained it. Though a few of them had taken higher degrees and even taught at the university, they took very seriously the Action Française's pretension to correct and even to replace this official body. The Action Française's appeal to students was not regarded as a sign of its eccentricity, and must be seen rather in terms of the movement's tacit transfer of its ambitions from the realm of political action to that of national education in the widest sense. The journalistic approach of many of the Action Française writers never implied a departure from dedication, and did not usually interfere with comparatively high standards of scholarship and style.[114] The election to the Academy of many of them not only greatly increased their prestige, but also provided an indication of some kind of public approval. Bainville, Bellessort, Bertrand, Maurras, Gaxotte were elected, and between the wars and just afterwards, the Academy became almost an Action Française domain, since Octave Aubry, P. de Nolhac, P. de La Gorce, Georges Lenôtre, Henry Bordeaux, Louis Madelin, Abel Bonnard, Léon Bérard, the duc de La Force, Henri Massis and the military members were all friendly to the movement. Benoist, Funck-Brentano and Halévy were elected to the Académie des Sciences morales et politiques.

The Action Française has been compared with Port-Royal, and the comparison is not too far-fetched. Schools grouped around an individual, a doctrine, or later, a newspaper have been almost the units with which French intellectual history has been made, and it can be argued that the importance of the Action Française as a school of this kind outweighs its significance as a movement of social reaction and political protest; or rather that its social reaction and political protest expressed themselves best and most successfully, and perhaps inevitably, in the form of a literary movement. In the history of 'committed' literature from Voltaire to Sartre, the writers of the Action Française occupied a prominent but peculiar position, for the political movement to which they had committed themselves had far more decisively committed itself to them.

Notes

1. Obvious opportunities were in August 1914, in 1919 and in February 1934.

2. See for example chapter VI, 'Au sein de "L'Inaction française" in Lucien Rebatet, *Les Décombres* (Paris, 1942).

3. Despite the prestige of the movement in 1919, of the dozen seats aimed at only one, that contested by Léon Daudet, was won; in 1924 no Action Française candidate was elected, and votes cast for them were notably less than those cast previously for traditional royalists.

4. *L'Action Française*, 6 October 1910.

5. Charles Maurras, *Quand les Français ne s'aimaient pas* (Paris, 1926), p. 178.

6. Maurras, *La Contre-Révolution spontanée* (Lyon, 1943), pp. 138–9; Maurras, *Gaulois, Germains, Latins* (Paris, 1926), pp. 85–7.

7. Louis Dimier, *Vingt ans d'Action Française* (Paris, 1926), p. 84.

8. Ibid., p. 186.

9. *Non, l'Action Française n'a bien servi ni l'Eglise ni la France* (Paris,

n.d.), p. 94. The comte de Paris is said to have shared this opinion; see L. Dumont-Wilden, *Le crépuscule des maîtres* (Brussels, 1947), p. 173.

10. Georges Valois, *L'homme contre l'argent* (Paris, 1928), p. 18. By this time Valois had broken with the movement.

11. See Léon S. Roudiez, *Maurras jusqu'à l'Action Française* (Paris, 1957), p. 195.

12. 'Ce logicien, ce raisonneur est avant tout, un créateur de mythes', wrote Robert Brasillach, *Portraits* (Paris, 1935), p. 30. See below for Brasillach's association with the Action Française.

13. Maurras, *Enquête sur la Monarchie* (Paris, 1911), p. 146.

14. See, Dimier, op. cit., pp. 17, 70, 187.

15. Many leaders and members of the movement were of course sincere and practising Catholics, and some of these abandoned it after the papal condemnation of 1926–7.

16. *Cahiers de la Nouvelle Journée*, no. 10, (1927), p. 76.

17. See Stephen Wilson, 'History and Traditionalism: Maurras and the Action Française', *Journal of the History of Ideas*, xxix, No. 3 (July–Sept., 1968).

18. Maurras, *Au signe de Flore* (Paris, 1931), pp. 101, 117 and 162.

19. Thibaudet, 'Refléxions', *La Nouvelle Revue Française* (January–June, 1931), p. 104. Thibaudet's *Les idées de Charles Maurras* (Paris, 1919) is sympathetic but detached; and still the best book on Maurras.

20. Maurras, *La démocratie religieuse* (Paris, 1921), p. 545.

21. Maurras, *Enquête sur la Monarchie*, introduction.

22. E.g. Maurras, *La Contre-Révolution spontanée*, p. 98.

23. Xavier Vallat, *Charles Maurras, Numéro d'écrou 8321* (Paris, 1953), p. 64.

24. Maurras, *Au signe de Flore*, préface; M. de Roux, *Charles Maurras et le nationalisme de l'Action Française* (Paris, 1927), pp. 30–1 and 80–4.

25. Vallat, op. cit., p. 129.

26. Ibid., p. 199.

27. R. Girardet, 'L'héritage de l'Action Française', *Revue Française de Science Politique*, vii, no. 4 (1957). Girardet himself passed through the Action Française.

28. E. Beau de Loménie, *Maurras et son système* (Bourg, 1953), p. 73.

29. Thierry Maulnier, *La Table Ronde* (January 1953), cited by I. P. Barko, *l'Esthétique littéraire de Charles Maurras* (Geneva, 1961), p. 219.

30. Gérard de Catalogne, *Notre Révolution* (Montreal, 1941–4), 1, 158.

31. Jean Longnon, 'L'histoire et la vie', *Revue critique des idées et des livres* (March–April 1924). Barrès's influence on the early Action Française was considerable, though to some extent that of Maurras worked against it—see Wilson, op. cit.

32. Lucien Dubech, *Pourquoi je suis royaliste* (Paris, 1928), pp. 28–31. See Stephen Wilson, *The Historians of the Action Française*, unpublished thesis (Cambridge, 1966).

33. Maurras, *Pages littéraires choisies* (Paris, 1922), p. 139; *Les Conditions de la Victoire* (Paris, 1916–18), ii, pp. 58–9.

34. Eugen Weber, *Action Française* (Stanford, 1962), pp. 183–4. Any student of the Action Française must express his debts to this volume.

35. *Revue critique des idées et des livres* (July 1919).

36. Truc wrote in his *Apologie pour l'Action Française* (Paris, 1926), p. 11: 'Quelles que soient une admiration et une gratitude croissantes pour les hommes de l'Action Française, nous n'appartenons point à leur groupement...'

37. His *Cathérine de Médicis* (Paris, 1940) recently earned tribute from N. M. Sutherland, *Catherine de Medici and the Ancien Régime* (London, 1966), 36, for helping to present a more historical picture of Catherine, though the author says quite wrongly that his book lacks notes, references and bibliography.

38. The *Revue du Siècle* had as its own semi-political organizations, a Bureau politique internationale, a Comité de Défense des classes moyennes and a Comité de Défense des intérêts régionaux.

39. *Revue Universelle* (1 April 1920).

40. *Le Procès de Charles Maurras* (Paris, 1946), p. 77.

41. For their association with the Action Française, see below.

42. Guiraud was later editor of *La Croix*, which gave the Action Française temporary support. He was also professor of history at the University of Besançon, and his *Histoire partiale, histoire vraie* (Paris, 1911–17), 4 vols., and his history textbooks played an important part in the campaign against 'official' republican historiography and history teaching, led by the Action Française.

43. Dom Jean-Martial Besse has a claim to fame as the man who converted Huysmans to Catholicism; see Joseph Daoust, *Les débuts bénédictins de J-K. Huysmans* (Abbaye de St. Wandrille, 1950).

44. Many also belonged to local academies and provincial history societies; for example, the marquis de Roux was president of the Société des Antiquaires de l'Ouest; Louis Dimier, after his break with the Action Française, became a member of the Académie de Savoie and President of the Société des Antiquaires de France.

45. Maurras dedicated part of *Jeanne d'Arc, Louis XIV, Napoléon* (Paris, 1937) to Lévis-Mirepoix, 'Pour ses livres royaux'; these included *Francois Ier* (Paris, 1931) and *Philippe le Bel* (Paris, 1936). Lévis-Mirepoix was fittingly elected to Mauras's chair in the Academy in January 1953.

46. E.g. Léon Daudet, *Panorama de la Troisième République* (Paris, 1936); and André Bellessort, *Le Collège et le Monde* (1941).

47. This collection was directed by Marcel Boulenger and P. Bessand-Massenet, and included works by Bellessort, Louis Madelin, and Jean Lucas-Dubreton.

48. Other Hachette collections in which Action Française writers were prominent were *Récits d'autrefois*, which included works by Lucas-Dubreton and Bainville, and *Hier et Aujourd'hui*, which included works by Funck-Brentano, Bainville and Bertrand.

49. Maurras, *Quand les Français ne s'aimaient pas*, p. xiii; Maurras,

Gazette de France (12 December 1901), cited by W. C. Buthman, *The Rise of Integral Nationalism in France* (New York, 1939), p. 252.

50. Maurras's deafness may have had something to do with this attitude: 'Maurras est un sourd, comme l'Angleterre est une île . . .' wrote Andre Gide, *Journal* (Paris, 1948), p. 753.

51. See Claude Digeon, *La crise allemande de la pensée française* (Paris, 1959), pp. 472–3.

52. W. Morton Fullerton, Preface, Bainville, *L'Angleterre et l'Empire britannique* (Paris, 1938) ; Mme la Générale Noguès, unpublished MS.

53. Maurras, *Jacques Bainville et Paul Bourget* (Paris, 1937), p. 56; and a letter from Daniel Halévy to Marcel Guérin, 19 August 1916, *Bibliothèque Nationale, Collection Marcel Guérin*, NAF 24,839, fo. 336.

54. See Valois, *L'homme contre l'argent*, p. 28; Rebatet, op. cit., pp. 53 and 114; and Jean Drault, *Drumont, La France Juive et La Libre Parole* (Paris, 1935), p. 298.

55. Livre de poche still publish two Bainville, two Gaxotte and one Louis Bertrand today.

56. E.g. Bainville, *La Fortune de la France* (Paris, 1937), pp. 97–8 and passim.

57. See Georges Lecomte, *Ma traversée* (Paris, 1949), pp. 576–92.

58. Given the Action Française's traditionalist cult of the family Léon Daudet's own divorce and that of his sister were ironic to say the least.

59. Alphonse Daudet and Edmond de Goncourt who had a great influence on Léon were not, of course, free of antisemitism.

60. Léon Daudet had written for Mme Adam's *Nouvelle Revue*, for *Le Figaro*, and for Arthur Meyer's *Le Gaulois* among others.

61. See Léon Daudet, *Le Poignard dans le dos. Notes sur l'affaire Malvy* (Paris, 1918).

62. Testimonies to Daudet's charitable nature abound. See for example: Bainville, *Doit-on le dire?* (Paris, 1939), p. 207; Marcel Wiriath, *Silhouettes* (Paris, 1949), pp. 25–8; J-H. Rosny (aîné), *Mémoires de la vie littéraire* (Paris, 1927), pp. 45–9; and Valois, op. cit., pp. 22 and 160–3; Valois's lasting sympathy for Daudet was in marked contrast to his persistent denigration of all his other former colleagues at the Action Française.

63. Henri Massis, *Maurras et notre temps* (Paris, 1961), p. 233.

64. André Germain, *Les Croisées modernes* (Paris, 1958), p. 15.

65. In 1948 Maurras referred to Gaxotte as 'un garçon remarquable et qui m'est toujours fidèle'. Vallat, op. cit., p. 35.

66. Auriant, *Mercure de France* (15 August 1939).

67. Dimier was a Savoyard and expressed his debts to his 'petite patrie' in a *Histoire de Savoie* (Paris, 1913).

68. *Le Nationalisme littéraire et ses méfaits chez les Français.*

69. Selim Ezban, *Les débuts littéraires de Pierre Lasserre*, Publications of the Modern Language Society of America (December 1947).

70. The expression is Lasserre's; see *Mise au point*, pp. 26–34.

71. *La Jeunesse d'Ernest Renan, Histoire de la crise religieuse au XIXᵉ siècle* (Paris, 1924–32), 3 vols.

72. Beau de Loménie, op. cit., p. 77.

73. R. Brasillach, *Notre Avant-Guerre* (Paris, 1941), p. 218.

74. Bellessort, *Les Intellectuels et l'avènement de la Troisième République* (Paris, 1931), pp. 238–9.

75. Bellessort, *Le Collège et le Monde* (Paris, 1941), pp. 158–60.

76. Andre Chaumeix, 'André Bellessort', *Revue des Deux Mondes* (15 February 1942).

77. Various writers, for example Brasillach, Drieu La Rochelle and Rebatet, also evolved from the Action Française to 'fascism', but this movement was by no means a general rule.

78. See Louis Bertrand, *Le Sens de l'ennemi* (Paris, 1917). It is interesting to see how far French nationalism was linked with the Eastern frontier in terms of personalities. Barrès, Bertrand, Gaxotte, Funck-Brentano—and also Lyautey and Poincaré—all came from the East.

79. Bertrand, *Devant l'Islam* (Paris, 1926), pp. 72–3; Bertrand, 'L'eternel champ de bataille', *Revue des Deux Mondes* (15 August 1915).

80. See Bertrand, 'Les minutes heureuses', *Revue des Deux Mondes* (15 November 1937); and *BN, Papiers Brunetière*, v, NAF 25,031, fos. 520–1.

81. See Bertrand, 'Le centénaire du Cardinal Lavigerie à la Sorbonne', *Revue des Deux Mondes* (1 December 1925); and Bertrand, 'Pour le centénaire de Flaubert, Discours à la Nation Africiane', ibid. (1 December 1921).

82. Bertrand, 'La Riviéra que j'ai connu', *Revue Universelle* (1 March 1931).

83. Bertrand, 'Vers l'unité latine', *Revue des Deux Mondes* (15 September 1916).

84. See Maurras, *Louis XIV ou l'Homme-Roi* (Paris, 1939).

85. See Bertrand, *Devant l'Islam*; Bertrand, *Idées et Portraits* (Paris, 1927), introduction; and Maurras, 'Le système de Gobineau', *Gaulois, Germains, Latins*, pp. 29–30.

86. Bertrand, 'Vers l'unité latine', *Revue des Deux Mondes* (15 September 1916); Bertrand, *Le sens de l'ennemi*, préface and pp. 34–40.

87. For example, in October 1932 he attended a conference on European reconstruction arranged by the Italian Academy and under the auspices of the Duce. Bertrand, 'Vieillir', *Revue des Deux Mondes* (15 September 1933).

88. Bertrand, *Hitler* (Paris, 1936). In the same year Bertrand, then *directeur* of the French Academy, delivered a paper at Hans Keller's Nazi-inspired Nationalist International. Bertrand, *L'Internationale—ennemie des nations* (Zürich, 1936).

89. Bertrand's publications in these various fields included: *L'invasion* (Paris, 1907); *Saint Augustin* (Paris, 1913); *Histoire d'Espagne* (Paris, 1932); and *Les Villes d'Or* (Paris, 1921).

90. Bertrand, 'Sur un livre de Paul Adam', *Revue des Deux Mondes* (1 July 1922).

91. René Johannet, *Vie et mort de Péguy* (Paris, 1950), pp. 254–7.

92. See Daniel Halévy, *Pays Parisiens* (Paris, 1932), pp. 155–204; and *Apologie pour notre passé, Cahiers de la Quinzaine*, 10ᵉ cahier, 11ᵉ série (April 1910).

93. Johannet, op. cit., pp. 169–70.

94. Halévy published his first article on Nietzsche in 1891, and several others around the turn of the century. See Halévy, *Nietzsche* (Paris, 1944), préface; and G. Bianquis, *Nietzsche en France* (Paris, 1929).

95. See Halévy, *La vie de Proudhon* (Paris, 1948); and *Le mariage de Proudhon* (Paris, 1955).

96. Halévy demonstrated this dissatisfaction by unconventional dress and behaviour. Wiriath wrote of him in 1949: 'Il porte une rédingote d'avant 1900, paraît dépaysé dans le présent', *Silhouettes*, pp. 36–7. See also Pieter Geyl, *Encounters in History* (London, 1963), pp. 183 ff.

97. Halévy, *Apologie pour notre passé*, pp. 86–90.

98. Halévy, *Courrier de Paris* (Paris, 1932), pp. 303–13.

99. His friend Proust wrote to rebuke him for this, seeing it as a betrayal of what they had fought for in the Dreyfus affair. Proust–Rivière, *Correspondance* (Paris, 1955), p. 51.

100. Vallat, op. cit., p. 87.

101. Halévy, *Courrier de Paris*, pp. 1–17.

102. Daniel Guérin, *Front Populaire, Révolution manqueé* (Paris, 1963), p. 49. See also Fidus, 'Daniel Halévy', *Revue des Deux Mondes* (15 June 1936), which confirms this testimony.

103. See Halévy, *Trois épreuves* (Paris, 1942); and *La France de l'Esprit* (1943).

104. Chanoine Aristide Cormier, *La vie intérieure de Charles Maurras* (Paris, 1955), p. 160.

105. E.g. Halévy, *Décadence de la Liberté* (Paris, 1931).

106. J.-M. Besse, *Les Rapports de l'Eglise et de l'Etat dans l'ancienne France* (Paris, 1907), pp. 7–9.

107. Halévy, *La république des ducs* (Paris, 1937), pp. 201–2.

108. After a fairly distinguished career as a politician and ambassador, Benoist announced his adhesion to the Action Française in 1928. His best-known book was *Le machiavélisme* (1907–37), 3 vols.

109. Roux, op. cit., p. 264; Massis, op. cit., pp. 112–24.

110. Vaugeois, who died during the Great War, founded the Action Française with Maurice Pujo, though Maurras soon assumed predominance; Moreau was also an early member and leader.

111. As Dimier said: 'Bon nombre de royalistes, qui ne pouvaient pas nous souffrir, nous regardèrent comme on regarde le peinture cubiste au Salon.' *Vingt ans d'Action Française*, p. 70. Léon de Montesquiou was one of the few members of the old aristocracy to take a leading part in the Action Française.

112. See Valois, *D'un siècle à l'autre* (Paris, 1921), p. 104; Maurras, *Oeuvres Capitales* (Paris, 1954), pp. 1, 37.

113. Vallat, op. cit., p. 221.

114. This is not to say that the Action Française did not specialize in polemic and abuse: 'Nous n'insultions pas. Nous *diffamions* ouvertement, catégoriquement . . .'. Maurras, *Pour un jeune Français* (Paris, 1949), p. 114. But the attitude of the Action Française had nuances even here, as Daudet, who excelled in journalistic abuse, explained: 'J'ai horreur de cabotinage, mais je crois qu'il n'y a rien à faire, en politique anti-démocratique, sans coups de tonnerre et actes vilement représentatifs.' *Au temps de Judas* (Paris, 1920), p. 167.

7. MAXIME WEYGAND AND THE ARMY–NATION CONCEPT IN THE MODERN FRENCH ARMY

by Philip C. F. Bankwitz

The Republic since 1870 has been more intimately dependent upon the army than upon any other single institution. Memories are short and this proposition may seem questionable. But there was a time when the French army enjoyed a prestige—albeit very different from that of the Prussian army—that had no parallel among the armed forces of other nations. Rooted in the historic and revolutionary past, this prestige survived the not very brilliant decades of the earlier nineteenth century, even the débâcle of 1870–1871. Paradoxically it was around the shattered army of the année terrible *that the nation gathered to reconstitute itself as a great power. Though the civil-military relationship was badly strained in the political warfare at the turn of the century, and although the professional army may well have sustained in those post-Dreyfus years some spiritual wound forever unhealed, the army's triumph in the Great War of 1914–1918 carried it to the summit of its reputation. Thereafter the realities of social change, ideological conflict, economic troubles, and national political insecurities bore down upon the officer corps, bringing about a new uncertainty as regards its place, its mission, and, finally, its competence. The stunning collapse of 1940 opened up a period of tense civil-military relations, amid changing regimes and in a climate of divisiveness sometimes approaching that of incipient civil war. The tradition of "the great silent service," if not brought to a close, was at least intermittently suspended over some twenty years.*

Philip C. F. Bankwitz illuminates the crisis of the civil-military relationship and the origins of the breakdown of what once had

*seemed, at all events, to be the aloof, disciplined, unquestioning
attitude of the army. Professor of History, Trinity College, Hart-
ford, Connecticut, he is the author of* Maxime Weygand and Civil-
Military Relations in Modern France *(Cambridge, Mass., 1967) and*
The Alsatian Autonomist Leaders Between France and Germany,
1919–1947 *(Kansas, 1977) and various scholarly articles on the
history of contemporary France. This paper first appeared in* French
Historical Studies *2 (1961): 157–188. It is reprinted by kind permission of the author and the editor of* FHS.

When a recent article on French military affairs stated that the
only way to overcome the Army officer's deep "sadness" and sense of
"injustice" was the reaffirmation of the "contact . . . between Army
and Nation," [1] it touched on one of the central ideas in the evolution of French civil-military relationships during the past half-
century. This idea, the fusion in military minds between Army and
Nation, furnishes one of the keys to the complex process of the
politicization of French military life in recent times. Using the
experience of General Maxime Weygand, peacetime commander of
the French Army from 1931 to 1935 and Generalissimo in June,
1940, this article proposes to trace the development of the Army-
Nation idea from its origins in the nineteenth century through the
troubled period of the thirties to its emergence in 1940 and its
adoption and implementation by the officer corps in the years following the Defeat.

I

. The first element in the progression of steps that leads to the
fusion between Army and Nation is the recognition that the barriers
between civilian society and the military institution are broken down
in the era of mass, conscript armies, an era in which war includes
"all measures of political, economic and military order." [2] From
this state of affairs, two concepts arise. One deals with the participation of the nation in the preparation and waging of war. This
idea, the "nation in arms," is usually accorded the most attention
in writings on French civil-military affairs. With original Jacobin
roots and always championed in some form by the Left, it developed,
as Challener's definitive treatise has shown, into a highly articulated
socio-political phenomenon with a complex history of its own in

modern French life.[3] The other concept, sometimes overlooked by civilian writers but always accorded some attention by the soldiers, is that of the Army as a microcosm of the nation.

The receptacle of all able-bodied males generation after generation, the Army as described by writers since the early part of the nineteenth century, is the concrete physical representative of the nation in peace and war.[4] It is, as Weygand often wrote, the "perfect emanation of the *Patrie*"; it is the "pays total" in the words of Jean Fabry, a soldier turned civilian minister; it is the "French people" as Edouard Daladier stated to the Chambre in 1937.[5] Even more important, the Army is the "moral" as well as the "material" armature of the country at all times, since it is considered to contain the best and most vigorous elements in the nation. From this point, it is but a step to the assumption that the Army is the historical carrier of the inner content, the spiritual values of the nation itself: It "personifies national feeling" and is the "most complete expression of the spirit of a society," in De Gaulle's words.[6] No army officer, whatever his rank or political sympathies, needed to be reminded of Barrès' famous statement that "when a regiment passes . . . the honor of the country is contained therein." [7]

The Army, then, is the repository of national virtue in time of peace. In time of war, it rises to even more sublime heights. By the symbols "inscribed on [its] standards: Honor, Country, Value, Discipline," it protects the "material and moral integrity" of the nation and thus, in Weygand's words, has performed a vitally important part in "making France what she is." [8] In both peace and war, the Army insures that these symbols and ideals are inculcated in its civilian conscripts and thus maintained in the nation. The mission of impregnating the nation with patriotism and what was called at the time of the 1871–1873 military reforms "universal discipline" originated in the task of national "moral regeneration" which the Army was summoned to perform after the defeat of the Franco-Prussian war.[9] This mission was extended in the new educative duties assigned to the soldiers, epitomized by Marshal Hubert Lyautey's famous article, "Du rôle social de l'officier" of 1891.[10]

This complex of attitudes erected on the basis of the Army-Nation concept concerning the superior values and integrity of the Army formed a cohesive whole in the minds of every officer in the Third Republic's military force. Echoing de Vigny and Psichari, Jules Roy has written that "in a world corrupted by bargaining and the negation of the spiritual, it [the Army] always had its law: disinterest; its mystique: the nation; its role: discipline; and its ethics:

honor." [11] Weygand reaffirmed this thought when he wrote that the Army was like the priesthood in that "it obeys a vocation, fulfills a sacerdotal function," that in it, "honor" and the "higher interest of the country" form a "single word." [12] On this basis, it was indeed possible, by a judicious choice of phrases and by omitting troublesome reformist ideas, for the soldiers to borrow support from the many civilians who firmly believed in the nation in arms theory. Hence, that paladin of civilianism, Jaurès himself, could appear to reinforce the Army-Nation concept when he wrote that "there is no army more powerful and more capable of endowing its leaders with moral authority and prestige . . . than an army which is the armed nation itself." [13]

II

This was the concept, then, of what a later military rebel, General André Zeller, called the "moral fusion" between Army and Nation.[14] From the beginning, the military mind incorporated into it the idea of the separation of nation from régime, of the "essence" of power from the "constitutional" form of government, with the nation assuming the higher value.[15] Identification-cum-separation had, along with political neutrality and passive obedience, permitted the Army to adjust to and survive the seven changes of régime between 1814 and 1871.[16] Carried over into the army of the Third Republic, this enlarged Army-Nation concept was reinforced in a dominating nucleus of anti-republican and ultra-conservative *bien pensant* officers when the Army took a stand on the opposite side from the political majority in the great schism at the end of the nineteenth century.[17] By 1914, at least in this select and powerful minority of anti-Dreyfusard and *Déroulèdiste* officers, the fusion of Army with Nation had already produced the elements of what might be called a split image of loyalty. While it is true that this image existed primarily as a feeling rather than as an idea at this time, seldom verbalized and then only by rare eccentrics, it was a definite state of mind and carried with it a disturbing functional corollary: conditional rather than passive, or automatic obedience to the régime. This split image and its version of obedience, pointing inevitably toward an arbitral role for the Army in national affairs, did not, of course, disappear during the conflicts between the command and the civilians over the conduct of the war of 1914–1918, over the terms of the peace that followed, and over the organization and

development of the post-war Army.[18] Indeed, the dangerous potentialities of the Army-Nation idea were immeasurably increased by
the difficult conditions of the post-war period where a troubled
Army as in de Vigny's time, was "searching for its soul and could
not find it." [19]

The soldiers bitterly resented the fact that, from their point of
view, the "politicians," after having obtained the military institutions they desired in 1928, proceeded first to ignore the threat of a
new war these laws created and then to threaten to push the
country into an unequal conflict before adequate material and spiritual preparation, a *réveil national,* could take place.[20] The officers
were aghast at the legislative measures and the disarmament negotiations which, especially during the period from 1932 to 1934,
threatened to reduce the cadres, effectives, and equipment of the
Army below the survival limit and to alter its traditional role of pro-
tector of the peace in Europe and defender of the country against
the reviving German military menace.[21] Their defensiveness against
political attack was complicated and aggravated by simultaneous
assaults on their doctrinal orthodoxy after 1933 from political
quarters, spurred on by such rare military rebels as De Gaulle.
Worse still, the state itself had suffered a scandalous collapse of
authority in the riots of February, 1934 and had failed to recover its
prestige. Undergoing the social turmoil, industrial strikes, and street
clashes of 1936–1937, France to its horrified and despairing soldiers
seemed to be forsaking all discipline, losing its morale, and sinking
toward the level of "sick man of Europe." [22]

These tensions, fears, and resentments were summed up in 1937–
1938 in a major scare in the officer corps over an allegedly im-
minent Communist military coup, and in the discovery of a clandestine network of cells devoted to purge action against Communists
and antimilitarism in the ranks, to the "cleansing" of the officer
cadres, and to patriotic propaganda to prepare the nation for the
coming war.[23] The members of this network (called "Corvignolles")
felt "betrayed" by the politicians who, in the striking phrase of one of
the leaders, (a member of Pétain's personal staff, Commandant
Georges Loustaunau-Lacau), had transformed the victorious and vigorous military institution of 1918 into an "armé assise." [24] These
officers were determined to maintain the "hinge between army and
nation." Moreover, they had, apparently, intimate connections with
a much more blatantly anti-régime civilian group, the Comité secret
d'action révolutionnaire, the C. S. A. R. (popularly known as the
"Cagoule"), whose military sympathizers included several members

of the nation's highest military body, the Conseil Supérieur de la Guerre, (among them, the Inspector of the Infantry and of Tanks, General J. Dufieux), and the two living marshals, Franchet d'Esperey and Pétain himself.[25]

The above elements had conspired, by the mid-thirties, to produce a real although still partially concealed schism between the Army and the régime. The situation was made all the more dangerous by the progressive erosion, particularly pronounced after the sixth of February, of the national consensus regarding the acceptability of the Third Republic as the nation's political régime.[26] The political conditions of the post-sixth of February era, which President Albert Lebrun has described in a masterpiece of understatement as one "not particularly characterized by calmness and sagacity," [27] accentuated anti-parliamentarianism, anti-régime feelings and indifference toward the Republic's fate in all sections of the population and gave rise to a desperate quest for authoritarian leaders, for what Alfred Fabre-Luce once called a "common denominator for France." [28] Quite obviously, then, the concept of fusion between the Army and the Nation would create grave problems for the reflective officer of the time. Would it have any effect on his course of action? For the first time, voices appeared expressing themselves on this issue in direct terms, and they were not confined to subordinate levels.

An example was that of General Eugène Debeney, Weygand's predecessor as Chief of the General Staff, who, in an article on the "mystique" of the officer corps published in the first issue of the *Revue militaire générale* of January, 1937, wrote that the Army, a "qualified representative" of the nation, had at the present time a distinct nonmilitary mission to execute. It was that of healing the social and political divisions of the nation, discord which, in the General's opinion, was "threatening to become mortal." In what can only be described as prophetic words he stated that the "recompense" of the Army "impregnated" by this inspiring task would come "that solemn day when the vibrant voice of the nation in arms proclaims 'here are those whom I have chosen to unite my children!' " [29]

From the point of view of what occurred three years later, in 1940, and again in 1958, a critical stage was now reached. Debeney was a typical member of the older military generation who probably intended his writings to convey only an exalted and slightly romanticized version of the *union morale* tradition of national regeneration through the Army mentioned above, and to express concern over the current social conflicts and what the soldiers felt to be the

growing vacuum of political authority. Even Daladier was to proclaim to the Chamber in the next month that despite political diver-
gencies, "the real unity of France always forms again around its
Army." [30] Debeney must have believed that he had avoided the
implication of political involvement by a passing reference to the
non-political status of the officer corps.[31]

Nevertheless, especially when placed beside the platitudes on the
same subject, or the silence toward it observed by the other contributors to the issue (constituting a veritable roll call of honor in
the Command—Pétain, Franchet d'Esperey Weygand, Gamelin, Admirals Castex and Lacaze *et al.*), what was implied in Debeney's
article was nothing short of revolutionary. For here, responding to
what the soldiers felt to be the political and social disintegration
of the nineteen-thirties, the Army becomes the active, galvanizing
factor in the peacetime life of the nation. It is no longer a passive
instrument merely helping to re-educate and reform the country
as in the past century. As the "one remaining bulwark which held
society together," [32] the Army now deprives the unsteady régime
of the role of the dominant element in the work of achieving national union. Now representing the interests of the nation on the
active level, the Army *becomes* the Nation, the *réelle*, the true
France, which it henceforth nurtures and protects against the régime,
the distrusted and secondary *pays légal* of French reactionary political theory. The régime, never more than the "instrument of national destinies" and never having a right to exist by or for itself
according to the soldiers, can now be dominated by that other national "instrument," the Army.[33] The inevitable result of the officer
corps' Army-Nation identification, including the traditional separation between the *Patrie* and the *régime* which "exploits it" in the
terms of one officer, has finally occurred.[34] Form, reality and depth
have now been given to the feelings of distrust, aloofness, alienation,
and unenthusiastic obedience, to the whole state of mind charac-
terizing the nineteenth-century Army.[35]

III

It is easy to see, in retrospect, that at this point, through the
back door of philosophizing over the mystical identification between the institution and the community, the Army was, for the
first time in its successive "examinations of conscience" since 1898,
embarking again on the perilous road which, in words attributed

to de Vigny, "leads it periodically from disdain to honor," from isolation to involvement in national affairs.[36] Subjected to the same pressures as Debeney, having had to function from 1930 to 1935 in a system that even Gamelin publicly (but, as always, diplomatically) described at this time as "hesitant," [37] Weygand was certainly aware of the problem. His entire reasoning in the question of De Gaulle's *métier* force during the period from 1934 to 1937, reasoning which emphasized the links between Army and country, pointed toward it.[38] So too did his extensive criticism of national conditions in his writings during his retirement years after 1935, criticisms which indirectly impugned the régime.[39] What was his answer to the problem of temptation to political engagement posed by the Army-Nation concept during this difficult period?

On the one hand, Weygand did not quite follow the orthodox formula dating from the politically sterilizing experience of the nineteenth century. Rather than a complete reversion to this formula of disciplined silence, isolation and passivity, he counselled frank recognition of the "parallel" but mutually exclusive existence separating soldier from civilian and of the burden of distrust it carried. He urged the undertaking of a conscientious effort to overcome these barriers. His prescription, while not novel or particularly brilliant, was broad in its approach, ranging from the creation of high-level study sessions and seminars bringing together military men and civilians to examine outstanding problems of national defense, to the recognition by a revitalized and "strong State" of the Army's legitimate demands for material and moral support from it, to the familiar *union morale* through common devotion to the ideals of "Discipline, Patriotism, Duty." [40]

But, on the other hand, Weygand was in complete agreement with Gamelin and others on the essential point unwittingly raised by Debeney, that suggesting the active involvement of the Army in the political and social problems of the nation. Although he did not answer Debeney directly, the phrase or its equivalent applying to the rightful role of the Army, "penetrated with the grandeur of its duties and protected from politics" occurs repeatedly in his writings at this time. He stated clearly that the Government alone possessed the means and the right to execute the necessary task of inspiring the "fervent collaboration of the country." [41]

Weygand's answer was theoretically impeccable, based as it was upon the Clausewitzian ideal of the relations between the Army and the State of his youth. According to this theory, the civilian authority was unique, ultimate, and superior in power to the military which, to be sure, was given a great deal of internal autonomy and was placed upon a higher moral "pedestal" because of its courage, service, honor, and abnegation.[42] Weygand's answer also derived from his awareness that there now existed temptations to political "engagement" in a situation of increasing *embourgeoisement* and "civilianism" in the officer corps,[43] of mounting impatience with what was looked upon as an "archaic" attitude of isolation, of growing eagerness to espouse current social and political doctrines, most of them reactionary.[44] Conscious of his own resentment at the recent "catastrophic" trials of the Army and its "persecution" by civilians and, possibly, influenced by the contemporary example of the German Army and its political involvement of the past decade,[45] Weygand could not have been too astonished at the "Corvignolles" and "Cagoule" affairs of 1937–1938. Like all *bien pensant* nineteenth-century officers, he had never to be reminded of Barrès' celebrated prophecy at the end of *L'appel au soldat:* "Boulanger is nothing but an incident. We will find other Boulangisms again." [46]

Weygand's "traditionalist" answer was shared by most of the members of the Command, excluding, however, one of the few among them proceeding along new lines, Pétain, who laid down in various public speeches during this period the "conditions of national revival" which included the "reforging of a single national soul by the Army and the schools." [47] But events were shortly to prove that Weygand and the others had not gauged the momentum and power of the forces favoring military involvement in French political affairs any more accurately than did that of the new theories of the use of armored and air masses in warfare. The reasons for this failure illustrate the complexities and dangerous potentialities of the relationships between civilians and soldiers in France during the thirties.

First, Weygand did not grasp the full force of the anti-régime hostility imbedded in the very reasoning he used in refusing to proceed further with the Army-Nation identification. For the next step, literal implementation of the concept itself, violated the soldiers' traditional sense of separateness and distinction from the rest of national life by bringing the Army into direct contact with the alien civilian world and the political régime it had spawned. Weygand must have felt that this régime was responsible for the "evil divorce" between two naturally symbiotic entities, for the Army-Nation identification was absolute in military minds and powerful because of its "symmetry and internal consistency." [48] All of the unhappy tensions and friction borne by the Army since the nineties of the last century, all of the "unjust comprehension" shown it by the nation, could be explained away as the result of interference by "external" elements which, in the last analysis, turned out to be "political" ones associated with the régime.

In a certain sense, the soldiers believed the past and the current "persecution" of the Army and the dread scourge of antimilitarism itself to be inevitable phenomena arising from the intrinsic nature of the régime.[49] For the majority of the politician-civilians believed that naturally virtuous and pacific man was able to solve all of his problems, including that of war, by the application of his own rational powers. They were largely indifferent to spiritual matters and to the fact that traditional patriotism was fast disappearing as the central focus of unity shifted from the concrete geopolitical entity of the Nation to what a nineteenth-century mind like Weygand's regarded as the unfamiliar and impalpable realm of international causes and ideologies.[50] They seemed unwilling to arrest the erosion of the old national and military ideals in a community which Franchet d'Esperey once described as "detesting constraint and rejecting discipline." [51] In their hopelessly naïve and sanguine rationalism, humanitarianism, and internationalism, their "enfantillage" in Weygand's direct word at the time, the politicians were "misleading" the national will, as von Seeckt had pointed out in relation to the German civil-military situation a decade earlier.[52] They were corrupting the moral forces and military voluntarism that a generation of French military authorities, especially Weygand's mentor Foch, had taught were the prime elements in national life, whether in peace or in battle.[53]

And yet, it was because of these very ideals that Weygand had known the culminating moment of his life, the Armistice of 1918: it was because of the "confidence in God and faith in the destiny of France that [I] was able to experience this sublime hour." [54] He was dominated by the values and attitudes summed up in the term *esprit militaire* which, as an early writer on the Army-Nation idea had asserted, reposed on "order, morality, discipline, respect for authority . . . absolute devotion to the flag which is the emblem, not of a certain form of government, but of the common motherland." [55] It is no wonder that Weygand was close to the Maurrassian viewpoint that a death struggle between the régime and the Army was inevitable,[56] although he did not publicly reveal his concern over these incompatibilities until the nineteen-fifties when he brought up twice the difficulties of adjustment between a "partisan and demagogic" democracy and the military institution. Both times, echoing a familiar theme of the nineteenth-century officer and of nineteenth-century political thought, he quoted Renan's famous lines: "Democracy is the strongest dissolvent of the military organization . . . founded on discipline. Democracy is the negation of discipline." [57] Such sentiments repeated those expressed earlier and more directly by another officer involved in the problem of the thirties, General Jean Perré, "I never met a real soldier who was a real democrat." [58] They were echoed by a more forceful statement on the subject by the Commander-in-Chief of N. A. T. O. forces in Central Europe from 1956 to 1960, General Jean Valluy, *"torn between Democracy and the 'Patrie,' we prefer the latter when it is in danger."* [59]

This was the most powerful reason explaining why Weygand and most of his colleagues held to the attitude of the previous century that although it was the nation, the Army should maintain its special characteristics, its own "mystique" and "morals" as Ernest Psichari had vehemently insisted it should in *L'appel des armes;* it should be kept aloof from the rest of the community.[60] The Army's leaders were convinced that they must maintain what de Vigny described as the "nation within the nation; the vice of our times," what a post-war writer has called "coexistence without intimacy." [61] Otherwise, the Army would become corrupted by the "vices and weaknesses" of the régime, by the alien values, concepts, attitudes, and behavioral characteristics of a "flabby" civilian world if it entered public affairs.[62] If this occurred, not only would the independent inner functioning of the Army come to an end, and "objective" civilian control give way to what Huntington has called "subjective" civilian control: that is, ubiquitous civilian supervision of the minutest details through politicized and fanatical commanders.[63] Worst of all, the soul of the Army would be destroyed, its essential nature, its *esprit militaire*, its professionalism, all of which derived from its status as "refuge and monastery." Its physical collapse would be merely a matter of time.[64] The Army as a mystical union so strong that, in Malraux' words, it seemed separated from the rest of European life by a "frontier of blood," the Army as an "Order," the Army as the only "real" family for one with Weygand's harsh and empty childhood, would cease to exist.[65]

Beyond Weygand's failure to grasp the fact that the sacred concept of separateness aggravated anti-régime hostility in himself and his brethren was an inability to recognize the profound transformation of the classic civil-military relationship since the end of the First World War. He did not realize that the increased technical complications, the "technical uncontrollability" of war itself,[66] and the special political conditions of the post-1919 period—dilution of political authority, instability of cabinets, the fears, timidity, and technical incompetence of many civilian ministers of war—had transposed the dominating weight of power in the relationship to the military side.[67] Although partially concealed, this transposition was nonetheless amply indicated in a general sense by a marked rise in the influence of the military in national affairs, measured, as Huntington has pointed out, in terms of connections with other groups, increasing control of the economic life and financial affairs of the country, penetration into positions of authority in non-military sectors and (in direct contrast to the feelings of the soldiers on the subject) the respect and prestige actually accorded by civilians.[68] It was also specifically proved by phenomena in which Weygand had either been directly involved or to which he had paid a great deal of attention: his own determining influence on the government's policy in the disarmament and effectives crises of 1932–1934,[69] governmental passivity in the questions of doctrinal and organizational reform after 1933,[70] and its total dependence upon the soldiers during the Rhineland crisis of 1936.[71] In its analysis of the problem, the post-1945 Investigating Commission (Commission chargée d'enquêter sur les événements survenus en France de 1933 à 1945) did not hesitate to describe the General Staff of this period as a "real State within a State." [72]

Finally, Weygand's failure to react in a sufficiently forceful manner to the problem of political involvement depends upon the fact that he was not fully aware of the powerful external pressure for political action now being exerted by a deeply troubled society which, in an age of the "obliteration" of State authority, assigned to the officer corps a "monopoly" of prestige and power because it was the only national group still in a condition of "complete moral homogeneity." [73] The asseverations of his many enemies in the Army and the political world notwithstanding,[74] Weygand was quite blind in this respect. He really did not perceive the dangers of the new *appel au soldat* coming from a combination of new and old anti-parliamentarian and anti-régime classes and groups heavily influenced by authoritarian and Caesarean aims.[75] He did not grasp the fact that the experience of the soldiers—their old role of moral regeneration of the nation after 1871, their historical sympathies for their Rightist and nationalist allies in the struggles over military organization since 1889 and in the pre-1914 *réveil national*—rendered them deeply vulnerable to use in a future crisis by "ardently patriotic" elements now espousing "direct access" to power.[76]

A frank recognition of the above points, the anti-régime hostility imbedded in the notion of separateness, growth of military power, external pressures for political action, would have alerted Weygand to the fact that a crisis between the Army and the State was approaching. But he faced grave difficulties in arriving at this realization. Separateness was part of the very fibre of his military being. Refusal to face intellectually and emotionally the effects of what the soldiers themselves called the "diminution of the State" [77] on the civil-military relationship protected him from guilty misgivings concerning first, his aggressive, provocative, and generally misunderstood behavior when in command before 1935 and, second, his implied criticism of the régime in his extensive writings after retirement. Blindness to external political pressures (which, after all, had long been resisted successfully by the Army) was part of the strict construction of the term, the "good soldier."

It was, probably, no more possible for Weygand to overcome these obstacles and inhibitions than to realize that the Army-Nation identification itself could be appropriated by other individuals and movements in national life—Laval and the Resistance of 1940–1944 are two examples. For the Army-Nation identification was really only an extension of the values and standards, the prejudices and biases of one group to the nation and as such a complete misrepresentation of fact. What the French officer corps needed to be reminded of at this time, and, manifestly, later on, was Clemenceau's blunt statement in his plea to the jury at the Zola trial in 1898: "The only reason for the existence of the soldier is to defend the principles that civilian society represents." [78] But only a Clemenceau could have uttered these words in the present situation where the commanders of the Army were desperately seeking for their prime professional and psychological need, authority, and were finding little or none of it. As Weygand stated long afterward to his civilian questioners in the post-1945 Investigating Commission, "I reproach the Reynaud government for but one thing: not knowing how to command. It is your weakness that makes you [politicians] so suspicious." [79]

IV

As a result, Weygand did not sense the ease by which the Army could fulfill the old Rightist dreams of military messianism dating from the last century, the hopes of Maurras contained in the famous conclusion to the 1924 edition of *L'enquête sur la monarchie:* Here in a moment of national military catastrophe, the *pays réel,* by "coolly and deliberately bringing together certain serious measures" could destroy the *pays légal.*[80] He did not perceive the power of the "reflex attitudes" being built up within him and others for political action, attitudes based upon an overpowering conviction of the soldier's personal responsibility for the welfare of the nation. Guardians of the persecuted Army, the members of the Command had inevitably become guardians of the suffering community as well. They had long since lost the essential "reciprocal confidence" of the civil-military relationship. They no longer felt themselves to be the instrument of the government's policy but the true representatives of the nation itself.[81]

These reflex attitudes became apparent to Weygand only in 1940 when, in a moment of desperation and what to him was an utter "absurdity of conditions," [82] he carried out what was only implicit in Debeney's article: He implemented the results of the Army-Nation identification to their fullest extent. He frankly drew upon two assertions: first, that the "Army was the Nation," as he wrote later describing his disgust at the civilian ministers' unfavorable reaction to his appeal for an armistice at the cabinet meeting at Cangé on June 12, 1940; and second, that the Reynaud cabinet did not represent the country, as he declared to the Premier in a passionate exchange of words at Bordeaux on June 15.[83] Weygand momentarily abjured his faith in the traditional military system of values. He broke the two fundamental laws of the old civil-military relationship, those forbidding the political "deliberation" of the military power and its disobedience of the civilian authority, even if the orders involved were, allegedly, "illegal." [84] He brought to an end in France what Mosca called the "great modern fact" of the standing Army as the eternal custodian of civilian law.[85]

Weygand entered politics to "save the country" from the régime, convinced that he was, at the same time, saving the Army from destruction. In this dual task, he was "doing his duty." [86] He was certain that he was engaged in what the Chief of the Armed Forces General Staff at the time of the 1958 crises in Algiers, General Paul Ely, called a struggle between "two different conceptions of the future," between "two civilizations." Despite the fact that his victory would result in the collapse of the eternally "fragile links between the State and the Army," Weygand felt he must win this struggle because he was "responsible to the Nation." [87]

After the dramatic crisis in June, 1940, Weygand had exactly the same hopes of restoring the intimate links between Army and Nation of the pre-Dreyfus era that the Reichswehr leaders entertained during the first years of the Third Reich, when they looked forward to the return of the close contact of the Wilhelmian era.[88] Weygand, had, at last, as a like-minded officer wrote in a remarkable article on civil-military relations published in 1943, a political system whose leader satisfied "one of the Army's deep sentimental needs." He had a régime whose political doctrine was "in accord" with military "principles" and under which "one no longer had the right to be antimilitaristic." [89] Quite naturally, then, Weygand went on to work for the fusion of the Army and the Nation. As Minister of Defense and Generalissimo during the summer of 1940, he vigorously supported a new united veterans' organization, the Légion française des combattants. This organization, he hoped, would be a counterweight to the projected *parti unique* of Marcel Déat he opposed and would become the "moral infrastructure" of the "new social régime" for which, in late June, 1940, he had drawn up a blueprint based upon his reflections and writings of the previous decade.[90]

But in carrying one step further the Army ideals of a *relèvement moral* inherited from the post-1871 era, Weygand had committed the act of disobedience which, as Minister of the Interior Eugène Frot had prophesied in the troubles of 1934, would mean the "end of the State." [91] He thus opened up the Army to the very dangers of civilian contamination he so dreaded. Huntington's phrase, "the generals and admirals may triumph but not the professional military ethic" describes the situation perfectly.[92] For discipline broke down, ideology vanquished *esprit militaire*, and political intrigue rapidly divided the Army to a degree not seen since the Revolution itself.[93] The result was the spiritual demise of the classic military institution to which, in a heartfelt statement made toward the end of his life, Weygand confessed "I owe my being what I am." [94]

V

When the Republic was reconstituted in 1944, it found itself faced not only with much the same problems of power disparities and ideological tensions between it and a physically revived military establishment, but also with a new set of military attitudes, among which was conditional obedience. As a young paratrooper lieutenant involved in the upheaval of 1958 has written, the Army would obey the civilian power only if its orders were compatible with the military concept of "honor." [95] These attitudes were part of that emergent set of concepts concerning the civil-military relationship which the old leaders had tried to ignore during the nineteen-thirties but to which they had nonetheless conformed in the Defeat. The above-cited confrontation of honor versus obedience stems from the original one made by Weygand before Reynaud on June 15, 1940, at Bordeaux, where the former refused, on the grounds of military ethics, to follow the latter's "suggestion" that France imitate the Dutch example of surrender of the land forces by the commander-in-chief and the withdrawal overseas of the Government.[96] These new attitudes were supported after 1945 by an expanded view of war itself, now held to involve a "horizontal" component of politics and ideology as well as the traditional "vertical" one of national conflict between organized bodies of troops.[97]

Prominent military spokesmen now urged the Army to abandon its "ivory tower" retreat, its *Grande Muette* "passive obedience" which were deemed responsible for the "rupture" between it and country in 1940.[98] Still the *"armature of the nation,"* it must become fully integrated with the political power and "politically prepared" to engage in "psychological" and "ideological" action. This action included not only suppression of civil war and revolution and the fulfillment of the old apostolate of youth education and dissemination of patriotic propaganda, but also the defense of French "intellectual positions" against any totalitarian "aggression." [99] The Army was to destroy, now, the "political-military" base of the enemy by "revolutionary politico-military" operations and "civil-military unity of action." [100]

As the crisis between the civil and military authorities deepened during this post-1945 period, alarm was manifested over the effects upon discipline of conditional obedience. Urgent appeals were heard from both civilian and military sources for the civilians to recognize the central issue of the age of "simultaneous war and peace," the "political" transformation of war. It was now vitally necessary to destroy the intellectual barriers between the political élites and the Command and to adopt "positive" civil-military institutions and "total" concepts of national defense which would "integrate" the Army into the political life of the nation.[101] Similarly, military sources warned that the Army must abandon its particularist ideas and attitudes, so obviously incompatible with the community. It must become "really republican," thoroughly committed ideologically to the preservation of the régime. It was enjoined to overcome its historic sense of distinctiveness, to integrate itself completely with the régime as a "gage of its loyalism." It must learn the "difficult task" of tolerating the inevitable and "necessary divisions" within the nation.[102] Only by these adjustments and by spurning the temptation to "control the country's activities under the cover of national defense" in Marshal Jean de Lattre de Tassigny's sage words, could it avoid the approaching "convulsions," the explosive "movement." [103]

But other opinions were also heard. These, more familiar, were based upon the opposing traditional thesis of fusion between Army and Nation. One of these warning opinions came from General Lionel Chassin, ranking general in the Air Force, military historian, and one of the leaders of the anti-régime groups in the late fifties. In 1956, Chassin did not hesitate to publish in the country's leading military journal, the *Revue de défense nationale*, an extraordinarily frank article on the role of the Army in history with broad applications to the rapidly evolving politico-military situation in France. Here, during a period of "decline" and "disintegration," the Army prevents the nation's "death by suicide and death by murder" for "long centuries" by periodically seizing power to "put the nation back on the tracks each time a unanimous feeling of defensive reaction tells it to do so." [104] The only remnant of the attitudes so important twenty years before was the rather perfunctory assurance that the Army, in its new role, could keep its identity by resisting "depersonalization" and "denationalization," and by remaining "disciplined, patriotic, national." [105]

By this time, the Army-Nation concept was an integral part of the thinking of the officer corps not only about the stinging defeat of 1940 (which was blamed on the "politicians"), but also about the humiliating *guerre pourrie*, the festering colonial conflicts in Asia and Africa. For the soldiers, in the words of a defense lawyer in the "Procès des Barricades" of 1960–1961 trying those responsible for the uprising in Algiers in January, 1960, "It was the nation that counts, this warm and living entity, not the State, cold and abstract." [106] The responsibility for these colonial conflicts, which the officers felt were separating the Army physically and spritually from the nation to a degree unknown since the Second Empire, was placed on what most of them now called the "Système," the régime of "political intrigue." Algeria was now, according to Lucien Rebatet, the man who had written so scathingly of the Army of 1940 in *Les décombres*, "the only possible redemption for these insulted banners, dragged from burlesque routs to miserable abandonment." [107]

In May, 1958, the Army made its second entrance into politics in modern French history. Avoiding an overt putsch and open seizure of power, it nonetheless performed the role of what even its most fanatical civilian partisans admitted was that of a "political 'pressure group.' " [108] It did so because, again in its civilian defenders' words, it chose the "imperative of national salvation" over service to the "legal State." [109] The Chief of Staff of the Armed forces, General Paul Ely, noted that by intervening at this moment in the name of "national continuity," the Army thus exhibited "profound respect for true legality." [110] This interpretation was only a slightly amended version of that contained in the proclamation of Louis-Napoleon Bonaparte on December 2, 1851. Here, the new dictator announced that the soldiers, the "Élite of the nation," had not "violated the laws" but had made prevail the "first law of the country, national sovereignty, of which I am the legitimate representative." [111]

Shortly after this event, another article appeared in the *Revue de défense nationale*, containing the full theoretical justification for military interference in politics and based upon the evolving Army-Nation concept of the past century. Apotheosizing De Gaulle as the living personification of the Army as Nation, a high-ranking admiral wrote:

> At grave hours, when the sovereign voice of the people can no longer express itself, the ARMY suddenly becomes aware of what it is: the People under the Flag.
> Then, the Army takes responsibility for the People.[112]

VI

Despite his experience of 1940, Weygand confined himself to the old pre-war themes in the articles he was called upon to write in the military journals and in other publications during the nineteen-fifties. He was thoroughly aware of the mounting crisis between Army and Régime and of the introduction of politics into the Army, a phenomenon he characteristically blamed on the Liberation governments and their *épuration* policies.[113] Along with Marshal Alphonse Juin, he took an uncompromising and public stand on the side of those advocating an *Algérie française*, as his sponsorship of several groups devoted to this aim (and to the twin thesis of an "amnesty" for those condemned in the "Terror" of 1944–45) would indicate.[114] But, eschewing discussion of the real dangers of the situation and reference to the Army-Nation concept that had governed his own behavior so recently, Weygand still counselled the adoption of the same palliatives he had advocated before 1940: the reinforcement of patriotism to produce real leaders, character formation in the officer corps, observation of the principle of superior civilian power.[115] Even after what he inaccurately but understandably termed the "first political initiative" [116] of the Army of 1958, Weygand continued to refuse to examine the problem in terms of the power relationships involved. In a speech to the École de Guerre in 1959, made in his capacity as the rehabilitated dean of the Army, he advised the soldiers, instead, to avoid the "petty politics" of party struggle and to concentrate on "high politics" of party struggle and to concentrate on "high politics." By this last term, he meant questions of truly national significance raised in specific civil-military institutions or posts: the Institut des hautes études de défense nationale, the Chief of the General Staff of National Defense directly responsible to the Premier, the combined committee of chiefs of staff of the three military arms. The régime, indeed, had only to be disciplined, patriotic, favorably disposed toward the Army and willing to command to be obeyed by its soldiers.[117]

These ideas concerning civil-military cooperation were the outgrowth of those which had influenced him, several years earlier, to become honorary president of a political and business pressure group, the Centre d'études politiques et civiques under the guidance of his good friend René Gillouin, Maurrassian, nationalist municipal councillor of Paris at the sixth of February and one of Pétain's "best confidants" at Vichy. This group, which Weygand no doubt saw as a new version of Paul Desjardin's and Lyautey's Union pour la Verité of the Ralliement period of the early nineties, had a marked interest in "politics in the Army" and in the *Algérie française* thesis. Its avowed purpose was the formation of a military-civilian élite "in contact with the workers and social questions" and engaged in "noble politics for the benefit of the national community." [118] Such activities and ideas suggest what may be Weygand's whole view of the problem of the political engagement of the French Army. Here, military politics is seen as a minor and incidental part of a larger process by which the military institution lifted itself above the deadening *fonctionnairisme* of the nineteenth century. In order to justify its existence as national "guide and tutor" in a new and complex era, the Army merely broadened its range of interests in the mid-twentieth century as it had at the end of the nineteenth, and did so in the same spirit of idealism and generosity. At this point, Weygand's *rôle politique de l'officier* of the fifties joins together with Lyautey's *rôle social* of the nineties to form the new task of the modern Army.[119]

Such an interpretation would, of course, omit the definitive changes in the values and self-concept of the officer corps this process of politicization had brought about. It would skirt the supremely perplexing difficulties of maintaining discipline, of keeping the independent military personality free of ideological "infection," and above all, of avoiding the garrison state and the Caesars by confining the enthusiastic "guardians of the nation's moral patrimony" to Weygand's "high" or "noble" politics.[120] The General's interpretation, further, would fail to make reference to the many obstacles in the long road to what may be an eventual point of equilibrium where the "political integration of the Army would be part of the general custom." [121] Finally, such a limited interpretation would fail to identify the military evolution toward ideology and politics as part of the rationalization and extension of the concept of war from what Gerhard Ritter calls *politischen Krieg* to *kriegerischen Politik*, from the restricted French level of nationalism versus humanitarian ideology to the international plane of "defense of Western civilization" versus "freedom for all mankind." [122]

It is, perhaps, permissible to conclude that Weygand could see his own important role in this entire question as simply that of the continuator of the nineteenth-century military traditions of moral reformism and national regeneration, as that of the man who restored the Army as the "conscience of the nation," never as that of a revolutionary.[123] Only in these terms could he accept the entrance of what the soldiers call the "democratic and social"—and the civilians, the "revolutionary"—Army into politics.[124] Only with this view of his own role could Weygand make what may have been a subtle allusion to his activities in his speech to the École de Guerre cited above: "I thus leaned on a door which opened and I am entirely happy to have done so." [125] He, and the many older officers who supported this qualified interpretation of the Army's new role, could never recognize or accept openly the victorious conquest of the military institution by civilian ideologies which now encompassed the ideals of discipline and patriotism of yesteryear. Weygand could never state frankly, as did Juin at a veterans' meeting in Paris in November, 1960, as a fresh crisis developed between the military leaders and the "new *Système*," that the "Army must maintain its unity and complete cohesion, for it will perhaps intervene for the salvation of France." [126] He could never urge, as did Valluy at this time, that the Army must be "politicized in its totality" to avoid the danger of disunion.[127]

Weygand's limited recognition of his own role as the first commander to carry out the full consequences of the Army-Nation concept also illustrates a monstrous irony. By imposing once, and once only, his particularist interpretation of "honor and security" over the civilian version of it, thus re-enacting the famous confrontation of civilian and military "justice" summed up in the Zola trial during the Dreyfus Affair, Weygand completed the destruction of the Republic which, as Julien Benda had pointed out long ago in a penetrating phrase, could survive only by making "authority civil by nature, subordinating the military element." [128] Weygand fulfilled the curious prophecy contained in the antimilitarist classic of Urbain Gohier written at the time of the Affair, *L'Armée contre la nation,* that power would eventually be taken from the hands of the régime by "overwhelming the nation [with] the national army." [129] And, in the sense that the old army perished in its involvement in the nation's destiny in 1940, Weygand also carried out the equally prophetic words of one of the earliest writers on the subject of Army-Nation relations, General Théodore Iung, who wrote during the nineties that the "Army will be republican or it will not exist." [130]

The final twist to the whole problem of Weygand and the fusion of Army and Nation is furnished by the fact that the man who believed that he had fought hardest against political involvement as he understood it is, after all, the one originally responsible for the "great historical fact," the politicization of contemporary French military life, a fact which is, in François Mauriac's words, the "greatest misfortune that could happen to the French nation." [131] It was no accident that a phrase of Weygand, hurled at the deliberating ministers during the cabinet meeting at Cangé on June 12, 1940, should be displayed as a frontispiece to a recent brochure entitled "Contre-Révolution." This guide to action, decorated with the cross and Sacred Heart and published secretly at Liége in 1957, was circulated to a large number of clandestine anti-régime military and civilian groups in France before the upheaval of May, 1958. It described in minute detail a coup d'état which would be mounted by a politically-inspired Army with its vital *"Army-Nation* contact," the "indispensable instrument" of revolution.[132] For it was Weygand the tragic actor who, born into the politically neutral *Grande Muette* of the age of nations, introduced into it in the age of global war the Caesarean outlook he most abhorred.

Notes

1. Dr. André Gros and Georges Guéron, "Quelques réflexions sur l'officier français," *Revue de défense nationale,* XVI (Nov., 1960), 1770.

2. Lt. Col. J. Stagnaro, "Une conception de la défense nationale," *ibid.*, V (Aug., 1947), 52.

3. See Richard Challener, *The French Theory of the Nation in Arms, 1866–1939* (N.Y., 1955), especially pp. 184–210, 234–44; and Joseph Monteilhet, *Les institutions militaires de la France (1814–1932)* (Paris, 1932), pp. 109–450 *passim*.

4. Alfred de Vigny, *Servitude et grandeur militaires* (in *Œuvres complètes*, Paris, 1914), pp. 21, 26; Paul Marguerite, "L'officier français," *Journal des sciences militaires*, III (June, 1908), 372; Gen. Bourelly, "L'armée, est-elle, doit-elle être la nation?," *Le Correspondant*, CLXXI (Apr., 1902), 193; Raoul Girardet, *La société militaire dans la France contemporaine, 1815–1939* (Paris, 1953), p. 48.

5. France, *Journal officiel de la République francaise. Chambre des Députés. Débats parlementaires. Compte rendu in extenso.* (Paris, 1871–1942) (Hereafter cited as *J. O. C. Debs.*), Feb. 2, 1937, p. 294; Jean Fabry, "La 'stratégie générale,' affaire de gouvernement," *Revue militaire générale*, I (Apr., 1937), 388; Gen. Maxime Weygand, *La France est-elle défendue?* (Paris, 1937), p. 47; and his "L'unité de l'armée," *Revue militaire générale*, I (Jan., 1937), 18.

6. Charles de Gaulle, *Vers l'armée de métier* (Paris, 1934), p. 229; Bourelly, *op. cit.*, p. 209.

7. Maurice Barrès, *Les taches d'encre* (Paris, 1884), p. 33.

8. Weygand, preface to J. Goulven, *Lyautey l'Africain* (Nancy, 1935), unnumbered page; Chef d'escadron Dassonville, "L'officier dans la nation," *Revue militaire générale*, III (Jan., 1938), 99.

9. Monteilhet, *op. cit.*, pp. 132–3.

10. Marshal Hubert Lyautey, "Du rôle social de l'officier," *Revue des deux mondes*, CIV (Mar. 15, 1891), 443–58. See also, Weygand, preface to Lyautey, *Le rôle social de l'officier* (Paris, 1935); Captain Pierre Viannay, "L'armée, école professionelle de la nation," *Revue de défense nationale*, VIII (Mar., 1949), 323; Margueritte, *op. cit.*, p. 372; Bourelly, *op. cit.*, pp. 199–202; Girardet, *op. cit.*, pp. 148–52, 180–1, 247, 296.

11. Jules Roy, *Le métier des armes* (Paris, 1948), p. 211; Ernest Psichari, *L'appel des armes* (Paris, 1911), p. 32; see also, de Vigny, *op. cit.*, pp. 26–32, 84, 264–5.

12. Weygand, "Les constantes du comportement du chef et de la troupe," *Revue militaire générale*, VII (July, 1959), 165, 168; and his *Forces de la France. Vocation de la France* (Paris, 1951), p. 164.

13. Jean Jaurès, *Democracy and Military Service* (tr. G. G. Coulton of *L'Armée nouvelle*) (London, 1916), p. 38; see also, Gaston Moch, *L'armée d'une démocratie* (Paris, 1900), pp. 22–30; Émile Boutroux, "Démocratie et armée," in C. Bouglé, E. Bourgeois and E. Boutroux, *La nation armée* (Paris, 1909), pp. 73–93.

14. Gen. André Zeller, "Armée et politique," *Revue de défense nationale*, XXIV (Apr., 1957), 504–7.

15. Admiral Darlan's son wrote that for the Admiral at the critical

juncture in 1940, "France above and first of all was the land itself with its people, its history, its memories." Alain Darlan, *L'amiral Darlan parle* (Paris, 1952), p. 47. On this point, see François Kuntz, *L'officier dans la nation* (Paris, 1960), pp. 144–5, 179; Albert Vallet, *Le problème militaire de la 4ᵉ république* (Lyon, 1947), p. 46; Zeller, *op. cit.*, p. 517; Girardet, *op. cit.*, p. 121.

16. De Vigny, *op. cit.*, pp. 25, 32, 81; Girardet, *op. cit.*, pp. 122, 230; Pierre Chalmin, *L'officier français de 1815 à 1871* (Paris, 1957), pp. 361–2; and his "Crises morales de l'armée française au 19ᵉ siècle," *Revue de défense nationale*, X (May, 1950), 556, 562, 570.

17. Joseph Reinach, *Histoire de l'affaire Dreyfus* (Paris, 1906–8), VI, 391–415; Gerhard Ritter, *Staatskunst und Kriegshandwerk. II. Die Hauptmächte Europas und das Wilhelminische Reich (1890–1914)* (Munich, 1960), 30–1; Girardet, *op. cit.*, pp. 57–9, 86, 144, 196–8; Kuntz, *op. cit.*, pp. 73–6; John Cairns, "International Politics and the Military Mind: The Case of the French Republic, 1911–1914," *Journal of Modern History*, XXV (Sept., 1953), 279, 283–5.

18. The behavior of Foch at Versailles in 1919 is especially instructive in this respect and is covered in Raymond Recouly, *Le mémorial de Foch. Mes entretiens avec le Maréchal* (Paris, 1929), pp. 282–4; Weygand, *Foch* (Paris, 1947), p. 293; Jean Martet, *Monsieur Clemenceau peint par lui-même* (Paris, 1929), pp. 243, 251. See also, Ritter, *op. cit.*, pp. 35–42; and Gen. Jean Perré, "L'armée, l'état et la nation," *Revue des deux mondes*, LXXIII (Jan. 1, 1943), 10.

19. De Vigny, *op. cit.*, p. 24; see also, De Gaulle, "Du prestige," *Revue militaire française*, CXX (June, 1931), 395.

20. Pétain's speech of June 20, 1940, in his *Quatre années au pouvoir* (Paris, 1949), p. 49; testimony of Gamelin (Dec. 11, 1947); Georges (Feb. 5, 1948); and Weygand (May 24 and June 9, 1949) in Assemblée Nationale, *Commission d'enquête parlementaire sur les événements survenus en France de 1933 à 1945. Rapport. Témoignages et documents* (Paris, 1951–4) (this work contains reports, documents and testimony and will be cited hereafter as *Commission . . . Rapport*, or *Commission . . . Témoignages*), II, 434, III, 626–7; VI, 1676, 1713, 1771. Also, Gen. Édouard Requin, *Combats pour l'honneur (1939–1940)* (Paris, 1946), p. 196; Gen. A. Laffargue, *Justice pour ceux de 1940* (Paris, 1952), pp. 225–33; René Bertrand-Serret, "L'armée et le régime," *Écrits de Paris*, No. 173 (July-Aug., 1959), 69.

21. Weygand's reaction to these crises is traced in his *Mémoires* (Paris, 1950–7), II, 375–435; his *Rapport . . . sur l'état de l'armée établi le 10 février 1934 . . .* in *Commission . . . Rapport*, I, 92–3, 105–6; his statements in séance spéciale du Conseil supérieur de la guerre du 5 janvier 1935, in *ibid.*, I, 121–5. See also Gen. Auguste Laure *Pétain* (Paris, 1941), pp. 362, 379, 386–93; Gen. Henri Niessel, *Le déséquilibre militaire* (Paris, 1937), pp. 40–1; Jacques Minart, *Le drame du désarmement . . . La revanche allemande (1918–1939)* (Paris, 1959), pp. 23, 201–2, 210.

22. Weygand, *La France est-elle défendue?* (Paris, 1937), pp. 20–1, 29–31, 47; Gen. Maurice Gamelin, *Servir* (Paris, 1946–7), II, 221–66 *passim;* speeches grouped under the title, "Avertissements, 1934–9" in Pétain, *Paroles aux Français: messages et écrits, 1934–41* (Lyon, 1941), pp. 3–37; Gen. Eugène Debeney, *La guerre et les hommes* (Paris, 1937), pp. 376–8; Gen. Henri Mordacq, *Faut-il changer le régime?* (Paris, 1935), p. 247; Gen. Édouard Requin, *D'une guerre à l'autre, 1919–1939* (Paris, 1949), pp. 201–6, 223, 249.

23. The "Spanish document" affair concerning the Communist "coup" is summed up in Gamelin, *op. cit.*, II, 261–3; testimony of Gen. Gérodias and Daladier (Mar. 25, 1942) in Pierre Mazé and Roger Génébrier, *Les grandes journées du procès de Riom* (Paris, 1945), pp. 227–8; and Gen. Victor Bourret, *La tragédie de l'armée française* (Paris, 1947), pp. 137–8. For the secret network, see Cdt. Georges Loustaneau-Lacau, *Mémoires d'un Français rebelle, 1914–1948* (Paris, 1948), pp. 110–11; and the summary of a sub-dossier on Loustaneau-Lacau in the Pétain dossier of 1945 in Louis Noguères, *Le véritable procès du maréchal Pétain* (Paris, 1955), p. 48 (note 1).

24. Loustaneau-Lacau, *op. cit.*, p. 117.

25. The interrelations of the several groups included in the general term "Cagoule" with "Corvignolles," and the involvement of the soldiers were not revealed until the post-1945 era. In the extensive literature on the subject, much of which implicates Pétain as a most important figure not only here but also in the "Spanish document" affair, see Gamelin, *op. cit.*, II, 303–4; III, 532–3; Loustaneau-Lacau, *op cit.*, pp. 112–6; Noguères, *op. cit.*, pp. 49–53; Maurice Garçon, *Histoire de la justice sous la 3e république* (Paris, 1955–7), III, 266–77; Col. Groussard, *Chemins secrets* (Mulhouse, 1948), pp. 106–27.

26. Raoul Girardet, "Pouvoir civil et pouvoir militaire dans la France contemporaine," *Revue française de science politique*, X (Mar., 1960), 38; Jean Meynaud, "Les militaires et le pouvoir," *Revue française de sociologie*, II (Apr.-June, 1961), 85; André Siegfried, *De la 3e à la 4e république* (Paris, 1956), pp 59–62.

27. Testimony of Lebrun (May 27, 1948), *Commission . . . Témoignages*, IV, 950.

28. Alfred Fabre-Luce, *Journal de la France* (Paris, 1942), II, 52. Among the numerous treatments concerning this period of decline, see especially Bertrand de Jouvenel, *Après la défaite* (Paris, 1941), pp. 115–25; Marc Bloch, *L'étrange défaite* (Paris, 1946), p. 206; Raoul Girardet, "Notes sur l'esprit d'un fascisme français," *Revue française de science politique*, V (July, 1955), 540; Stanley Hoffmann, "Aspects du régime de Vichy," *ibid.*, VI (Jan., 1956), 51–2; *Commission . . . Rapport*, I, 85.

29. Gen. Eugéne Debeney, "La mystique de notre corps d'officiers," *Revue militaire générale*, I (Jan., 1937), 22–3.

30. *J. O. C. Débs.*, Feb. 2, 1937, p. 289.

31. Debeney, *op. cit.*, p. 25.

32. Challener, *op. cit.*, p. 75.

33. Perré, *op. cit.*, p. 3.

34. Col. J. Revol, *Chroniques de guerre (1939–1945)* (Paris, 1945), p. 241.

35. Vallet, *op. cit.*, p. 46.

36. See Maurice Mégret, "Fonction et intégration politiques de l'armée," in Centre de sciences politiques de l'Institut d'études juridiques de Nice, *La défense nationale* (Paris, 1958), p. 157.

37. Speech of Gamelin at St. Cyr, Mar. 5, 1936, *Revue des deux mondes*, XXV (Mar., 1936), 141.

38. Weygand, *France?*, p. 23; "Unité," *op. cit.*, p. 18.

39. See his *France?*, pp. 20–47 *passim;* his *Comment élever nos fils?* (Paris, 1937), pp. 2–44 *passim;* his preface to Lyautey, *op. cit.*, p. xix.

40. Weygand, *France?*, p. 47; and *Comment?*, p. 24. See also his *Forces*, pp. 163–4.

41. Weygand, *Histoire de l'armée française* (Paris, 1938), p. 392; his "L'armée d'aujourd'hui," *Revue des deux mondes*, XXXIX (May 15, 1938), 335–6; preface to Lyautey, *op. cit.*, p. xvi; Gamelin's speech at St. Cyr, Mar. 5, 1936, *op. cit.*, p. 140. De Gaulle's shift of opinion from the orthodox "retreat" to "national renewal" led by the "new Army" is recorded in his "Prestige," *op. cit.*, pp. 395, 404–5, 412; and his *Armée de métier*, pp. 229–30.

42. De Gaulle, "Prestige," *op. cit.*, pp. 405. See also Karl von Clausewitz, *Vom Kriege* (Berlin, 1832–4), I, 108; III, 1120; Bourret, *op. cit.*, p. 130; Henry Contamine, *La revanche, 1871–1940* (Paris, 1957), p. 20; Samuel P. Huntington, *The Soldier and the State* (N.Y., 1957), pp. 83–5, 94; Girardet, *op. cit.*, pp. 255, 320.

43. Girardet, p. 318; Guy Chapman, "The French Army and politics," in Michael Howard, *Soldiers and Governments* (London, 1957), pp. 66–7, 71–2.

44. Col. M. Alerme, *Les causes militaires de notre défaite* (Paris, 1941), p. 37; Pierre Cot, *Triumph of Treason* (N.Y., 1944), pp. 196–7; Gen. Jean Perré, "Les officiers de carrière et la nation," *Écrits de Paris*, No. 146 (Feb., 1957), 54; and his "Armée-État," *op. cit.*, p. 14.

45. Werner Gembruch, "Deutsches soldatentum in Leben der Nation seit der Jahrhundertwende," *Wehrwissenschaftliche Rundschau*, X (Sept., 1960), 470–2. See also, Hans von Seeckt, *Landesverteidigung* (Berlin, 1930), pp. 92–4; Wilhelm Ritter von Schramm, *Staatskunst und bewaffnete Macht* (Munich, 1957), pp. 114–5; John Wheeler-Bennett, *Nemesis of Power: The German Army in Politics, 1918–1945* (London, 1953), pp. 182–256; Ritter, *op. cit.*, pp. 118–31.

46. Maurice Barrès, *L'appel au soldat* (Paris, 1901), p. 540.

47. Pétain, p. 20; other important speeches by him are found in M. A. Pardee, *Le maréchal que j'ai connu* (Paris, 1952), pp. 103, 107–9, 113.

48. Wilfred Trotter, *Instincts of the Herd in Peace and War, 1916–1919* (London, 1953), pp. 179–81; Admiral Raoul Castex, *Théories stratégiques* (Paris, 1913–1933), IV, 515; Gen. Jean Valluy, "Le corps

des officiers devant la nation," *Revue militaire générale*, VI (Dec., 1958), 598; Perré, "Armée-État," *op. cit.*, p. 12.

49. Bertrand-Serret, *op. cit.*, pp. 64–8; Perré, "Armée-État," *op. cit.*, pp. 11–12; Girardet, pp. *op. cit.*, 213–35, 257–66.

50. See Weygand, "Constantes," *op. cit.*, p. 169; Raymond Aron, "On treason," *Confluences*, III (1954), 280–94; Roger Marlin, "A la recherche d'un État français," *Écrits de Paris*, No. 142 (Oct., 1956), 39–40.

51. Louis Franchet d'Esperey and Gabriel Hanotaux, *Histoire militaire et navale* (vol. 8 of *Histoire de la nation française*) (Paris, 1927), p. 444.

52. Von Seeckt, *op. cit.*, pp. 66–7; Weygand, preface to Gen. Max Hoffmann, *La guerre des occasions manqués* (Paris, 1927), p. 13.

53. Marshal Ferdinand Foch, *Principes de guerre* (Paris, 1903), pp. 286–8. See also, Weygand, *Historie*, p. 391; Perré, "Armée-État," *op. cit.*, p. 15; Cairns, *op. cit.*, pp. 283–4.

54. Weygand, *Mémoires*, I, 645.

55. Bourelly, *op. cit.*, p. 209.

56. Charles Maurras, article on "Armée," in his *Dictionnaire politique et critique* (Paris, 1932), I, 95, 99, 104–5.

57. Weygand, *Forces*, p. 163; and his "Constantes," *op. cit.*, p. 177. See similar opinions of Gen. François-Charles du Barail cited in Kuntz, *op. cit.*, p. 73; and Perré, "Officiers," *op. cit*, p. 32. Cf. Monteilhet, *op. cit.*, pp. 121–8.

58. Perré, "Armée-État," *op. cit.*, p. 9.

59. Gen. Jean Valluy, *Se défendre? contre qui? pour quoi? et comment?* (Paris, 1960), p. 140.

60. Psichari's opinions are cited in Girardet, *op. cit.*, p. 306; see also, Alerme, *op. cit.*, p. 103; and Bourelly, *op. cit.*, p. 219.

61. Kuntz, *op. cit.*, p. 128; de Vigny, *op. cit.*, p. 21.

62. Charles Maurras, *La seule France, chronique des jours d'épreuve* (Lyon, 1941), p. 23; Joseph Caillaux, *Mes mémoires* (Paris, 1942–7), III, 244.

63. Huntington, *op. cit.*, pp. 80–5.

64. Bourelly, *op. cit.*, p. 211; n.f.n. Calender, "Évolution de la condition militaire," *Revue de défense nationale*, XIV (Mar., 1958), 441–2.

65. André Malraux, preface to Gen. P. E. Jacquot, *Essai de stratégie occidentale* (Paris, 1953), p. ix.

66. Gerhard Ritter, "Das Problem des Militarismus in Deutschland," *Historische Zeitschrift*, CLXXVII (Feb., 1954), 39; Charles E. Merriam, "Security without Militarism" in Jerome Kerwin, ed., *Civil-Military Relationships in American Life* (Chicago, 1948), pp. 156–72; Mégret, *op. cit.*, p. 145: Meynaud, *op. cit.*, pp. 78–9.

67. Bourret, *op. cit.*, p. 132; testimony of Albert Sarraut (Feb. 10, 1948), *Commission . . . Témoignages*, III, 671; Paul Reynaud, *La France a sauvé l'Europe* (Paris, 1947), II, 438. Warnings concerning this state of affairs are found in Reynaud, *Le problème militaire français* (Paris, 1937), pp. 82, 88; and Alain's *Propos de politique* for Apr. 8, 1925, cited

in J. de Soto, "Pouvoir civil et pouvoir militaire," in Centre de sciences politiques de l'institut d'études juridiques de Nice, *La défense nationale* (Paris, 1958), p. 118. The principle of dilution of authority in the laws concerning civilian control over the military is discussed in *ibid.*, pp. 116–7. Weygand's opinions are found in his *France?*, p. 44; and his "Unité," *op. cit.*, p. 15. Similar ones are expressed by Gen. Louis Maurin, Minister of War in 1935–6, in his testimony (May 20, 1948), *Commission . . . Témoignages*, IV, 916–9.

68. Huntington, *op. cit.*, pp. 86–9. The legal limitations on military authority, contained in the Declaration of the Rights of Man, various constitutions to 1946 and Duguit's *Précis de droit constitutionnel*, are discussed in de Soto, *op. cit.*, pp. 120, 123–5. The rise in the military's prestige throughout the decade (so great, according to one account, that the Army was able to persuade *bien pensant* opinion to accept Daladier, the "murderer" of the sixth of February, as Premier in 1938), is indicated in Jacques Debu-Bridel, *L'agonie de la 3ᵉ république, 1929–1939* (Paris, 1948), pp. 436–8; Jacques Bainville, *La 3ᵉ république, avec un complément sur les années 1936–1940 par Jean Ratinaud* (Paris, 1960), p. 314; Girardet, *op. cit.*, pp. 316–8.

69. See Enclosure No. 2 in Doc. No. 428 (Nov. 14, 1933); and Doc. No. 415 (Apr. 30, 1934), in Great Britain, Foreign Office (E. L. Woodward and Rohan Butler, eds.) *Documents on British Foreign Policy 1919–1939* (London, 1946ff), ser. 2, VI, 53, 682; André Scherer, "Les mémoires du général Weygand," *Revue d'histoire de la 2ᵉ guerre mondiale*, IX (1959), 68; Georges Castellan, *Le réarmement clandestin du Reich, 1930–1935* (Paris, 1954), p. 522; Gamelin, *op. cit.*, II, 107; Gen. Maurice Duval, "Le général Weygand et le général Gamelin," *Journal des débats*, Jan. 21, 1935–6; André Tardieu, *Sur le pente* (Paris, 1935), p. 112.

70. Fabry, *op. cit.*, p. 389; Gen. Tony Albord, *Pourquoi cela est arrivé, ou les responsabilités d'une génération militaire* (Nantes, 1947), pp. 120–3; Reynaud, I, 419, 542–3; Bloch, p. 201; S. T. Possony, "Organised Intelligence: The Problem of the French General Staff," *Social Research*, VIII (May, 1941), 236; *Commission . . . Rapport*, I, 89; Charles de Gaulle, *Mémoires de guerre* (Paris, 1954–9), I, 4.

71. See Raymond Recouly, "Les leçons d'une crise," *Revue de France*, XVI (1936), 535–40; P. Dhers, "Du 7 mars à l'île de Yeu,'" *Revue d'histoire de la 2ᵉ guerre mondiale*, II (Jan., 1952), 18–21; and the conclusions of the Post-war Commission in *Commission . . . Rapport*, I, 82, 85, 89.

72. *Commission . . . Rapport*, I, 67; similar conclusions are found in Gen. André Zeller, "Armée et politique," *Revue de défense nationale*, XXIV (Apr., 1957), 505.

73. Trotter, *op. cit.*, pp. 179–81, 193–4, 205–8.

74. Gamelin, *op. cit.*, I, 370–1; II, xvii, 58, 75, 106–9; Reynaud, *op. cit.*, II, 434–5, 439; Léon Blum, *L'œuvre de Léon Blum* (Paris, 1955), I, 112; interview with Daladier on June 22, 1940 in M. Tony Révillon,

Mes carnets (juin-octobre 1940) (Paris, 1945), p. 72; Bourret, *op. cit.*, pp. 44, 131–2; Cot, *op. cit.*, pp. 266–7.

75. Eugen Weber, "The Right in France," *American Historical Review*, LXV (Apr., 1960), 562, 565–7; and his "New wine in old bottles: les familles spirituelles de la France," *French Historical Studies*, I (1959), 209–13; René Rémond, *La droite en France de 1815 à nos jours* (Paris, 1954), pp. 218–9; Girardet, pp. 122–3, 163, 202–13, 314–5; J. Vialatoux and J. Lacroix, "Le mythe Pétain," *Esprit*, XIX (Sept., 1951), 382; Pierre Drieu la Rochelle, *Chronique politique 1934–1942* (Paris, 1943), p. 25; Henry Bordeaux, *Weygand* (Paris, 1957), pp. 101, 135, 147.

76. Maurras, article on "Armée" in *Dictionnaire*, I, 104–5; Eugen Weber, *The Nationalist Revival in France* (Berkeley, 1959), pp. 153–4. See also, "Pertinax" (André Géraud), *Les fossoyeurs* (N.Y., 1944), I, 331; II, 11; Charles Odic, *Le Maréchal Défaite* (Paris, 1945), pp. 221–2.

77. Niessel, *op. cit.*, pp. 223–5; Debeney, *op. cit.*, p. 376; De Gaulle, "Prestige," *op. cit.*, p. 405.

78. Testimony of Georges Clemenceau (Feb. 13, 1898), in *L'affaire Dreyfus. Le procès Zola . . . Compte-rendu sténographique et documents annexes* (Paris, 1898), II, 418.

79. Testimony of Weygand (June 30, 1949), *Commission . . . Témoignages*, VI, 1927.

80. Charles Maurras, *L'enquête sur la monarchie* (Paris, 1924), p. 571; (the title of the chapter under consideration is "Le coup de force et l'opinion").

81. Gen. Marcel Boucherie, "Les causes politiques et morales d'un désastre: 1940," *Revue de défense nationale*, XIV (Mar., 1958), 415–6; Calender, *op. cit.*, pp. 438, 443; Mégret, *op. cit.*, p. 157; Gen. Jean Mordacq, *Politique et stratégie dans une démocratie* (Paris, 1912), p. 272.

82. Weygand, *Forces*, p. 163.

83. Weygand, "Exposé succinct des faits depuis l'arrivée du général Weygand jusqu'à la demande qu'il a adressée au Gouvernement pour la conclusion d'une armistice. . . ," in *Commission . . . Raport*, II, 412, (this is Weygand's deposition for the Cour suprême de justice sitting at Riom); his *Mémoires*, III, 213, 225–6; and his testimony (June 21, 1949), *Commission . . . Témoignages*, VI, 1854.

84. Duguit, *Précis de droit constitutionnel*, IV, 597, cited in de Soto, *op. cit.*, p. 124; Prosper Weil, "Armée et fonction publique," in *ibid.*, p. 200.

85. Gaetano Mosca, *The Ruling Class. (Elementi di scienza politica)* (N.Y., 1939), p. 229.

86. Weygand at the reception in his honor given by the Union des intellectuels indépendants on Jan. 19, 1957, cited in *Revue des deux mondes* (Feb. 1, 1957), p. 563.

87. Weygand, *Mémoires*, III, 86; Gen. Paul Ely, "Notre politique militaire," *Revue de défense nationale*, XXV (July, 1957), 1050–1; Zeller, *op. cit.*, p. 504.

88. Gembruch, *op. cit.*, pp. 68–70, 473.

89. Perré, "Armée-État," *op. cit.*, pp. 11, 17, 19. See Pétain's description of himself as the "incarnation" of the *Patrie* in a proclamation to the Army of Africa in 1942, cited in Noguères, *op. cit.*, p. 520.

90. Weygand's "program" is found in his *Mémoires*, III, 298–9; for the Légion, see *ibid.*, 306, and Xavier Vallat, *Le nez de Cléopatre. Souvenirs d'un homme de droite, 1918–1945* (Paris, 1957), pp. 196, 296.

91. France, Commission d'enquête chargée de rechercher les causes et les origines des événements du 6 février 1934 . . . . , *No. 3383. Rapport général . . . Annexes. (Procès-verbaux de la Commission)* (Paris, 1934), II, 2769.

92. Huntington, *op. cit.*, p. 93.

93. See Groussard, *op. cit.*, p. 62; Roy, *Métier*, p. 149; Valluy *op. cit.*, p. 597; Gen. Paul Ely, "L'Armée dans la nation," *Revue militaire d'information*, No. 297 (Aug.-Sept., 1958), 8; Col. Château-Jobert, "Les Centurions s'expliquent," *Rivarol*, No. 489 (May 26, 1960), p. 10.

94. Weygand in Centre d'etudes politiques et civiques *Hommage au général Weygand . . . à l'occasion de son 90ᵉ anniversaire* (Paris, 1957), p. 35.

95. Interview with Paratrooper Lieutenant G. in *L'Express*, No. 488 (Oct. 20, 1960), p. 10. See also, Girardet, "Pouvoir," *op. cit.*, pp. 8–15, 33; and a report on a lecture on conditional obedience delivered at the École interarmes in 1958 in Gen. Edmond Ruby, "Loyalisme et discipline," *Écrits de Paris*, No. 165 (Nov., 1958), 21–2.

96. Weygand, *Mémoires*, III, 223–8; Reynaud, *La France*, II, 337–47.

97. Col. Nemo, "La guerre dans le milieu social," *Revue de défense nationale*, XXII (May, 1956), 730; Cdt. Jacques Hogard, "L'armée française devant la guerre révolutionnaire," *ibid.*, XXIV (Jan., 1957), 83; Stagnaro, *op. cit.*, p. 52; Megret, *op. cit.*, pp. 154–6; Valluy, *op. cit.*, p. 212.

98. Valluy, "Corps," *op. cit.*, pp. 594, 605.

99. Col. Archard-James, "Possibilités et volonté." *Revue de défense nationale*, XXV (Nov., 1957), 1684–91; Claude Delmas, "Notes sur les fondements d'une doctrine de défense nationale," *ibid.*, XIV (June, 1958), 924; Claude Bessières, "Commandement et État-major," *ibid.*, XV (Feb., 1959), 257; Hogard, *op. cit.*, p. 225; Zeller, *op. cit.*, p. 515–7.

100. Ely, "Armée," *op. cit.*, p. 8; and his "Le Chef et l'évolution de la guerre," *Revue militaire d'information*, No. 284 (June, 1957), 13–18. See the entire issue of *ibid.*, No. 281 (Feb.-Mar., 1957) entitled "La guerre révolutionnaire." On "psychological action," see Jean Planchais, *Où en est l'armée?* (Paris, 1959), pp. 119–28; Valluy, pp. 233–6; Capt. F. Pophillat, "Pour une psychologie sociale dans l'armée," *Revue militaire d'information*, No. 293 (Apr., 1958), 72.

101. Col. Allemane, "La direction des forces armées et la conduite supérieure des opérations," in Centre de sciences politiques de l'Institut d'études juridigues de Nice, *La défense nationale* (Paris, 1958), pp. 505–7; also, Mégret and Weil, *ibid.*, pp. 150, 158, 163–80, 203.

102. Calender, *op. cit.*, p. 441; Germain Jousse, *Considérations sur l'armée de demain* (Paris, 1945), p. 68; XXX, "De l'indiscipline des chefs," *Écrits de Paris*, No. 150 (June, 1957), 22.

103. Marshal Jean de Lattre de Tassigny, "Essai d'adaptation de l'organisation militaire," *Revue de défense nationale*, IV (Apr., 1947), 440–1; Capt. Bernard Delègue, "Interpénétration des pouvoirs civils et militaires aux États-Unis," *ibid.*, IX (Nov., 1949), 425–6; Jean-Marie Domenach, "Réponses à l'enquête," and Jean Lacroix "L'armée et la politique," *Esprit*, XVII (May, 1950), 727, 752–3.

104. Gen. Lionel Chassin, "Du rôle historique de l'Armée," *Revue de défense nationale*, XXIII (Oct., 1956), 1199; also, Gen. André Zeller, "L'armée de terre liée à la nation," *ibid.*, XV (June, 1959), 966.

105. Chassin, *op. cit.*, p. 1199.

106. Quoted in *Rivarol*, No. 530 (Mar. 9, 1961), p. 9. On the theme of 1940, see Bertrand-Serret, "Armée-régime," *op. cit.*, 69; and Gen. Alfred Conquet,

"À propos de la thèse: nous pouvions vaincre en 1940," *Écrits de Paris*, No. 160 (May, 1958), 82–5. The classic presentation of the military case against the "politicians" is found in Gen. Henri Navarre, *Agonie de l'Indochine* (Paris, 1956), pp. 316, 319–22, 333–5.

107. Lucien Rebatet, "Feue l'Armée française," *Rivarol*, No. 524 (Jan. 26, 1961), p. 5. See also, XXXX, "L'armée française passé, présent, conditionnel," *Esprit*, XVIII (May, 1950), 770, 778, 780, 905, (this entire issue is devoted to the Army under the title "Le chemin sans retour: Armée française"); excerpts from articles cited in *Revue militaire d'information*, No. 283 (May, 1957), 102–3; Ely, "Armée," *op. cit.*, pp. 9–11; Marshal Alphonse Juin, *Mémoires* (Paris, 1956–60), II, 171, 211, 290–307, 366–7; letter to the Président du Counseil of the Comité d'action des associations nationales d'anciens combattants (Mar. 18, 1958), in *Caravane, revue des anciens de la 2ᵉ division blindée française*, No. 186 (Feb.-Mar., 1958), 7.

108. Thierry Maulnier, "Du 13 mai au 28 septembre," *Revue de défense nationale*, XIV (Nov., 1958), 1660.

109. *Ibid.*, p. 1660.

110. Ely, "Armée," *op. cit.*, p. 9. Also, Juin, II, 318, 323; René Bertrand-Serret, "L'armée et la politique," *Écrits de Paris*, No. 168 (Feb., 1959), 44, 52; letter of the President of the Association in *Caravane*, No. 189 (June, 1958), 2.

111. Proclamation to the Army of Dec. 2, 1851, in L. Cahen and A. Mathiez, *Les lois françaises de 1815 à 1914* (Paris, 1933), p. 120.

112. Admiral Ortuli, "Le général de Gaulle, soldat-écrivain-homme d'État," *Revue de défense nationale*, XV (Apr., 1959), 584. Also, Gen. Mirambeau, "L'esprit de Leclerc," *Caravane*, No. 189 (June, 1958), 5; Valluy, *op. cit.*, pp. 139, 141.

113. Weygand, *Forces*, pp. 154, 163; Weygand in Centre d'études, *Hommage à Weygand*, p. 36.

114. Weygand's and Juin's actions and public statements are noted in

Rivarol, No. 456 (Oct. 8, 1959), pp. 1–8; and No. 507 (Sept. 29, 1960), p. 3; *L'Express* (Oct. 29, 1959), p. 7, and (Nov. 5, 1959), p. 11; *New York Times* (Oct. 29, 1959), p. 4; Juin, *op. cit.*, II, 290–307, 336–7.

115. Weygand, "Des chefs?," *Revue de défense nationale*, XXIII (Dec., 1956), 1447–9; and his *Forces*, pp. 163–4.

116. Weygand, "Constantes," *op. cit.*, p. 183.

117. *Ibid.*, pp. 172, 178, 180, 184–8. See also, interviews with "Gen. X" and "Cdt. M." in Claude Dufresnoy, *Les officiers parlent* (Paris, 1961), pp. 191–7.

118. Weygand in Centre d'études, *Hommage à Weygand*, pp. 16, 32. Related ideas concerning the joint education of a military-civilian "élite" are found in François Gromier, "Une conception archaïque," *Les cahiers de la République*, V (Nov.-Dec., 1960), 27–30; Valluy, *op. cit.*, pp. 225–32; Mégret, *op. cit.*, pp. 176–81; Kuntz, *op cit.*, pp. 182–3.

119. See Weygand, "Constantes," *op. cit.*, pp. 180, 185; Girardet, *op. cit.*, pp. 295–6.

120. These difficulties are minimized in Thierry Maulnier, "L'armée, L'Algérie et la nation," *Revue de défense nationale*, XVI (Mar., 1960), 397; they are emphasized in G. Berger, "Hommes politiques et chefs militaires. Étude psycho-sociologique," in Centre de sciences politiques de l'Institut d'études juridiques de Nice, *La défense nationale* (Paris, 1958), p. 29; Ruby, *op. cit.*, p. 22; Meynaud, *op. cit.*, pp. 80, 85–6. On the Caesarean outlook, see especially Jean Lartéguy, *Les centurions* (Paris, 1960), pp. 258, 411.

121. Mégret, *op. cit.*, p. 182; also, Morris Janowitz, *The professional soldier, a social and political portrait* (Glencoe, Ill., 1960), pp. 435–40; Harold Lasswell, "The Garrison State," *American Journal of Sociology*, XLVI (1941), 455.

122. Gerhard Ritter, *Staatskunst und Kriegshandwerk. I: Die altpreussische Tradition* (1740–1890) (Munich, 1954), 23. Also Girardet, pp. 310, 323, 326; Janowitz, *op. cit.*, pp. 235–6; Mosca, *op. cit.*, pp. 229, 242, 468–9; Jules Roy, *La guerre d'Algérie* (Paris, 1960), pp. 135–9; 159–60, 170, 210–11.

123. The phrase describing the Army as the nation's "conscience" is from Jules Lemaître, *Opinions à répandre* (Paris, 1901), cited in Kuntz, *op. cit.*, p. 77. See also, Girardet, *op. cit.*, pp. 156, 162–5, 322; Cairns, *op. cit.*, pp. 274, 283–5.

124. Ely, "Armée," *op. cit.*, p. 11; Girardet, "Pouvoir," *op. cit.*, p. 15.

125. Weygand, "Constantes," *op. cit.*, pp. 187–8.

126. Juin in *L'Express*, Nov. 24, 1960, p. 8; and his *Mémoires*, II, 315–30, 336–7; see also, Michel Dacier, "L'armée et le nouveau système," *Écrits de Paris*, No. 171 (May, 1959), 8.

127. Valluy, *op. cit.*, pp. 144, 147. See also, declarations of Valluy, cited in *Rivarol*, No. 521 (Jan. 5, 1961), p. 11; of Gen. Salan, *ibid.*, No. 511 (Oct. 27, 1960), pp. 3, 11; of Gen. Augustin Guillaume, *ibid.*, No. 514 (Nov. 17, 1960), p. 3.

128. Julien Benda, *Esquisse d'une histoire des Français dans leur volonté d'être une nation* (Paris, 1932), pp. 195–6.

129. Urbain Gohier, *L'armée contre la nation* (Paris, 1899), p. v; see also his *L'armée nouvelle* (Paris, 1897), p. 66.

130. Gen. Théodore Iung, *La république et l'armée* (Paris, 1892), p. 357.

131. François Mauriac, "Bloc-notes," *L'Express*, No. 489 (Oct. 27, 1960), p. 44.

132. *** (Pierre Joly), *Contre-révolution. Stratégie et tactique* (Liége, 1957), pp. 60–2.

8. WAS THE VICHY REGIME FASCIST? A TENTATIVE APPROACH TO THE QUESTION

by Roger Bourderon

Translated by John F. Flinn

The military defeat of the French and their allies in the great battle of 1940 led to the occupation of France (completed just over two years later in 1942), armistices with Germany and Italy, and a fundamental change of regime at home. There is no more painful, bitter, and controversial episode in contemporary French history than the still far from fully known story of the ill-fated Etat fran-çais, *1940–1944, commonly called the Vichy regime. In the end it proved no more than an interruption in the history of the Republic. But it was by no means a mere freak of nature, accidental, rootless, the creature of Hitler's European empire. Or rather, it was all those things, while issuing directly out of the Third Republic and trans-mitting not a little of its elements to the Fourth and Fifth Republics that came after. Around Vichy for more than thirty years has hung an uneasy silence, broken almost incessantly by the small sound of small-scale scholarly contributions to its history, periodically by some storm of reawakened passions occasioned by an anniversary, an obituary, a film, even an important book emerging from the rela-tively obscure world of academia into the common light of day. All the same, it is the silence that has been most impressive. In the midst of a contemporary history quite extraordinarily revealed by the opening of public and private papers in many countries, the Vichy regime remains half-hidden still, an unwelcome ghost in the later twentieth century. Just what it was in all has been hard to say and no consensus is yet in sight.*

The author of this article places the Etat français *squarely in the overall European experience and seeks by the comparative method to define its characteristics. Roger Bourderon, Maître-assistant d'histoire contemporaine, Université Paul Valéry, Montpellier, has published numerous articles on the Vichy regime in general and on its various aspects in Languedoc and the Department of the Gard in particular. This paper first appeared in the* Revue d'histoire de la deuxième guerre mondiale *23, no. 91 (1973): 23–45. It is reprinted by kind permission of the author and of the editor and publisher of that periodical.*

The upheavals that the spread of fascism brought about in Europe between the two wars, followed by those that resulted from the onrush of the Nazi wave in the period between 1938 and 1942, profoundly changed the structure of most of the states of Europe and the conduct of international relations. They also caused a complicated overlapping of the elements of evolution, the internal ones (which may be encountered, at least in part, in each of those states) and the external ones (which were determined especially by the successes and then the reverses of the Axis powers, that is to say, essentially of Hitler's Germany). In particular, the creation of dependency upon Nazi Germany weighed heavily not only on the external policies of the states that accepted it or had it imposed upon them, but also on their internal policies. We may therefore wonder whether German domination was or was not an element in rendering uniform the attitudes of the governments of the subject countries. On the other hand, the generalized implantation of authoritarian and socially reactionary regimes, from the accession to power of fascism in Italy to the dictatorship of the Arrow Cross in Hungary in October 1944, before or after the beginning of the Second World War, with or without the intervention of the Nazis, leads us to look for affinities between those regimes and at the same time to define their specific characteristics.

Consequently, beyond the indispensable study of each country, utilization of the comparative method may permit a fruitful approach to the areas of convergence and to the specific characteristics of the various elements of the mosaic that Hitler's Europe seemingly constituted. Despite the criticisms that may be made of them, Ernst Nolte's works on fascism [1] demonstrate the interest of this method. In trying in this way to define the place of the Vichy regime, however, we make no secret of the difficulties, hazards, and limits of the undertaking. These are due at one and the same time to our incomplete knowledge about the different European states during the War—Vichy France included—the important differences, both in quantity and quality, among the available publications in such a vast field, the risks of systematizing points apparently common to national situations, which in other respects cannot be reduced to any system, the danger of the intrusion of ideologies into considerations on a subject in which polemics and the adoption of positions on emotional grounds can destroy the scientific attitude. We shall therefore not claim to present definitive conclusions; rather we hope to suggest some considerations for a comparative analysis of the *Etat français* and the different regimes in Hitler's Europe. We have deliberately left aside the problem of the "intimate convictions," which have given rise to so much controversy, of the men who in those regimes had the responsibilities of power, keeping to the more solid though sometimes shifting ground of the facts that enable us to characterize policies, public attitudes, ideologies.

In Europe under German domination, France, as we well know, was the only country whose relations had been defined by an armistice reached by the legal government. France was also the only defeated country that was not completely occupied, at least until November 1942, and in which consequently a sector with complete sovereignty (at least in theory) continued to exist for the government in office, alongside the occupied zone where the sovereignty of that government, though recognized in principle, was limited under the terms of the armistice agreement and the occupation. To this, naturally, was added authority over the territories of the French Empire. Hence in 1942 at the height of Hitler's power, France, which was officially out of the war, was in a different situation both from that of countries such as Denmark, whose government had placed its neutrality under the protection of Germany in April 1940 [2] and was completely occupied, and from allied countries such as Bulgaria or Rumania, where the presence of German troops on the whole of their territories took on the form of a regular occupation.[3] But it is proper to put Vichy France also in Hitler's Europe seen as a whole, in order to define the limits of its incontestably unique status.

In 1942 Europe was in fact a mosaic in which political statutes varied greatly: There were countries administered directly by Germany, occupied countries whose administration, while under the supreme control of Reichskommissars, nevertheless continued in large measure to be assured by officials who were natives of the country, new states whose creation depended exclusively on the will of the victor, intent on breaking up the Versailles system, and allied states in which German troops were—or were not—stationed, not to mention "nonbelligerent" Spain. France apparently had a privileged status, since alone among the defeated nations, and even when allies of Germany were occupied, she retained a fraction of her territory free of a German military presence. This "privilege" was, however, reduced, as we know, by the proliferation of armistice commissions that assured a German presence, often a far from discreet one, in the Southern Zone. Above all, the great diversity of treatment meted out to the European nations resulted from the Germans' desire not to impose the same yoke everywhere. It was through a deliberate calculation that Hitler, even before the armistice, announced his intention of doing everything to ensure that a legal government remained in France. We know that subsequently, on various occasions, he feared lest some striking action by this government or the head of state might come along to compromise his French policy.[4] For the Nazis the principal objective, if only for running the war, was to assure by the most appropriate means the maintenance of order and the administration in the different countries of Europe, so as to allow them to be exploited economically—to be pillaged—with the maximum efficiency. The future fate of those countries and racist ideology were probably reflected in the way they were treated at that time. But that treatment was determined in the first place by economic, political, and strategic imperatives, by the war's direction. As a result, the Hitlerians in many cases maintained a certain prudence in their relations with the vanquished or satellite countries, in order not to compromise the future. The existence of the Vichy government thus resulted exclusively from a political decision that had as its aim not to run into direct collision with the French and to bring them to participate, with the acquiescence of their legitimate authorities, in their own subjection. But one can measure by this to what an extent the dice were loaded from the very beginning, how relative was the independence of such a government, how purely formal was the variety in the political status of the countries in Hitler's Europe, a variety that depended in a way only on the opinion, a political one, that the Nazis formed of the difficulties and risks that too severe a treatment would give rise to, and in particular the resistances it would be liable to stir up.

By the simple fact of its existence every government in Hitler's Europe thus served in actual fact (whether unknowingly or knowingly is not the point) the Nazis' plans for its own country. From this viewpoint, invoking the "Polonization" of France to justify Pierre Laval's policy, as the defenders of the Vichy regime often do, does not seem convincing to us, because it implies passing over the capital fact of Hitler's political choice to keep a legitimate government in France after the defeat, if possible, and to exclude "Polonization" except as a means of blackmail. It is proper, besides, to compare the "moderation" with which Hitler treated France to different but comparable practices, such as the refusal to install National-Socialist movements in power automatically when they did not have a sufficiently strong base or did not offer all the desirable guarantees: Such was the case in Holland (Anton Mussert never succeeded in taking power there), Norway (Vidkun Quisling did not become the head of government until February 1942), and Rumania (in January 1941 Hitler supported General Antonescu's dictatorship against the attempt by the Iron Guard to seize complete power).[5] Without maintaining that German policy was constantly coherent, without overlooking the part of improvisation, without forgetting the role of the conflicts inside Nazism, the traces of which could easily be seen in the occupied countries, we can nevertheless say that the guideline in dealing with the political organization of occupied Europe was *to adapt* to the economic, social, political situation (as well as to the historical past) of each country, and to do so all the more as the economic or strategic interest of the country was great (France, Hungary, Rumania, Bulgaria are to our mind prime examples). This resulted in the relative diversity of Hitler's Europe. The ambassador and Reichskommissar in Hungary, Veesenmayer, summer up this guideline very well when in March 1944 he considered that the Hungarian army should not be disarmed because "it is more important to maintain order in Hungary and to make use of the country's forces until the very end than to create through dangerous measures a new and irreversible situation." [6]

On the other hand, the fundamental objectives of Nazi policy were identical everywhere, and the implementation of economic exploitation scarcely varied from one country to another. When the conference held on April 19, 1944, in the German Ministry of Foreign Affairs shows, in discussing the economic exploitation of Hungary, indifference to the risks of inflation in the long term and concern not to provoke galloping inflation in the short term,[7] we are struck by the way in which these preoccupations concorded exactly with those expressed about France.[8] Interference in the nation's economy, acquisition of interests in companies, control of the means of transport, setting-up of commissions to supervise agriculture and industry, seizure of control of external trade and so-called clearing agreements, demands for manpower were the common lot of the subject countries, defeated or allied. Even occupation expenses were borne, after being considerably overestimated, by the countries in which units of the *Wehrmacht* were stationed, even if the *Wehrmacht* was officially presented as being an allied force: For formerly neutral countries (with the exception, however, of Denmark), defeated enemies with or without a government, allies of the Reich, the treatment was the same. At that level Vichy France lost all originality and merged with the mass of nations subjected to the systematic application of the plans for pillage.[9]

That France's original status in Hitler's Europe could not confer on her any special advantages resulted moreover from the conditions of complete inequality under which Franco-German relations were carried on. A comparison of these relations with those that the Reich maintained at the same time with Bulgaria, Rumania, and Hungary is rather illuminating. The Nazis had at their disposal considerable means to put pressure upon all those countries. First of all, the Fascist parties or movements, which were completely at the disposal of the Germans, constituted a first-class means of stimulating the zeal of those governments or of encouraging their comprehension. In each country the Nazis thus disposed of political troops whose agitation was a permanent threat to the government and who could accede to power at the right moment. In France the *Parisian collaboration* played that role through its constant attempts to outdo the Vichy regime and its virulent verbal attacks upon it. In Rumania Hitler did indeed take Antonescu's side against the Iron Guard, but it and other movements always remained an army in reserve for the Nazis. In Hungary the Germans overthrew Admiral Horthy's regime in October 1944 and replaced it with the dictatorship of the Arrow Cross.

To this indirect but constant intervention by the roundabout way of pro-Nazi movements were added means of applying pressure according to the international situation of each country. Germany thus made use of the Balkan and Danubian countries' territorial claims by bringing into play, in turn or simultaneously, promises of territorial expansion or threats of dismemberment to speed up their acceptance of the *New Order* and their economic and military participation in it. In this way she reinforced her domination in a zone that was of capital importance for her economic and strategic interests. Thus in the question of Transylvania, for example, Hungary received a partial settlement only when the Germans consented to it, but not without receiving important economic and political guaran-

tees in return, whereas Bulgaria paid very dearly for the participation of her troops in the occupation of Yugoslavia and Greece.
Moreover, in this case we are dealing with countries whose governing groups were lured on by the revision of the "Versailles system":
From a certain point of view they had reason to think that they
would profit from it. German pressures on Rumania, which was very
much isolated diplomatically, were more brutal, and they led to the
acquiescence of the Rumanian government in the surrender of whole
territories: It is true that alignment on the antisoviet policy of the
Third Reich could give it the hope at least of recuperating Bes-
sarabia and Northern Bukovina. Those countries had in addition
some winning cards in discussions with the Nazis, since the Nazis
were also seeking something, were trying to obtain participation of
their own accord by Hungary, Bulgaria, and Rumania in the war
effort, and consequently the three countries retained a certain margin of maneuver. The Berlin government was fully aware of this:
For example, while very much hoping that Hungary would take part
in the war against the USSR, Germany did not ask her to declare
war in order to avoid having to negotiate concessions with Admiral
Horthy. The declaration of war was obtained through an act of
provocation planned by the Nazis. Let us also recall that, probably
in large part because the traditionally Russophile sentiments of the
population were well known, the Bulgarian government was able to
avoid engaging openly in the war against the USSR, while promis-
ing to join in the conflict at the "opportune" moment, which never
arrived. Even in the position of weakness where they found themselves, those countries therefore retained some possibilities of
maneuver. The results were slight: If they all discussed the German
requests, if they tried to negotiate, they obtained with difficulty only
limited—or illusory—concessions that did not prevent the Nazis
from profiting to the maximum from each of them. Even Bulgaria,
which remained outside the conflict, did not escape this rule.

Let us note in passing that those discussions were similar to the
ones that the Vichy authorities had with the Germans and that they
went off according to the same pattern: requests for a lightening of
occupation costs, attempts to negotiate prices and quantities of de-
liveries, etc., before falling into line essentially, if not on everything, with the Nazi demands, and passing legislation to that effect.
Clearly it is only by twisting language that the word *resistance* can
be used to describe the rearguard actions that Germany's allies conducted, just as Vichy did, dictated by the most elementary concern
to defend the interests of the groups directing the economy of each
country. Yet the situation of the Vichy government facing the Ger-

mans seems to us in many respects to have been more precarious even than that of the Danubian allies. Very rapidly, because they are well known,[10] we shall recall some of the considerable means of pressure that the Germans had at their disposal (the harshness of the armistice terms, made worse by the way they were applied, the fact that the Northern Zone was in reality outside the authority of the Vichy government, the possibility of transforming the demarcation line into a hermetically sealed frontier between the two zones, etc.). But we shall recall them only to underline the fact that the Germans were thus able to take measures whenever they wanted that had immediate repercussions on the life of the country, simply through the victor's *Diktat,* whereas the pressures—which, it is true, were considerable—that the Danubian allies were subjected to were part of a diplomatic game that was more classical, even if it was strongly affected by the brutality of the Nazi methods.

At the same time, in choosing through its policy of collaboration to situate itself within the framework of the *New Order* in Europe, in giving proof of good will toward the Germans, and indeed in offering its services, in cherishing the hope in so doing of obtaining preferential treatment after the final German victory, the Vichy regime deprived itself of the only possibilities it had of negotiating with some winning cards in its hand—the fleet and the empire. In addition, it put itself in the position of a seeker of favors. Now, and in our eyes this was an important difference between the relations between Germany and Vichy and those between Germany and Hungary or Bulgaria, on the level of general policy the Germans were not seeking anything from the Vichy regime. In particular they never envisaged seriously its entering the war on their side.[11] What we are saying is that the weakness inherent in any government that followed in the wake of the Third Reich, a weakness that was accentuated by the relationship between victor and vanquished resulting from the armistice, was increased still further by the complete distortion between Vichy's political options and the hopes that they gave rise to, on the one hand, and Hitler's plans for France, on the other. If the authoritarian regimes in Hungary, Bulgaria, and even Rumania could expect territorial aggrandizement in return for their political and military participation in the elaboration of the *New Order,* Vichy France, in a particularly weak position, had nothing to hope for from the participation she tried to bring about but which the German partner was not asking for and, still more, did not want.

The inequality in the relations between the Third Reich and the other states was not limited to international relations: If the occasion arose, Germany did not hesitate to intervene in their internal politics. It is possible to distinguish some general tendencies that show up in an examination of the Nazis' attitude in this area with respect to France and the Danubian states that were their allies.

Throughout the period of the Axis successes, at the time when their victory seemed assured or at least within reach, the Nazis left the governments of those countries a certain independence in the field of internal politics, within the framework of inequality that has been outlined. Apparently the Germans were not interested in the internal politics of each state as long as there was no danger of those politics hindering their economic or strategic interests. We know that the creation of the Vichy regime, on July 10, 1940, went ahead without any interference from them. If they showed some real agitation when Laval was dismissed in December 1940, they did not demand his return once they were reassured of Vichy's political intentions. No more were they responsible for his recall to office in April 1942. The institution of the *Révolution nationale* was carried out without any pressure from the Germans in favor of any particular measure. This state of affairs also prevailed at the same period in the Danubian states, whose internal legislation (in particular, repressive measures, and anti-Semitic measures when they existed) were not dictated by the Germans. Such independence, however, was only relative: Its limits can be perceived everywhere. On the one hand, it was certain that the Germans would not allow any decision that might be prejudicial to their interests (we know their reticence about the *Légion française des combattants* [a veterans' organization], which they were afraid of seeing become a hotbed of *revanchisme*). Independence within a country was conceived of, on the other hand, within the perspectives of the *New Order;* for their part, too, the regimes that subsisted were authoritarian ones, more or less openly Fascist or tending toward fascism, whether those dictatorships were already old ones such as that of Admiral Horthy, or quite recent ones such as that of Marshal Pétain. But above all direct intervention in the internal life of the states came very quickly. If Hungary seems to have been secure from these acts of interference—probably because of the proofs of its Fascist sympathies, which the Horthy regime had long furnished, both within and without the country—on the other hand, Bulgaria and Rumania, like Vichy France, were subjected to demands that were incompatible with their independence. Thus, for example, the most important governmental decisions in Bulgaria were taken in the presence of the German ambassador. Above all, the choice of the political personnel and senior high officials depended upon the consent of the Germans, who demanded and obtained the dismissal of those they judged undesirable. The harshest intervention during this period took place in Rumania, where the Nazis imposed the entry of the Iron Guard into the government, before supporting Antonescu against it some months later.

If an exception is made of the states that were created from nothing, such as Slovakia or Croatia, it was undoubtedly in Rumania that complete reduction to the status of a satellite on the political level was carried out the most quickly. But the process speeded up everywhere after the turning point of 1942–1943 through more and more overt interventions in the internal life of the states that still existed. This evolution was linked with the development of internal resistance within the countries, which undermined the authority of the governments in place, as well as with the inclinations or attempts on the part of those governments to disengage themselves.[12] From the summer of 1943 till the spring of 1944, German surveillance became tighter. Thus in Bulgaria, after the death of Boris III the ambassador, Beckerle, intervened directly in the formation of the council of regency and the government. In France, which after November 1942 was completely occupied, the arrival of the "counselor" to the Vichy government, Cecil von Renthe-Fink, led up to direct intervention by the Nazis in governmental changes and to the entry into the government of the Parisian collaboration. In the spring of 1944, along with accepting military occupation, Hungary had to agree to negotiate a change in the government with Ambassador Veesenmayer. These political changes were directed particularly toward emphasizing the struggle against the resistance movements, developing the machinery of repression for that purpose, and reinforcing links with the Reich to prevent any of these countries deserting the German side. They were not consented to spontaneously; Everywhere the governing groups tried to bargain, or to avoid a worsening of their state of dependence. At Vichy they gave in completely after Pétain's "strike" in November 1943, while Horthy for his part succeeded in reaching a compromise and in keeping out of his ministerial team formed in March 1944 certain of the Nazis' confidential agents. But could one still speak of independence? Hungary's case shows exactly how narrow was the remaining margin for maneuver: The Nazis accepted arrangements only if the policy followed was strictly in conformity in every way with their views. The application of this principle led quite naturally to the fall of Admiral Horthy in October 1944 and his replacement by the Arrow Cross dictatorship.

Beginning with different situations, at least on the formal level, for we have already noted the fundamental standardization of treatment in economic matters, it seems possible to conclude that there was some sort of standardization of treatment in the political status of the countries in Hitler's Europe: Reichskommissars, counselors, or ambassadors, at the end of 1943 and in any event by the spring of 1944, dictated the policy to be followed, whether there was a government or not. Though born of Hitler's desire to preserve a legitimate government in France, the Vichy government did not escape the continual worsening of its dependent state. In Hitler's Europe it appeared less free in its movements than Admiral Horthy's Hungary, closer to despoiled Rumania than to a Bulgaria that was able to avoid total engagement on the side of the Third Reich, weaker than those three states, whose political collaboration Hitler was seeking, and finally losing all originality, sunk in the general leveling imposed by the Nazis. But could it be otherwise? Every policy of collaboration, whatever its motives—which are not in question here—contained within it a process of satellization that was constantly pushed further and further, given the objectives and methods of Hitlerian imperialism. Only those who understood that fact or whose material or social interests did not bind them, even temporarily, to the victor, were able to disengage themselves in time; what is more, at any moment, refusal meant one's downfall. But the others were drawn into a veritable flight forward, causing their country to lose even the shadow of independence. From this particular point of view, if we limit ourselves to two essential aspects, and if we admit that such was their objective, the failure of those governments was all the more complete as finally they avoided nothing, either on the economic plane or in the matter of repression. This observation is as valid for Admiral Horthy's Hungary as for Marshal Pétain's France.

The governments that subsisted in Hitler's Europe were all authoritarian. Their existence, as we have seen, could not be other than dependent. Under these conditions, could the ruling groups fail to be favorable to the *New Order* (at least in its general lines) that the Nazis were setting up in Europe? Did governing not mean engaging in a process, more or less rapid, of turning a country Fascist? Certainly one must guard against the indiscriminate use of the term *Fascist*. But one must not hesitate either to use it when a sufficient accumulation of details justifies its use. Besides, the designation cannot be used in reference to a model that does not exist, since each country engendered its own form of fascism, but rather in recognition of a certain number of common characteristics that allow us to identify the phenomenon over and above national particularities. We shall now try to situate the Vichy regime among the dictatorial regimes of Hitler's Europe in order to define its nature and examine the problem of its insertion in European fascism.

A precaution of methodological nature must be observed before we characterize the *Révolution nationale*. The historian cannot trust the affirmations of originality, indeed of irreducible specificity, which its originators and then its defenders have often put forward, because such affirmations have been thrown about in all directions, from one country to another, by all the movements that are characterized by fascism. To the extent, in fact, that one of the essential ideological components of fascism is the glorification of radical nationalism, Fascist movements have been represented as plunging their roots deep into national traditions. But to limit ourselves to one example that deceived people for a long time, the touchy proclamations by José Antonio Primo de Rivera about the independence and the specific nature of the Falange did not prevent him, as Max Gallo has discovered, from being an agent in the pay of Fascist Italy.[13] Simply referring to the sources of the *Révolution nationale* does not seem sufficient to us either: The fact that beyond the ideas of Charles Maurras we find, along with ultraism, the French ideologues of the social doctrine of the Church (in particular René de La Tour du Pin), but also openly proclaimed borrowings from Proudhon's form of socialism, certainly enables us to show that the *Révolution nationale* took its ideological themes from certain currents in the nation's thinking, even to the point where, upon inspection, all originality disappears. One is tempted to conclude from this that it was therefore fundamentally very French. In reality this brings up one of the difficulties that we constantly experience in this kind of approach when we ask ourselves about Fascist ideology. In fact, even for Germany, where nevertheless the doctrinal radicalism, which was pushed to extremes, and the violence with which racism was asserted conferred an undeniable originality on Nazism, we discover that that originality becomes diluted and even disappears as analysis is brought to bear upon its national sources, where one finds absolutely everything that made up its doctrine. But can we be satisfied when we discover that *National-Socialism* is German, *Fascism* Italian, *National-Syndicalism* Spanish, the *Révolution nationale* French? Do we still not have to wonder about their remarkable simultaneity at least? We shall consequently endeavor to go outside the national framework in which the

Révolution nationale asserted itself and developed, and not let ourselves be caught up solely in the game of historical French references, in order to compare the *Révolution* with the other regimes
that were in place at the beginning of the 1940s. In so doing we shall
retain as a guiding principle the idea that in every country fascism
presented a specific aspect, style, and formulation that were due to
the country in which it had its roots and which sometimes even
made it, in appearances, very different from its neighbor. At the
same time we shall keep in mind the idea that the ideological
themes, the way in which power was exercised, the economic and
social objectives, support in society, were fundamentally the same
from one country to another despite some minor variants.

The propagandists of the *Révolution nationale* presented it to
the French from the beginning as an original experiment indeed,
profoundly French and therefore one that could not be applied
elsewhere. But we are struck by their concern to link it up with
what they considered to be the great events then occurring. The
publications that celebrated in 1941 and 1942 the merits of the new
regime and that were particularly abundant at the time of its first
anniversary—but that were at the same time hostile to the Parisian
collaboration—most often kept their distance from the German and
Italian regimes and pointed out the new regime's specifically
French character. At the same time they underlined the interest of the
German and Italian experiments and most often the relationship of
the *Révolution nationale* with them. Still more, they often took
pleasure in remarking that ideologically at least the French were in
many respects precursors. In *La France, la guerre et la paix* (Editions Lardanchet in 1942), Thierry Maulnier wrote: "We have been
the last in Europe to carry out our revolution, but our political
theorists, from Maurras to Sorel, have been the guiding lights
of contemporary revolutions" (p.98). The same idea is contained in
R. Valéry-Radot's book *Source d'une doctrine nationale* (Editions
Sequana, 1942): "This synthesis of the national and the social,
thanks to which Germany and Italy were going to save their states
from capitalism and Marxism, we shall find all its elements in the
dialectic of a Proudhon, a La Tour du Pin, a Georges Sorel, a Charles
Péguy. Péguy, Sorel: Mussolini always had them within reach
beside Nietzsche on his work desk" (p.18).[14] Had not the head of
the *Etat français* himself set the fashion at the very beginning of
the Vichy regime, in an article published by the *Revue des Deux
Mondes* of September 15, 1940, and in which he declared that when
France examined "the principles which have assured her adversaries'

victory . . . , she would be surprised to recognize throughout them her own works, her purest and most authentic tradition"? Thus the authors and propagandists of the *Révolution nationale* voluntarily situated themselves in the field of action of fascism and National-Socialism, all the while proclaiming their refusal to imitate them.[15] The works published since then on the *Action française* (whose great influence on Vichyism we know) and particularly those of Ernst Nolte, which show it to be an archetype of fascism,[16] allow us to maintain that those declarations were not stylized expressions arising from the circumstances of the period but the recognition of membership in the same family.

After all, the ideology of the *Révolution nationale*, stuffed as it was with references to France's past, to the point of leaving room for practically nothing else—except the universal Church—contained all the essential themes that we find in the Fascist, Nazi, National-Syndicalist ideologies. A rapid enumeration of those themes is conclusive: glorification of exclusive nationalism (summed up in Maurras's slogan *la seule France*) and of the country's world mission; anti-Marxism, anticapitalism and corporatism; hierarchical organization of the social body; individual rights and liberties defined by the duties to the state; enrollment of the individual in the family, local, professional, national communities; denunciation of democracy, glorification of the elites, cult of the leader, the authoritarian, social and national state; revolutionary phraseology (the entire operation bestowing upon itself, moreover, the title of *Révolution*) announcing the establishment of a *New Order*, although it was deeply anchored in the nation's past and traditions,[17] as a third way between socialism and capitalism and social difficulties which the myth of the class struggle could not resolve; the prevention of parasites on the body social from doing harm (this theme opening the way quite naturally to the kind of racism characterized by xenophobia and anti-Semitism). Taken separately, these themes are obviously not specifically Fascist. But encountering them all together in the same ideological current enables us to recognize definitely a variant of fascism and gives them a coherence as a whole that is in addition emphasized by constant reference to the national *mystique* to which each belonged: the appeal to the irrational that the *Révolution nationale* made abundant use of, as did fascism and National-Socialism.

Does this mean that the ideology of the *Révolution nationale* presents no originality, if we abstract its integration into the nation's past? Not exactly. It was distinguished first of all by a style that was generally rather moderate, often soothing, paternalistic, and that tried to be reassuring (although that was far from being an absolute rule) both in its writings and its propaganda rallies. For doctrine one naturally refers to Charles Maurras, but he is not alone, far from it. For rallies one thinks of Georges Lamirand's proclamations during the youth meetings, of which we have a striking example in the film *Le chagrin et la pitié*.

In addition, the *Révolution nationale* developed some themes of its own, of which we shall mention only the principal ones. Contrition in defeat, a sort of morose delectation aiming at public confession of France's many and varied sins and a necessary stage before addressing one's self to regeneration, which was possible only with a pure heart and a tranquil mind, was one of the predominant elements at the beginning of the Vichy regime. This element was displayed immoderately at that time, but became distinctly less noisy; indeed, it became simply an underlying one in the publications in 1941 and 1942. Moreover, if the glorification of small and medium-sized property, in the hands of the artisans and *paysans*, was found in all the Fascist ideologies, in the *Révolution nationale* it became the affirmation of a fundamental vocation of France and attained the dimensions of a myth with *le retour à la terre*. This glorification of craftsmen and *paysans*, moreover, modified the corporatist theses, which were most often developed with the invocation of a French Golden Age represented by the corporations before 1789. But this addiction to the past, which seemed to reveal the most antiquated traditionalist attitudes, did not prevent Vichy's form of corporatism from appearing as the only viable solution between capitalism and socialism. In that respect it was undeniably linked with the corporatism of the Fascists.[18]

Finally we come to the Catholic permeation, which was so great in Vichy and which so strongly affected the style as well as the themes of the *Révolution nationale*. But at this point it seems to us necessary to dispel an ambiguity nourished by the conflicts that arose between the Fascist states and the Church: the proclaimed adherence to Christian values was not in itself a sign of non-fascism. Without taking the extreme case of the Ustachi dictatorship in Croatia, one will recall that Spanish National-Syndicalism, while proclaiming its membership in the Fascist family, made its profession of the Catholic faith one of the essential axes of the ideology of the new Spain, that Fascist Italy claimed its dual heritage from ancient Rome and Catholic Rome, and that the Nazis themselves referred to a *constructive Christianity*.[19] Even though it plunged deep into the national counterrevolutionary tradition, to the extent of appearing to be simply a legacy from ultraism, and despite its recuperation of French socialism (which it initiated), the ideology of the *Révolution nationale* seems to us to be a variant of the Fascist one, because we find in it all the constituent parts of the ideology of Fascist movements recognized as such.

What do we learn from the way in which power and the means of governing were exercised? The process of setting up the *Etat français* was not limited to the classical operations that changes of regime had followed up till then, that is to say, in the main, remodeling of institutions, a purge of the administration, repressive measures against opponents. Vichy claimed that it was undertaking a complete reorganization of French society through the intervention of the new regime in all sectors of the country's life, all in the name of an all-embracing vision of society. In this single project to remodel institutions and customs, called a *Révolution nationale*, were included both organization of the economy and athletic education. There resulted a period of more or less brutal but always energetic implementation, concentrated into a relatively short period of time, since almost everything was set up within a few months. It was based upon the systematic intervention of the state, directly through the usual channels of government and its administration, indirectly thanks to the use of semi-official or government-influenced organisms.

This considerable extension of the legislating activity and of the State's presence, made possible by the total concentration of powers in the hands of the head of the *Etat français* following the *Actes constitutionnels* of July 11, 1940, had no precedent in France at that time. It shows Vichy's originality as compared with previous regimes or periods of political and social reaction. In fact, it seems to us that if the Vichy regime is related by its references, certain aspects of its style, indeed certain of its practices, to the Second Empire and especially to the *Ordre moral* of the early Third Republic, it is very clearly marked off from them by its intervention in all areas of public life, and even in many sectors of private life. It did not question, any more than had its predecessors, the social and economic foundations of French society, particularly the system of property-holding; but through the complete remodeling, institutionally, politically, ideologically, morally, socially, economically, that it undertook and that gave the *Révolution nationale* a totalitarian character, the Vichy regime instituted a *radicalization* of the tendencies, attitudes, and practices, openly expressed or latent, of the regimes or authoritarian periods that had preceded it. Finally, the work of *national reconciliation,* which befitted any attempt at an *"Ordre moral,"* took on new dimensions with Vichy, not so much through the presence in the corridors of power of former Socialists or trade unionists, who had belonged to the *"planisme"* or neo-Socialist tendency, as through the emphasis placed on the reconciliation of classes, which was pushed very far, the institution of the corporatist system, the taking-over of "French" socialism, the announcement that the *Ordre nouveau* would carry true socialism into effect, the use of the word *Révolution* to designate the whole undertaking. These characteristics and especially the last one, excluded only reference to the *Ordre moral,* to which the very term of revolution is in complete contradistinction. In declaring that it was founding a national and social state, Vichy was endeavoring to reinsert the popular classes of society, and particularly the working classes, into the body of the nation. National reconciliation was not only a moral imperative or a simple requirement born of the necessities of the hour: For the state it included recognition of its fundamentally social character, and for the regime, recognition of its truly revolutionary orientation. Consequently the order to be installed would be *new*—and not *moral;* this concern with appearing revolutionary was completely foreign to the attempts to restore the monarchy at the outset of the Third Republic.

Vichy cannot thus be confined to a simple return to past forms of government. Moreover, in the generalization of intervention in public—and private—life, which corresponded with a totalitarian concept of power and its exercise, in the radicalization of tendencies and practices of earlier authoritarian regimes, in the attempt to integrate the masses into a national and social state and to bring about a national revolution, we recognize some essential traits common to Fascist regimes.

The means used to establish the regime seem to us to confirm this observation. The few founding months were spent bringing into line organized bodies, public opinion, and individuals, and the methods employed make this period similar to the one that turned Italy Fascist—although that was notably more protracted—and to the *Gleichschaltung,* which was much more brutal, in Germany. We shall mention some of those methods in order to justify this comparison: It will be seen that they do not bear upon details of the government's action, but that on the contrary they concern its essential aspects. The systematic hammering-away at the French through a massive propaganda campaign, keeping in mind the means that existed (radio, cinema, posters, a many-sided iconography, spectacular meetings), the efforts to implant Vichyite ideas even in the most remote parts of the country regions by developing a network as tightly knit as possible of local correspondents, militant members of the Marshal's *Service de propagande*, reveal a desire to seize control very rapidly of public opinion, to eradicate from it the aftereffects of the *ancien régime*, as it was then called, and to proceed with its standardization on the basis of the objectives of the *Révolution nationale*. This was an undertaking of a totalitarian nature, which was accompanied by attempts to enroll certain categories of the French population indirectly through official or semiofficial organisms such as the *Légion française des combattants* or the *Compagnons de France*.[20] Enrollment, but also surveillance.[21] The most zealous of the members of the *Légion*, like the activists of the *Service de propagande*, whose role was very important, brought the good and the bad among the French population to the attention of the authorities, asked for sanctions against those persons who were "nostalgic for the *ancien régime*," urged that municipal councils be purged, sought to assume positions of responsibility. Thus, despite the absence of a single party, a form of political surveillance different from the classic model created by police services developed. It was the work of militants, whose enlistment in the *Révolution nationale* led them to accept base police work, when they did not themselves take the initiative. Here we are clearly dealing with one of the roles assigned to Fascist parties after the seizure of power; the absence of a unified movement at Vichy did not prevent the fact from existing, unquestionably facilitated by the origins of the personnel put in positions of responsibility in the new organisms of the *Révolution nationale*, who in fact most often belonged before the war to political formations on the extreme right, tending toward fascism, or Fascist: above all the *Action française* and the *Parti social français*. In the absence of a mass party before the coming to power, then for want of a single party, the *Révolution nationale* took root in the political sphere on the spot as it were, thanks to a few zealous members of the *Légion* and the members of the *Service de propagande*. This is an extremely interesting detail, which situates the *Etat français* between the single-party regimes, Fascist, Nazi, Falangist, and those that assumed more classical authoritarian forms, such as in Hungary or Bulgaria. Those militants, propagandists, and informers, ready to fill the prisons, place Vichy clearly in the Fascist camp. They substituted themselves for the official authorities, who in their eyes were sometimes too much concerned with observing legalities. Thus they would be the first to become the "gangsters" of the regime when new efforts to create structures would lead them to the *Service d'ordre Légionnaire* and then to the *Milice*. Thus we see an original form of Fascist activism develop, without a mass party but present as soon as a militant showed up. And he, without too much self-searching, if indeed he did not ask to be allowed to do so of his own accord, would go from using the pen and the spoken word to handling the submachine gun and the blackjack.

The other measures for establishing a system of controls over the country and bringing it into line are likewise ascribable to methods and objectives that were different from those of the authoritarian regimes that had previously appeared in France within the framework of the bourgeois society. Indeed those regimes no longer questioned the representative system of parliamentary government or even universal suffrage, but were prepared to manipulate them.[22] Vichy, on the contrary, initiated a thorough examination of universal suffrage and the representative parliamentary system, envisaged for some later date a reorganization of the elective system on new principles, and at the time distributed from above all forms of authority, at all levels, by investing *Chefs* with office; in short, it took up the criticisms and applied the recommendations formulated in France in the prewar period by the Fascist or Fascist-inclined movements and abroad by all Fascist-type parties. The dissolution of political parties, trade unions, local councils that were considered undesirable even if they had pledged allegiance to the new regime, the abolition of the councils at the levels of the department and *arrondissement*, the prorogation sine die of the parliamentary *Chambres* and then the abolition of their permanent secretariats, a purge of the civil service bodies, preliminary measures for setting up an authoritarian hierarchical system to replace the representative system, a considerable extension of the prefects' powers, laws on October 12, 1940, concerning the administrative commissions for the departments, on November 16 concerning municipal delegates, on January 24, 1941, creating the *Conseil national*: After a year in power the *Etat français* had reached the point where Mussolini's state was around 1930 in destroying the previous political system —whether that system had been liberal or authoritarian in applying its laws—and in constructing a new system.[23] It had gone further than the Horthy regime, which kept political parties (even the Social-Democratic party) along with parliament until the ministerial change that accompanied the German occupation in March 1944; or than Boris III's Bulgaria where, despite the abolition of political parties in 1934, parliament was maintained, while representatives of the opposition could still be elected, since in July 1941 the election of nine of them was annulled.[24]

The concept and practice of justice and the police also derived in very large part from fascism. Certainly the Vichy regime did not treat indiscriminately as criminals, as did the Nazis, the different categories of offenders (common law, political, associal, racial).[25] From the beginning, however, by recognizing as an offense the fact of belonging to certain groups, which struck whole categories of Frenchmen according to discriminatory criteria based on political, ideological, or racial grounds, the Vichy regime excluded from the national community *pariahs*—to use Henri Michel's expression. These were forbidden under civil law to exercise certain professions by virtue of their origin; they fell foul of laws or decrees that had been created expressly against them; and at the same time they were delivered up to public obloquy by propaganda that accused them of being responsible for all of society's ills: a process of simplification and mystification that the neighboring dictatorships practiced without exception. At the same time the creation of the first exceptional courts and the multiplication of police tasks and services added to the arsenal of repressive weapons that were not special to fascism. The appearance, with Colonel Groussard's *groupes de protection*, of parallel police forces, however, gave the *Révolution nationale* its first militia, still in the embryonic stage, short-lived since it had to be dispersed after Laval was dismissed, but revealing of the profound tendencies of the regime. In other respects the setting in motion in the autumn of 1940 of vast police operations to hunt down Communists, the great roundups of which the victims were the Spanish Republicans who had taken refuge in the departments of the regions of Aquitaine and Languedoc; likewise in the autumn of 1940, the systematic application of the procedures providing for forced residence and detention while awaiting trial, and especially the generalized use against undesirables of administrative internment, which was ordered independently and sometimes in defiance of court decisions by authority of the prefects, who could thus order imprisonment in France or deportation to Algeria but also set at liberty as they thought proper, without going through the normal channels of the courts—all these things were the sure signs of the process of making the state machinery Fascist. This state aimed at providing itself with the means of eliminating unyielding, hence irrecoverable opponents, getting rid of undesirables—*parasites*—who were represented as such for ideological reasons, and creating in its nationals a permanent feeling of insecurity apt to prevent open opposition or even simple murmurings of discontent.

With undeniable ideological particularities, without a single party and thus without a party militia, but with its activists and its *groupes de protection*, the Vichy regime at its beginnings seems to us to show numerous essential traits of fascism, as much by its ideology as by its means of governing, despite the fog of deliberately moderate language and the reassuring image conferred by an old man who looked more like the father of a country than a Fascist leader. We are deliberately leaving aside the problem of future institutions, the examination of the way the government worked, the phenomenon of bureaucratic proliferation that resulted from the multiplication of controls of every sort. Those various aspects would allow us to make fruitful comparisons that are impossible in the limited space of this article. The process of converting to fascism that was subsequently observed and that kept on increasing until the creation of the *Milice* and the use of open terrorist violence against opponents who were more and more numerous seem to us therefore to result, not from the *Révolution nationale* going off course, but from the development of its fundamental tendencies and dispositions in keeping with its internal dynamism, with the gradual loss of its base in the mass of the population, with the development of the Resistance, with German pressure.

Thus far we have kept to the political shape of the regime and the ideology that it expressed. An examination of its economic and social initiatives and its supports in society should enable us to situate it better. The installation of a corporatist system was the key piece in the socioeconomic achievements of the *Révolution nationale*. The Vichy brand of corporatism had several facets. We must put aside the *corporation paysanne*: Keeping certain democratic forms in it was all the less a problem since before the war the people in view played an important role in the organizations of the peasantry; moreover, it was intended to encourage the attachment of the peasants to a regime that in its propaganda held country life in esteem and celebrated the virtues of the soil. On the other hand, the anticapitalist and antisocialist declarations, accompanied by praise of small property, industrial and commercial handicrafts, were suited to keeping the middle classes in the regime's orbit. The corporatist reorganization of industry appeared destined essentially to liquidate the working-class movement, to remove all class consciousness from the proletariat, to strengthen the employers' powers. The dissolution of the trade unions and the suppression of the right to strike broke up the structures and the means of action that the working-class movement had acquired for itself. The proclamation of the association of capital and labor, the affirmation of class collaboration in the national and social state played the role of a substitute ideology, which the measures on this account were to make credible (in particular, the joint social committees), while in other ways official concern for the most unfortunate demonstrated the attention of the public authorities to social problems and promoted the realization of national unanimity.[26] But the *Charte du Travail* provided explicitly for the integration of trade unionism into the state (Article 1) and attributed no role for making demands to the professional trade unions (Article 14). On the other hand, the untouchable nature of the employers' conduct of business was clearly stated. Class collaboration stopped well short of the threshold of property.[27] Thus, with special ways and means (separate and obligatory professional trade unions by categories, joint social committees) the Vichy regime realized a corporatist system that in its theoretical justification, its organizational principles, its social significance, differed in no way from the corporatism of the Fascist states; a comparison of the different labor codes or the main explanatory publications allows us to verify this profound degree of convergence, even with Nazi corporatism.

Vichy likewise proceeded from fascism in the pursuit, attested by the preferred axes of its economic and social propaganda, of a mass base in the middle classes and the peasantry—with quite particular insistence on the latter. The reality of power was, however, elsewhere; the denunciation of the great economic and capitalistic *féodalités* went hand in hand with the setting-up of the *comités d'organisation*, run by the representatives of the country's most important economic interests. Should we see in this apparent contradiction the proof of divergent tendencies in Vichy's ruling group? We see in it rather another aspect of Fascist power, whose economic policy consolidated the largest private interests and developed concentration of businesses, while at the same time its propaganda vigorously denounced capitalism and the misdeeds of its cosmopolitan and monopolistic tendencies. But at that level the convergence seems to us to have been still more fundamental. In the Fascist countries the state's economic intervention did not mean either a removal of the economy from the private sector or even a "bringing into line" of the industrialists. State intervention consisted rather of uniting the strength of the great private industrial interests with that of the state, enabling it to confront the new conditions born of the development of capitalist concentration as concerns the economic conjuncture. But at no time was private initiative questioned;

it remained the mainspring of the economic system, and in the middle of the war in Germany it remained largely secure from totalitarian initiatives—not only that, it was also able to develop under the protection of those initiatives.[28] Was not the *Etat français* a comparable adaptation, whose origin lay in the general causes listed above, the deep uneasiness that the social crisis in 1936 had created in the milieus running the economy, and the consequences of the defeat (particularly on the plan of economic relations with Germany)? In fact we note the presence in the government and the ministerial staff of men who had come directly from the most important business circles—a new phenomenon. We note the organization of professions by sectors of activity in the *comités d'organisation* under the guidance of the most important industrial groups—a tendency that was also found in Germany and Italy— and also the state's intervention on behalf of those same great interests to organize the professions, control economic activities, regulate production, while at the same time continuing to recognize the absolute authority and freedom of initiative of business leaders, without any measure ever being taken that might have risked doing any real damage to the capitalists' interests. All those things dispose us to emit the hypothesis that the *Etat français* was closer to the Italian Fascist and the Nazi states, where were to be found the same predominant groupings and that osmosis between the business circles and the machinery of state, than it was to Franco's state and the dictatorships of Danubian Europe, whose structures seem more traditional to us.

To conclude very briefly, we shall recall the *final phase* of the different regimes in Hitler's Europe. It presents interesting analogies among the different countries. In all of occupied Europe the presence and the demands of the Hitlerians became more and more oppressive. Everywhere racial persecution became worse, and repression against the rising forces of opposition and resistance was speeded up. The process of turning states Fascist became more pronounced. It was particularly characterized by the excessive expansion of the state police machinery, which is borne out by the generalized use of auxiliary forces. In Bulgaria, for example, the creation at the beginning of 1944 of special police forces, one military, the other civil, corresponded to that of the *Milice* of the *Etat français*.

Against this background the evolution of the different regimes remaining did not follow an absolutely straight line. Certainly the process of satellization went on inexorably. But at the same time, as the victory of the coalition against Hitler appeared inevitable and internal tensions, the forces of opposition, even armed resistance increased, the ruling groups, sometimes governments themselves, sought the means to save themselves as best they could and explored the possibilities of getting out, either by overtures to the Western Allies or by approaches, more or less seriously pursued, to opposition circles of a more or less broad political spectrum. These transactions were aimed at saving from the debacle individuals who were compromised in the German *New Order* and assuring the survival of the existing social system, though concessions dictated by circumstances might have to be made.

These approaches were a general phenomenon, and the example was set by the upper circles of fascism with the series of contacts that were made as early as the summer of 1942 with the British by former ruling circles in Italy and a certain number of highly placed Fascist dignitaries, and then with the conspiracy that was to lead to Mussolini's fall in July 1943 and bring about, initially, a very limited transformation of the regime. In the Danubian states the same external contacts were made, and in Hungary they assumed such great importance that they brought about the fall of Miklos Kallay's government and the German occupation in March 1944. Inside those states efforts sometimes went very far to reach a compromise with the opposition, including the coalitions of the *National Front* kind under Communist impulsion. The Regent Horthy took the initiative of such contacts himself in August 1944, shortly before his fall. On September 2 of that year the Bulgarian regents offered the Communists a place—unsuccessfully—at the time of the formation of the Mouraviev government. In Rumania things obviously happened outside the legitimate government of Antonescu, yet the king's entourage negotiated with all the forces of the opposition, including the Patriotic Front, and reached an agreement with them as early as June 1944, which facilitated Antonescu's fall in August.

In those countries, then, the situation was relatively clear: the ruling groups had been an integral part of the regime up till the very end. If, faced with the change in relationships of internal and external forces, they were brought to seek a compromise, they could still present themselves, even though scheming outside the government, as holding the reins and the destiny of a state in their hands over against an opposition that might be powerful, have solid bases in the country (not always the case), and hope to take or share power, but that meanwhile could only make capital out of its very existence—which, it is true, was the deciding factor. Elsewhere, for the social groups running countries whose governments were in exile, the situation was likewise fairly simple: They identified themselves as being part of those governments, which thereby retained an undeniable legitimacy even when abroad. The fact that it was necessary to come to terms with other social and political forces, and even to give in to them, often in dramatic circumstances, did not change those previously established basic principles.

On the other hand, before June 6, 1944, the Vichy government's room for maneuver was extremely narrow, narrower than that, already limited, of the Danubian states. Indeed, within the country its authority was more and more reduced; entire areas were practically beyond its control. Its social foundations were collapsing; even the ruling groups that had supported it, if indeed they had not created it—individuals and social collectivities—were abandoning it, as the departure for Algiers of many of its officials attested. The truth is that while it had long been able to present itself as the legitimate government of the country, which it had actually been, the Vichy regime had seen a new form of legitimacy gradually develop in opposition to it, one that had sprung out of the Resistance and that took in all its constituent parts. This new form of legitimacy had had at its disposal since June 1943 a veritable government, the *Comité français de libération nationale*, a genuine area of sovereignty of which North Africa was the center, and since February 1944 even an armed force in France, the *Forces françaises de l'intérieur*. Under those conditions what could the people who remained in Vichy try to negotiate? The fact that they nevertheless tried to do so, like others at the same time, came from their hopes of stirring up fear of communism in order to try to avoid de Gaulle and rapidly cultivate the seeds of division within the Resistance. The last attempts made by Laval during the Liberation to win over Edouard Herriot, and by Admiral Auphan in Pétain's name, were prompted by the hope of achieving this second purpose. The discussions held in Vichy in November 1943 between the head of state's entourage and some Third Republic parliamentarians, contacts that went hand in hand with preparations for possibly dismissing Laval a second time, clearly revealed the first hope, which was even more unrealistic. If the draft constitution of January 1944 (where the principles of the *Révolution nationale* were in turn rejected for a representative system resurrected from the ashes of the Third Republic) was obviously inapplicable, it appears to us as a supplementary aspect of Vichy's attempts, while showing a certain willingness to compromise, to achieve a rapprochement, if not with a part of the Resistance, at least with a certain number of important people who were taking a wait-and-see attitude. But evidently these ventures remained very limited, fewer than those attempted by the ruling groups in the Danubian states, even by those most deeply compromised with the Nazis. The rulers in Vichy could make practically no serious attempt to save the regime. After being the only legitimate government in a defeated country, it had become the weakest and most completely abandoned of Germany's satellite states.

The Vichy regime's destiny was thus linked from beginning to end with the political decisions and the fate of the Nazi armies. In Hitler's Europe the margin of independence of the *Etat français* was sometimes less than that of the Danubian states; moreover, it had deprived itself of the trump cards that it might have used in its relations with the victor, relations that in any event were unequal. But in view of the nature of the state and its conditions of existence, how could things be otherwise?

Does this mean that Vichy was only a phantom state? We do not think so. The *Etat français* seems to us to have been fundamentally an attempt, under cover of Hitler's victory and within the framework of the *Révolution nationale*, to consolidate the dominant position of the largest private interests—an objective that in fact had been achieved in Italy and Germany thanks to fascism. To achieve that, the liquidation of most of the institutions inherited from classical liberalism went hand in hand with the establishment of a totalitarian system that through its social foundations, its aims and means, seems to us to constitute a particular form of Fascist state, with deeply rooted structures comparable to a remarkable degree with those in Germany and Italy.[29] For that reason, and even though its international situation reduced it to the rank of a dependent state under close surveillance, the *Etat français* was not simply a transmission belt for implementing the victor's wishes. On the other hand, did not the pursuit of more and more complete integration into the European *New Order*, under the best conditions possible for the social groups running the regime, form part of the initial premises? With that perspective, keeping in mind the starting point, that is to say the defeat, was it possible to envisage bringing pressure to bear on the victor? Did not the policy of collaboration derive directly from the nature of the Vichy government? In other words, in Hitler's Europe, was it possible for the *Etat français* to be different from what it was?

Notes

1. Ernst Nolte, *Three Faces of Fascism: Action Française, Italian Fascism, National Socialism* (New York, 1966), *Die Krise des liberalen Systems und die faschistischen Bewegungen* (München, 1968).

2. Henri Michel, *The Second World War* (New York, 1975), I: 74.

3. Cf. particularly the special numbers of the *Revue d'Histoire de la Deuxième Guerre Mondiale* (hereafter cited as *R.d'H.D.G.M.*) devoted to Hungary (#62), Rumania (#70), Bulgaria (#72), and Balkan problems (#74).

4. Cf. among others, Eberhard Jäckel, *La France dans l'Europe de Hitler* (Paris, 1968).

5. Cf. for the Danubian states the numbers already mentioned of the *R.d'H.D.G.M.*, and #66 for Holland and Norway.

6. G. Ranki, "L'Occupation de la Hongrie par les Allemands," *R.d'H.D.G.M.*, #62, p. 40.

7. Ibid., p. 36 et seq.

8. Cf. particularly P. Arnoult, *Les Finances de la France et l'occupation allemande (1940–1944)* (Paris, 1951).

9. For these questions, cf. especially Arnoult, op. cit.; Henri Michel, *Vichy année 40* (Paris, 1966); the numbers of the *R.d'H.D.G.M.* mentioned above.

10. Robert Aron, *Histoire de Vichy* (Paris, 1954); Michel, *Vichy année 40;* Michel, "La Révolution nationale, latitude d'action du gouvernement de Vichy," *R.d'H.D.G.M.*, #81, p. 3.

11. Cf. particularly Jäckel, op. cit., and Michel's restatement, *Pétain, Laval, Darlan, trois politiques* (Paris, 1972).

12. Cf. below, pp. 222-3.

13. Max Gallo, *Histoire de l'Espagne franquiste* (Paris, 1969), p. 53.

14. One could multiply examples. Among the most important: Jean Thouvenin, *Un An d'histoire de France* (Paris, 1941) and a fat collection of articles, *France 1941, la Révolution nationale constructive, un bilan et un programme* (Paris, 1941).

15. Some years earlier, the Spanish Falangists had proceeded in a way that was no different. José Antonio Primo de Rivera said of the Falange: "It coincides with fascism on essential points of universal value, but with each day it accentuates still more its own characteristics and is sure to find its most fruitful possibilities along this path" (note published in the Spanish press, December 19, 1934, quoted by D. Teissonnier, *J. A. Primo de Rivera ou le national-syndicalisme espagnol*, mémoire de maitrise, Faculté des Lettres de Montpellier, 1969).

16. Nolte, *Three Faces of Fascism*, pp. 29–141.

17. Hence the glorification of monarchical France, as were glorified Spain of the Golden Age, medieval and barbarian Germany, and ancient Rome.

18. This relationship is still clearer if one refers to its concrete propositions and achievements.

19. Point 24 of the Nazi Party Program.

20. Certainly there was no unification of youth movements; but we may recall that this was likewise true during the initial phase of establishing fascism in Italy and Germany. Semi-official movements, however, were encouraged: *Jeunes du maréchal, Jeunesse de France et d'outre-mer,*

Compagnons de France. In the Gard, for example, these movements had a very important place in the press, where they were frequently glorified, as well as in the propaganda services, at least until the middle of 1941. They appeared in that department as the true children of the *Révolution nationale.*

21. The following reflections are suggested by our research on the *Révolution nationale* in the department of the Gard, and more especially by the ongoing scrutiny of archives, of private provenance, of the *Service de propagande,* the *Service d'ordre légionnaire,* and the *Milice,* whose interest far exceeds this limited geographical area.

22. One of Louis-Napoléon Bonaparte's first acts after the December 2, 1851, coup d'état was to restore universal suffrage.

23. Cf., inter alia, Serge Bernstein and Pierre Milza, *L'Italie fasciste* (Paris, 1970), p. 205 et seq.

24. On Hungary: G. Ranki, "L'Occupation de la Hongrie par les Allemands," *R.d'H.D.G.M.,* #62, p. 39. On Bulgaria: E. Kamenov, "La Politique intérieure," *R.d'H.D.G.M.,* #72, p. 27.

25. With the development of opposition and Resistance, resistants and common law criminals would be placed in the same category. But while the Nazis based their amalgamation of the two on principle (every diversity, every opposition of any sort, political or not, implied a diminution of the national community and was therefore a crime), the Vichyites took their stand on the formal resemblance between certain acts of resistance and offenses under the common law.

26. Cf. the role of the *Secours national,* whose campaigns began with a great flood of advertising in which the public authorities and the prefectures had an important place.

27. Article 24 of the *Charte du Travail* specified that the attributions of the joint social committees *excluded any interference with the control and management of the business.*

28. The memoirs of Albert Speer cast light on the privileged relationships of big industry with the Third Reich, the large degree of autonomy left to it, the penetration of state machinery by technicians from the great industrial enterprises (cf. particularly chapter 15). On these points Speer confirms Charles Bettelheim's earlier study, *'L'Economie allemande sous le nazisme* (Paris, 1970). For Italy, see Bernstein and Milza, op. cit., who summarize very suggestively the mechanism for state intervention on behalf of the capitalist system (chapter 13, p. 256 et seq.).

29. René Rémond rightly stresses the pretechnocratic character that can be detected in the *Etat français* (*La Droite en France,* 2d ed. [Paris, 1963], p. 242). This remark seems to apply fully to the Nazi and Italian Fascist states.

9. TECHNOCRATS AND PUBLIC ECONOMIC POLICY: FROM THE THIRD TO THE FOURTH REPUBLIC

by Richard F. Kuisel

When the illusions and conflicts of the 1920s, 1930s, and 1940s had been set aside, as they had to be if the nation was to make its way again, move on, and adapt to the postwar world, it was clear that the France of Déroulède now had an antedeluvian air to it. There were legacies, of course, since the past is never wholly exorcised, but new forces were at work to regenerate a nation on which the troubles of the century had rained down scarcely less cruelly than on other European peoples. If there was a short, dispirited passage from the Liberation, 1944–1945, into the early 1950s, soon it was evident that France—which had so often concluded that its historic moment had passed, that it could not keep pace, that it had repeatedly sacrificed itself for the sake of others (as was so often and so unhealthily said for more than a generation)—was once more on the rise. The era of demographic decline had come to an end. Industrial and agricultural indicators were up. What was loosely referred to as modernization had set in. Social patterns were changing, a kind of siege mentality was disappearing. There were limits to all this, but an optimism had taken hold. And observers who had so lately subscribed to gloomy forecasts on what lay ahead for the French suddenly discovered that the changes becoming evident around them had their origin further back than they had guessed. Most particularly, the technocratic elite, present but scarcely given free rein in the Third Republic, unleashed in the illiberal Vichy regime, and given ever widening authority in the Fourth and Fifth Republics, was singled out for its signal role in getting France back into the world as a dynamic, if no longer great, power.

*Richard Kuisel suggests in this article how all this came about.
Associate Professor of History, State University of New York,
Stony Brook, he is the author of* Ernest Mercier: French Technocrat
*(Berkeley, 1967) and of various scholarly articles on the French
economy in the twentieth century. This paper was first published in
the* Journal of European Economic History *2 (1973): 53–99. It is
reprinted here in a shortened version by kind permission of the
author and the editor of that periodical.*

With the coming of the "New French Revolution", that is, the
enormous social and economic changes since the Second World War,
came a new issue for the student of modern France. Like the origins
of 1789 this latest French Revolution promises to attract a good deal
of scholarly attention. It is my contention that one answer to the
question of how and why "dynamic France" overcame "static
France" is that there was a change in elite behavior and popular
attitudes. Stanley Hoffmann originally suggested this line of inquiry with his provocative analysis of the breakdown of what he
called the "stalemate society".[1] Between 1934 and 1944, according
to Hoffmann, events like depression, defeat, and occupation over-
turned a consensus which had curbed both strong government and
rapid industrialization under the Third Republic. Out of the war
came a new scale of national priorities, with full industrialization
high on the list, and a widespread commitment to the interventionist
state.

My aim is to describe the dramatic change in the outlook and
behavior of the public officials who directed the state's industrial
policy under the Third and Fourth Republics. These *hauts fonctionnaires*, my main protagonists, were converted to technocracy,
penetrated the centers of public decision-making, and turned the
state into an instrument for rapid industrialization. The modernizers
began their ascent during the First World War, but arrived in power
only at the end of the Second World War. Even then the battle to
create their vision of France was barely joined; yet from that time
on their positions in the state were secure and their opponents were
on the defensive. There are gaps in such a long and complex story
and causes are often obscure. Here I wish only to clarify the
character, scope, timing, and general causes of this development.
The rise of the technocrats appears as a long-term, evolutionary, yet
discontinuous process.

Under the Third Republic public policy was what the French

called economic liberalism. The non-interventionist state, the free market, and individual entrepreneurship were all ideals. Indeed the state had little influence on private economic behavior given the minuscule public sector and its restrained use of fiscal and monetary controls. Yet in practice the state intervened. Its actions were normally to protect the status quo, however, and rarely, if ever, to promote industrialization or economic expansion. The state restrained rapid economic change, especially industrialization, because it would have harmed established interests, like a backward or timid branch of industry, or a powerful social stratum, like the farm vote. Legislation defended independent shopkeepers against the inroads of aggressive chain retailers; the tax structure helped small firms survive; interventions sheltered, subsidized, and salvaged hard pressed sectors; and high tariffs protected domestic producers against foreign competition. Private interests came to the state to request protection for their *situations acquises,* but assistance was only welcome when sought. Thus economic planning, by or through the state, or even collecting statistical information about industry was considered unwanted interference. With the state's toleration, private industry became heavily cartelized, curtailed competition, shared markets, and even sheltered smaller, less efficient, firms. Restriction and protection were essential to the functioning of French liberalism.

The official view of public finance held simply that expenditures and receipts should balance. . . . There was little notion of public finance as a means of social and economic action—except in a protectionist sense: thus taxes were for revenue, not for re-distributing income. The state consumed but never produced wealth: it was *un trou* that swallowed what Frenchmen created.

The wisdom of a balanced economy was enshrined as the semi-official ideology of the republic, and was supported by a broad consensus. This consensus held that God (or Nature, depending on your politics) had endowed France with the perfect mix of agriculture and industry, farm and city. Frenchmen saw no need to rush headlong after industrialization: they feared (among other things) the unrest and destruction of traditional virtue it might bring.

The liberal state was supported and perpetuated by a congruent educational system, where liberal economics was the ruling orthodoxy. The principal antechambers to high government service (especially the *grands corps* like the Inspection des Finances and the state engineers) were the elite educational institutions: the Ecole Libre des Sciences Politiques, the Ecole Polytechnique, and the law faculties. Clément Colson taught the course in political economy at the Ecole Libre for almost three decades, and his economics text was widely used elsewhere. In it he zealously defended the liberal faith in individual initiative and the free market as the best means of producing wealth. State intervention (*étatisme*) was to be avoided whenever possible because it killed private enterprise and usually served to protect special interests at the expense of taxpayers and consumers. . . . Jacques Rueff and Charles Rist, Colson's successors at the Ecole Libre in the 1930's, continued to teach the liberal orthodoxy. At the Faculté de Droit in Paris, another school for aspiring *hauts fonctionnaires*, the uncompromising liberals Gaston Jèze and Auguste Deschamps lectured on public finance and political economy during the interwar years.

Once entered upon their careers, the students of these men acted much as their professors would have wished. The Conseil d'Etat, for example, consistently obstructed the development of municipal socialism, curbing all efforts by local governments to operate public utilities. But the key corps in the economic administration was the Inspection des Finances, which dominated the Ministry of Finance and rigorously adhered to the liberal orthodoxy. It was drawn almost exclusively from the Parisian *grande bourgeoisie*, whose formality and traditionalism reflected its intense conservatism. Throughout the interwar period the Ministry of Finance guarded the treasury and the franc against the spending urges of other ministries, reputedly even infiltrating them with its inspectors for this purpose. Critics complained that the state was a "business run by the cashier".

Indeed, the Ministry of Finance was the most powerful of those whose primary task was the management of the economy. . . . Since the Minister of Finance himself, like other ministers, was often a transient at the ministry, real power accumulated with the semi-permanent heads of *directions* (the ministry's principal subdivisions), such as the Treasury or the Budget. There were, of course, other sources of public economic authority. There were the so-called "technical ministries", of which the most relevant to our subject was the Ministry of Commerce and Industry. The precedence of commerce over industry in the title is significant, for this ministry confined itself mostly to the promotion of exports and tariffs, while its responsibilities for the domestic economy were few and routine. And like other technical ministries, the Ministry of Commerce acted more as a representative of its constituency (in this case, of business interests) than as an agent of state control. Parliament, too, especially through the Finance Committe of the lower house, exercised some supervision over economic policy by virtue of its control over the annual budget. However, the committee itself was too politically divided to take charge of public policy. This multiplicity of decision-making centers meant that it was virtually impossible for the state to pursue a harmonious policy. Its inconsistencies were aggravated by the short duration of governments' tenure. Nevertheless there were a few sufficiently powerful institutions, working within the liberal ideological tradition, to determine the overall character of economic policy. Of these a word more about the finance inspectorate is in order.

Originally the inspectorate's primary duty had been the verification of public accounts, but it had come to assume responsibility for the management of the public sector of the economy. From 1890 on it formed the backbone of the ministry's principal *directions,* monopolized the major public financial institutions, represented France in international economic organizations, and helped to formulate most important economic and financial legislation. The ubiquitous inspectors regularly participated in political life as members of ministers' personal cabinets. They were admired for their expertise, esprit de corps, and honest dedication to public service. Finally many inspectors resigned from public administration to make second careers in influential positions at the major private banks and the most enterprising industrial firms. In short, this elite corps of roughly 250 inspectors had a centralizing, cohesive effect on French administration through its participation in numerous important sectors, public and private.

The First World War was an interruption in the prevailing style of private-public relations that anticipated the future. It is well-known that state intervention in economic life grew enormously between 1914 and 1918, with the institution of rationing, price and monetary controls, and even direct management of enterprises essential to the war effort. A less well-known aspect of the state's mobilization program is the long-range effect of the precedents it set upon the relationship of the public to the private sector of the economy, upon the course of industrial modernization, and upon the careers of future technocrats. The state's eagerness to raise the output of war manufacturers led it to introduce technological innovation and to standardize production methods and products. . . . To co-ordinate mobilization schemes, the republic sponsored new agencies, some of which were inter-Allied in character. Among the most significant were the consortiums, or associations of manufacturers and distributors who joined together under official supervision in order to purchase and allocate raw materials. These consortiums institutionalized cooperation among businessmen and consultation with the state. . . .

What might be called the first generation of technocrats made their debut in government service with the proliferation of such wartime offices. These men and their successors are the principal protagonists in this account of the transformation of the French state and economy. Some, such as André Tardieu and Pierre Mendès-France, were parliamentarians; there were a few private individuals who tried to shape government policy or entered public service temporarily; but the majority were *hauts fonctionnaires,* top-level career administrators who directed the major economic organs of the state. Of these, Jean Bichelonne, François Bloch-Lainé, Michel Debré, and Jean Monnet were the most commanding figures.

The term "technocracy" is a recent American import and carries a mildly derogatory meaning in French. The French *technocrate* thus usually repudiates this attribution and the stereotype that accompanies it.[2] But technocracy as an intellectual tradition in France dates back over a century to the Comte de Saint-Simon. As a doctrine technocracy has as its fundamental aim the creation of material abundance through the appropriate management and development of economic, especially industrial, resources. It further usually prefers rule, economic and even political, by an elite of experts. While technocracy is often regarded as a right-wing doctrine because of its elitism, its emphasis on production rather than distribution, and its interest in rationalizing rather than overturning capitalism, it has also displayed a strong socialist thrust. One can see this in Saint-Simon's own belief that the needs of "the poorest and most numerous" would be served by the improvement of human productivity through industry, science, technology, and central planning. Thus technocrats of the Left have looked to distributing the new abundance and to curbing, if not supplanting, the prerogatives of private enterprise.

In the 20th century French technocrats of both the Right and the Left have conceived of "modernization" as a single path forward: France must follow the lead of the "advanced" countries like the United States and Germany toward a future whose content is predetermined. Thus the planners who gained ascendancy after 1945 believed that imitation was the means for France to catch up and become "un pays moderne". They have further assumed that the process of modernization would carry them, as an expert elite, forward to positions of economic control. As forecasters of French modernization the technocrats were farsighted. The "rural exodus" could not be stopped; thus the balanced economy collapsed of its own weight. And the economic reawakening of France after the Second World War was almost inevitable: it occurred throughout Western Europe. Yet it was not so evident that the technocrats would head the modernization process, and not so certain that *dirigisme*, meaning state and expert control, would succeed. In fact these were features unique to France among the major countries of Western Europe during the 1950's. Neither the British, the West Germans, nor the Italians followed the French in their reliance upon state powers and officials, national planning, and public and private managers working in unison to accelerate and shape economic growth.[3] The technocrats' success in France was by no means inevitable, but was rather the result of certain contingencies, namely: the strength of the Saint-Simonian tradition itself; the intrusion of two wars and an occupation which stimulated *dirigisme*; the failure of business and government, especially in the 1930's, to make the economy perform satisfactorily; and the political adaptability of the technocrats.

Despite the persistent influence of Saint-Simonian thought upon their economic goals, modern technocrats were anything but doctrinaire in their choice of tactics: they could embrace both *dirigisme* and the free market as means to higher ends. In general they endorsed state action when private forces seemed unequal to the task—as was precisely the case with the task of mobilization during the First World War. . . .

The heavy public debt and ruinous inflation of the 1920's only intensified the republic's phobia about imbalanced budgets and distracted it further from the problem of industrial development. The staggering costs of the war absorbed public revenues that might otherwise have been employed in capital investment. But privately sponsored efforts at reform flourished, spurred by prospects of prosperity, by American and German competition, and by the perplexing inability of the politicians to meet postwar financial problems. For some the hallowed economic virtues of stability and balance began to fade before the attractions of affluence.

By far the most formidable effort launched by the capitalist neo-Saint-Simonians was that of Ernest Mercier. This naval engineer turned manager, . . . an admirer of America, recruited like-minded businessmen from the dynamic industries. Their well-financed pressure group, the Redressement Français, reached its peak of influence in 1926–27. Its program of national overhaul stressed the adoption of American methods of mass production, industrial concentration and research, and the elimination of marginal producers. State intervention was considered a danger, yet Mercier's group believed the republic could be managed more efficiently by freeing government from party politics and giving experts, especially *hauts fonctionnaires*, a greater say in determining policy. Despite a few successes, the Redressement was unable to persuade parliament, labor, or even the business community. . . .

The special needs of a war-torn country were more crucial than the efforts of the neo-Saint-Simonians in the state's rare decisions to intervene during this period. . . . Heavy expenditure for industrial renewal did result in considerable improvement in plant size and equipment. Reconstruction of the so-called Liberated Regions, however, was considered an emergency operation, and state direction terminated when the task was completed. . . . A few "mixed companies"—"mixed" because they combined public and private ownership and management—were established to undertake special large-scale tasks, like developing the Rhone valley, where private capital was reluctant to venture. Some of these enterprises . . . struggled along and eventually contributed greatly to industrial development; yet there was pressure on the state from liberals in business, academic, and political circles to abandon almost all its industrial and commercial functions.

At the same time, the Left was not satisfied with any halfway station toward public control. The trade union federation (Confédération Générale du Travail or CGT) produced its own scheme for the outright nationalization of key industries. In 1925 the CGT also inspired the establishment of the Conseil National Economique (CNE). Labor, capital, and the consuming public were represented on the council. Its aims were to study pressing economic and social questions, to recommend projects to the government, and to advise parliament on pending legislation. But parliament was suspicious of this potential rival, this quasi-parliamentary body based on interest group representation. Neither parliaments nor governments sought the council's advice, and the council itself was timid in offering it. Employers' associations were simply hostile. . . . The CNE had a stormy history. It barely survived subsequent right-wing governments. Revived for a moment by the Popular Front in 1936, it succumbed to the Vichy regime. . . .

The technocratic schemes and movements of the 1920's reached a characteristic climax with André Tardieu's government at the end of the decade. Tardieu, like so many others who had worked on wartime mobilization and especially those who had had contact with the Allies, had been awakened to the inferior capacity and incoherence of French industry. His inflexible attitude toward Germany, his intimacy with Clemenceau, his ties with big business, his arrogance and ambition, and his contempt for political parties had won him the distrust of the Left. As champion of the technocrats, e.g., the Redressement Français, Tardieu hoped to promote the mystique of economic growth, expedite the schemes of his expert advisers, and replace "lobbying" with official consultation between interest groups and the state. He was a right-wing deputy who appeared in a number of postwar governments usually as head of a technical ministry like Public Works. Then in 1929 he formed his own government composed largely of young parliamentarians from the Center and Right. The new premier announced that he would spend five billion francs from the treasury surplus to launch a five-year program of "national retooling" (*outillage national*), in which the government would commit itself to assisting the French in achieving a prosperity equal to America's. . . . Approximately equal amounts were to be spent on: public works, public welfare, and agriculture. The economic infrastructure would be renovated by improving the electrical and transportation networks. New health and educational facilities would be provided, with special emphasis on the improvement of rural communities. It is to be noted that Tardieu remained committed to a balanced budget and his program showed no clear preference for industrial development, as Monnet's would later. Yet Tardieu and his ministers did openly and firmly proclaim the obsolescence of economic liberalism. . . . Tardieu's bold "plan for national equipment", which broke with the liberal style of the republic, was never implemented: the political maneuvering he so despised blocked it. . . .

The depression would shelve all prospects of economic expansion. It would shift concern from industrial concentration, standardization and budgetary surpluses to falling exports, uncompetitive prices, unemployment, and budgetary deficits. The Third Republic responded initially with a reaffirmation of liberalism, sometimes tinged with "Malthusianism".[4] Yet the enormity of the collapse prodded many to search for alternatives. In the ferment of the 1930's the consensus supporting the immobile state disintegrated and the transition to *dirigisme* began. Impersonal economic forces thus intruded and in the long run served the technocrats' cause.

The republic's conduct of economic affairs between 1931 and 1935 was pathetic. French governments imitated neither the massive interventionism of Nazi Germany, nor the vigorous pragmatism of the American New Deal: their behavior was closer to the British "muddling through", but with less success. . . . At first the authorities tried to restore economic vigor through such traditional expedients as extending protection against imports, subsidizing hard pressed agricultural commodities and dampening industrial competition. The reflex response to growing deficits in the public budget was to compress expenses; the alternative of raising aggregate demand through deficit spending or tax relief was not seriously considered. While Great Britain and other nations benefited from devaluations in the early 1930's, France refused to modify the exchange rate in order to bring domestic prices in line with world prices. . . . Eventually, in 1935, the republic attempted full-scale deflation in order to bring prices down: the state set an example with a ten percent cut in all prices and wages under its control. Such ill advised action probably only aggravated the depression by discouraging investment and further contracting demand.

The advice from organized business and the "economics establishment" supported the government's orthodox response. . . . The basic liberal prescription for depression was to wait for the natural purge of unhealthy producers, to reduce state expenditures, and to deflate prices and wages while guarding the franc. Intervention would only aggravate a passing disequilibrium and turn it into a catastrophe. In its Malthusian variation, the prescription included direct government action, but only that which aimed at driving down production to meet reduced demand or reducing productivity to raise the employment rate. The state's few interventions of the 1930's corresponded in fact to these negative aims. . . .

Despite reaffirmations of liberalism, dissent spread in French society at large.[5] . . . Corporativism was a popular alternative among right-wing theorists. While the schemes of different groups and individuals varied, they agreed that the best way to avoid the anarchy of economic liberalism was to give natural economic groupings (for instance, associations of employers and employees within the same branch of industry), called "corporations", the legal authority to regulate themselves. Although the technocratic planning movement has sometimes been assimilated to corporativism, in fact their only point of contact was the desire (in common with all anti-liberals) for the ordering of economic life. Where the technocrats identified themselves with economic growth, spurred by technology, foreign trade, and state initiative, the corporativists were Malthusians and decentralizers who relied on semiautonomous corporations to reduce the state's economic responsibilities. Although corporativism had a wide and diffuse audience, that included some of the pseudo-fascist leagues, it failed to establish any institutional roots or win any elite or social stratum which could sustain it.

The Left preferred nationalization and state planning. These poli-cies were hailed as means to alleviate the depression and ameliorate capitalist exploitation, but again were rarely seen as instruments of expansion. Nationalization (or some form of public ownership and control of key sectors of the economy) had at least nominal support from many left-wing institutions, including the CGT, the Catholic trade unions, the Socialist party, and in a halfhearted way, the Radical party. Planning was more controversial. In 1934–35 the CGT added the idea of a planning agency to their program for liquidating the crisis and ending unemployment. CGT leaders tried in vain to induce the Socialist party to endorse planning; their efforts were seconded by an earnest minority of young planners within the party. . . . But Léon Blum and other Socialist leaders objected to planning in theory: with the Communists, they believed that it would fail within a capitalist system, and at the same time they worried lest it inadvertently help preserve capitalism. For most of the Left, moreover, the idea of planning implied a threat to freedom and a step toward fascism. . . . In 1935–36 when the three major left-wing parties formed the Popular Front electoral coalition, they agreed to exclude planning from their official platform.

Various non-political groups and unaligned individuals joined in dissent from prevailing economic policies. A spate of new reviews with titles like *L'Ordre nouveau, Esprit, Réaction,* and *Plans* ap-peared in the early 1930's. Here young intellectuals . . . expressed anti-establishment and anti-capitalist views, based on moral outrage. Laissez-faire capitalism stood condemned as wasteful, exploitative, divisive, and above all, conducive to selfish materialism. These youthful dissenters hoped to "place the economy in the service of man", some through planning or corporativism, some by a dose of technocratic expertise, some through a new labor code, and still others through a European federation. . . .

We have only been able to sample here the wide range of theoreti-cal non-conformism in the 1930's. The first actual departure from orthodox practice in this period occurred in 1936–37 under Léon Blum's Popular Front government. It was a crucial break, from which there was to be no complete return. The economic policies of the Popular Front are well-known: in summary, they represented a cautious movement to the Left. The public sector expanded slightly;

this expansion proved to be permanent. Less successful . . . were the Popular Front's attempts to improve the position of the working classes and to alleviate the depression. The Popular Front ended deflation and presided over a substantial boost in wages in order to "increase purchasing power", though deficit spending was not attempted. The long overdue devaluation also came, but without any exchange controls and only because it was forced on Blum. The function of overall coordination of the state's economic activities was assigned to the new Ministry of National Economy, headed by the Socialist Charles Spinasse and staffed with his technocratic friends. . . . But resistance from the other ministries, especially its arch rival on the Rue de Rivoli, prevented Spinasse's ministry from ever establishing its authority. In the end the mandate of the Popular Front expired before much of its program was ever implemented.

The Daladier governments of 1938–39 called their economic program the "last experiment in liberalism", as in some ways it was. They made serious efforts to balance the budget by increasing taxes and compressing expenses. They also reversed some Popular Front measures, such as the forty-hour week, which they rightly viewed as an obstacle to greater industrial output. For Daladier and his Minister of Finance, Paul Reynaud, were decidedly more production oriented, more expansionist than their predecessors before 1935, and they left much less to the automatic functioning of the market. Reynaud, for example, announced that "the state is responsible for the general orientation of the economy".[6] His staff included a liberal like Rueff but also rising technocrats like Michel Debré, Alfred Sauvy, and Claude Gruson. The government issued hundreds of economic decree laws and at one point entertained hopes of launching a ten-year development plan which in some ways resembled Tardieu's. . . . Another devaluation, massive spending on rearmament, and the general trend toward economic mobilization, especially after Munich, demonstrated that the old liberal era was over.

Legislation adopted in 1938 defined the vast powers of a wartime government and established the legal basis for the emerging *économie dirigée*. With the coming of war in 1939 a powerful Ministry of Armaments was created and endowed with virtual control over French production. As in the First World War, technocrats were summoned to staff it. Raoul Dautry, formerly head of the state railways, became minister and surrounded himself with young technocrats recruited largely from the elite engineering corps. After 1940 Dautry's ministry was easily transformed into Vichy's mighty Ministry of Industrial Production and many of Dautry's appointees, like Jean Bichelonne . . . were to stay on.

In retrospect the technocrats had failed to turn their cause into a mass movement or win political allies between the wars. In the 1920's business, labor, and the political parties repudiated the neo-Saint-Simonians. And neither the Right nor the Left was willing to rally behind Tardieu. During the 1930's the Right plunged into corporativism while the leaders of the major left-wing political parties were at best unenthusiastic about planning. Unable to attract wide support, the technocrats remained a small movement, poorly organized (at the level of study groups), and restricted largely to the administrative and business elites. Rejection also tended to nourish their conception of themselves as above parliaments and politics. Yet the technocrats had made some headway: they had formed cadres, gained experience in government service, added agencies and precedents, and profited from the growing dissatisfaction with liberal ways. The next turn of the historical kaleidoscope—the fall of France—offered them a chance to form a partnership with the traditional Right.

The unexpected collapse of the Third Republic in 1940 provided an opportunity for many of the political "outsiders" of the 1930's. Among the diverse factions that rallied to Marshal Pétain were the technocrats. Pétain wanted to bar the old guard of business, labor, and parliament from his National Revolution and preferred to let experts take charge of economic affairs. Thus he appointed young civil servants and business managers to positions like the Minister of Finance and they in turn co-opted others. Eager to use the state's authority for economic renovation, the technocrats installed an *économie dirigée* which surpassed that of the First World War.

At Vichy a grand Ministry of Industrial Production, a technocratic creation based partly on *directions* seized from other ministries, partly on new agencies, assumed far-reaching powers to regulate all phases of manufacture and marketing. The new ministry had authority to distribute scarce resources and to compel the standardization of production techniques. Its novel structure permitted close scrutiny of each branch of industry. The quiet revolution in the collection of economic statistics, begun in 1937, also advanced. During 1941–42 the ministry designed a ten-year plan for overhauling the nation's capital equipment. The technocrats, . . . including the formidable Jean Bichelonne, headed the ministry and staffed it with state engineers. This ministry and its personnel survived the war and the liberation almost intact to become "one of the chief governmental tools of expansion".[7]

But the creation of Comités d'Organisation (CO's) was the armistice regime's most ambitious attempt to reform industry. Its long-term aim was to organize employers and thereby enlist their participation in an *économie dirigée*. The CO's would help meet the wartime shortages and promote industrial recovery, protecting the French plant from usurpation by the German occupiers. Ultimately, they were to transmit a modernizing impulse. Each branch of industry came under a CO's authority, directed and financed by employers, but supervised by the Ministry of Industrial Production. The CO experience brought civil servants and employers together as never before: they became veritable industrial planners. At least in the more modern sector, especially in war-related industries where German and Vichy interests coincided, they effected mergers, raised productivity, and improved technology.

The CO's, however, were unable to prevent an absolute decline in industrial production. Shortages and restrictions hampered them and opposition harassed them. Nevertheless, during the liberation the Left was so impressed with their effectiveness that it preserved the CO's for another two years. . . .

Under Admiral Darlan's government of 1941, the technocrats extended their influence into political and diplomatic affairs. They did not accept Nazism as a political model, but they did admire Germany's industrial plant and its organization.[8] To their minds, France had either to overhaul her economy in order to become worthy of partnership with Hitler, or else she would suffer his domination. Meanwhile the technocrats' growing power, their clannishness, and their aggressive approach to modernization aroused a storm of opposition. . . . Pétain himself was distressed by their ambitions and policies; preferring to sustain small enterprises rather than big business, he joined the critics.

The technocrats resisted, but after Darlan's fall in 1942 they began to withdraw. Some were disenchanted with Vichy and collaboration or decided they could not fulfill their hopes at that time. Of the major figures only Bichelonne remained with Pétain till the end. Except for a few ministers and those who had engaged in high level negotiations with the Germans, the technocrats avoided the stain of collaboration. Most had worked quietly on economic and administrative reform, kept clear of politics, or departed before Vichy's credit was gone. In the end the technocrats at Vichy were denied their triumph by the war, and by the forces of conservatism, reaction, and fascism. But as of 1944 these forces were on the run. The technocrats emerged unscathed and politically unattached—free for the Left to adopt their program as a means of improving the lot of the working man. The technocrats in turn, frustrated with the Right, would accept the Left's support, yet insist on their autonomy and their political neutrality—a posture recommended by the lessons of the past twenty-five years. Thus they would entrench themselves safely in unexposed positions within the administration.

This opportunity was provided by the resistance organizations and reaffirmed during the liberation, when the forces for change which had been building momentum for over twenty years finally broke through. The aim of the resistance in economic matters was, in general terms, to provide a rational order to the economy: an *économie dirigée* (though not of Vichy's authoritarian stripe) must replace the wasteful and anarchic liberal order. Each major resistance group articulated its own program, yet it is possible to distinguish this as the overall direction. The Gaullists established several commissions charged with concerting efforts: newcomers joined early advocates of planning to study postwar problems. Those who had failed to convert the Left in the 1930's were now deciding policy. At the same time, the Commissariat of Armament and Supply, directed by Jean Monnet in Algiers, forged the nucleus of the postwar Planning Commission.

The resistance insisted that the new, managed economy msut serve the people, not selfish interests. From all quarters came condemnations of the parasitical "trusts" which had allegedly collaborated with the occupiers. There would be no independent trade unions, no free press or free market, they said, unless the power of the trusts was smashed. The resistance roundly attacked "all economic Malthusianism" and argued that a defensive, Maginot line mentality worked no better in economics than in war. The Left saw rejuvenation as the means of improving the lot of the masses, while the Gaullists envisioned it as a prerequisite of France's return to the ranks of the great powers. Thus reasons varied, but the ideal of the balanced economy had lost its hold on many minds. . . . Rejuvenation entailed a rise in productivity and wages, massive investments for the rebuilding and extension of industry, as well as streamlined marketing of consumer goods.

Such economic goals required fundamental structural change. An interventionist state would "direct" (or "orient" or "coordinate") the economy, but it must avoid *étatisation* with its overtones of bureaucratization and authoritarianism. Interventionism meant above all a partly nationalized economy, the "return to the nation" of monopolies held by the trusts and the seizure of the levers of command over the economy. There was disagreement on the scope and means of nationalization, yet a consensus existed on its necessity. Planning was a less common theme than nationalization; the Socialists warned that it must be participatory or democratic and "imperative", rather than obligatory. Indeed it was seen as an alternative to *étatisation*. Thus the resistance labored to free the directed economy from its associations with Vichy, fascism, and Stalinism.

Yet somewhat ironically, the resistance was in many ways the complement rather than the adversary of Vichy. The leaders of the two wartime movements shared the same impatience with the disorder and backwardness of the French economy, and with the impotence of the state under the Third Republic. Although the resistance was more inclined toward socialism than Vichy, they shared a technocratic thrust. . . . Even De Gaulle, who otherwise had no use for Vichy, acknowledged that in their attempt at economic renewal Pétain's "technocrats had despite all setbacks shown incontestable skill". The head of the future provisional government also realized that the economy had been "desperately out of date" in 1940 and that its renovation depended on the state.[9] . . .

Given the rivalries within the resistance (there were left-wing technocrats like Mendès-France and liberals like René Pleven on De Gaulle's team), the paucity of information about economic conditions in France, the hesitations of De Gaulle himself, and the complexity and enormity of the tasks which faced the incoming authorities, it is not surprising that their vision of the future was uncertain, their goals lacking in definition. There was, for example, no agreement or much concern about the precise nature and scope of either planning or nationalization. Some considered planning merely as a means of improving the allocation of resources during a time of shortages or as a catalogue of aims, while others conceived of it as a vast investment program for expanding and modernizing the industrial plant. De Gaulle and the Communists, furthermore, were not enthusiastic about planning and nationalization in principle. No decision had been reached concerning the fate of the CO's and other aspects of Vichy's legacy. Moreover, the appeal of *dirigisme* was contradicted by a common desire to end wartime regulations and dispose of a hated past. As a result the provisional government improvised much and its achievements did not measure up to its goals.

With the end of the war, France made a fundamental break with the economic policy of the past. The enthusiasm of the moment provided wide popular support for economic renovation and state action. . . . Institutional innovation vastly enhanced the apparatus of state direction, and at the same time technocrats won control of the new centers of economic decision making—and a few of the old. The drive toward administrative rather than political control over economic policy, which Vichy had stimulated, gathered momentum. Armed with new governmental organs, granted autonomy by De Gaulle, and backed by the public's desire for structural reforms, the technocrats had come to stay.

The parliamentary assemblies of those years readily concurred with the resistance planners' demand for nationalizations. A wave of legislation in 1945–46, much of it impromptu, established a large public sector, including gas and electricity, coal, credit, insurance, and much of transportation. Suddenly the state had become an enormous employer and producer in its own right, but it attempted to keep faith with the resistance slogan: "nationaliser n'est pas étatiser". Accordingly, tripartite governing boards of company personnel, consumers, and the state assumed direction of nationalized corporations; these boards were to provide autonomy and popular control. Their first managers, uninhibited technocrats like Louis Armand of the railroads . . . set dynamic precedents for their successors. The nationalized firms received sufficient financial aid from public sources to undertake large-scale improvements, such as electrifying the railway network and constructing hydroelectric plants.

Although national planning had been called for by the resistance, a year passed without much progress except for the preparation of piecemeal plans and purchasing orders by various government agencies. Only the intervention of Jean Monnet saved it from chaos and indifference. Monnet, former economic adviser to foreign governments and the League of Nations, served on Allied supply commissions in both wars and gained considerable influence in London, Washington, and Paris. His mediation among French and Allied political factions, his unqualified supranationalism, and his socialism separated Monnet from De Gaulle. Yet in December, 1945, as head of the French purchasing commission in the United States, he appealed directly to De Gaulle. His historic memorandum argued that in order for France to recover its place in world affairs and to raise its standard of living, the nation must pursue industrial reconstruction and modernization simultaneously.[10] France's already antiquated plant and production methods had fallen further behind during the war, while the other belligerents were experiencing "a veritable technical revolution"; therefore modernization and expansion were the only way to attack "the root of the problem", to raise consumption levels and pay for imports. Monnet further warned that special interests were already seeking protection rather than change, and that unless the government took advantage of its current position of strength, the economy would "crystallize at a level of mediocrity". He urged the co-ordination of piecemeal orders into a single grand plan. De Gaulle, realizing that economic recovery had been slower than anticipated, immediately appointed Monnet High Commissioner for Planning.

In this capacity Monnet quickly won the backing of the trade unions, of Léon Blum and the Socialists, and of the United States (which was anxious to see the best possible use made of its credits). His autonomous Commissariat became a new technocratic headquarters: Robert Marjolin, a professor who had studied Keynes at Yale, was Monnet's deputy, while his technical and financial advisers were the engineer and former manager Etienne Hirsch and the Inspector of Finance Paul Delouvrier. From the outset Marjolin explained that the Commissariat was but "une petite chose" which would not replace other government agencies, but would only help them implement their projects.[11] By posing as honest brokers and by limiting the size of their staff, the planners expected to avoid arousing the fears of established government services. The Commissariat could do its job with so few personnel because it would utilize the services of many others through Modernization Commissions created to help prepare the initial draft of the Plan. The commissions would continue the institutionalized consultation between business and government inaugurated by Vichy. Marjolin described the men he wanted to serve on them: not prominent office-holders but those who recommended themselves by the "knowledge which they have of industry, by their dynamism, by their willingness to do something modern". In the end hundreds of businessmen, technicians, civil servants, trade union and farm officials were to participate in these advisory commissions. . . .

Out of the efforts of the Modernization Commissions came the Monnet Plan, which aimed to eliminate obstacles to recovery and to permit long-term growth by modernizing and expanding the capital goods sector of industry. It channeled public funds into this sector at a time when private sources had all but dried up, and relied on other state powers and incentives to encourage the use of these funds. It was a crude design by later standards—ignoring for example the inflationary effects of massive spending—and was confined to a few, long-range goals. Its target industries were coal, power, steel, transport, building materials, and agricultural equipment. The Plan's strong industrial bias became overwhelming when its agricultural budget was later cut back.

In theory the nationalized enterprises and the preparation of the Plan were to be supervised by a new "superministry", the Ministry of National Economy. Mendès-France defined its powers, and he became its first minister in 1944. The Ministry of National Economy represented a resurrection of the Left's old scheme to subjugate the Ministry of Finance under an authority possessing a broader and more dynamic outlook. Its functions included numerous regulatory *directions;* in essence it was to provide overall orientation to the state's economic activity. Yet almost immediately the ministry suffered an ominous defeat. The liberal Minister of Finance, René Pleven, blocked Mendès-France's project to curb inflationary pressures through a drastic currency conversion. In April, 1945, after only four months in office, the volatile Mendès-France resigned his post. . . .

There were still other more substantial, though less publicized reforms during 1944–46. A small group of civil servants, led by Claude Gruson and Alfred Sauvy, began overhauling the state's apparatus for collecting and analysing economic and statistical data. The new demands on the state for economic management, and an awareness of French backwardness compared to British and American services, prompted them. Soon new agencies and up-to-date methods appeared—even within the inner sanctum of the Rue de Rivoli—for the preparation of national accounts, the budget, general statistical studies, and economic forecasts. In the same period the government founded or rejuvenated several scientific and technical research institutes. . . . In the long run, the efforts of these institutes were to help French industry reduce its technological lag.

As the enthusiasm generated by the liberation dwindled, opposition to continued regulations and to certain of the new institutions appeared. There was dissatisfaction, for example, with price and wage controls which failed to curb inflation between 1944 and 1948. And as the severe shortages faded, state intervention relaxed. . . .

In the early 1950's the Fourth Republic directed a sharply increased proportion of its budget towards capital formation. Much of this funding was Marshall Plan aid, whose use the United States prescribed, channeled through the Plan's Modernization and Equipment Fund. At the same time the Fourth Republic, unlike the Third, launched an effective "productivity drive" which used American aid for loan programs and study missions abroad. The big push came with the republic's most technocratic cabinet, that of Mendès-France in 1954–55, when new funds for reconverting obsolescent firms, retraining displaced labor, and promoting regional industrial development were established. The state also began to use its powers of taxation as an instrument of industrial reform. . . . Although the Fourth Republic was far too weak to sweep away the accumulation of privilege, a campaign against all forms of protectionism was begun. . . . But it was Monnet, the Planning Commissariat, and the nationalized sectors (among others) who championed the more important entry of France into the European Coal and Steel Community in 1951. This move not only reversed the restrictive commercial policy of the past, but opened the way toward the Common Market and European integration.

The major technocratic innovations of the liberation, the nationalized industries and the Plan, not only endured but prospered. The nationalized companies in the 1950's were expansionist in their own operations and in their effect on the French economy. . . . Most important, the example of public enterprise led private industry toward a pattern of high investment and a decisive break with prewar behavior. One economist surveying the machine tool industry of Renault, the Caravelle and Mystère jets, and EDF's high voltage power grid, concludes that "much of the stimulus for technological change came from nationalized industry".[12]

The Monnet Plan (1947–52) was at least a qualified success. Monnet's exhortations helped to reconcile the socialist-minded government of the early Fourth Republic with a conservative business elite disgraced by its wartime record. The planners succeeded in transmitting the expansionist message to other state agencies and to the business community. . . . This regular and continuous exchange of information through the planning mechanism signaled a further advance toward the *économie concertée*. If the Plan did not reach all its production goals, it came close. It achieved a high level of investment and pursued its modernization programs vigorously. Monnet's warning in 1945 about the economy "crystallizing" at prewar "mediocrity" was correct: had it not been for the Plan, it is likely that scarce resources would have been fruitlessly drained away in consumption or in the extension of out-moded industrial facilities.

The Second Plan (1954–57) has not received the universal acclaim of Monnet's. It was immoderate in encompassing all of industry and in trying to provide for general input-output coherence. And while the prestige of planning grew and its techniques improved, its real influence on industrial strategy declined. Yet for the most part it exceeded its ambitious targets for industrial production, and it continued to involve those most immediately concerned in its projects. By this time the Planning Commissariat had become a permanent and vital institution of economic decision making—one directed by administrators and largely free of parliamentary control. . . .

The state's behavior in the 1950's can be accounted for largely by the conversion to technocracy and *dirigisme* of the *hauts fonctionnaires* in charge of economic affairs. The major economic reforms of the liberation had not been inspired or even supported by a majority of the top officials. It was the enlarged economic responsibilities of the state, however, which soon forced interventionism and a general change in outlook on the upper levels of the administration. Defeat and occupation had provoked reflection on the reasons for national decline; then the contagious mood of reform during the liberation, new or reformed institutions for training civil servants, and the arrival of Keynesian theory also prompted the shift toward technocracy. It is also the pattern of change in French bureaucracy that innovation starts at the top where discretionary power is lodged. Credit for the state's record must, however, be shared with certain politicians, especially on the Left and Center. It was the political parties and movements of the resistance that introduced the economic and educational reforms which in turn transformed the duties and training of the *hauts fonctionnaires*. Ministers like Edgar Faure and Mendès-France also actively promoted the technocrats' cause, while parliamentarians voted for massive investments and allowed public officials to proceed unhampered.

A new graduate school for public administration, the Ecole Nationale d'Administration (ENA) was founded and replaced the Ecole Libre as the antechamber to the high civil service. Michel Debré designed the new institution. It was to democratize and centralize recruitment, i.e., end co-option by the caste-like *grands corps*, and to breathe unity and dynamism into the entire administration. Preparation was to be less specialized and more widely functional. The ENA proved more effective in promoting intellectual rather than social change. In fact the Parisian *haute bourgeoisie* crowded into the ENA much as it had the Ecole Libre. In this instance there was a fundamental shift in an elite's orientation without a corresponding modification in its social base. At the very moment when officials were obliged to take on greater responsibilities for the economy, Keynesian principles found a more receptive audience. Although the ENA did not teach Keynes as such, his ideas strongly influenced the new pragmatic approach which was now preferred to doctrinaire liberalism. . . . The new mentors were Sauvy, Armand, Gruson, Paul Delouvrier, and Bloch-Lainé. The enemy was Malthusianism; the way out was "flexible planning" and the *économie concertée*—a framework within which the state could make "constant adjustments . . . to assure maximum economic growth with social and financial stability".[13]

The ENA was not able to transform the attitudes of the entire administration in the 1950's. Some of its graduates were assimilated to a more traditional viewpoint. But many *hauts fonctionnaires*, especially graduates of the ENA, polytechnicians (who had always displayed a Saint-Simonian bent), younger men, and those in the economic, financial, and technical ministries, saw the state in a new technocratic light—as "the carrier of progress". The state was the agent of material and cultural uplift and when necessary might even tear the citizenry away from old habits. There were others, most evident in the judicial, diplomatic, and prefectoral corps, who retained the prewar view of the state as the "impartial arbiter" which maintained harmony and order among competing interests.[14] Nevertheless, ENA graduates soon populated the *grands corps*, and their preference for economic administration made the Ministry of Finance their stronghold.

The Inspection des Finances, the elite of the financial administration, abandoned classical economics to embrace a form of pragmatic or empirical *dirigisme:* the state intervened to liberate the economy for expansion whereas under the Third Republic the authorities had acted only to shelter it. The post-1945 generation of inspectors was the first to assimilate Keynes fully, especially Keynes' emphasis on investments. They also accepted the primacy of economics over finances, that is, they perceived budgetary problems as derivative of underemployment of manpower and productive capacity. The inspectorate asserted that only the state could insure large-scale, continuous, and productive investment; only it had the means to analyze *conjoncture*, make forecasts and harmonize development. The inspectorate remained attached to capitalism: the state was not to replace private initiative, only to correct it. But the archaic structure of French industry was to be demolished. Through tariff and fiscal reform the state could clear away the obstacles to competition, both internal and external, and assist the most profitable enterprises.

The new hero of this generation of inspectors was François Bloch-Lainé. He was a prominent inspector himself, former director of the Treasury, and head of the principal state investment bank. Bloch-Lainé praised the Plan and similar institutions for launching the "silent revolution" of the *économie concertée*. It was in the interest of the business community itself, he contended, to learn what the state knew and planned, and to advise it. An exchange of information would shape a "flexible plan" in which a "wide latitude of choice" would exist for those who implemented it. Relations between business and state would be both institutionalized and depoliticized. Bloch-Lainé endorsed a "pragmatic approach" which would end the sterile debate over liberalism and *dirigisme*.

The ultimate victory of the technocrats was the gradual conversion of the Ministry of Finance. From this vantage point the technocrats could use the state's control of credit to coerce reluctant industrialists into making proper investment decisions. Under the Fourth Republic ministers at the Rue de Rivoli were usually political centrists, yet most of them, especially after Edgar Faure's attempt to *relancer* the economy following the Korean war, were unqualified expansionists. The civil service staff, beginning in the early 1950's, began to acquire a new reputation as technocrats. . . . Again practice preceded theory: the Treasury's enlarged responsibilities for handling the Plan's funds, for forecasting, and for investment and credit in general converted officials to *dirigisme* and the *économie concertée*. Rivalry from the Planning Commissariat and the secretariat for economic affairs also prodded the Treasury to give itself an equally modern allure. Ministry officials continued, however, to deny their full cooperation to the planners. Only with the preparation of the Fourth Plan during the Fifth Republic did they co-ordinate their day-to-day decisions with the Plan's long-term goals. Then Gaullist technocrats like Michel Debré adopted the Plan and it became the *grand affaire* of the regime. . . .

During the Fourth Republic, the cause of industrial modernization spread beyond the administrative elite. The "productivity drive" led by zealous technocrats caught hold among businessmen who before the war rarely even knew the term itself. Alfred Sauvy's campaign against Malthusianism took hold, especially with the Left. The prolific and popular economist-statistician Jean Fourastié presented empirical data to prove that a rising standard of living depended on advances in productivity.

This flourishing technocratic propaganda coincided with a shift in popular attitudes which gave industrialization a high priority.[15] Otherwise the technocrats would have been ineffectual—much like Tardieu earlier. . . . Sociologist Raymond Aron became one of the earliest and most influential spokesmen for the "industrial society", which would eliminate poverty and enlarge opportunity. In 1955 the Swiss writer Herbert Lüthy provided a damning critique of the *situations acquises* in his widely-read work, *France Against Herself*. In the early 1950's the American scholars joined in exposing the "backwardness" of French business. The breadth of the attack against old ways indicated that the technocrats had finally found a receptive audience.

The technocrats' success in popularizing their view alarmed some Frenchmen. The dark forebodings of intellectuals like Jacques Ellul were part of a growing literary technophobia. Conservative social elements rallied to the Poujadists who displayed a strident, anti-technocratic rhetoric and scored major political successes in the mid-1950's. Social scientists, among others, posed the question of who ruled, or at least, who was going to rule? According to these apprehensive observers, the technocrats, identified as the administrative elite, challenged the parliamentary elite by seeking to transfer power to the most competent. The technocrats believed that the state was an affair to be managed, that class conflict would disappear through a combination of prosperity and social engineering, and that society's energies should be harnessed to creating abundance. In contrast politicians based their authority on the popular will rather than expertise and assumed that policy-making was a matter of conciliating competing interests and ideals rather than a scientific, and thus politically neutral, process. In an abstract sense the social scientists discerned the critical issue of social control which technocracy posed. Or as Karl Mannheim expressed it, "Who plans the planner?" [16] Yet the historical record reveals rather few proponents of the ideal technocracy, especially on the Left. And even on the Right advocates like Bloch-Lainé insisted that major economic decisions were political in character and that experts could only help prepare the options more rationally. There is evidence, moreover, that technocrats were not confined to public administration but appeared among the political, business and labor elites as well. Instead of competing for power these like-minded leaders were drawn together in the cause of modernization.

It is not my contention that after the war the state consistently pursued rapid industrial growth. There were lapses and contradictions in its behavior. Yet on the whole state policy turned the corner with the reforms of the liberation era: until then primacy had been given to stability and protection, while afterward the overriding concern was growth and modernization. France by the 1950's had moved from a liberal to a directed economy, from a protectionist to an interventionist state, from the idyll of a balanced economy to the promise and problems of an industrial society. Criticism of the state's economic activities continued, but except for an uncompromising few, the critics sought a better performance from the state in its new role rather than its exit from the economic scene.

Notes

1. Stanley Hoffmann, "The Effects of World War II on French Society and Politics," *French Historical Studies*, II (Spring 1961), 28–63. Only a small fraction of the notes to this essay are reprinted here. See the original publication for references.

2. The *Petit Larousse* (1959) defines *technocrate* as an "homme d'état ou haut fonctionnaire quie exerce son autorité en fonction d'études théoriques approfondies des mécaniques économiques, sans tenir un compte suffisant des facteurs humains." There is a digest of the beliefs of the contemporary technocrat by Jean Touchard and Jacques Solé, "Planification et technocratie," *La Planification comme processus de décision*, Cahiers de la Fondation Nationale des Sciences Politiques, No. 140 (1965), 31–33. This mock credo begins with, "One must be a realist," calls political parties, ideologies, nationalism, liberal capitalism, and Marxism all *dépassé*, declares belief in social mobility, efficiency, progress, and Alfred Sauvy, and concludes with "We are not technocrats." The major professional categories which popular opinion regards as technocratic are: officials of the economic administration, graduates of the Ecole Nationale d'Administration, state engineers, economists and statisticians, and "Eurocrats" (Bernard Gournay, "Technocratie et administration," *Revue française de science politique*, X [December, 1960], 884–885). Poujadists, Communists, and other critics regard the technocrats as heartless productivity maniacs who impose their will on others, depend on foreign trusts, blindly admire America, patronize supermarkets, know only Paris, and drink whisky and Coca-Cola (Touchard and Solé, p. 29).

3. Andrew Shonfield, *Modern Capitalism* (New York and London, 1965).

4. Malthusianism in this context refers to an underlying pessimism about both the possibility of improving the material lot of man and the use of restraint to avoid the danger of over-production.

5. For example, the program of the Fédération nationale des contribuables, which expressed middle-class discontent in the 1930's, while continuing to urge the state to divest itself of its economic functions, declared economic liberalism outmoded and embraced corporativism (William A. Hoisington, "Taxpayer Revolt in France, the National Taxpayers' Federation, 1928–1939," unpublished manuscript, 1972). Henry W. Ehrmann discusses how employers began to experiment with alternatives after the shock of the Popular Front (*Organized Business in France* [Princeton, 1957], pp. 43ff.).

6. Quoted in Paul Delouvrier and Roger Nathan, *Politique économique de la France*, Cours de droit à l'Université de Paris, 1957–58, fasc. I, p. 52.

7. Robert Catherine, *L'Industrie* (Paris, 1965), p. 21.

8. Bichelonne enjoyed the respect of his technocratic counterpart, Al-

bert Speer, the Nazi Minister of Armaments. In 1943 they joined forces against Fritz Sauckel, a Nazi ideologue and the Commissar-General for Labor, over the issue of raising industrial production in France.

9. De Gaulle, *Mémoires de guerre: Le Salut, 1944–1946* (Paris, 1959), pp. 111–112.

10. This memorandum can be found in De Gaulle, *Mémoires: Le Salut*, pp. 634–639.

11. Robert Marjolin, "Le Commissariat Général du Plan," *Cahiers français d'information*, June 1, 1946, pp. 17–20.

12. Charles Kindleberger, *Economic Growth in France and Britain, 1851–1950* (Cambridge, Mass., 1964), p. 159.

13. Jean-François Kesler, "Les anciens Elèves de l'Ecole Nationale d'Administration," *Revue française de science politique*, XIV (April, 1964), 249.

14. Bernard Gournay, "Un Groupe dirigeant de la société française: les grands fonctionnaires," *Revue française de science politique*, XIV (April, 1964), 229–231.

15. John Ardagh writes: "After decades of living in the past, the French have suddenly become passionate about modernizing their country" (*The New French Revolution* [London, 1968], p. xii).

16. Mannheim, *Man and Society in an Age of Reconstruction* (New York, 1940), p. 75.

BIBLIOGRAPHICAL NOTE

Among general surveys of recent French history both Alfred Cobban, *A History of Modern France*, vol. 3, *France of the Republics 1871–1962* (Harmondsworth, 1965) and Gordon Wright, *France in Modern Times, From the Enlightenment to the Present* (Chicago, 1974) remain outstanding, the latter being especially useful for its bibliographical chapters. Old but still rewarding are D. W. Brogan's sparkling narrative, *France Under the Republic: The Development of Modern France (1870–1939)* (New York, 1940) and David Thomson's thoughtful political and social analysis, *Democracy in France since 1870*, 4th ed. (New York, 1964). A long, conservative chronicle, full of interest, is Jacques Chastenet's *Histoire de la Troisième République*, 7 vols. (Paris, 1952–1963), which has reappeared with two additional volumes covering the post-1940 period as *Cent ans de la République*, 9 vols. (Paris, 1970). By contrast, volumes 10 to 18 of the work still in progress, *Nouvelle histoire de la France contemporaine*, reflect the social and economic concerns of recent historiography and seem certain to add up to the best overall account of the Republics at this time. Those that have appeared are, Jean-Marie Mayeur, *Les débuts de la IIIe République (1871–1898)* (Paris, 1973), Madeleine Rebérioux, *La République radicale (1898–1914)* (Paris, 1973), Philippe Bernard, *La fin d'un monde (1914–1929)* (Paris, 1975), Henri Dubief, *Le déclin de la Troisième République (1929–1938)* (Paris, 1976). Two excellent long essays should be singled out, Jean-Pierre Azéma and Michel Winock, *La IIIe République* (Paris, 1970) and Jacques Julliard, *La IVe République* (Paris, 1968).

On the problems of French demography in this period see the compact studies of André Armengaud, *La population française au XIXe siècle* (Paris, 1971) and *La population française au XXe siècle* (Paris, 1965). An outline social history that is brief but useful as an introduction is Georges Dupeux, *La société française 1789–1960* (Paris, 1964), which has been translated as *French Society 1789–1960* (New York, 1976).

Pierre Sorlin's two-volume study *La société française 1840–1968* (Paris, 1969–1971) is less schematic, more leisurely, a series of thematic essays. Of great interest also are the essays in Stanley Hoffmann et al., *In Search of France* (Cambridge, Mass., 1963), on a variety of topics from social change to foreign policy. Finally, to conclude this introductory section, one should mention Philip Ouston's comprehensive, synoptic *France in the Twentieth Century* (London, 1972), which provides an excellent overview, and Theodore Zeldin's discursive, richly informative work in progress, *France 1848–1945* (Oxford, 1973–), of which volume one, subtitled *Ambition, Love and Politics*, makes clear that this is a major work of synthesis and interpretation.

On the subject of French nationalism there is still justification for remembering Carlton J. H. Hayes's *France, A Nation of Patriots* (New York, 1930) half a century after its publication. Since that time a great deal of study has been devoted to the problem of nationalism in general, but it would be difficult to claim that a great deal of light has been shed on French nationalism, whether "old" or "new." Nevertheless, there is some debate on its diversity or essential unity. An important, suggestive essay is Raoul Girardet's "Pour une introduction à l'histoire du nationalisme français," *Revue française de science politique* 8 (September 1958): 505–528, which emphasizes the element of nostalgia for greatness and for unity. One should see also Girardet's prefatory remarks to his useful collection of texts, *Le nationalisme français 1871–1914* (Paris, 1966). Specialized studies of turn-of-the-century nationalist phenomena are Zeev Sternhell, *Maurice Barrès et le nationalisme français* (Paris, 1977) and Robert Soucy, *Fascism in France: The Case of Maurice Barrès* (Berkeley, 1972). Of interest is David R. Watson's electoral study of the triumph of the old nationalism in the capital early in the century, "The Nationalist Movement in Paris 1900–1906," in David Shapiro, ed., *The Right in France 1890–1919* (London, 1962), pp. 49–84. On the new nationalism, an early and still valuable work is William Curt Buthman, *The Rise of Integral Nationalism in France, with Special Reference to the Ideas and Activities of Charles Maurras* (New York, 1939). More recent are Edward R. Tannenbaum, *The Action Française: Die-Hard Reactionaries in Twentieth-Century France* (New York, 1962) and the superbly documented work of Eugen Weber, *Action Française: Royalism and Reaction in Twentieth-Century France* (Stanford, 1962). Of importance also is Weber's *The Nationalist Revival in France, 1905–1914* (Berkeley, 1959), which stresses the impact of foreign affairs and security problems on the growth of the new nationalism. In this connection, the conclusions of David E. Sumler should be read, "Domestic Influences on the Nationalist Revival in France, 1909–1914," *French Historical Studies* 6 (1970): 517–537. A suggestive essay, to conclude this section, is Stanley Hoffmann's "The Nation: What For? Vicissitudes of French Nationalism, 1871–1973," in his *Decline or Renewal? France since the 1930s* (New York, 1974), pp. 403–442.

The study of the great European empires flourishes on both sides of the Atlantic. A brief, succinct, and influential introduction to the problems of France's imperial enterprise is Henri Brunschwig, *Mythes et réalités de l'impérialisme colonial français 1871–1914* (Paris, 1960), translated as *French Colonialism 1871–1914: Myths and Realities* (London, 1964). Still more compact but of interest is Xavier Yacono, *Histoire de la colonisation française* (Paris, 1969). Jean Ganiage, *L'expansion coloniale de la France sous la Troisième République (1871–1914)* (Paris, 1968) is solid and authoritative. Stephen Roberts's large and learned study *The History of French Colonial Policy 1870–1925*, 2 vols. (London, 1929) has not been superseded by any one hand in its detail and grasp of the subject, though time has altered perspectives. Raymond F. Betts's *Assimilation and Association in French Colonial Theory 1890–1914* (New York, 1961) is straightforward and clear. Raoul Girardet's *L'idée coloniale en France* (Paris, 1970) is an important and stimulating study of changing attitudes toward empire. The same author's significant essay, "L'apothéose de 'la plus grande France': l'idée coloniale devant l'opinion française (1930–1935)," *Revue française de science politique* 18 (1968): 1085–1114, illuminates a critical turning point in the national perception of empire. William B. Cohen's *Rulers of Empire: The French Colonial Service in Africa 1888–1960* (Stanford, 1971) is a study of the virtues and, especially, failings of administrators in France's African empire. Concerning the motivations back of imperial activity, the current orthodoxy of stressing the place of prestige (as in Brunschwig) appears to be being challenged by a shift back toward renewed emphasis upon the economic factor, as in Jean Bouvier's "Les traits majeurs de l'impérialisme français avant 1914," in Bouvier and René Girault, eds., *L'impérialisme français d'avant 1914: Recueil de textes* (Paris, 1976), pp. 305–333. This point of view emerges forcefully too in L. Abrams and D. J. Miller, "Who Were the French Colonialists? A Reassessment of the *Parti Colonial* 1890–1914," *Historical Journal* 19 (1976): 685–725. Stuart M. Persell, who also attempts to count and place the members of the *Parti colonial*, "The *Parti Colonial Français*, 1889–1914: A Computer Study," *Third Republic/Troisième République* 1 (1976): 88–131, finds them to have been fairly typical parliamentarians. Finally, James J. Cooke, *The New French Imperialism 1880–1910: The Third Republic and Colonial Expansion* (Newton Abbot, 1975) is recent though not pathbreaking, while both Gifford Prosser and Wm. Louis Roger, eds., *France and Britain in Africa: Imperial Rivalry and Colonial Rule* (New Haven, 1971) and L. H. Gann and Peter Duignan, eds., *Colonialism in Africa 1870–1960*, 5 vols. (Cambridge, 1969–) include distinguished chapters on aspects of the French empire. As for the devolution of empire, there is of course an enormous specialized literature, but the brief study of Xavier Yacono, *Les étapes de la décolonisation française* (Paris, 1971), and the substantial general account of Rudolf von Albertini, *Decolonisation: The Administration and Future of the Colonies 1919–1960* (New York, 1971), the second half of which deals with the French empire, are useful. To conclude, mention should be made of Raymond F. Betts's imaginative article "The French Colonial Frontier," in Charles K. Warner, ed., *From the Ancien Regime to the Popular Front* (New York, 1969), pp. 127–143, which conveys some sense of the national appeal made by colonial enterprise, and of Charles-Robert Ageron's slight but interesting collection of texts, *L'anticolonialisme en France de 1871 à 1914* (Paris, 1973).

The economic history of France in the contemporary period is succinctly treated in two excellent books by Tom Kemp, *Economic Forces in French History* (London, 1971)—which supplements and corrects the pioneer and still useful account of J. H. Clapham, *The Economic Development of France and Germany 1815–1914* (Cambridge, 1913)—and *The French Economy 1913–1939: The History of a Decline* (London, 1972). Sections of David S. Landes's *The Unbound Prometheus: Technological Change and Industrial Development in Western Europe from 1750 to the Present* (Cambridge, 1969) are illuminating, as are parts of Charles P. Kindelberger's *Economic Growth in France and Britain 1851–1950* (Cambridge, Mass., 1964) and his essay "The Postwar Resurgence of the French Economy," in Hoffmann et al., *In Search of France*, pp. 118–158. Guy P. Palmade's long essay *Capitalisme et capitalistes français aux XIXe siècle* (Paris, 1961), translated as *French Capitalism in the Nineteenth Century* (New York, 1972), is stimulating as are parts of Charles Morazé's somewhat disjointed *Les Français et la République* (Paris, 1956), in translation as *The French and the Republic* (Ithaca, 1958), a lively and rather erratic work. Rondo E. Cameron's substantial *France and the Economic Development of Europe 1800–1914* (Princeton, 1961) supports in great detail some of the higher claims made by Morazé. A cautious revision of the more negative estimates of France's industrial performance continues and may be seen in René Girault, "L'homme d'affaires français vers 1914," *Revue d'histoire moderne et contemporaine* 16 (1969) : 329–349, and in the papers by Charles P. Kindelberger, David S. Landes, and Maurice Levy Leboyer in Edward C. Carter et al., eds., *Enterprise and Entrepreneurs in 19th and 20th Century France* (Baltimore, 1976). On the French economy between the two wars, in addition to Kemp, see the still useful Martin Wolfe, *The French Franc Between the Wars 1918–1939* (New York, 1951) and, above all, Alfred Sauvy's multivolume study *Histoire économique de la France entre les deux guerres*, 4 vols. (Paris, 1965–1975), which treats the subject in the broadest way, the third volume of which includes special studies by other scholars.

The general background history of the left before 1914 is conveniently found in such standard accounts as Georges Lefranc, *Le mouvement socialiste sous la Troisième République (1875–1940)* (Paris, 1963) and Daniel Ligou, *Histoire du socialisme en France (1871–1962)* (Paris, 1962). On the central experience of the Great War's impact, Merle Fainsod, *International Socialism and the World War* (Cambridge, Mass., 1935) remains useful, and Georges Haupt, *Socialism and the Great War:*

The Collapse of the Second International (Oxford, 1972) is up to date. On the formation of the French Communist party, the fundamental study is Annie Kriegel, *Aux origines du communisme français*, 2 vols. (The Hague, 1964), and Robert Wohl, *French Communism in the Making* (Stanford, 1966) is a fine scholarly account. Of importance is George Lichtheim's penetrating study of ideas, *Marxism in Modern France* (New York, 1966), while David Caute's *Communism and the French Intellectuals 1914–1960* (London, 1964) is a broad and lively, but rather glancing, survey. A recent general study of the whole period is Ronald Tiersky, *French Communism 1920–1970* (New York, 1974). Annie Kriegel's *The French Communists: Profile of a People* (Chicago, 1973) is authoritative, balanced, and readable. Less solidly documented than these studies is Jacques Fauvet's brief survey, *Histoire du parti communiste français*, 2 vols. (Paris, 1964–1965). Daniel R. Brower, *The New Jacobins: The French Communist Party and the Popular Front* (Ithaca, 1968) is useful for that era, while the older studies of Angelo Rossi [Tasca], *Physiologie du Parti Communiste Français* (Paris, 1948), *Les communistes pendant la drôle de guerre* (Paris, 1951), and *La guerre des papillons: quatre ans de politique communiste 1940–1944* (Paris, 1954), remain important for their close, if hostile, acquaintance with the subject and the documentation used. On the whole, however, the literature is, with notable exceptions, fairly tendentious, apologetic or polemical, and episodic. A recent attempt to come to grips with the known and the unknown is Roland Gaucher, *Histoire secrète du Parti Communiste français 1920–1974* (Paris, 1974), but the title implies more than the text delivers.

The *Front populaire* has given rise to a large literature, although scholars continue to wait for the opening of official archives relating to the 1930s. Comprehensive, though not unbiased, accounts include Georges Lefranc, *Histoire du Front populaire*, 2d ed. (Paris, 1974) and J. Delperrié de Bayac, *Histoire du Front populaire* (Paris, 1972). Through its survey and analysis of the press, Louis Bodin and Jean Touchard's *Front populaire* (Paris, 1965) conveys something of the contemporary atmosphere. Nathanael Greene, *Crisis and Decline: The French Socialist Party in the Popular Front Era* (Ithaca, 1969), Peter J. Larmour, *The French Radical Party in the 1930s* (Stanford, 1964), and Daniel Brower, *The New Jacobins* all help illuminate the political ramifications of the rather strange alliance. On Léon Blum, Joel Colton's sympathetic biography, *Léon Blum, Humanist in Politics* (New York, 1966), is the fullest general account, to be supplemented by the papers appearing in the important symposium *Léon Blum, chef de gouvernement 1936–1937* (Paris, 1972), in which both scholars and former associates make their contribution. Two papers by Irwin Wall throw light on the Blum government's relations with the civil service, "Socialists and Bureaucrats: The Blum Government and the French Administration 1936–1937," *International Review of Social History* 19 (1974): 326–346, and on the reasons for Blum's resignation, "The Resignation of the First Popular Front Government of

Léon Blum," *French Historical Studies* 6 (1970): 538–554, though Georges Dupeux, "L'échec du premier gouvernement Léon Blum," *Revue d'histoire moderne et contemporaine* 10 (1963): 35–44, presents another interpretation. A careful estimate of the economic unwisdom and the political inevitability of the forty-hour legislation is in Jean Charles Asselain, "Une erreur de politique économique: la loi de quarante heures de 1936," *Revue économique* 25 (1974): 672–705. Jean Bouvier discusses the matter in "Un débat toujours ouvert: la politique économique du Front populaire," *Mouvement social*, no. 54 (1966): 175–181. As for the theme that Blum threw away his opportunity to make a social revolution, the best-known study is Daniel Guérin, *Front populaire, révolution manquée* (Paris, 1963), a point of view that is discussed by Pierre Broué and Nicole Dorey, "Critiques de gauche et opposition révolutionnaire au Front populaire (1936–1938)," *Mouvement social*, no. 54 (1966): 92–123. Somewhat censorious is Colette Audry, *Léon Blum, ou la politique du juste* (Paris, 1955).

There has been a great deal of writing about the extreme right, and especially about Maurras and his associates. A brief and helpful introduction is Edward R. Tannenbaum, "The Myth of Counterrevolution in France 1870–1914," in Richard Herr and Harold Parker, eds., *Ideas in History* (Durham, 1965), pp. 266–287. Among the many studies of the *Action française* movement Eugen Weber's *Action Française* is certainly the most impressive single work, a prodigious piece of research and a beautifully written book. His essay "France" in Hans Rogger and Eugen Weber, eds., *The European Right: A Historical Profile* (Berkeley, 1965), pp. 71–127, offers a broad panorama of right-wing movements. The indispensable general study here is René Rémond, *La droite en France* (Paris, 1954), which has been periodically revised and appears in translation as *The Right Wing in France: From 1815 to de Gaulle* (Philadelphia, 1966). Well-informed and comprehensive, also, is Malcolm Anderson, *Conservative Politics in France* (London, 1974), a judicious work of research and synthesis. On the varieties of Fascist or so-called Fascist movements in France, Plumyène and Raymond Lasierra's *Les fascismes français 1923–1963* (Paris, 1963) is a convenient guide, while Paul Sérant, *Le romantisme fasciste* (Paris, 1960), discusses the intellectuals of this persuasion. Mention should be made of two articles that remain helpful orientations, Raoul Girardet, "Note sur l'esprit d'un fascisme français 1934–1939," *Revue française de science politique* 5 (1955): 529–546, and Robert Soucy, "The Nature of Fascism in France," *Journal of Contemporary History* 1, no. 1 (1966): 27–55, however differently the latter views the problem from the former and from Rémond. Only Jacques Doriot's *Parti populaire français* has had a substantial study to date, Dieter Wolf, *Doriot* (Paris, 1971), but doubtless other movements will soon be as carefully studied. Finally, two books that convey a sense of what it was like to be swept up by the apparent dynamism of the extreme right in those days are, Robert Brasillach, *Notre avant-guerre* (Paris, 1941)—on Brasillach see William R. Tucker, *The Fascist Ego: A Political Biography of Robert Brasillach* (Berkeley, 1975)—and Jean-Pierre Maxence, *Histoire de dix ans (1927–1937)* (Paris, 1939).

The vicissitudes of the army in the course of the Fourth and Fifth Republics have brought forth a large and polemical body of writing about civil-military relations. There is no better introduction to the subject than the admirably balanced essay by Raoul Girardet, *La société militaire dans la France contemporaine 1815–1939* (Paris, 1953). A fuller general history is to be found in Paul-Marie de la Gorce, *The French Army, A Military-Political History* (New York, 1963). For the earlier period of the Third Republic, David B. Ralston's *The Army of the Republic: The Place of the Military in the Political Evolution of France, 1871–1914* (Cambridge, Mass., 1967) is careful and fair-minded. For the period of the Great War and its immediate aftermath, see Jere C. King, *General and Politicians: Conflict Between France's High Command, Parliament and Government, 1914–1918* (Berkeley, 1951) and *Foch versus Clemenceau: France and German Dismemberment, 1918–1919* (Cambridge, Mass., 1960), both of them lively and readable. Rather sketchy, but interesting, is Jacques Nobécourt and Jean Planchais, *Une histoire politique de l'armée 1919–1967*, 2 vols. (Paris, 1967). A monographic study of some aspects of the interwar period is Judith M. Hughes, *To the Maginot Line: The Politics of French Military Preparation in the 1920s* (Cambridge, Mass., 1971). The republican theory of civil-military relations is methodically exposed in Richard D. Challener's excellent study *The French Theory of the Nation in Arms 1866–1939* (New York, 1955), while the older work of J. Monteilhet, *Les institutions militaires de la France (1814–1932): de la paix armée à la paix désarmée* (Paris, 1932), though reflecting a certain mood on the eve of the General Disarmament Conference of that time, remains a valuable discussion. Philip C. F. Bankwitz's *Maxime Weygand and Civil-Military Relations in Modern France* (Cambridge, Mass., 1967) is the most thoroughly documented work on the broad question of the army's role in the recent history of the Republic, a superb study that leads directly toward works concerning post-1945 events, such as John Ambler, *The French Army in Politics 1945–1962* (Columbus, 1962), James H. Meisel, *The Fall of the Republic: Military Revolt in France* (Ann Arbor, 1962), and George D. Kelly, *Lost Soldiers: The French Army and Empire in Crisis 1947–1962* (Cambridge, Mass., 1964). Brief, but of interest, is Raoul Girardet, "Civil and Military Power in the Fourth Republic," in Samuel P. Huntington, ed., *Changing Patterns of Military Politics* (New York, 1962). Finally, on the unhappy episode of the "Armistice Army" during the Second World War, there is the important work of Robert O. Paxton, *Parades and Politics at Vichy: The French Officer Corps under Marshal Pétain* (Princeton, 1966).

Study of the *Etat français* remains somewhat provisional, largely because of the continued difficulty of obtaining free access to the official archives for that period. Nevertheless, important studies have appeared, based upon German, American, British, and other archives, and one may suppose that the principal outlines are now fixed. The best general studies are Robert O. Paxton, *Vichy France: Old Guard and New Order, 1940–1944* (New York, 1972) and Eberhard Jaeckel, *La France dans l'Europe de Hitler* (Paris, 1968). Robert Aron's older account, *Histoire de Vichy* (Paris, 1954), translated as *The Vichy Regime* (London, 1957), remains worth reading, but its documentation is less solid, while its point of view is more favorable to the marshal. Henri Michel's *Vichy année 40* (Paris, 1966) is a very substantial account of the first stage of the regime. Alan S. Milward, *The New Order and the French Economy* (Oxford, 1970) is a thorough analysis of France's role in Hitler's empire. Studies of the principal personages of the regime have been numerous, but few are really solid. Richard Griffiths's *Marshal Pétain* (London, 1970) is a fair estimate, but largely derivative from other French works. Two of these that are superior are Pierre Bourget, *Un certain Philippe Pétain* (Paris, 1966) and Henri Amouroux, *Pétain avant Vichy—la guerre et l'amour* (Paris, 1967), while Jacques Isorni, *Philippe Pétain*, 2 vols. (Paris, 1972–1973) is a full and admiring biography by the marshal's principal defender, the most active advocate of official rehabilitation. Biographies of Laval have been partisan, but to date Geoffrey Warner's excellent *Pierre Laval and the Eclipse of France* (London, 1968) remains the only scholarly estimate. Memoirs abound, but the means of checking them are not yet to hand. Richard Kuisel has examined and disposed of the rumors that the regime was controlled by a sinister cabal of technicians, "The Legend of the Vichy Synarchy," *French Historical Studies* 6 (1970): 365–398. For the question of collaboration, there is the illuminating press study by Michèle Cotta, *La collaboration* (Paris, 1964), and various penetrating papers in Stanley Hoffmann's *Decline or Renewal?*, as well as Peter Novick's study of the denouement, *The Resistance Versus Vichy: The Purge of Collaborators in Liberated France* (New York, 1968). Concerning the Resistance, of course, a steadily growing literature exists, stemming from seminal studies of Henri Michel—for example, *Histoire de la Résistance en France* (Paris, 1950), *Les courants de pensée de la Résistance* (Paris, 1963)—and his collaborators.

About post-1945 France Raymond Aron once remarked that with the exception of the USSR, his was "the most commented-upon country in the world." There has been no lack of studies of the French recovery, reflecting the stages of France's progress away from the ruin of the 1939 war, and some of them now have value only as *pièces d'occasion*. Still worth reading, however, are Herbert Luethy's *France Against Herself* (New York, 1955) and Raymond Aron's reply to it, *France Steadfast and Changing: The Fourth to the Fifth Republic* (Cambridge, Mass., 1960). Edward R. Tannenbaum's *The New France* (Chicago, 1961) remains full of interesting observations, and John Ardagh's *The New French Revolution* (New York, 1969) is an informed and readable general survey. A great deal of literature has come forth about the modernization of France. On the transformation of agriculture, see especially Gordon Wright, *Rural Revolution in France: The Peasants in the Twentieth Century* (Stanford, 1964), Pierre Barral, *Les agrariens français de Méline à Pisani* (Paris, 1968), Marcel Faure, *Les paysans dans la société française* (Paris, 1966), Jean Meynaud, *La révolte paysanne* (Paris, 1963), and Henri Mendras, *The Vanishing Peasant: Innovation and Change in French Agriculture* (Cambridge, Mass., 1970). For the broadly changing rural scene there is the celebrated study by Laurence Wylie, *Village in the Vaucluse* (Cambridge, Mass., 1957) and a second study written by his students and himself, *Chanzeaux, A Village in Anjou* (Cambridge, Mass., 1966), as well as Robert T. and Barbara G. Anderson's *Bus Stop for Paris* (New York, 1965) and Edgar Morin's *Commune en France: la métamorphose de Plodémet* (Paris, 1967), translated as *The Red and the White: Report from a French Village* (New York, 1970). Among the many studies of planning and industrial change, see John Sheahan, *Promotion and Control of Industry in Postwar France* (Cambridge, Mass., 1963), John and Anne-Marie Hacket, *Economic Planning in France* (Cambridge, Mass., 1963), P. Bauchet, *Economic Planning: The French Experience* (London, 1964), and Stephen S. Cohen, *Modern Capitalist Planning: The French Model* (Cambridge, Mass., 1969). In the ongoing debate about the economic recovery and progress of contemporary France, Michel Crozier casts a certain shadow over the scene, blaming the civil service in his *La société bloquée* (Paris, 1970), translated as *The Stalled Society* (New York, 1973). Ezra N. Suleiman's *Politics, Power and Bureaucracy in France: The Administrative Elite* (Princeton, 1974) is a study of the massive powers lodged in the civil service and argues that it has been co-opted by the prevailing political groups and has come to play an important political role. For another discussion of this phenomenon, see the brief essays by Jeanne Siwek-Pouydesseau and Daniel Derivry in Mattei Dogan, ed., *The Mandarins of Western Europe: The Political Role of Top Civil Servants* (New York, 1975).

INDEX

ABOUT THE EDITOR

John C. Cairns is professor of history at the University of Toronto. He received his B.A. and M.A. degrees at the University of Toronto and his Ph.D. at Cornell.

seriously believed that 'l'expédition à Fez n'etait pas autre chose qu'une colonne de secours, qu'aussitôt nos compatriotes délivrés et la garnison chérifienne secourue, les troupes françaises se hâteraient de rejoindre leur base de départ et de regagner la côte'. His naiveté caused a good deal of amusement in the Ministry of Colonies, which had no doubt about the eventual outcome.[132] Berteaux, however, had no illusions about the expedition which he proposed to Cruppi. According to Victor Bérard, a usually reliable observer of Moroccan affairs, Etienne was present at the meeting between Berteaux and Cruppi when the decision was taken. Berteaux, said Bérard, 'a cédé aux instances d'Etienne parce qu'il était candidat à la présidence de la République et qu'il avait besoin des 40 voix du parti colonial'.[133] There is no reason to doubt Bérard's account; both Etienne's manoeuvre and Berteaux's reaction were entirely in character. In 1897 Etienne and his fellow Algerian deputy Thomson had used the promise of their votes to purchase the removal of the Governor-General, Jules Cambon, whom they had found insufficiently disposed to follow their instructions.[134] Berteaux, the object of Etienne's advances in 1911, had on previous occasions used bribery to further his political career.[135]

The expedition's orders were signed on 17 April. 'Les ministres convoqués en conseil de cabinet le 23 avril seulement', wrote Messimy later, 'ne purent que sanctionner le fait accompli.' [136] L'Humanité was not the only French newspaper to detect evidence of colonialist pressure. Even before the expedition was ordered, the usually conservative *Revue des Deux Mondes* reported that 'les partisans d'une politique d'intervention militaire au Maroc . . . ne perdent aucune occasion de pousser le gouvernement dans le sens de leurs vues et . . . à tort ou à raison comptent sur leur impressionnabilité'. Etienne's tactics were most accurately analysed, however, by the English *Nation:*

> The art of conducting this game lies in creating at each stage a situation which leads inevitably to the next . . . It avoids the presentation of a clear issue to the electorate and Parliament, with whose consent to the ulterior plans the manipulators of the manoeuvre contrive to dispense. There can be little doubt that if the French people or the French Chamber were asked to answer with a 'Yes' or 'No' whether they desire to embark upon the conquest of Morocco, their decision would be an emphatic and nearly unanimous negative.[137]

By the time French troops reached Fez most European diplomats already saw that a French protectorate was inevitable. This realization prompted the German Government to send a gunboat to Agadir in an attempt, as Kiderlen-Wächter put it, 'to thump the table' and force the French to offer compensation. The Agadir crisis ended in November 1911 when Germany recognized the French protectorate and received a large slice of the French Congo in return. The *parti colonial* was agreed both in deploring the sacrifice and in accepting it as a necessary consequence of the Government's earlier hesitation in Morocco. A few colonialists, as a sign of their displeasure, voted against the treaty in the Chamber, safe in the knowledge that it would go through nonetheless. But the whole of the *parti colonial* accepted Barrès distinction of the issues at stake: 'Le Maroc: question nationale. Le Congo: question coloniale.' [138]

Colonialist influence was as obvious in the organization of the Moroccan protectorate as in its origins. General Lyautey, a prominent member of the *Comité de l'Afrique Française,* was chosen as the first Resident-General. Both the President of the Republic and the Prime Minister had their own candidates for the post but were overruled by their colleagues, who were perhaps influenced by the *Comité du Maroc*'s press campaign in favour of Lyautey.[139] Instead of establishing an office in Paris on the lines of the *Office Algérienne* or the *Office Tunisienne,* Lyautey at first used the *Comité du Maroc* as his official representative.[140] When business grew too large for the *Comité du Maroc* to handle and an *Office Marocaine* had to be set up, its first secretary was Auguste Terrier, the secretary-general of both the *Comité du Maroc* and the *Comité de l'Afrique Française.*[141]

The establishment of the protectorate, however, removed the last issue capable of reconciling the differences within the *parti colonial.* During 1912 the old dispute over the *indigénat* re-emerged in an acute form. In December the *indigénophiles* in the Chamber formed a new *groupe parlementaire d'étude des questions indigènes,* swiftly denounced by its opponents as 'cet instrument de guerre contre les colons'.[142] At almost the same moment the *groupe colonial* disintegrated once again. In its place there emerged at the beginning of 1913 a new *groupe interparlementaire des représentants des colonies,* which by 1914 called itself simply the *groupe colonial.* Thus the wheel had turned almost full circle since the 1880s. Before the foundation of the *groupe colonial* in 1892, the colonial deputies had already formed a cohesive bloc, dominated by Etienne and the Algerians. When the *groupe interparlementaire des représentants des colonies* re-emerged in 1913, it was attended by representatives of all parts of the Empire *except* Algeria.[143] The reason why Etienne and the other Algerians boycotted the new group is simple. Unlike